shiho. Sugiura's

Silver diamond

2: master & servant

By Shiho Sugiura

TOKYOPOP®

HAMBURG // LONDON // LOS ANGELES // TOKYO

SILVER DIAMOND Vol. 2
Created by Shiho Sugiura

Translation - Shirley Kubo
English Adaptation - Karen S. Ahlstrom
Fan Consultant - The SD Fan Advisory Group
Retouch and Lettering - Star Print Brokers
Production Artist - Michael Paolilli
Graphic Designer - Chelsea Windlinger

Editor - Alexis Kirsch
Pre-Production Supervisor - Vicente Rivera, Jr.
Print-Production Specialist - Lucas Rivera
Managing Editor - Vy Nguyen
Senior Designer - Louis Csontos
Senior Designer - James Lee
Senior Editor - Bryce P. Coleman
Senior Editor - Jenna Winterberg
Associate Publisher - Marco F. Pavia
President and C.O.O. - John Parker
C.E.O. and Chief Creative Officer - Stu Levy

A **TOKYOPOP** Manga

TOKYOPOP Inc.
5900 Wilshire Blvd. Suite 2000
Los Angeles, CA 90036

E-mail: info@TOKYOPOP.com
Come visit us online at www.TOKYOPOP.com

ISBN: 978-1-4278-0966-7

First TOKYOPOP printing: October 2008
10 9 8 7 6 5 4 3
Printed in the USA

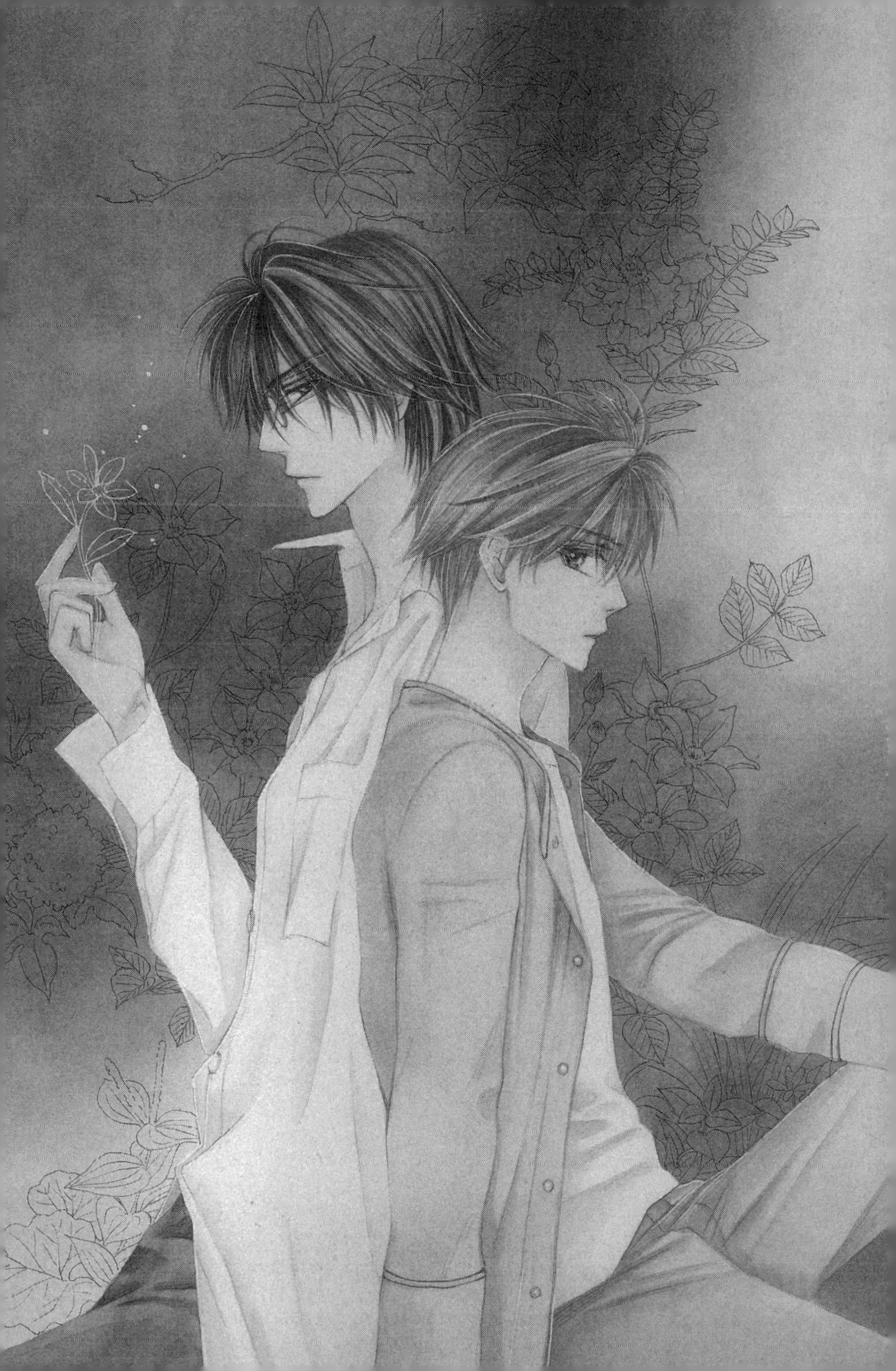

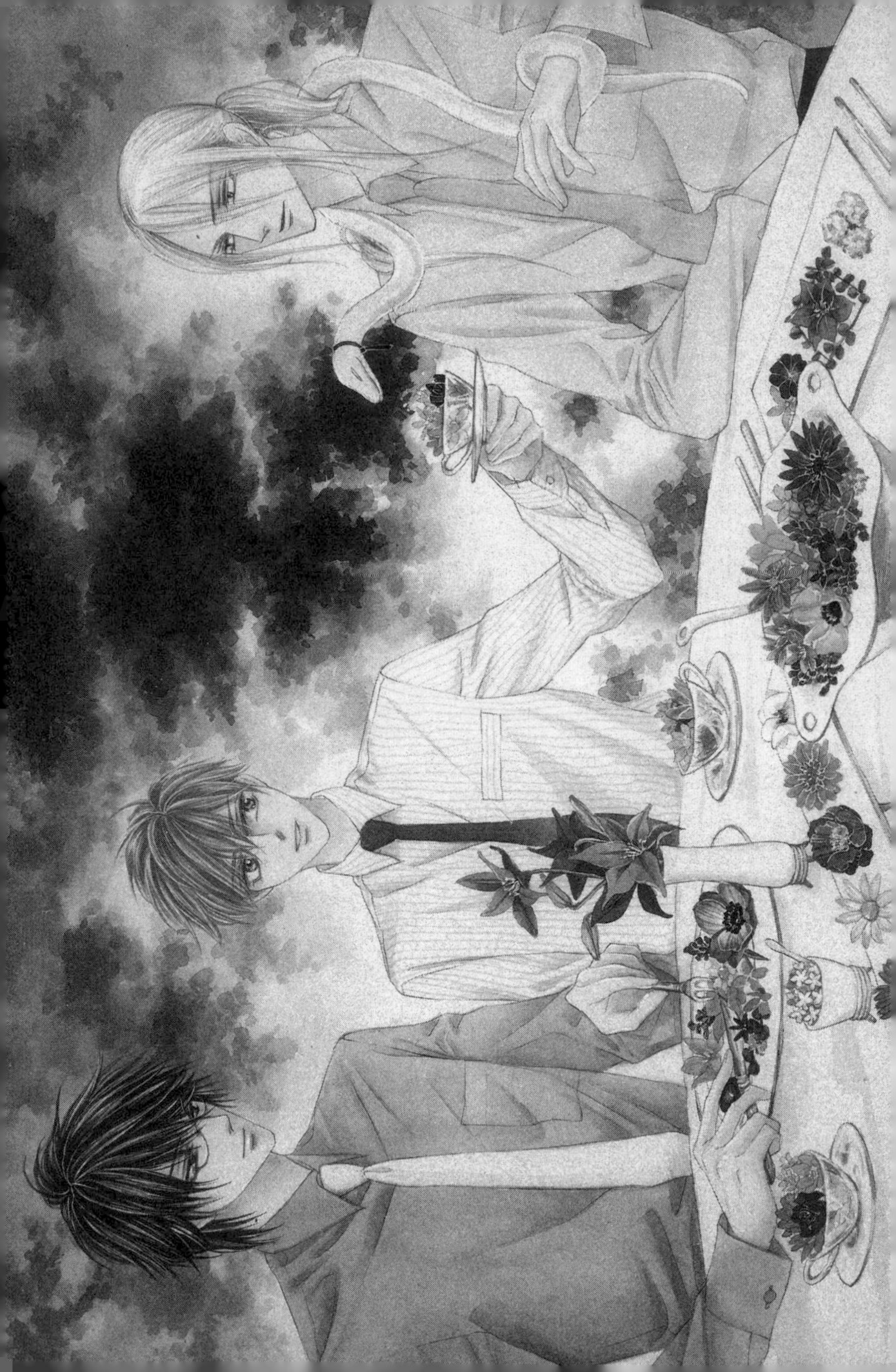

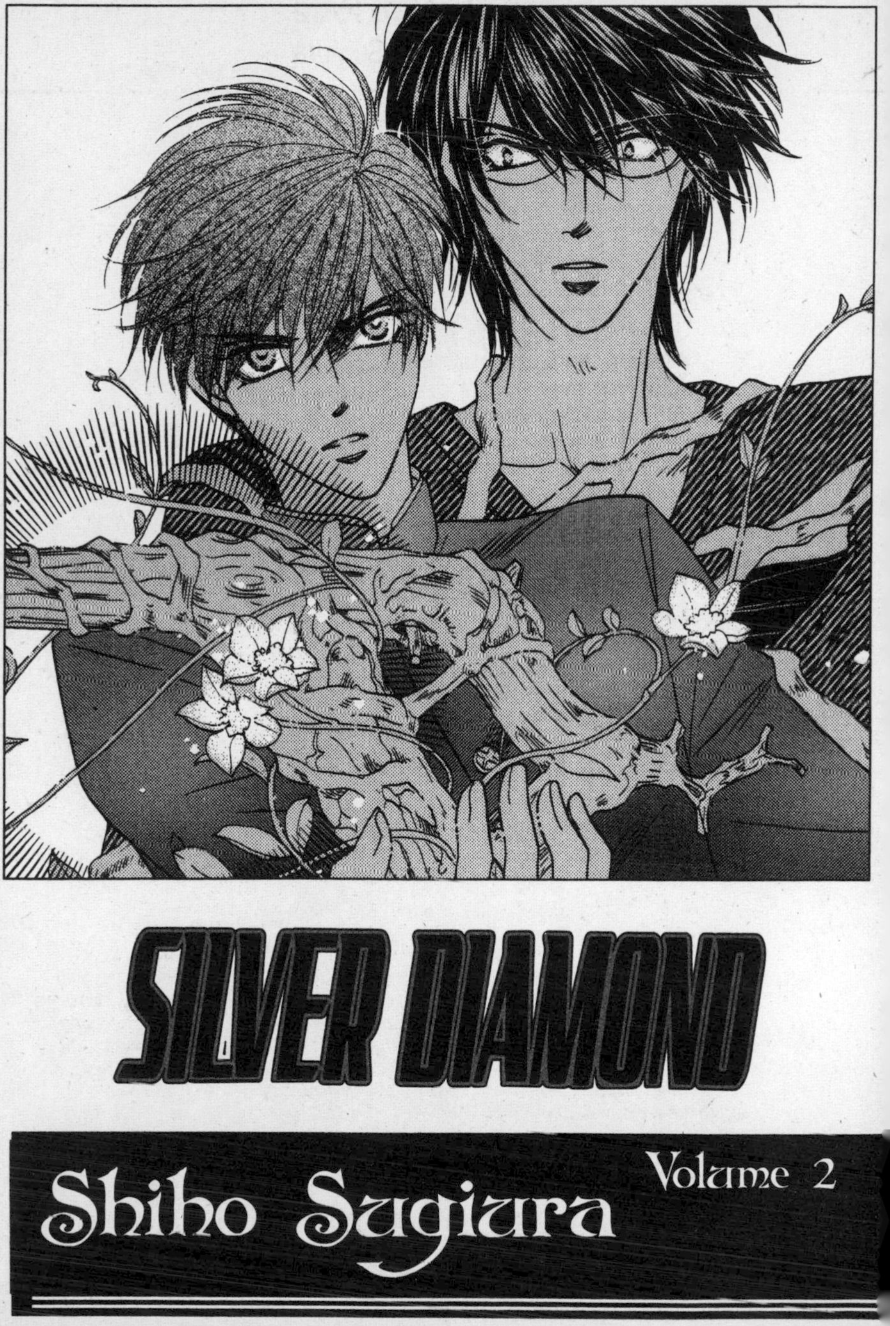

SILVER DIAMOND

Volume 2

Shiho Sugiura

Contents

Silver Diamond

**TO KEEP *SILVER DIAMOND* AS AUTHENTIC AS POSSIBLE, JAPANESE NAME ORDER (FAMILY NAME FIRST) AND HONORIFICS WILL BE MAINTAINED THROUGHOUT THE TEXT. FOR FURTHER EXPLANATIONS OF SPECIALLY-MARKED DIALOGUE(*), PLEASE CHECK THE GLOSSARY AT THE END OF THE VOLUME.

SILVER DIAMOND

シルバーダイヤモンド

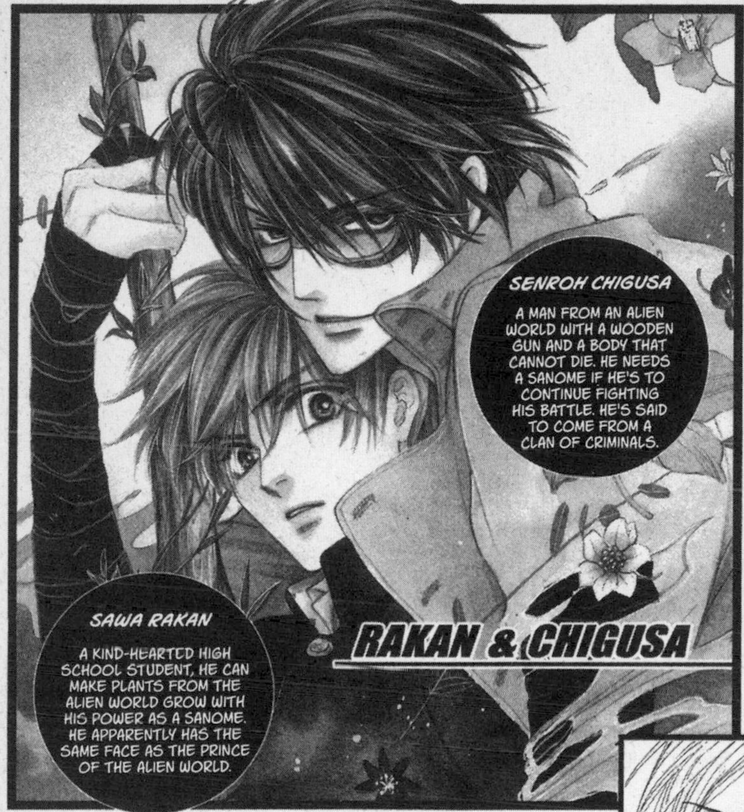
SENROH CHIGUSA
A MAN FROM AN ALIEN WORLD WITH A WOODEN GUN AND A BODY THAT CANNOT DIE. HE NEEDS A SANOME IF HE'S TO CONTINUE FIGHTING HIS BATTLE. HE'S SAID TO COME FROM A CLAN OF CRIMINALS.
RAKAN & CHIGUSA
SAWA RAKAN
A KIND-HEARTED HIGH SCHOOL STUDENT, HE CAN MAKE PLANTS FROM THE ALIEN WORLD GROW WITH HIS POWER AS A SANOME. HE APPARENTLY HAS THE SAME FACE AS THE PRINCE OF THE ALIEN WORLD.

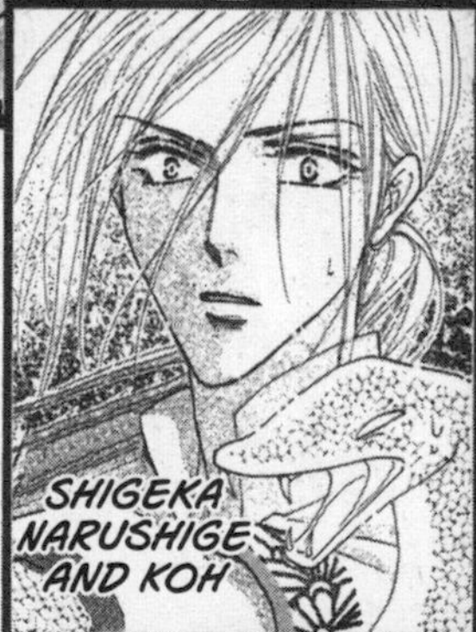
SHIGEKA NARUSHIGE AND KOH

◆ RAKAN LIVES ALONE IN A HOUSE WITH A JUNGLE-LIKE YARD. ONE DAY, A MAN WITH A WOODEN GUN FALLS INTO HIS YARD FROM ANOTHER WORLD. THIS MAN, NAMED CHIGUSA, IMMEDIATELY TRIES TO ATTACK RAKAN, WHO LOOKS EXACTLY LIKE THE PRINCE FROM HIS OWN WORLD. BUT WHEN CHIGUSA SEES THAT RAKAN MADE HIS WOODEN GUN GROW INTO A GIANT TREE, HE RECOGNIZES HIM AS A SANOME AND REALIZES HE'S NECESSARY FOR THE BATTLE HE MUST FIGHT. TO MAKE THINGS WORSE, NARUSHIGE AND KOH FALL IN AS WELL, AND RAKAN'S DAILY ROUTINE TURNS INTO A STRANGE ONE.

◆ WHEN AN ALIEN CREATURE APPEARS LATER ON, CHIGUSA SUSTAINS HEAVY INJURIES PROTECTING RAKAN. THOUGH RAKAN IS DEEPLY WORRIED, CHIGUSA'S WOUNDS HEAL COMPLETELY IN THE BLINK OF AN EYE, AND HE REVEALS THAT HIS BODY CANNOT DIE. HE EXPLAINS THAT BECAUSE HIS BODY IS HALF PLANT, IT CAN BE REGENERATED OVER AND OVER BY THE POWER OF A SANOME. AT THIS, RAKAN CRIES AND GETS ANGRY, SAYING THAT CHIGUSA SHOULDN'T TREAT HIS BODY LIKE THAT. AFTER EXPERIENCING RAKAN'S KINDNESS, CHIGUSA AND NARUSHIGE BOTH THINK, "IF ONLY THIS CHILD WERE THE REAL PRINCE."

PLEASE READ VOLUME 1 FOR MORE!!

STORY and CASTS

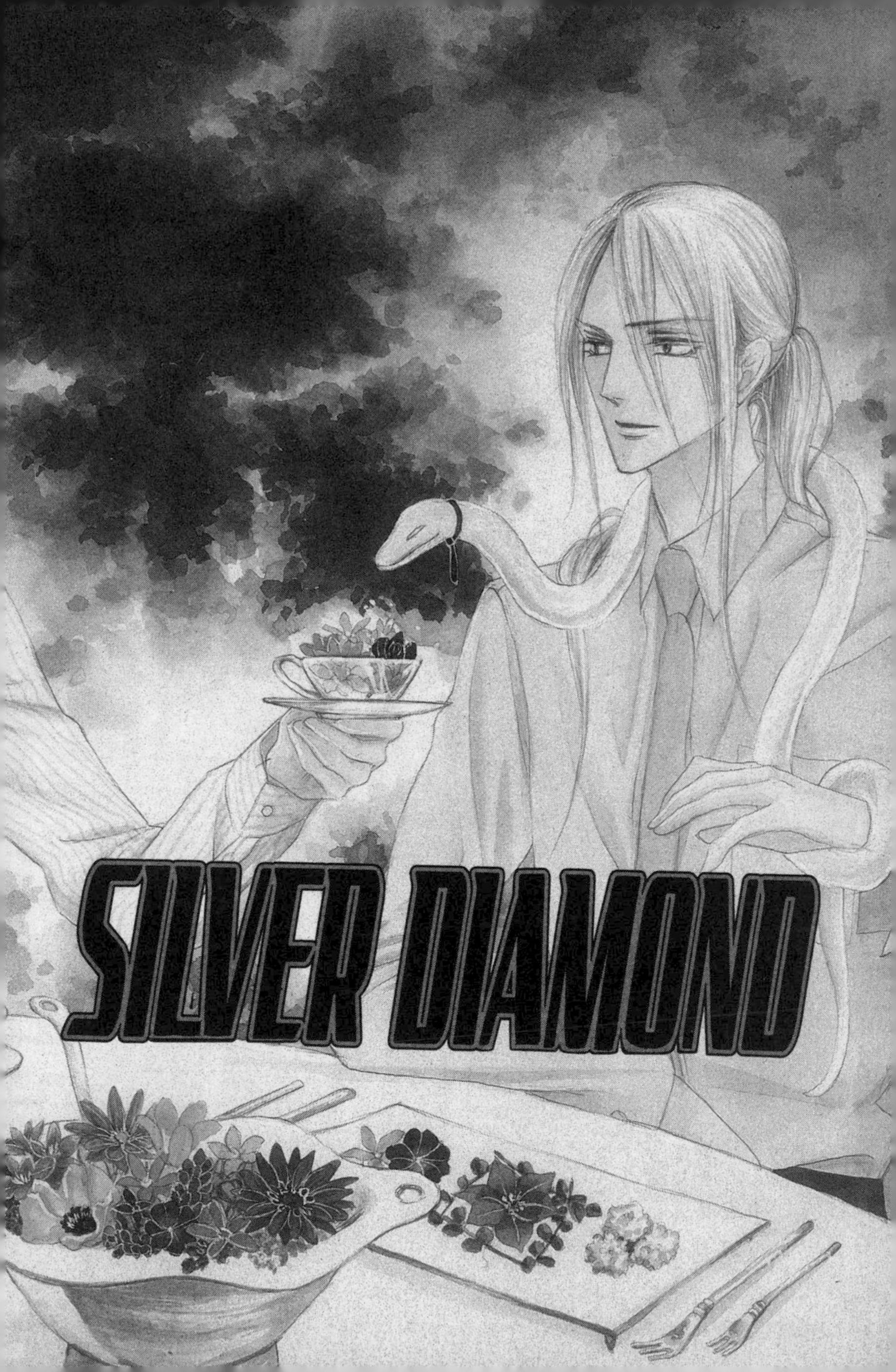
SILVER DIAMOND

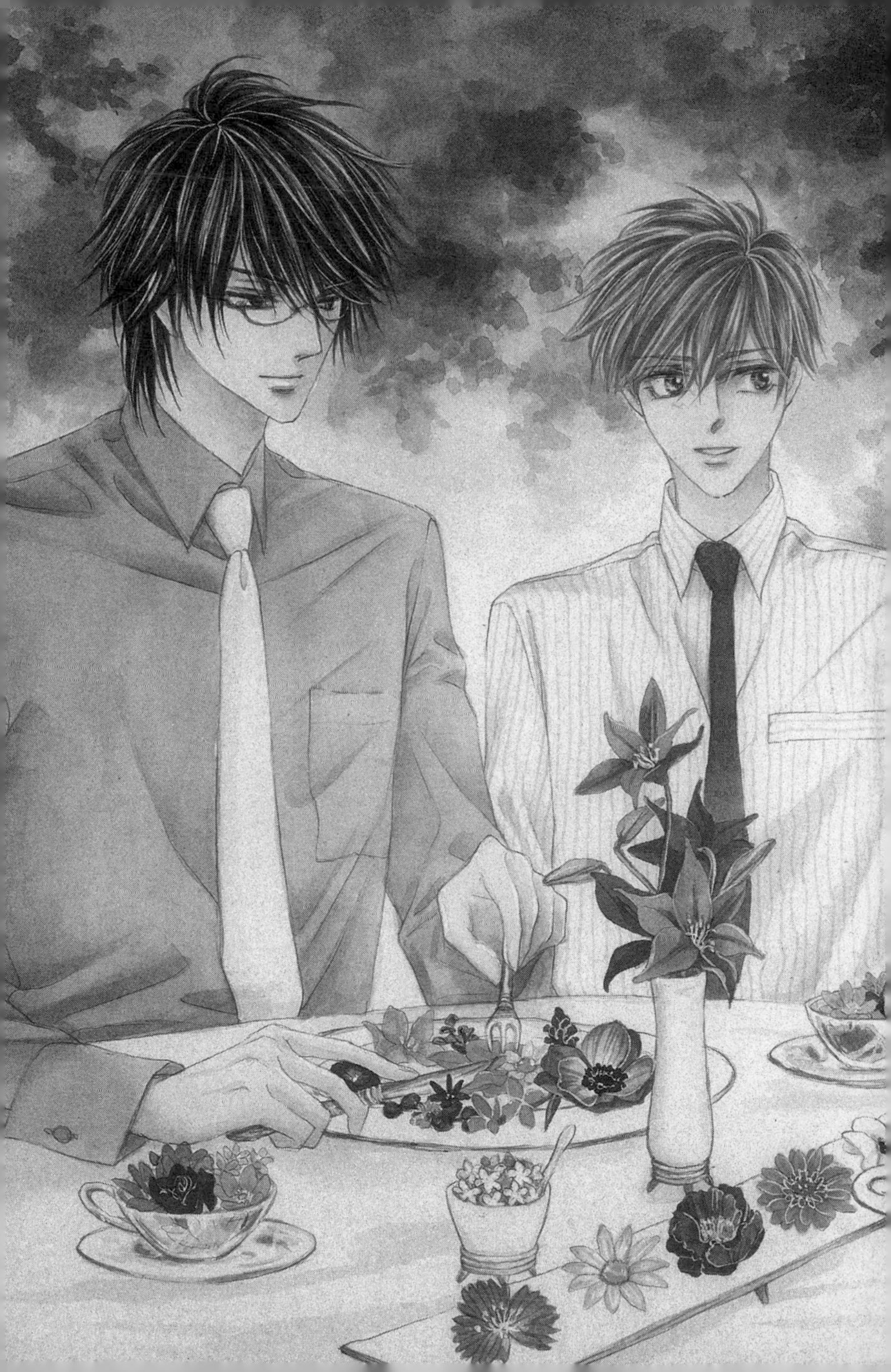

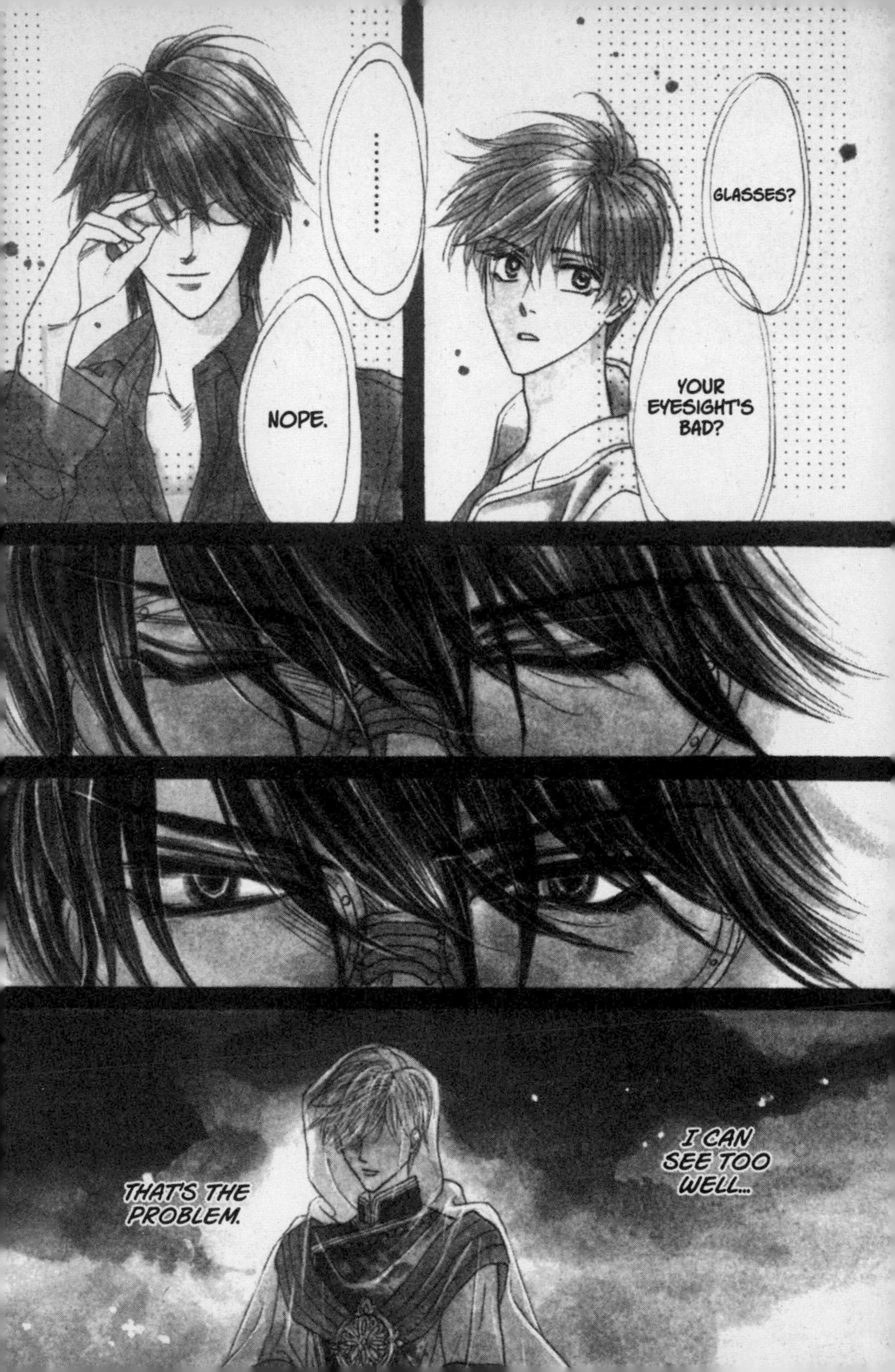
GLASSES?
YOUR EYESIGHT'S BAD?
......
NOPE.
I CAN SEE TOO WELL...
THAT'S THE PROBLEM.

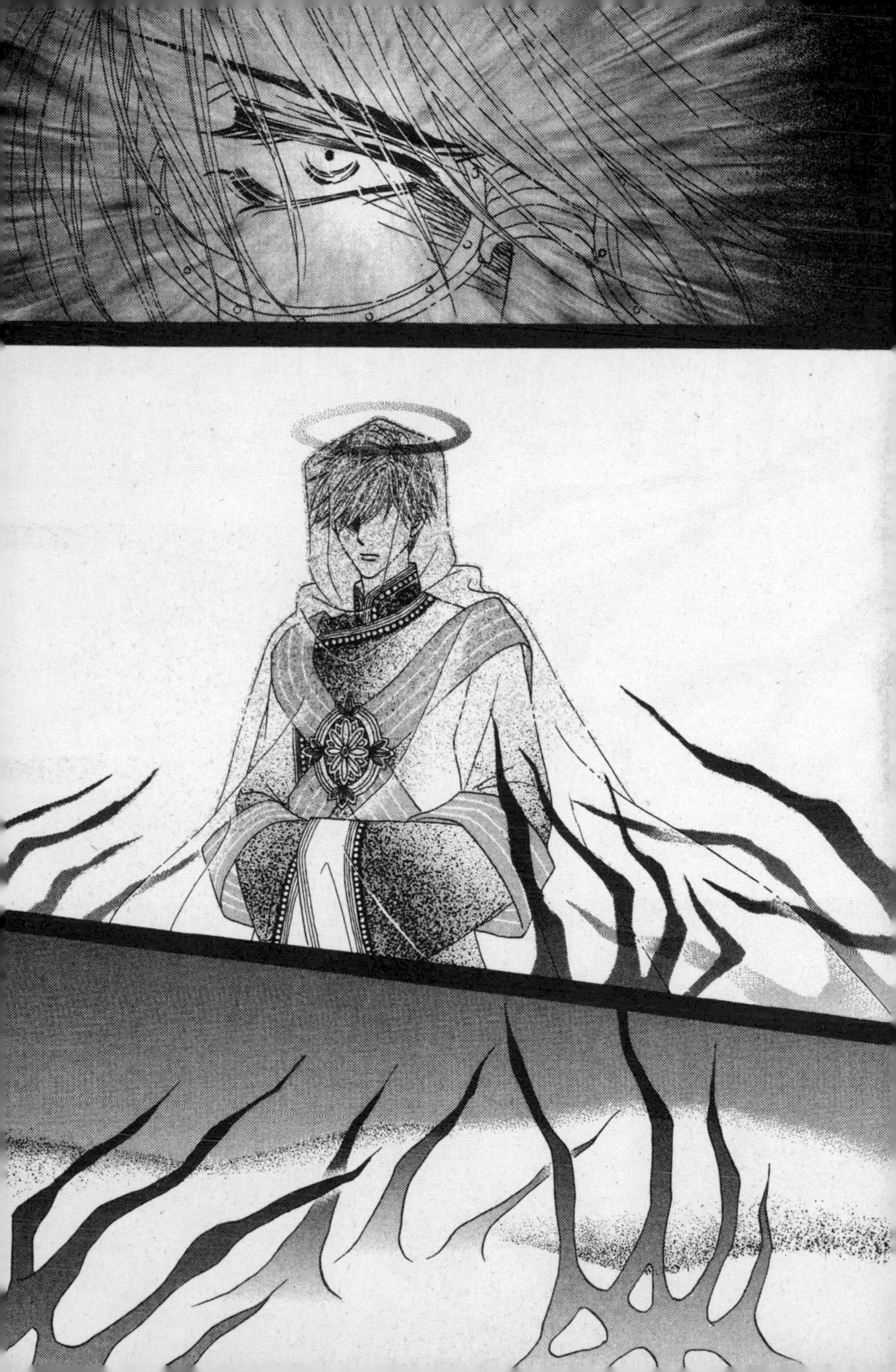

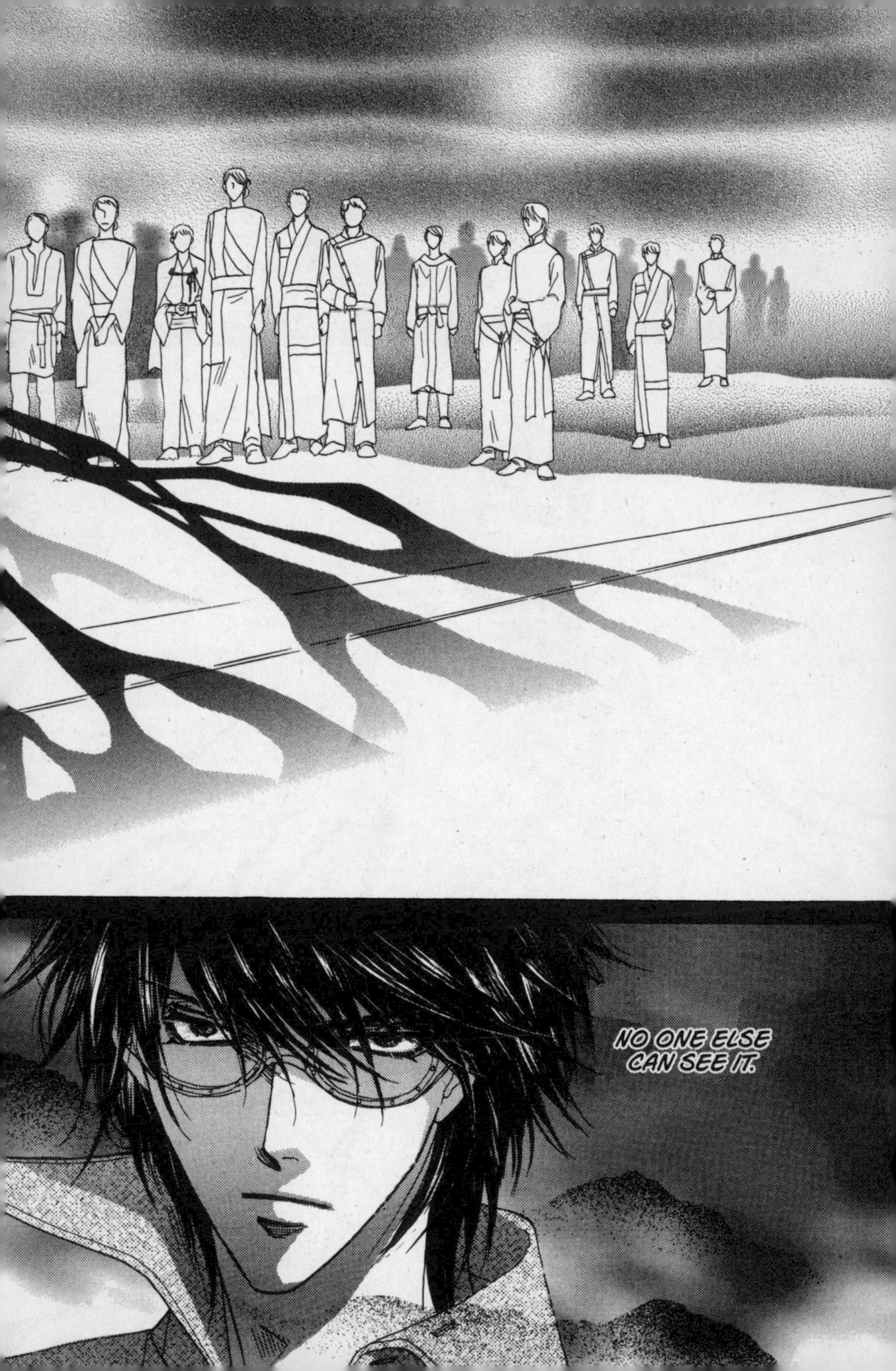
NO ONE ELSE CAN SEE IT.

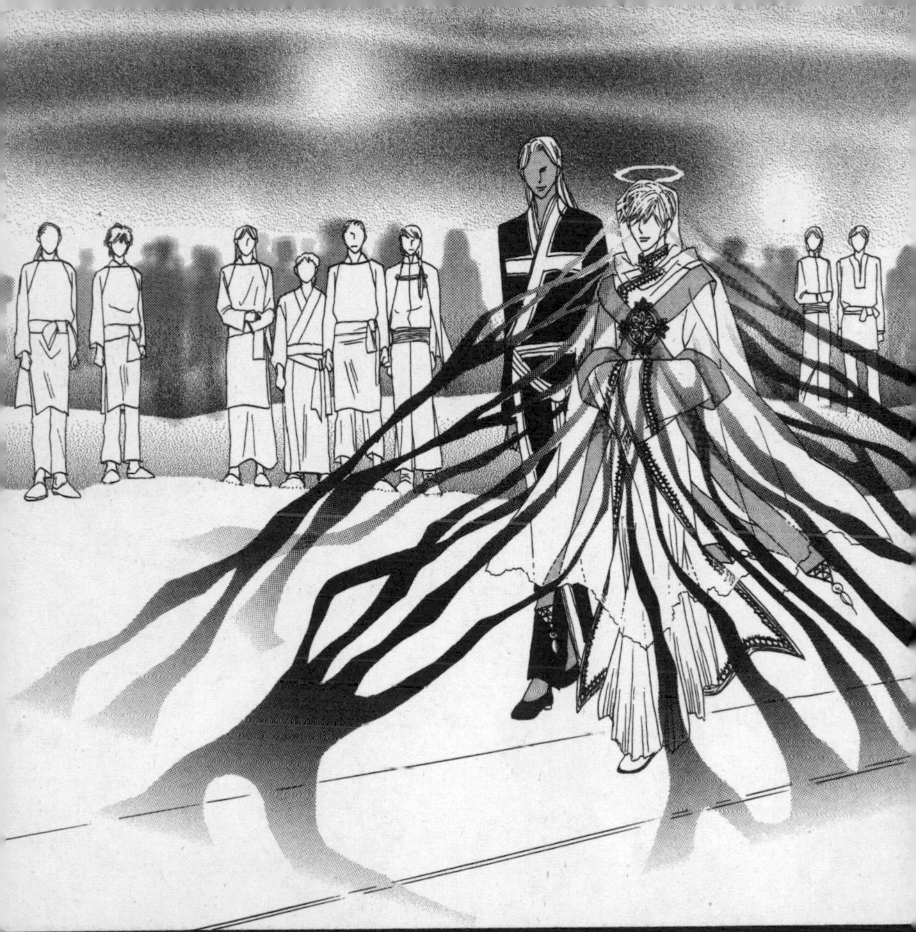

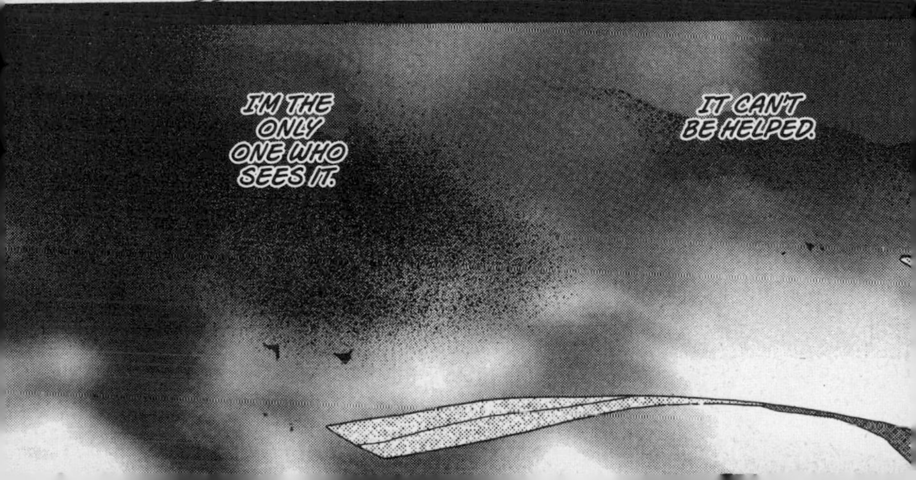
IT CAN'T BE HELPED.
I'M THE ONLY ONE WHO SEES IT.

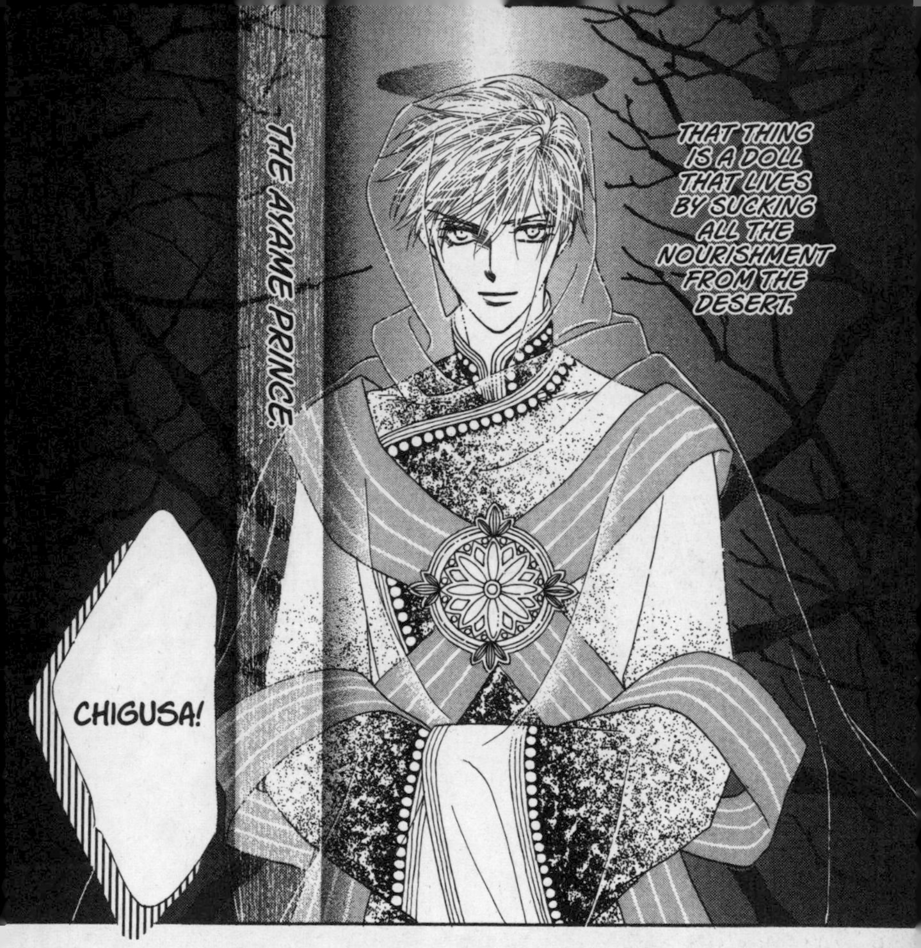
THAT THING IS A DOLL THAT LIVES BY SUCKING ALL THE NOURISHMENT FROM THE DESERT.
THE AYAME PRINCE.
CHIGUSA!

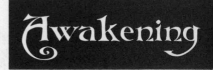

Awakening

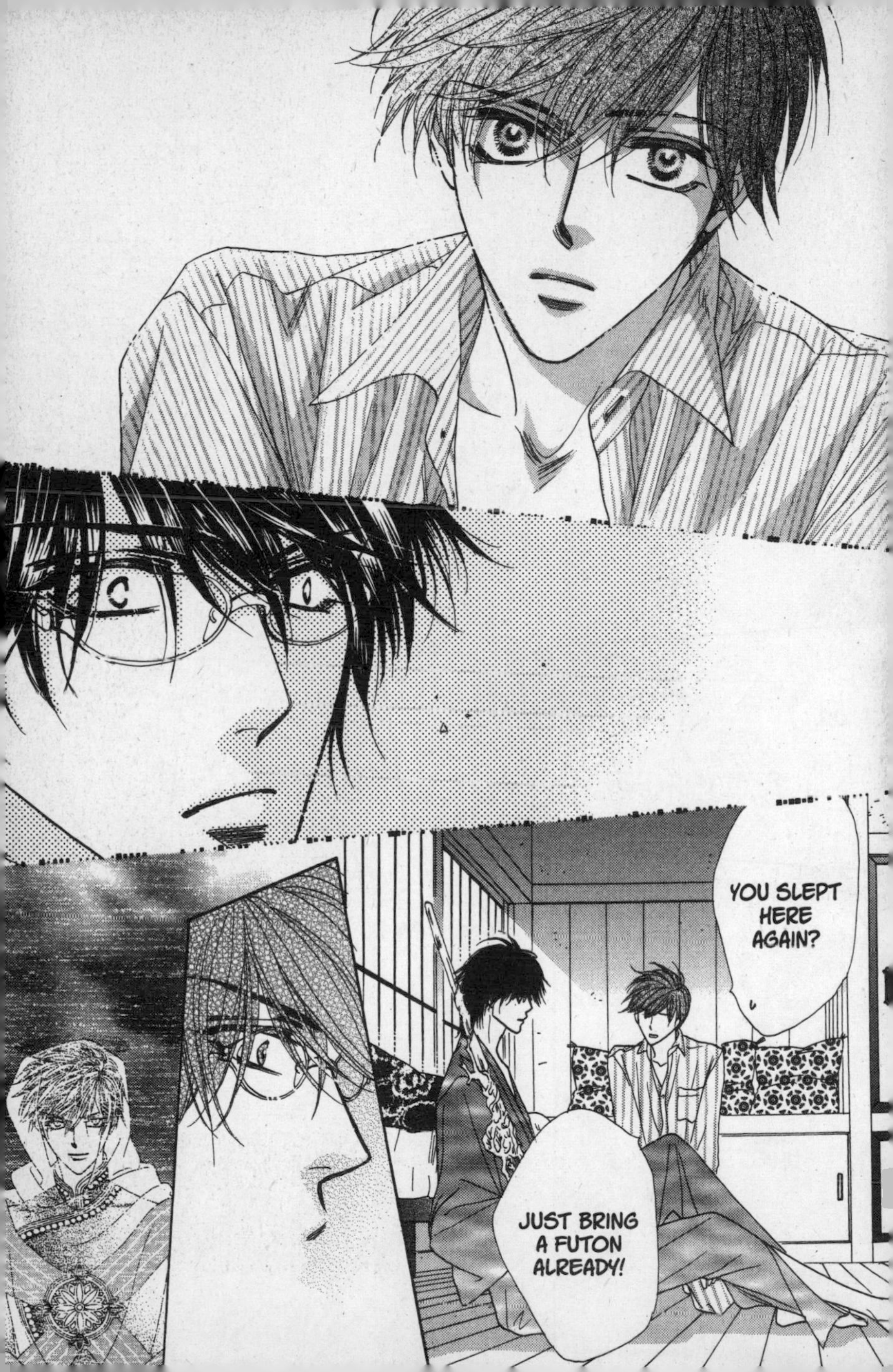
YOU SLEPT HERE AGAIN?
JUST BRING A FUTON ALREADY!

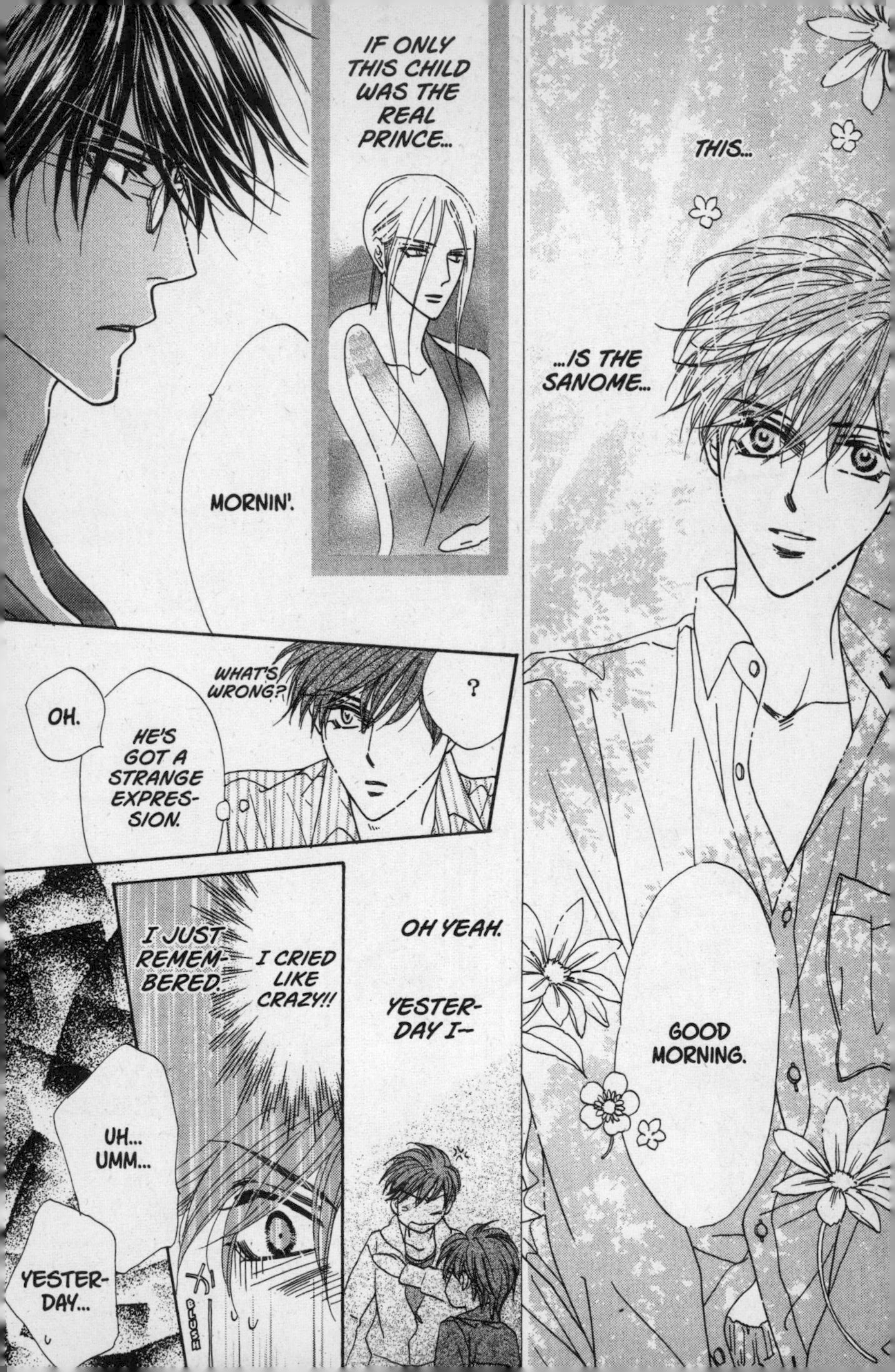
THIS...
...IS THE SANOME...
GOOD MORNING.
IF ONLY THIS CHILD WAS THE REAL PRINCE...
MORNIN'.
?
WHAT'S WRONG?
HE'S GOT A STRANGE EXPRES-SION.
OH.
OH YEAH.
YESTER-DAY I--
I CRIED LIKE CRAZY!!
I JUST REMEM-BERED.
UH... UMM...
YESTER-DAY...

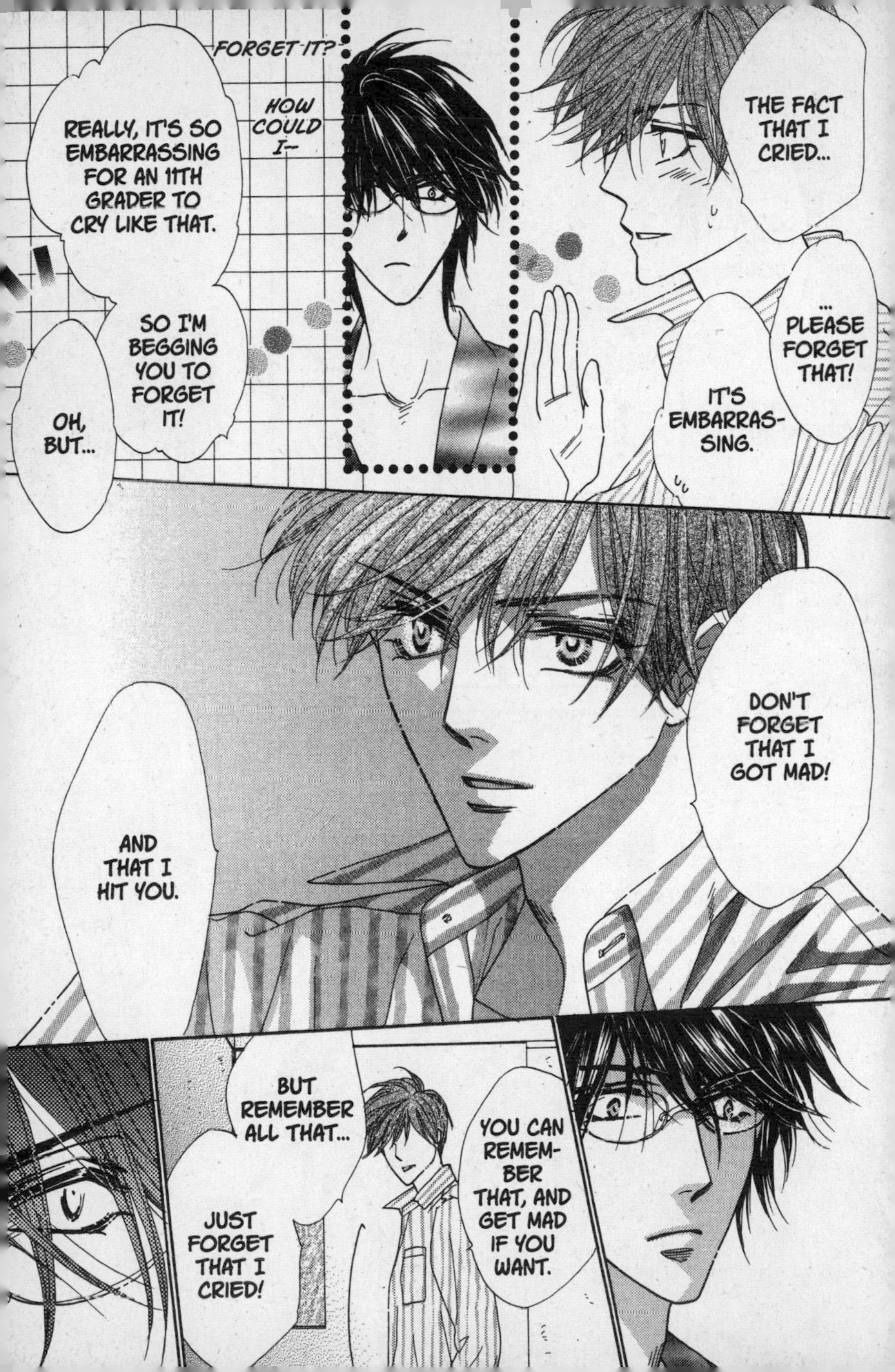
THE FACT THAT I CRIED...
...PLEASE FORGET THAT!
IT'S EMBARRAS-SING.
FORGET IT?
HOW COULD I–
REALLY, IT'S SO EMBARRASSING FOR AN 11TH GRADER TO CRY LIKE THAT.
SO I'M BEGGING YOU TO FORGET IT!
OH, BUT...
DON'T FORGET THAT I GOT MAD!
AND THAT I HIT YOU.
YOU CAN REMEMBER THAT, AND GET MAD IF YOU WANT.
BUT REMEMBER ALL THAT...
JUST FORGET THAT I CRIED!

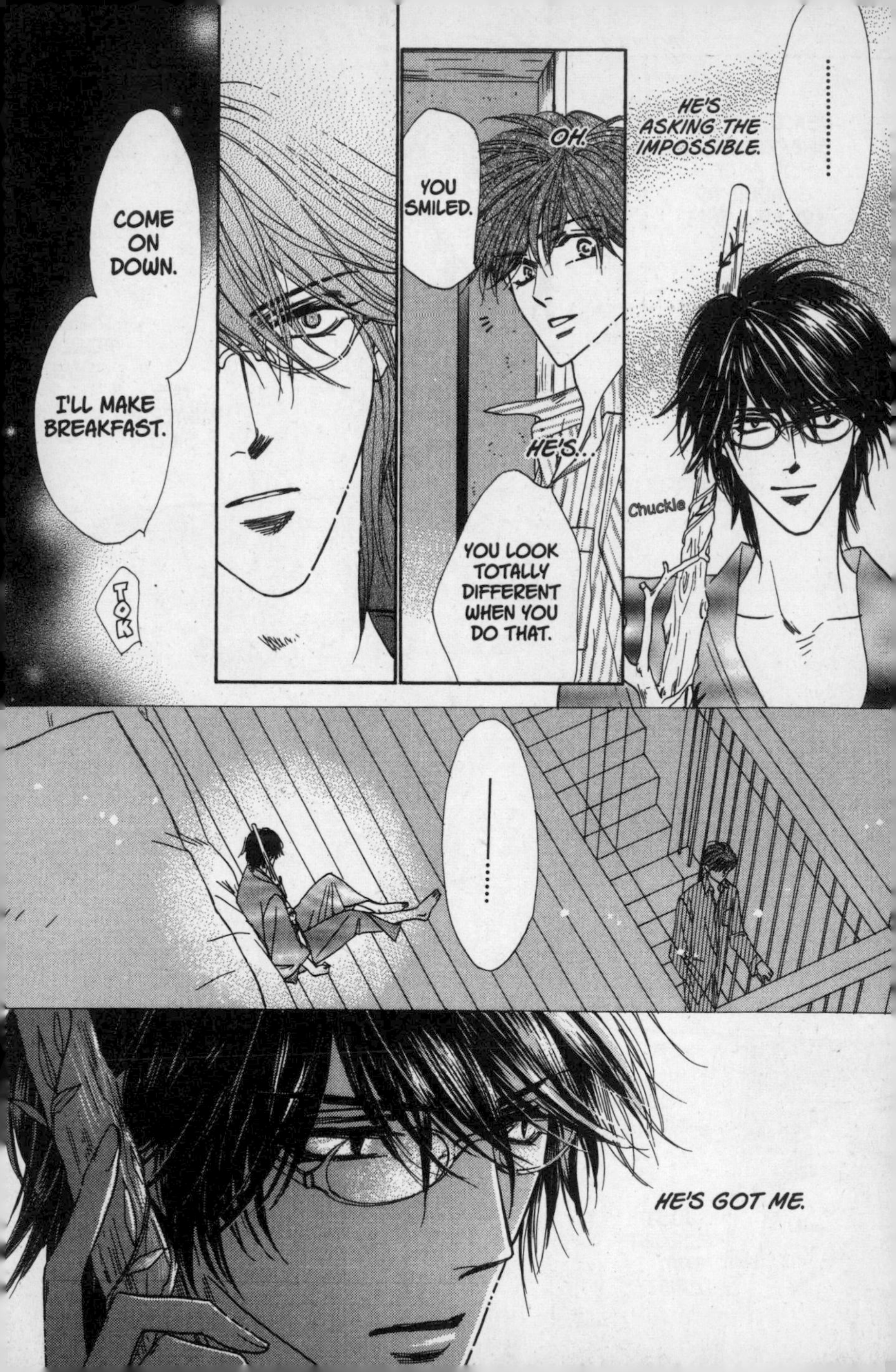
......
HE'S ASKING THE IMPOSSIBLE.
Chuckle
OH.
YOU SMILED.
HE'S...
YOU LOOK TOTALLY DIFFERENT WHEN YOU DO THAT.
COME ON DOWN.
I'LL MAKE BREAKFAST.
TOK
......
HE'S GOT ME.

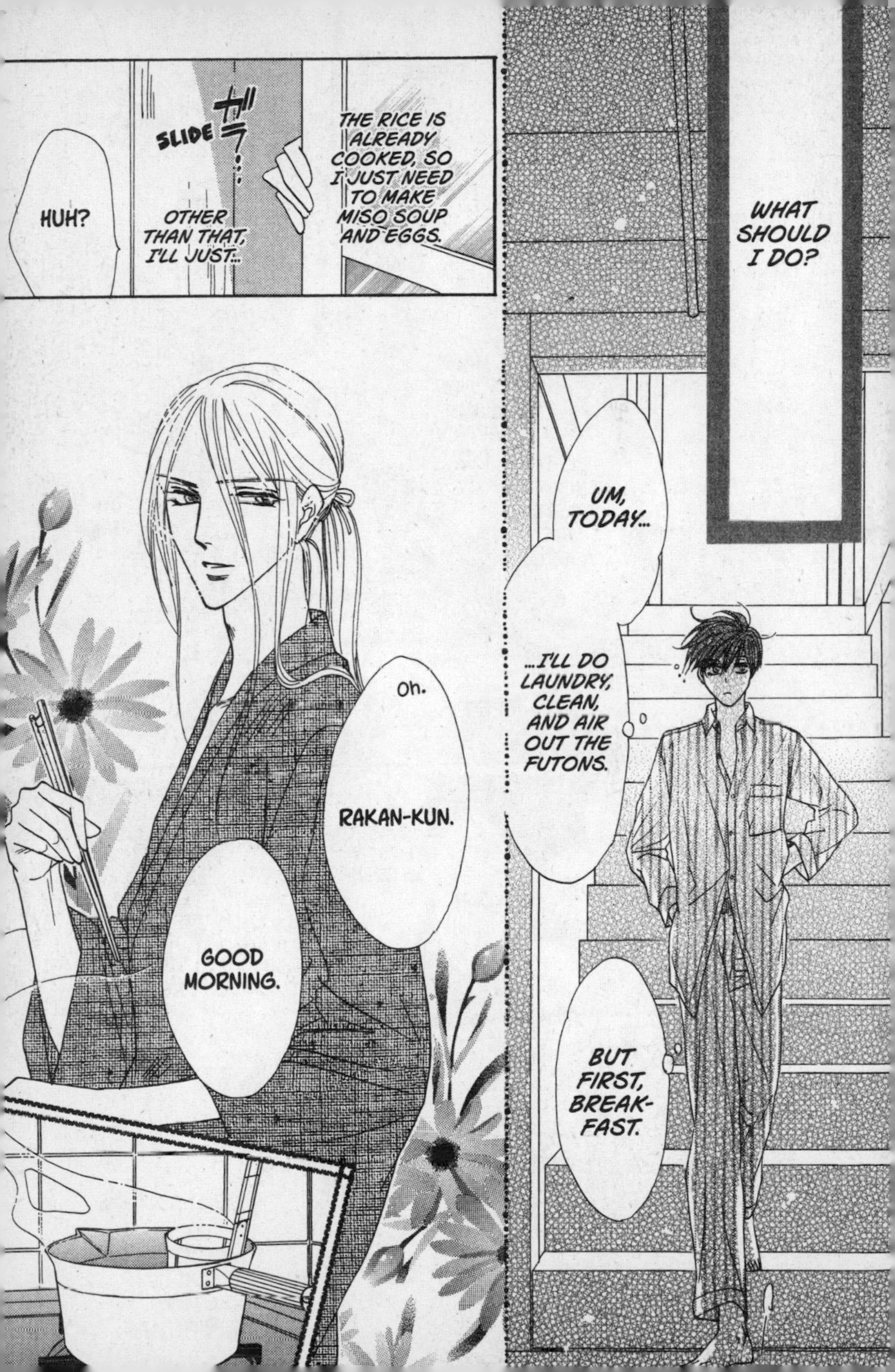
WHAT SHOULD I DO?
UM, TODAY...
...I'LL DO LAUNDRY, CLEAN, AND AIR OUT THE FUTONS.
BUT FIRST, BREAKFAST.
THE RICE IS ALREADY COOKED, SO I JUST NEED TO MAKE MISO SOUP AND EGGS.
SLIDE
OTHER THAN THAT, I'LL JUST...
HUH?
Oh.
RAKAN-KUN.
GOOD MORNING.

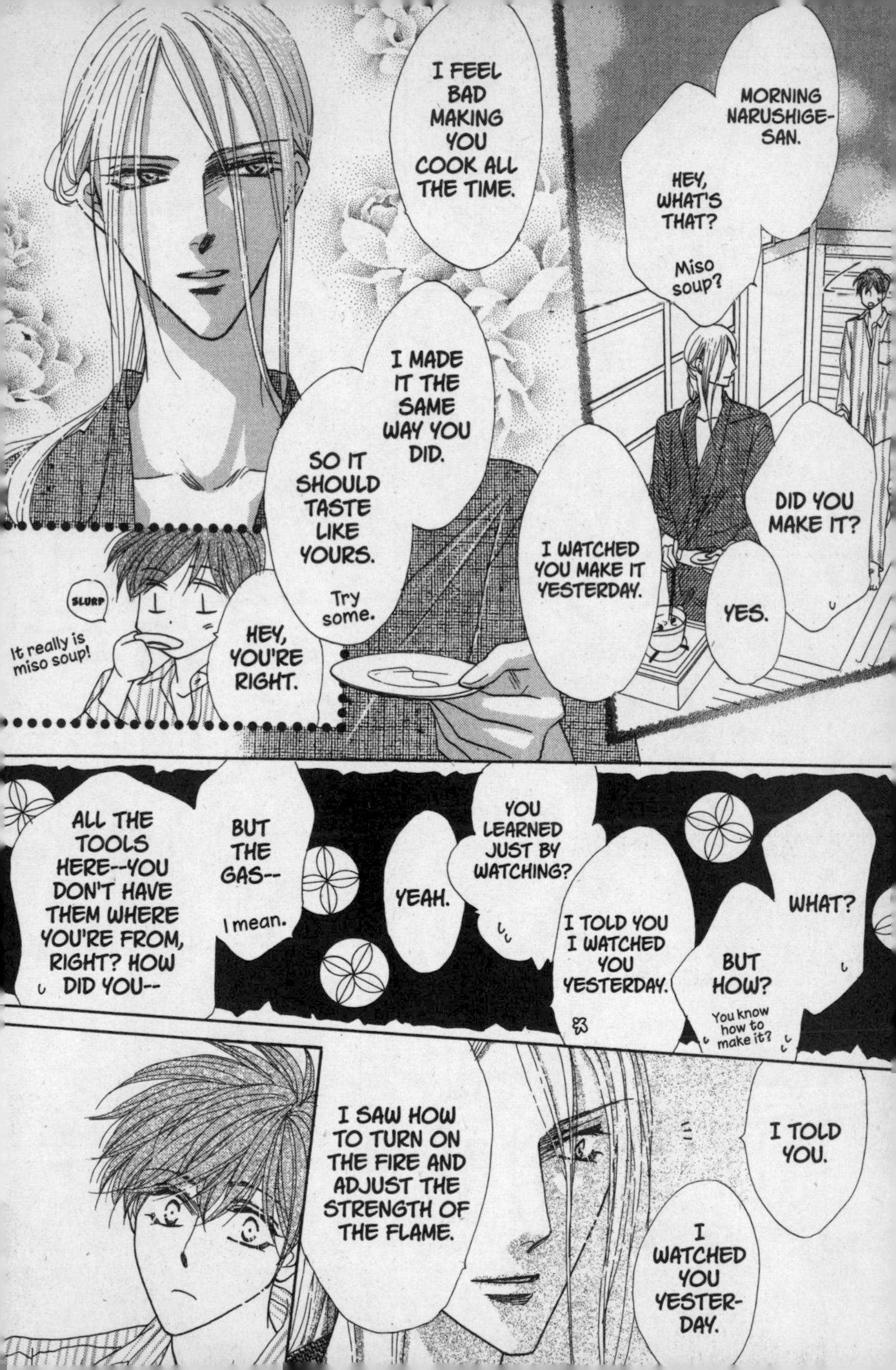

MORNING NARUSHIGE-SAN.
HEY, WHAT'S THAT?
Miso soup?
DID YOU MAKE IT?
YES.
I WATCHED YOU MAKE IT YESTERDAY.
I FEEL BAD MAKING YOU COOK ALL THE TIME.
I MADE IT THE SAME WAY YOU DID.
SO IT SHOULD TASTE LIKE YOURS.
Try some.
SLURP
HEY, YOU'RE RIGHT.
It really is miso soup!
WHAT?
BUT HOW?
You know how to make it?
I TOLD YOU I WATCHED YOU YESTERDAY.
YOU LEARNED JUST BY WATCHING?
YEAH.
BUT THE GAS--
I mean.
ALL THE TOOLS HERE--YOU DON'T HAVE THEM WHERE YOU'RE FROM, RIGHT? HOW DID YOU--
I TOLD YOU.
I WATCHED YOU YESTER-DAY.
I SAW HOW TO TURN ON THE FIRE AND ADJUST THE STRENGTH OF THE FLAME.

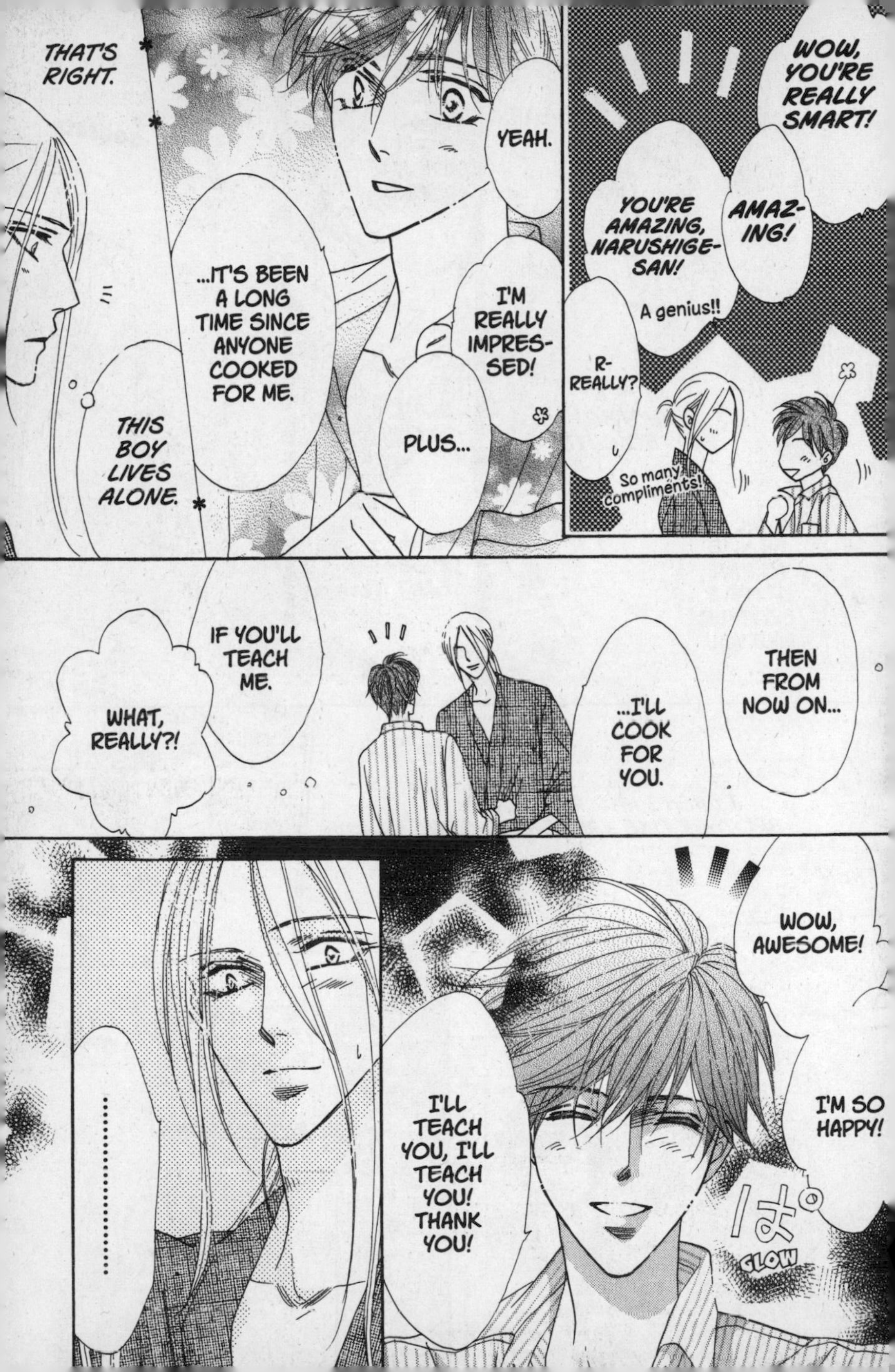
WOW, YOU'RE REALLY SMART!
AMAZ-ING!
YOU'RE AMAZING, NARUSHIGE-SAN!
A genius!!
R-REALLY?
So many compliments!
YEAH.
I'M REALLY IMPRES-SED!
PLUS...
...IT'S BEEN A LONG TIME SINCE ANYONE COOKED FOR ME.
THAT'S RIGHT.
THIS BOY LIVES ALONE.
THEN FROM NOW ON...
...I'LL COOK FOR YOU.
IF YOU'LL TEACH ME.
WHAT, REALLY?!
WOW, AWESOME!
I'M SO HAPPY!
ぱ
GLOW
I'LL TEACH YOU, I'LL TEACH YOU! THANK YOU!
....

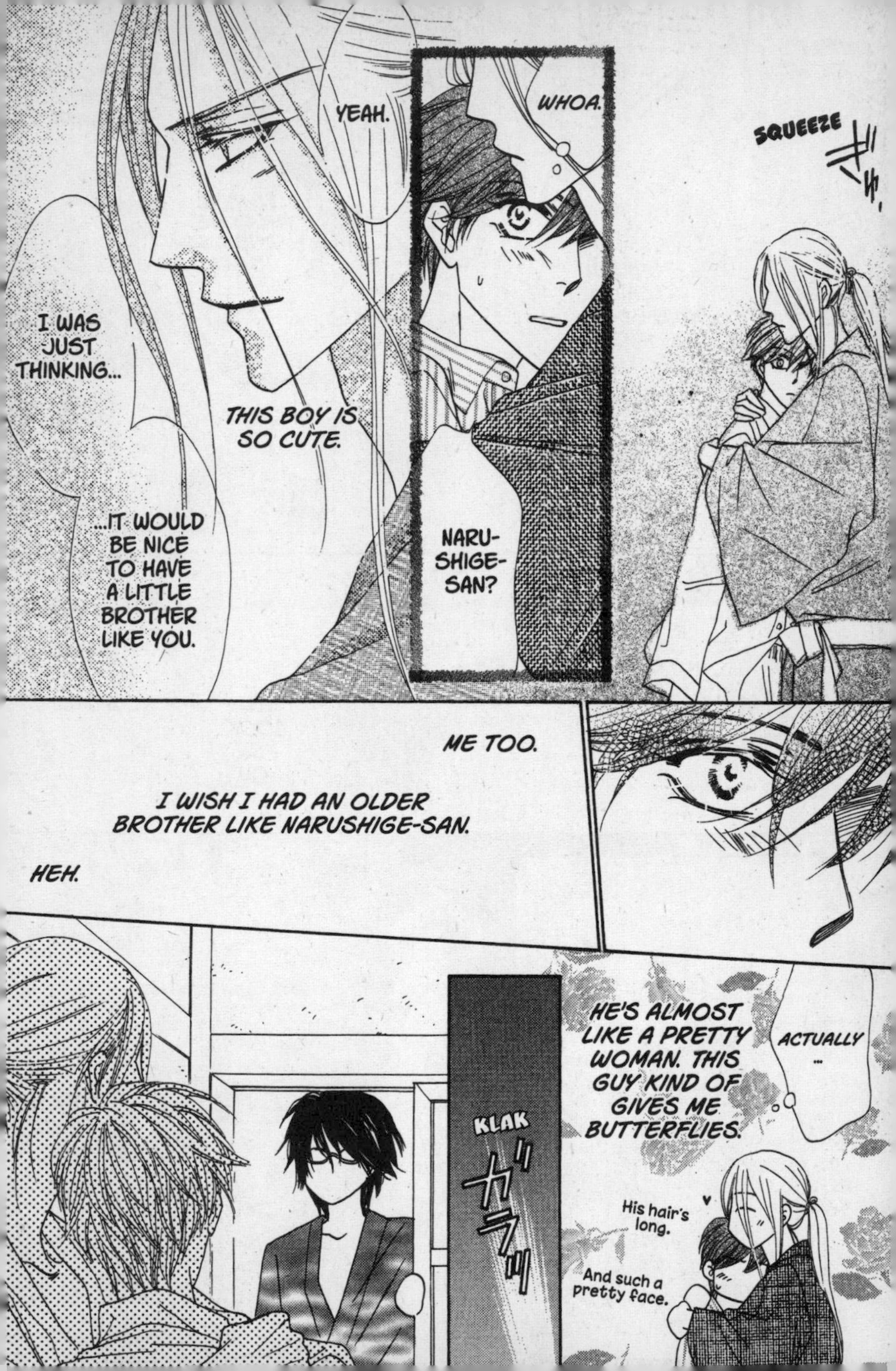
SQUEEZE
WHOA.
NARU-SHIGE-SAN?
YEAH.
I WAS JUST THINKING...
THIS BOY IS SO CUTE.
...IT WOULD BE NICE TO HAVE A LITTLE BROTHER LIKE YOU.
ME TOO.
I WISH I HAD AN OLDER BROTHER LIKE NARUSHIGE-SAN.
HEH.
ACTUALLY...
HE'S ALMOST LIKE A PRETTY WOMAN. THIS GUY KIND OF GIVES ME BUTTERFLIES.
His hair's long.
And such a pretty face.
KLAK

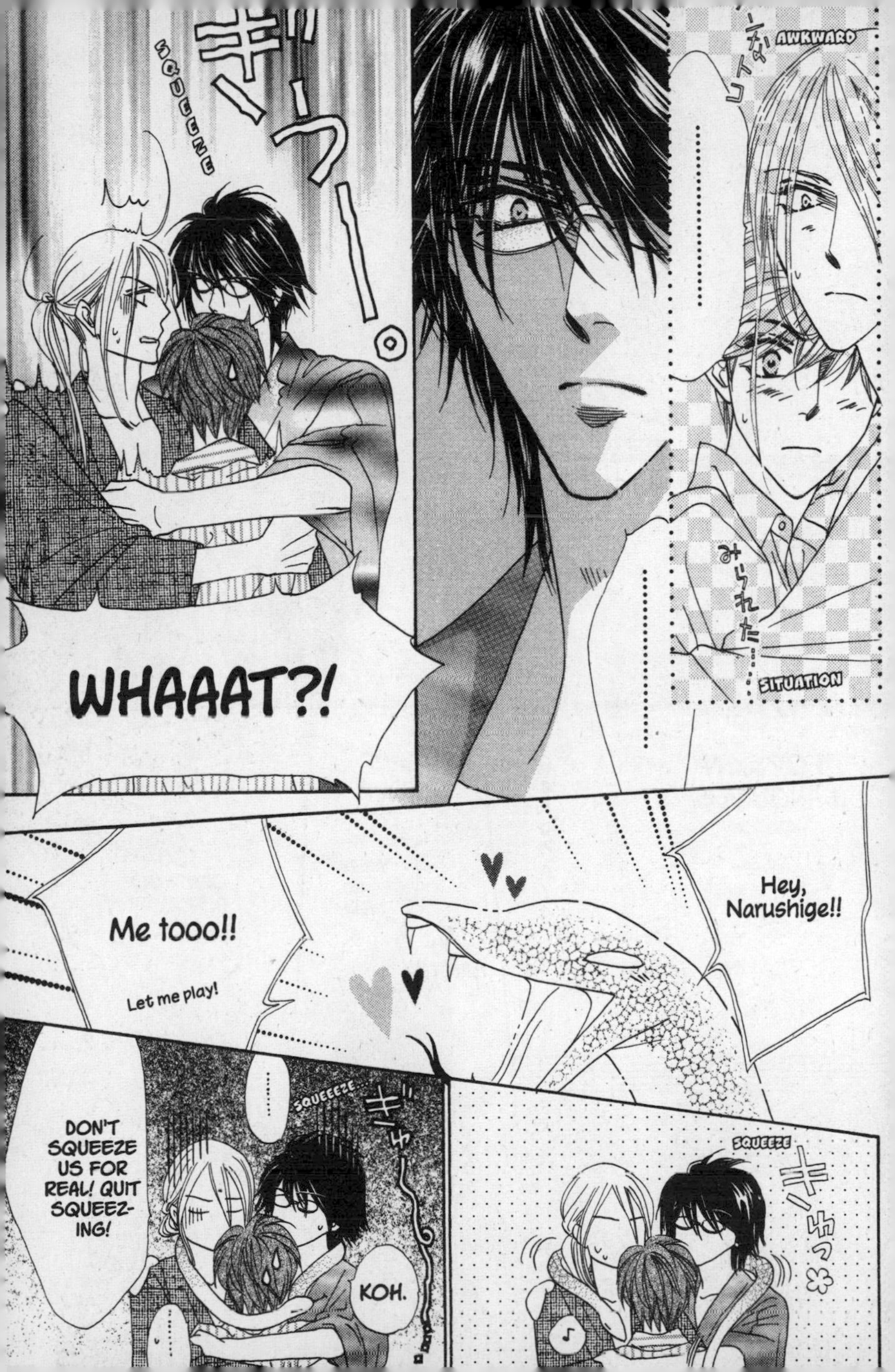
AWKWARD
……
みられた…
SITUATION
SQUEEEZE
WHAAAT?!
Hey, Narushige!!
Me tooo!!
Let me play!
SQUEEZE
SQUEEEZE
……
KOH.
DON'T SQUEEZE US FOR REAL! QUIT SQUEEZ-ING!

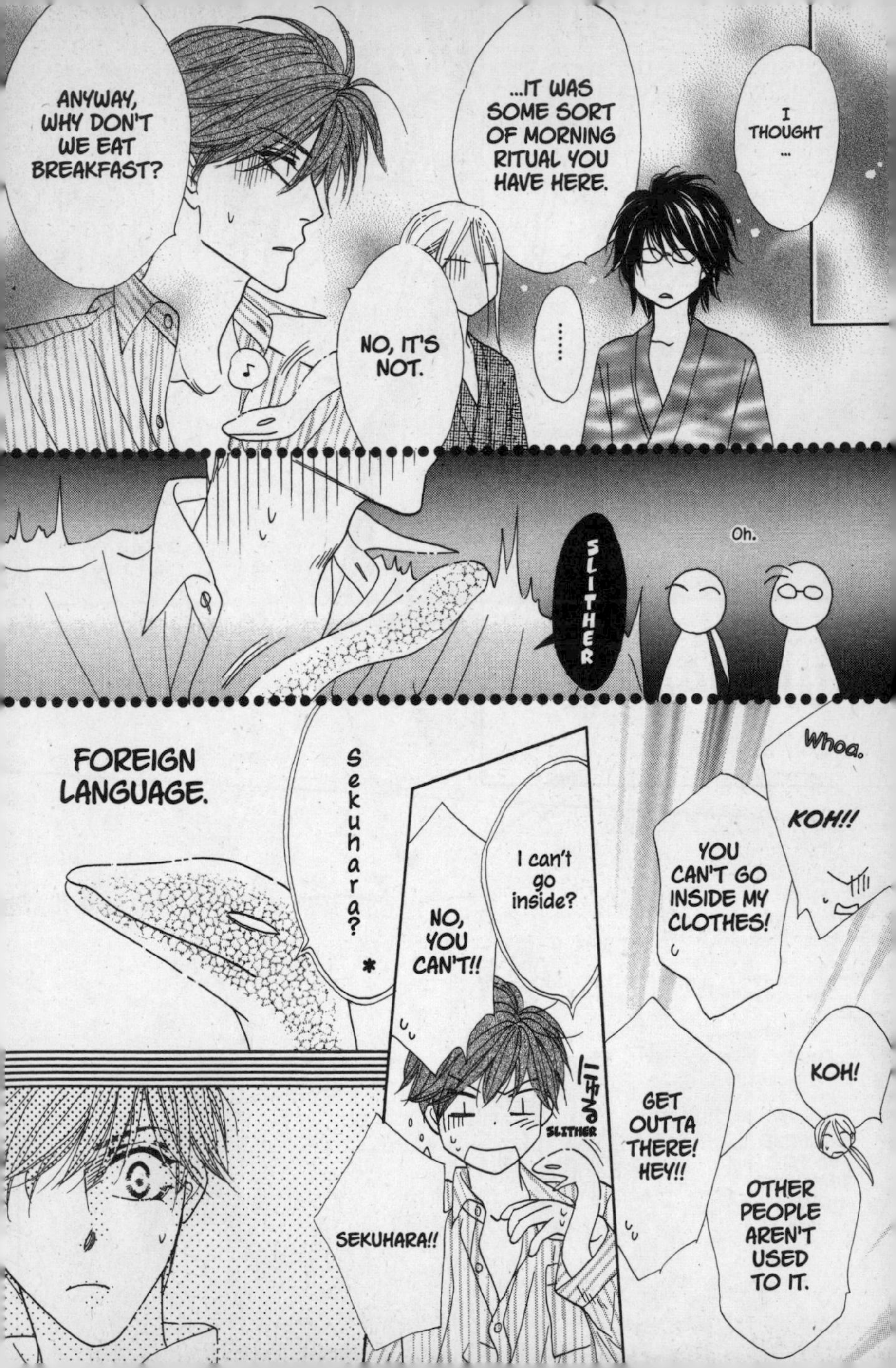
I THOUGHT ...
...IT WAS SOME SORT OF MORNING RITUAL YOU HAVE HERE.
......
NO, IT'S NOT.
ANYWAY, WHY DON'T WE EAT BREAKFAST?
Oh.
SLITHER
Whoa.
KOH!!
YOU CAN'T GO INSIDE MY CLOTHES!
KOH!
OTHER PEOPLE AREN'T USED TO IT.
GET OUTTA THERE! HEY!!
I can't go inside?
NO, YOU CAN'T!!
SLITHER
SEKUHARA!!
Sekuhara?
*
FOREIGN LANGUAGE.

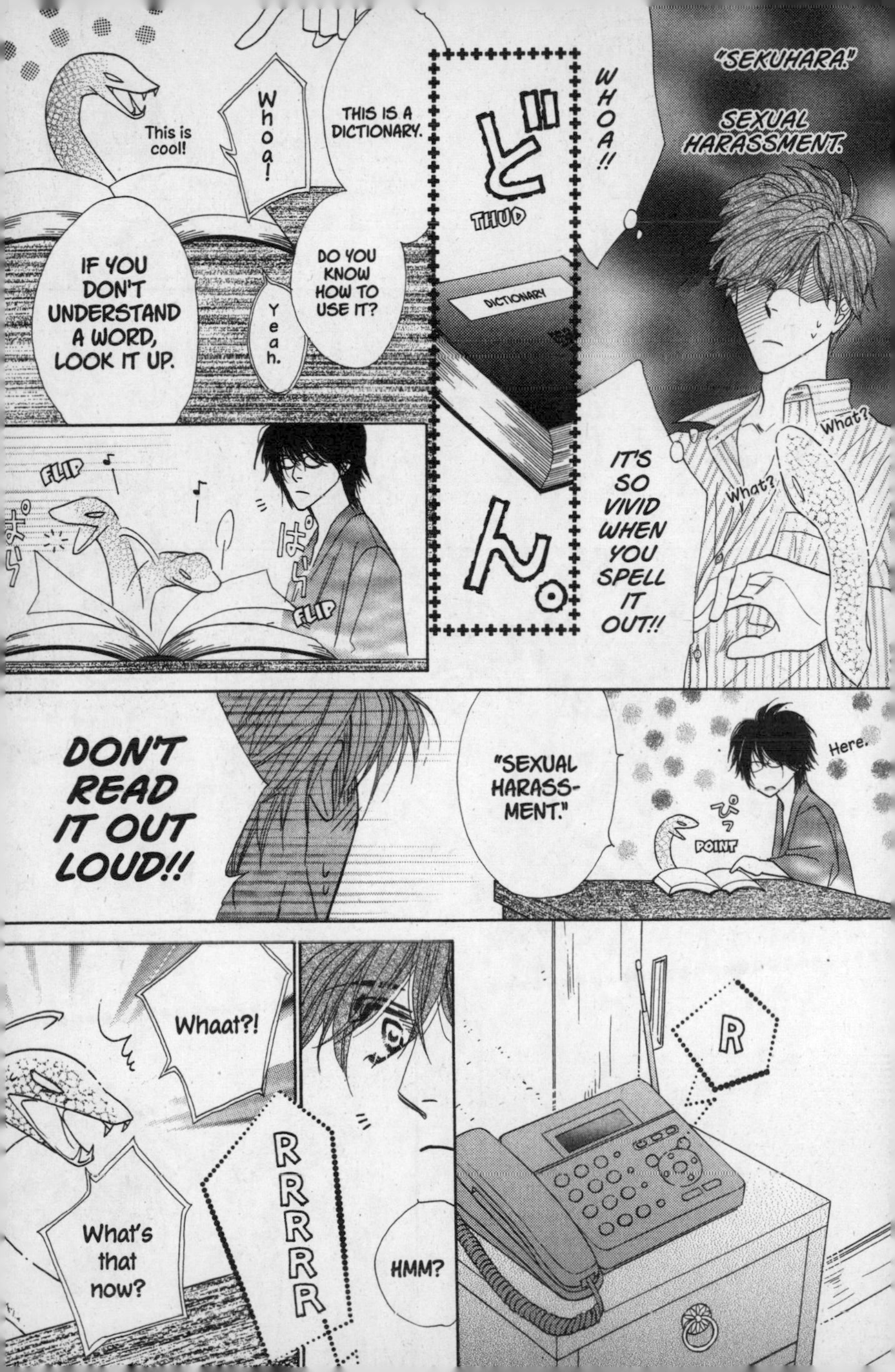
"SEKUHARA."
SEXUAL HARASSMENT.
WHOA!!
What?
What?
IT'S SO VIVID WHEN YOU SPELL IT OUT!!
どん。
THUD
DICTIONARY
THIS IS A DICTIONARY.
Whoa!
This is cool!
DO YOU KNOW HOW TO USE IT?
Yeah.
IF YOU DON'T UNDERSTAND A WORD, LOOK IT UP.
ぱら
FLIP
ぱら
FLIP
Here.
ぴっ
POINT
"SEXUAL HARASS-MENT."
DON'T READ IT OUT LOUD!!
R
RRRRR
HMM?
Whaat?!
What's that now?

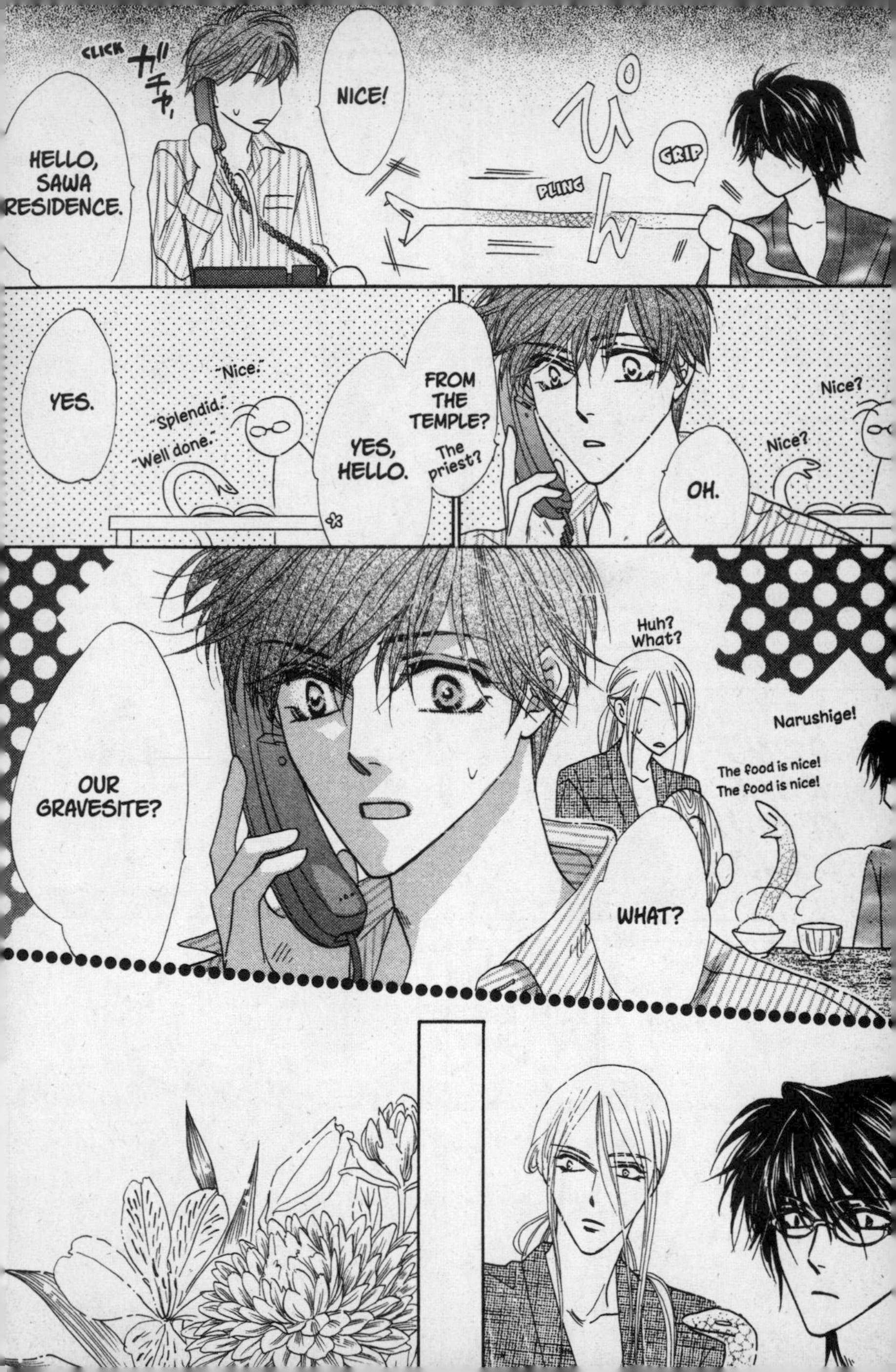
ぴん
GRIP
PLING
NICE!
CLICK
ガチャ
HELLO, SAWA RESIDENCE.
Nice?
Nice?
OH.
FROM THE TEMPLE?
The priest?
YES, HELLO.
"Nice."
"Splendid."
"Well done."
YES.
Narushige!
The food is nice! The food is nice!
Huh? What?
WHAT?
OUR GRAVESITE?

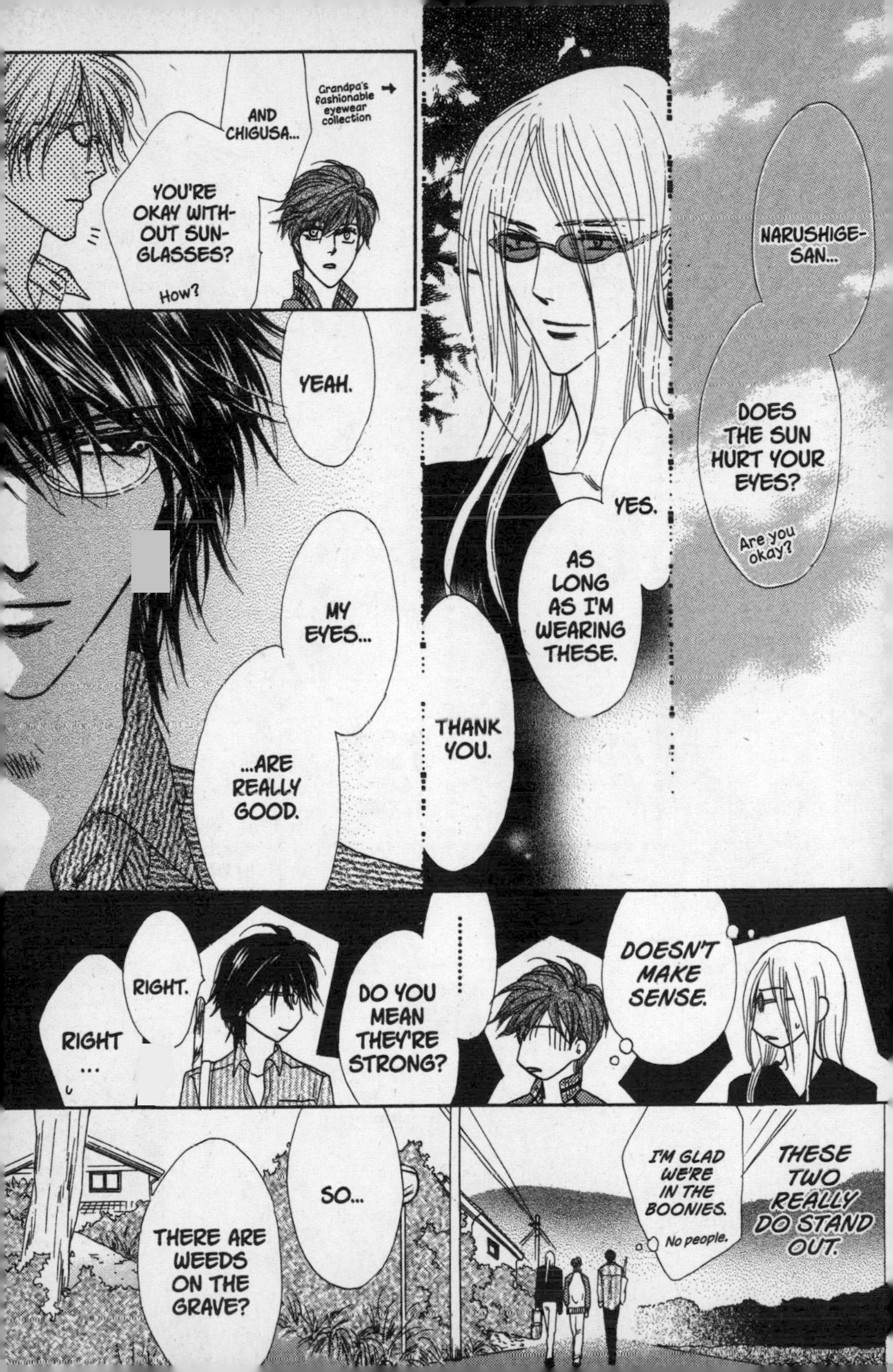
NARUSHIGE-SAN...
DOES THE SUN HURT YOUR EYES?
Are you okay?
YES.
AS LONG AS I'M WEARING THESE.
THANK YOU.
AND CHIGUSA...
YOU'RE OKAY WITH-OUT SUN-GLASSES?
How?
Grandpa's fashionable eyewear collection
YEAH.
MY EYES...
...ARE REALLY GOOD.
DOESN'T MAKE SENSE.
......
DO YOU MEAN THEY'RE STRONG?
RIGHT.
RIGHT...
THESE TWO REALLY DO STAND OUT.
I'M GLAD WE'RE IN THE BOONIES.
No people.
SO...
THERE ARE WEEDS ON THE GRAVE?

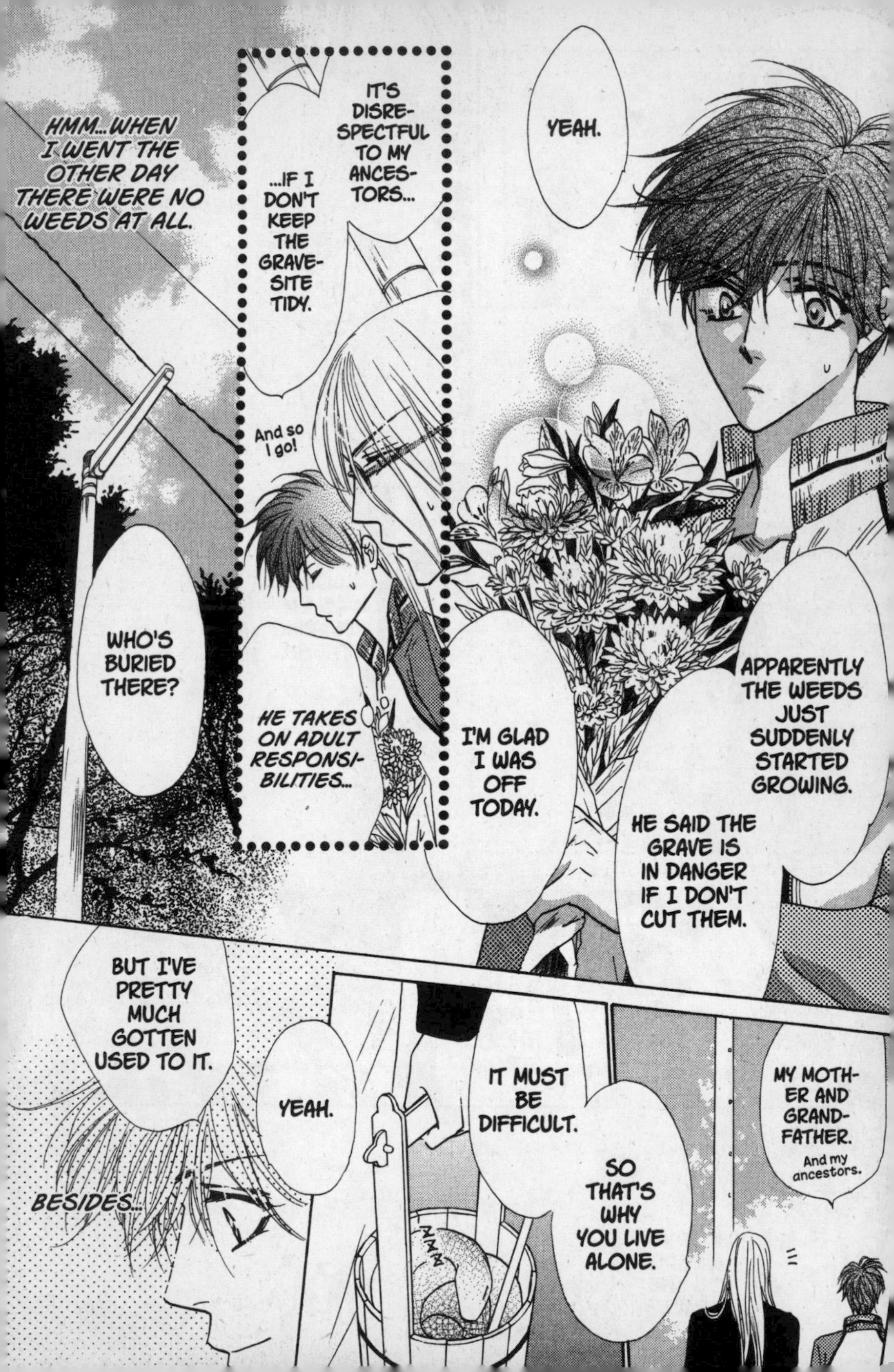
YEAH.
APPARENTLY THE WEEDS JUST SUDDENLY STARTED GROWING.
HE SAID THE GRAVE IS IN DANGER IF I DON'T CUT THEM.
I'M GLAD I WAS OFF TODAY.
IT'S DISRE-SPECTFUL TO MY ANCES-TORS...
...IF I DON'T KEEP THE GRAVE-SITE TIDY.
And so I go!
HE TAKES ON ADULT RESPONSI-BILITIES...
HMM...WHEN I WENT THE OTHER DAY THERE WERE NO WEEDS AT ALL.
WHO'S BURIED THERE?
MY MOTH-ER AND GRAND-FATHER.
And my ancestors.
SO THAT'S WHY YOU LIVE ALONE.
IT MUST BE DIFFICULT.
YEAH.
BUT I'VE PRETTY MUCH GOTTEN USED TO IT.
BESIDES...

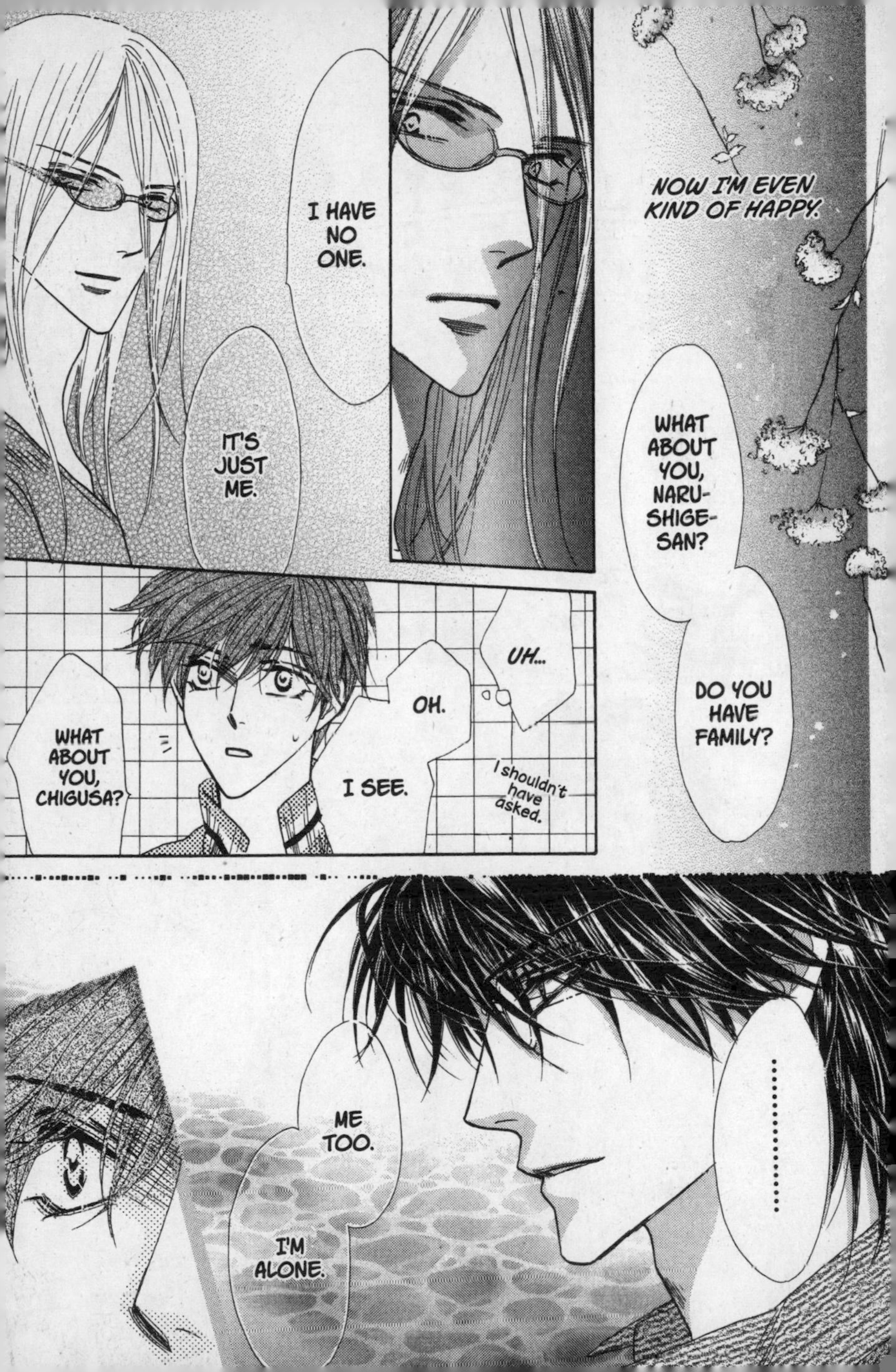
NOW I'M EVEN KIND OF HAPPY.
WHAT ABOUT YOU, NARUSHIGE-SAN?
DO YOU HAVE FAMILY?
I HAVE NO ONE.
IT'S JUST ME.
UH...
OH.
I SEE.
I shouldn't have asked.
WHAT ABOUT YOU, CHIGUSA?
......
ME TOO.
I'M ALONE.

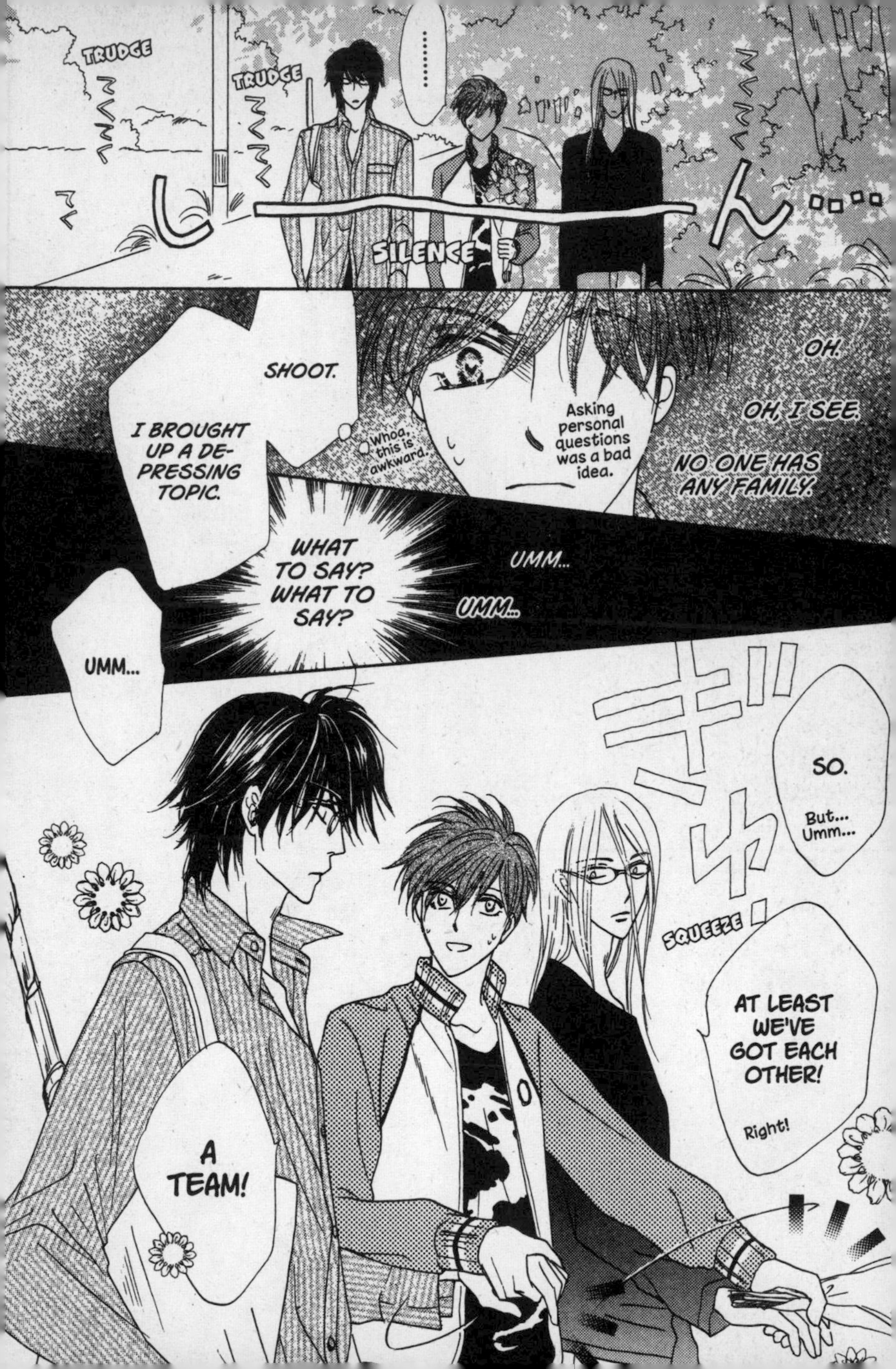
......
TRUDGE
TRUDGE
SILENCE
OH.
OH, I SEE.
NO ONE HAS ANY FAMILY.
Asking personal questions was a bad idea.
Whoa, this is awkward.
SHOOT.
I BROUGHT UP A DE-PRESSING TOPIC.
UMM...
UMM...
WHAT TO SAY? WHAT TO SAY?
UMM...
SO.
But... Umm...
SQUEEZE
AT LEAST WE'VE GOT EACH OTHER!
Right!
A TEAM!

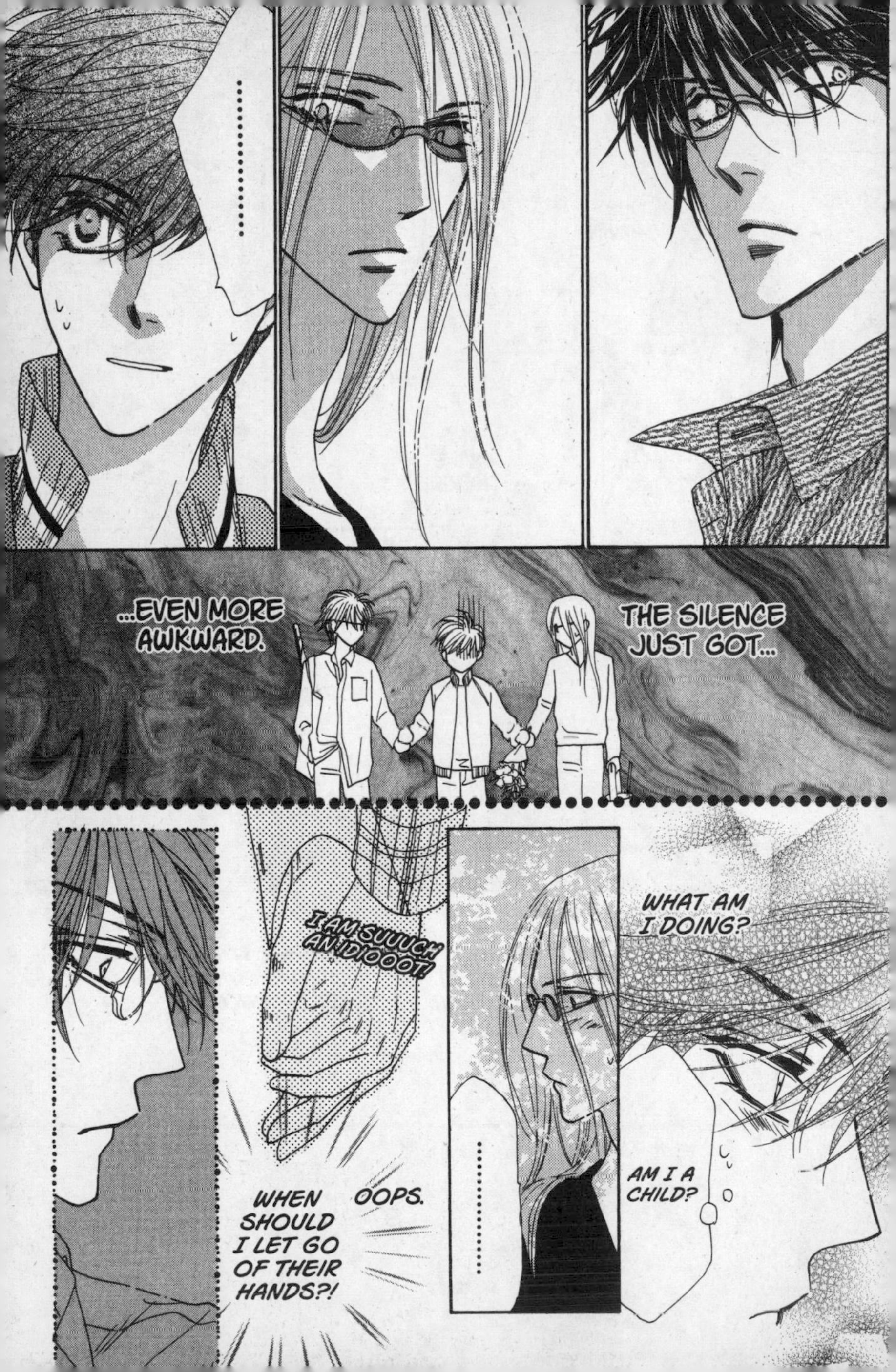
......
THE SILENCE JUST GOT...
...EVEN MORE AWKWARD.
WHAT AM I DOING?
AM I A CHILD?
......
I AM SUUUCH AN IDIOOOT!
OOPS.
WHEN SHOULD I LET GO OF THEIR HANDS?!

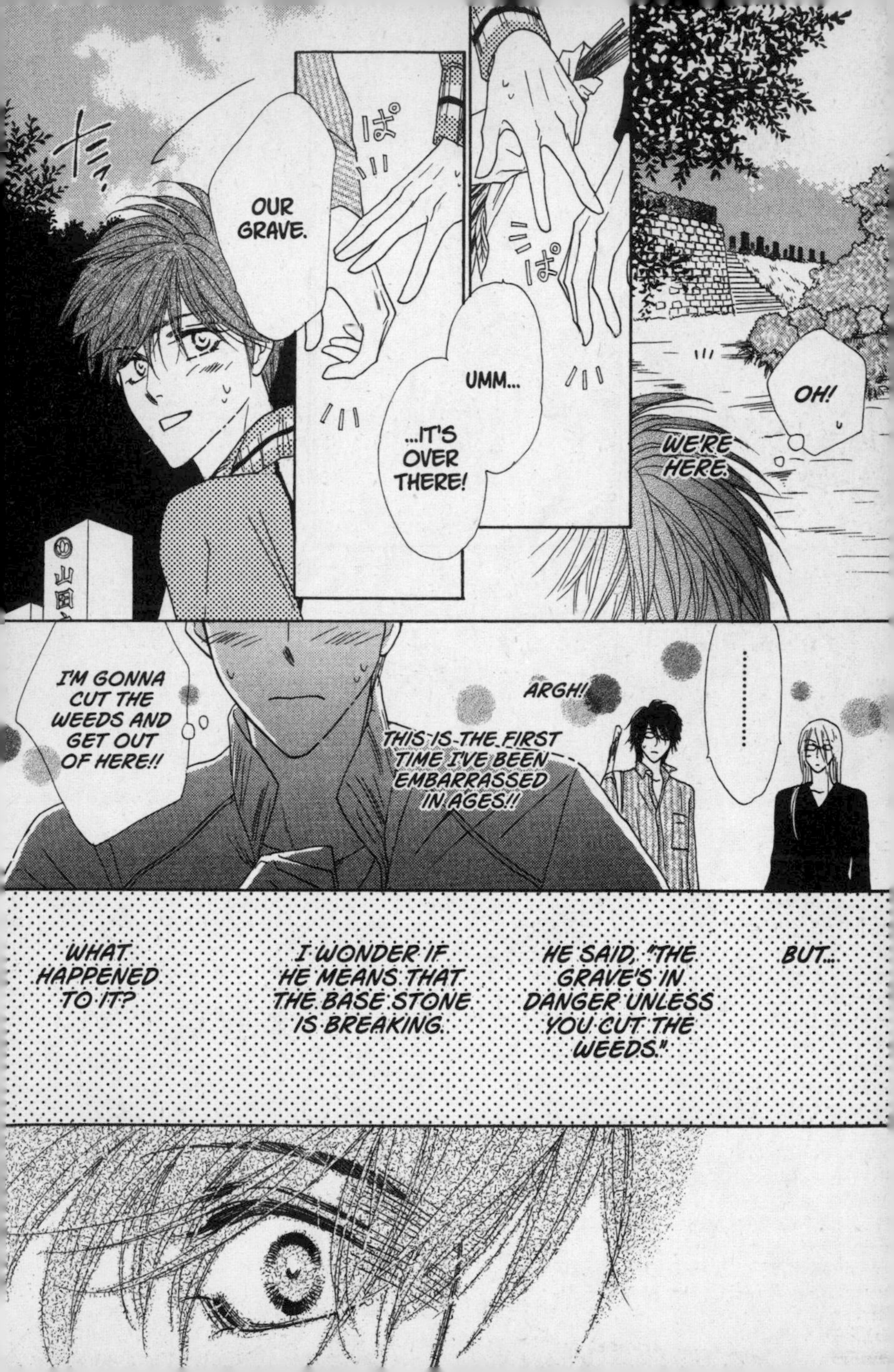

OH!
WE'RE HERE.
ぱ
ぱ
UMM...
...IT'S OVER THERE!
OUR GRAVE.
......
ARGH!
THIS IS THE FIRST TIME I'VE BEEN EMBARRASSED IN AGES!!
I'M GONNA CUT THE WEEDS AND GET OUT OF HERE!!
BUT...
HE SAID, "THE GRAVE'S IN DANGER UNLESS YOU CUT THE WEEDS."
I WONDER IF HE MEANS THAT THE BASE STONE IS BREAKING.
WHAT HAPPENED TO IT?

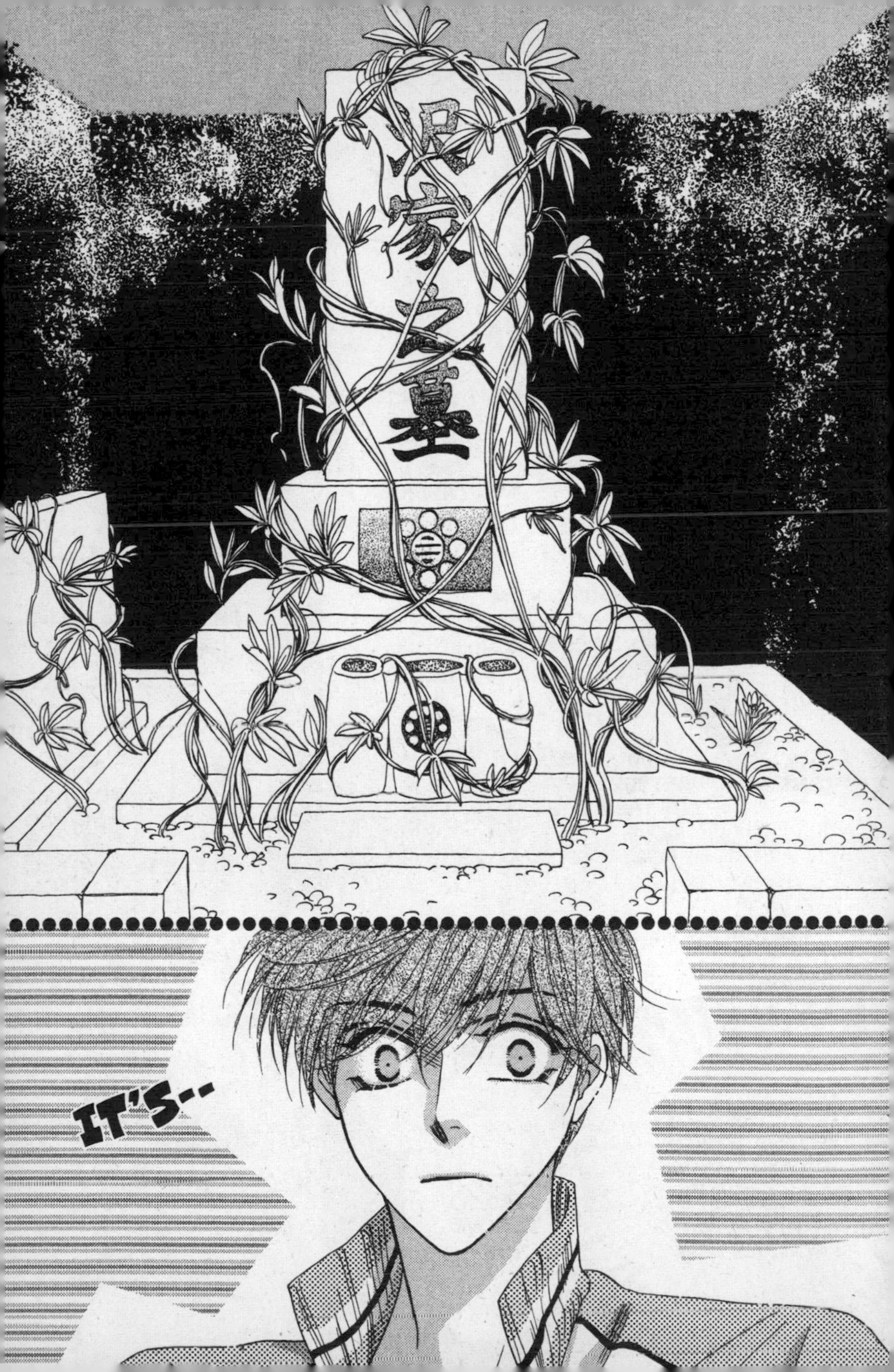
IT'S--

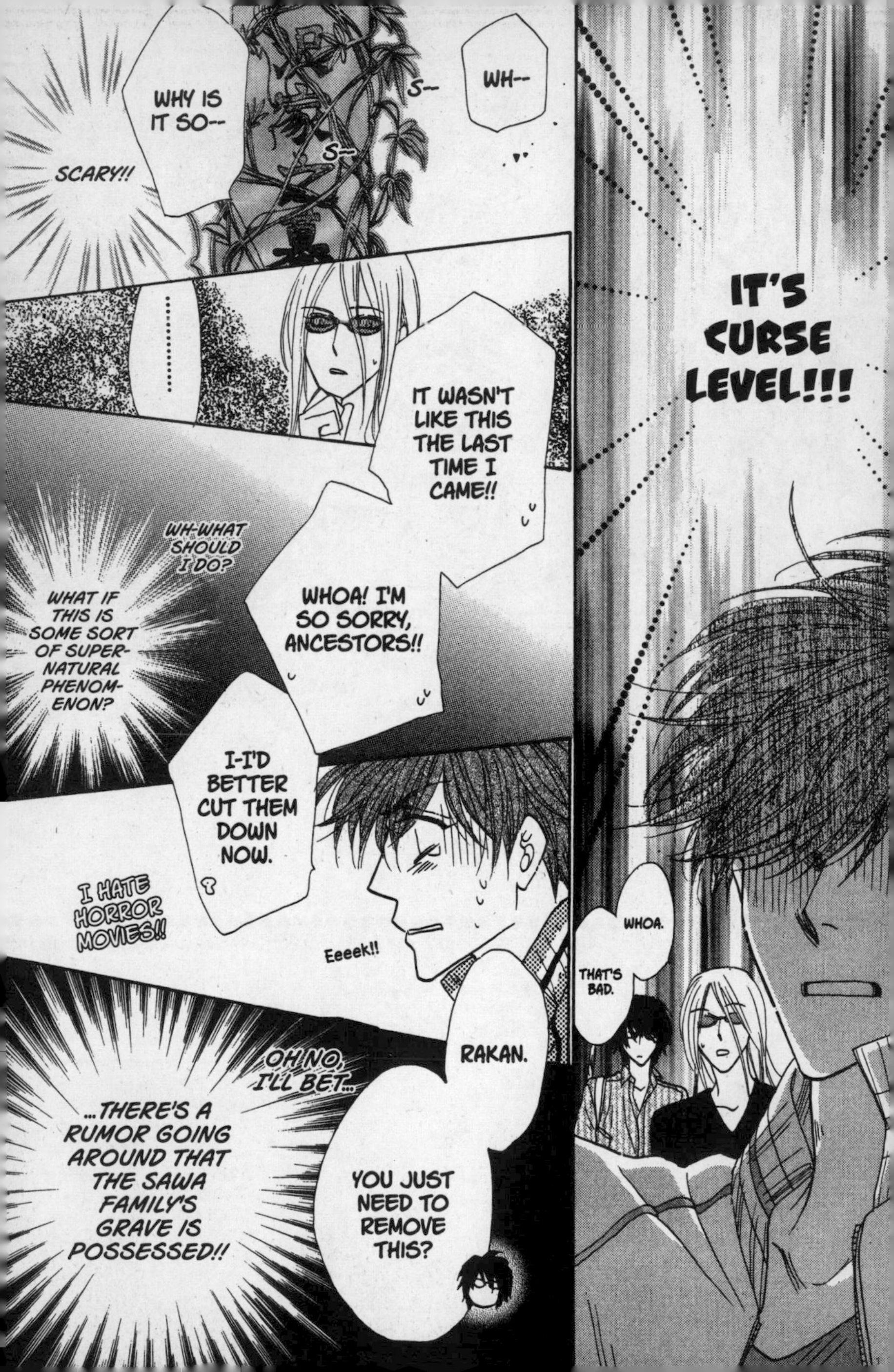
IT'S CURSE LEVEL!!!
WHOA.
THAT'S BAD.
WH--
S--
S--
WHY IS IT SO--
SCARY!!
IT WASN'T LIKE THIS THE LAST TIME I CAME!!
......
WHOA! I'M SO SORRY, ANCESTORS!!
WH-WHAT SHOULD I DO?
WHAT IF THIS IS SOME SORT OF SUPER-NATURAL PHENOMENON?
I-I'D BETTER CUT THEM DOWN NOW.
Eeeek!!
I HATE HORROR MOVIES!!
RAKAN.
YOU JUST NEED TO REMOVE THIS?
OH NO, I'LL BET...
...THERE'S A RUMOR GOING AROUND THAT THE SAWA FAMILY'S GRAVE IS POSSESSED!!

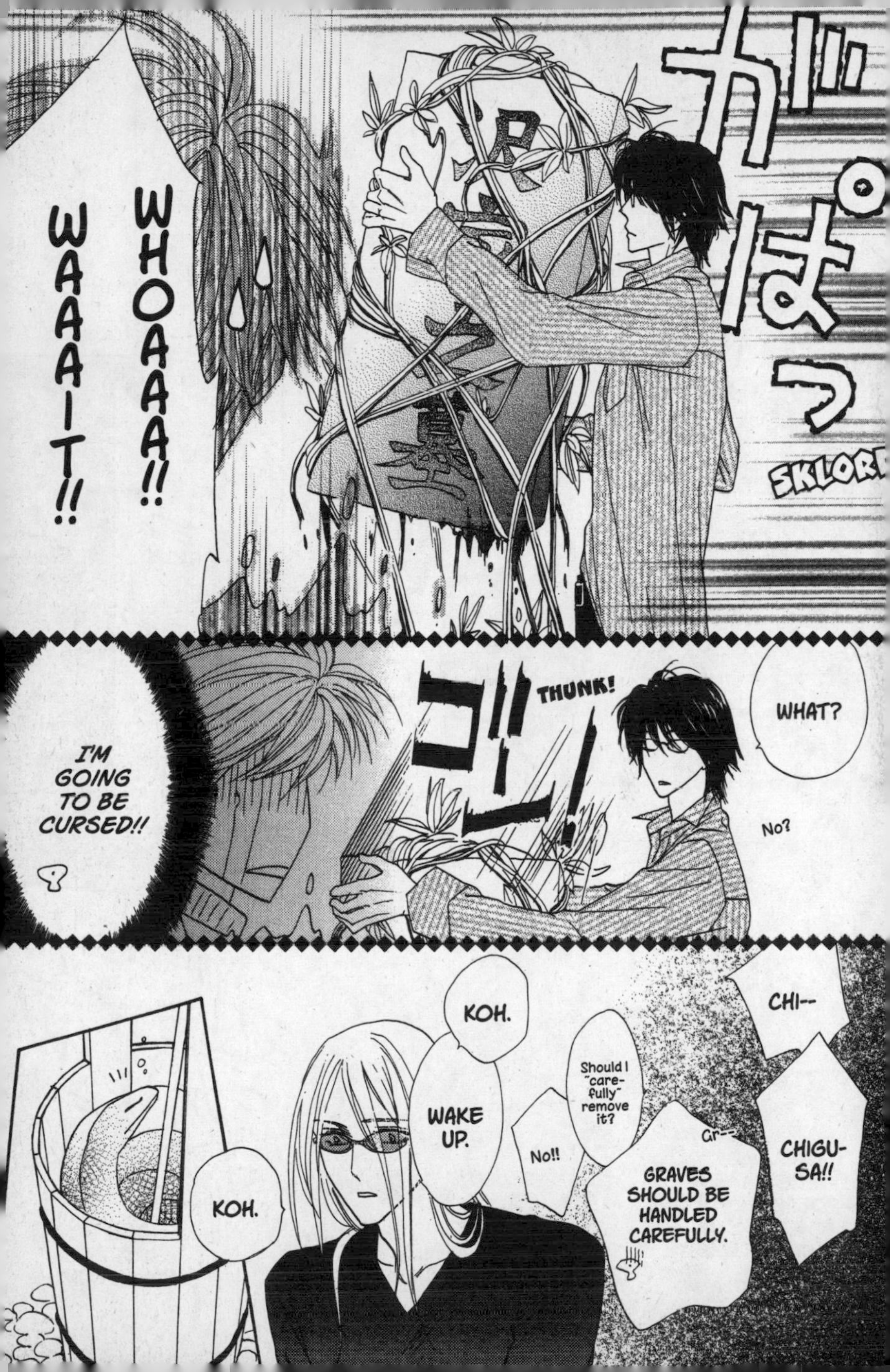
がぽっ
SKLOR
WHOAAAA!! WAAAAIT!!
WHAT?
No?
ゴン!
THUNK!
I'M GOING TO BE CURSED!!
CHI--
CHIGU-SA!!
GRAVES SHOULD BE HANDLED CAREFULLY.
Gr--
Should I "carefully" remove it?
No!!
KOH.
WAKE UP.
KOH.

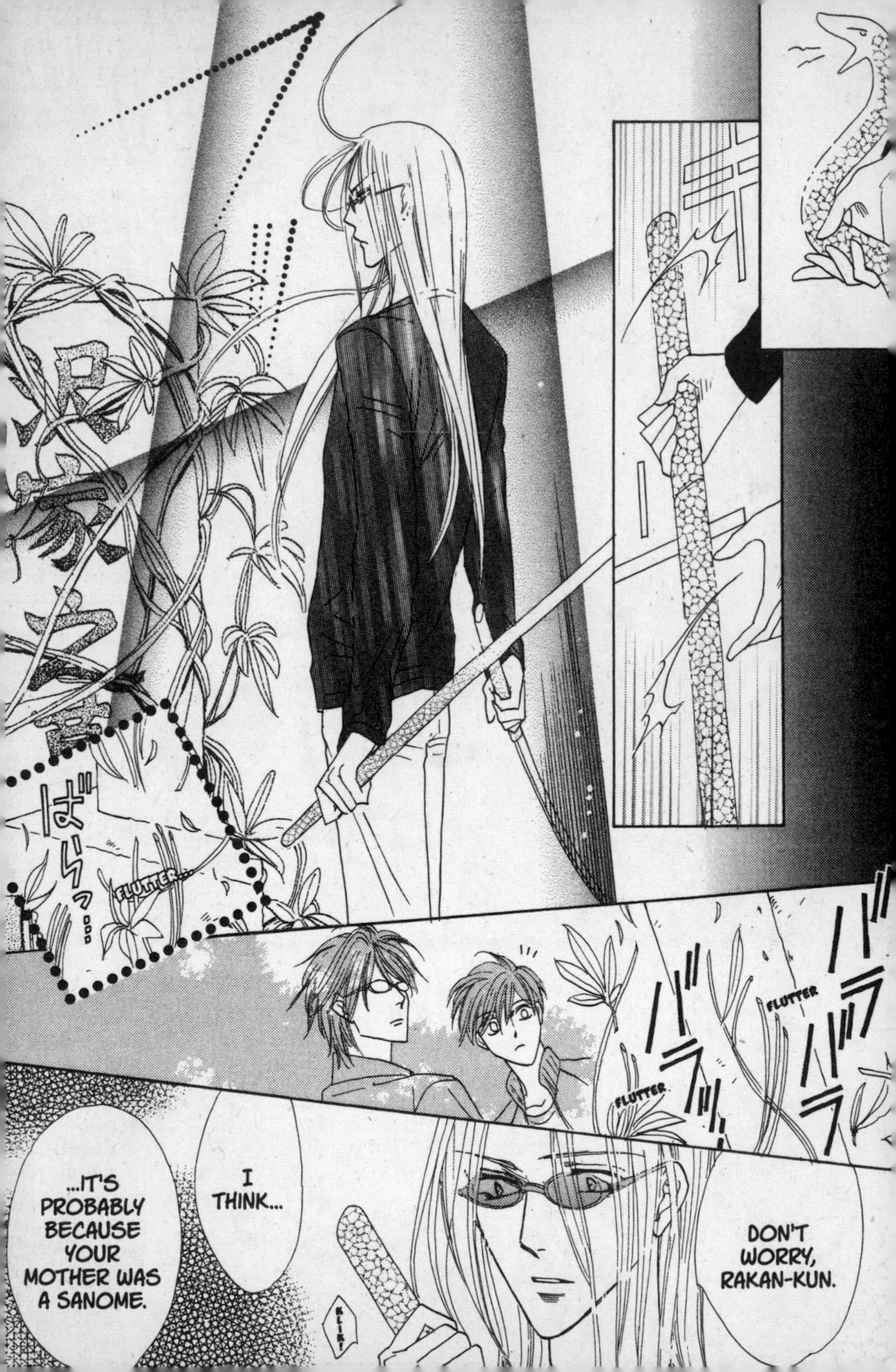

ばらっ...
FLUTTER...
バラッ
FLUTTER
バラ
FLUTTER
DON'T WORRY, RAKAN-KUN.
I THINK...
...IT'S PROBABLY BECAUSE YOUR MOTHER WAS A SANOME.
KLIK!

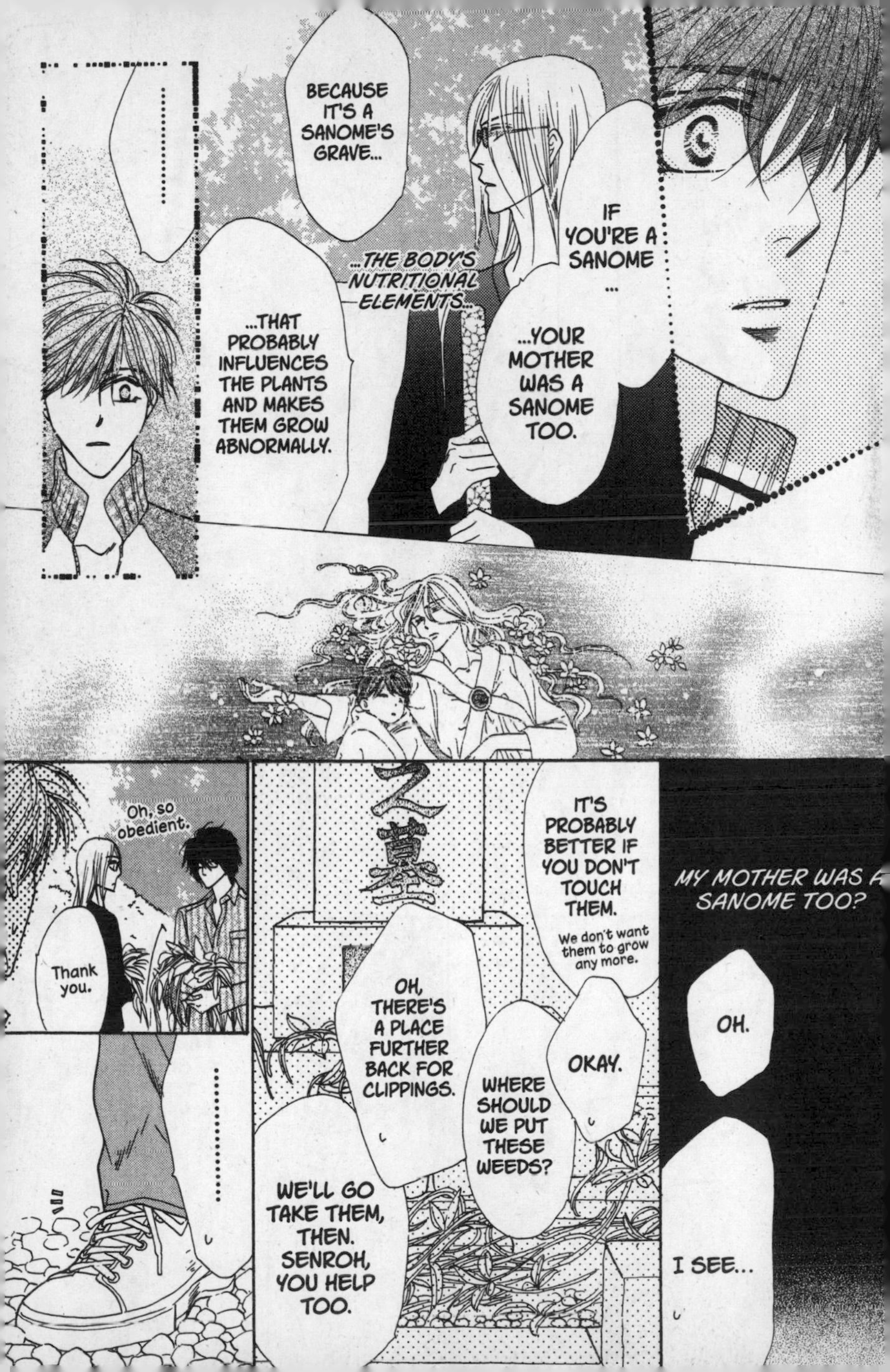
BECAUSE IT'S A SANOME'S GRAVE...
...THE BODY'S NUTRITIONAL ELEMENTS...
...THAT PROBABLY INFLUENCES THE PLANTS AND MAKES THEM GROW ABNORMALLY.
IF YOU'RE A SANOME ...
...YOUR MOTHER WAS A SANOME TOO.
......
MY MOTHER WAS A SANOME TOO?
OH.
I SEE...
IT'S PROBABLY BETTER IF YOU DON'T TOUCH THEM.
We don't want them to grow any more.
OKAY.
WHERE SHOULD WE PUT THESE WEEDS?
OH, THERE'S A PLACE FURTHER BACK FOR CLIPPINGS.
WE'LL GO TAKE THEM, THEN. SENROH, YOU HELP TOO.
Oh, so obedient.
Thank you.
......

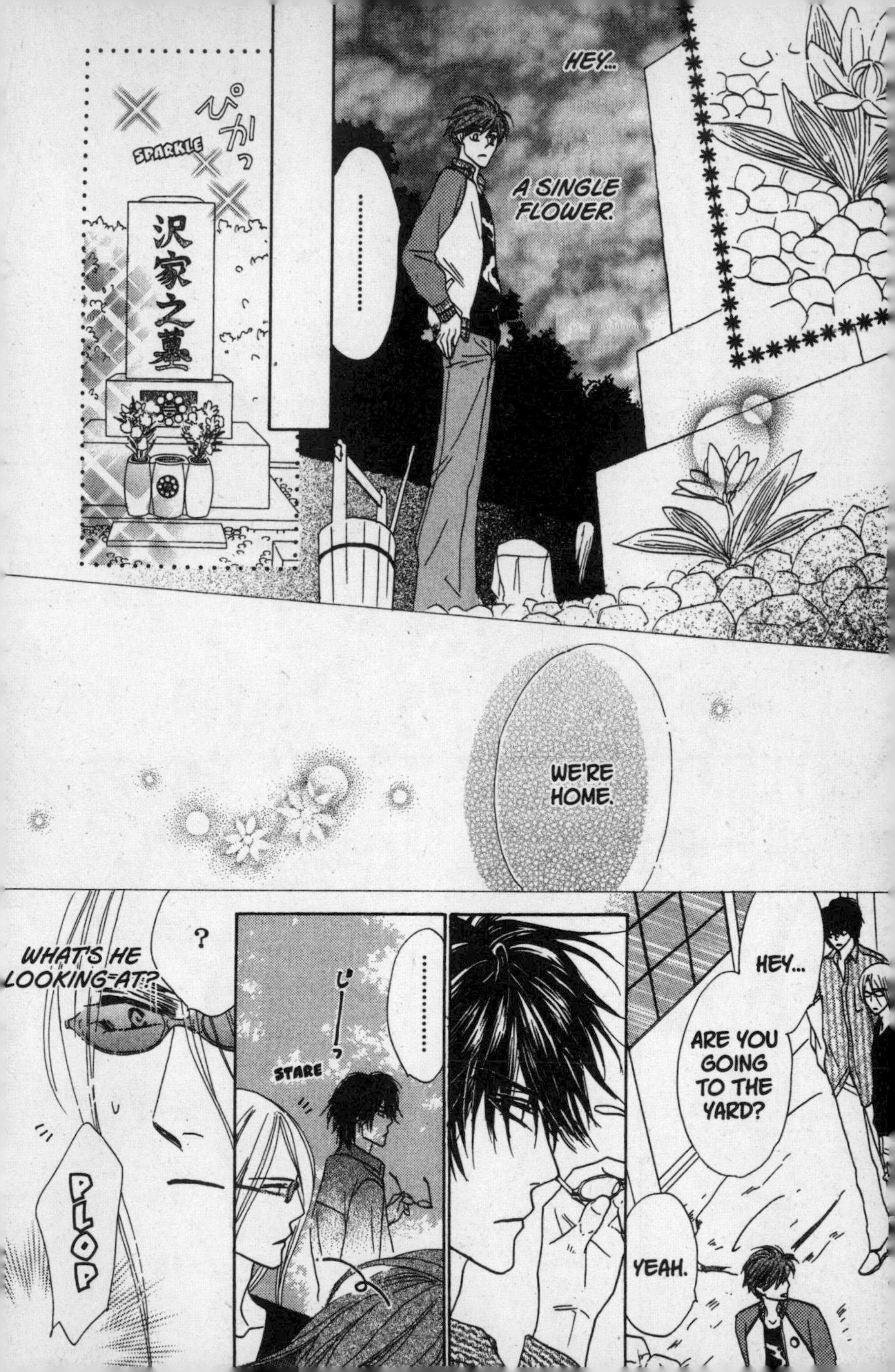
HEY...
A SINGLE FLOWER.
....
ぴかっ
SPARKLE
沢家之墓
WE'RE HOME.
HEY...
ARE YOU GOING TO THE YARD?
YEAH.
....
じーっ
STARE
?
WHAT'S HE LOOKING AT?
PLOP

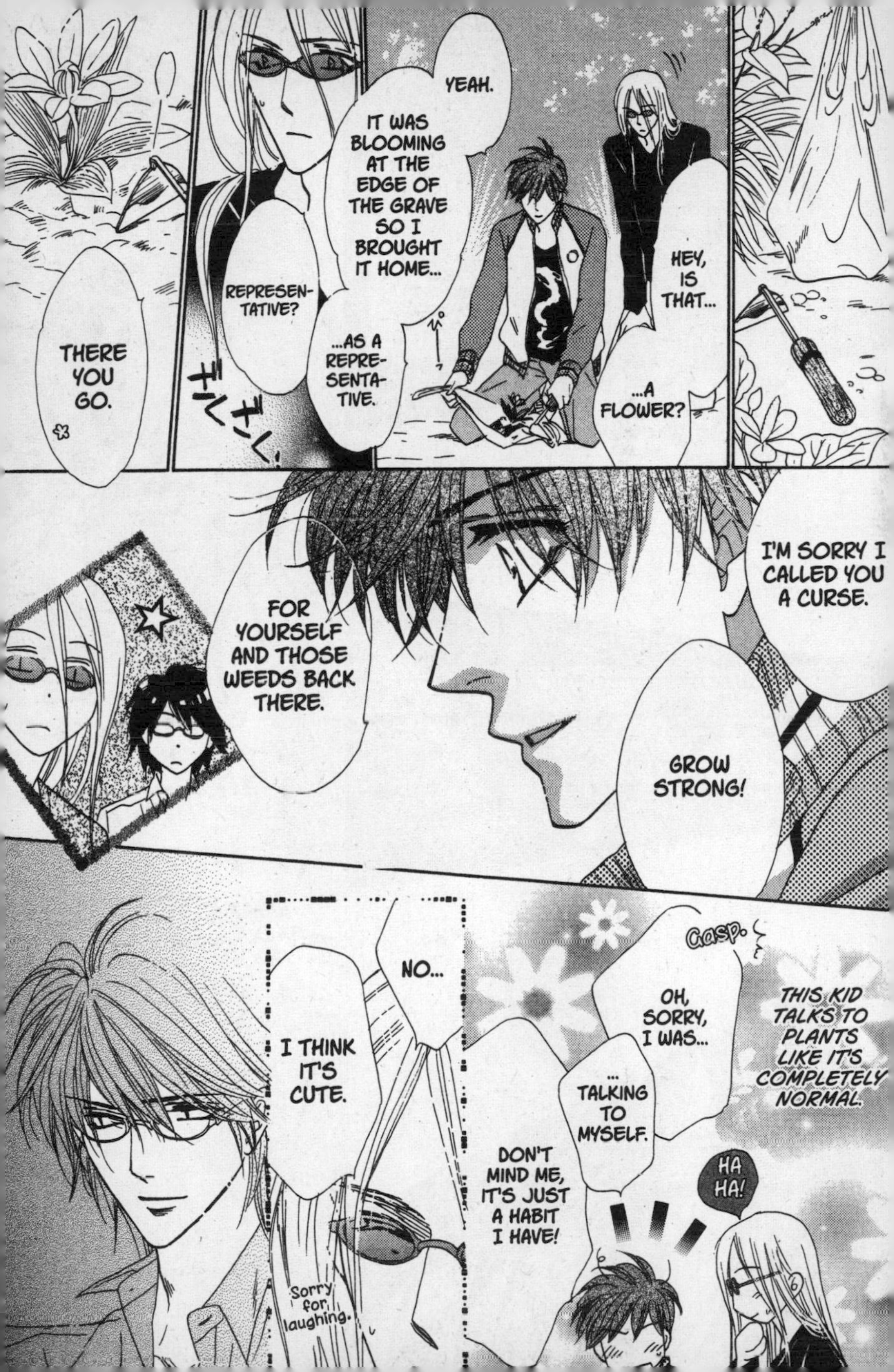

HEY, IS THAT...
...A FLOWER?
YEAH.
IT WAS BLOOMING AT THE EDGE OF THE GRAVE SO I BROUGHT IT HOME...
...AS A REPRESENTATIVE.
REPRESENTATIVE?
THERE YOU GO.
I'M SORRY I CALLED YOU A CURSE.
GROW STRONG!
FOR YOURSELF AND THOSE WEEDS BACK THERE.
Gasp.
THIS KID TALKS TO PLANTS LIKE IT'S COMPLETELY NORMAL.
HA HA!
OH, SORRY, I WAS...
...TALKING TO MYSELF.
DON'T MIND ME, IT'S JUST A HABIT I HAVE!
NO...
I THINK IT'S CUTE.
Sorry for laughing.

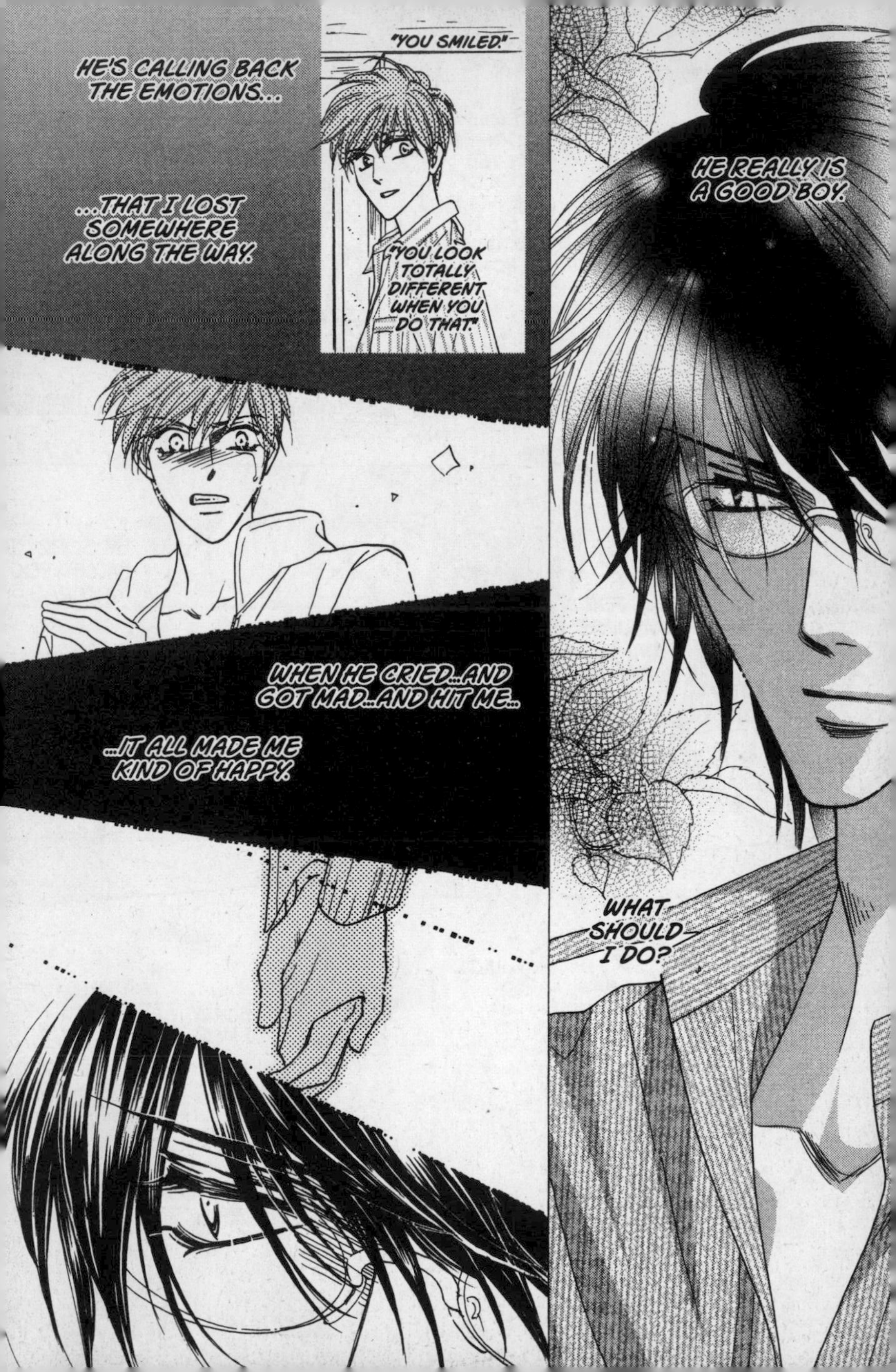
HE REALLY IS A GOOD BOY.
WHAT SHOULD I DO?
"YOU SMILED."
"YOU LOOK TOTALLY DIFFERENT WHEN YOU DO THAT."
HE'S CALLING BACK THE EMOTIONS...
...THAT I LOST SOMEWHERE ALONG THE WAY.
WHEN HE CRIED...AND GOT MAD...AND HIT ME...
...IT ALL MADE ME KIND OF HAPPY.

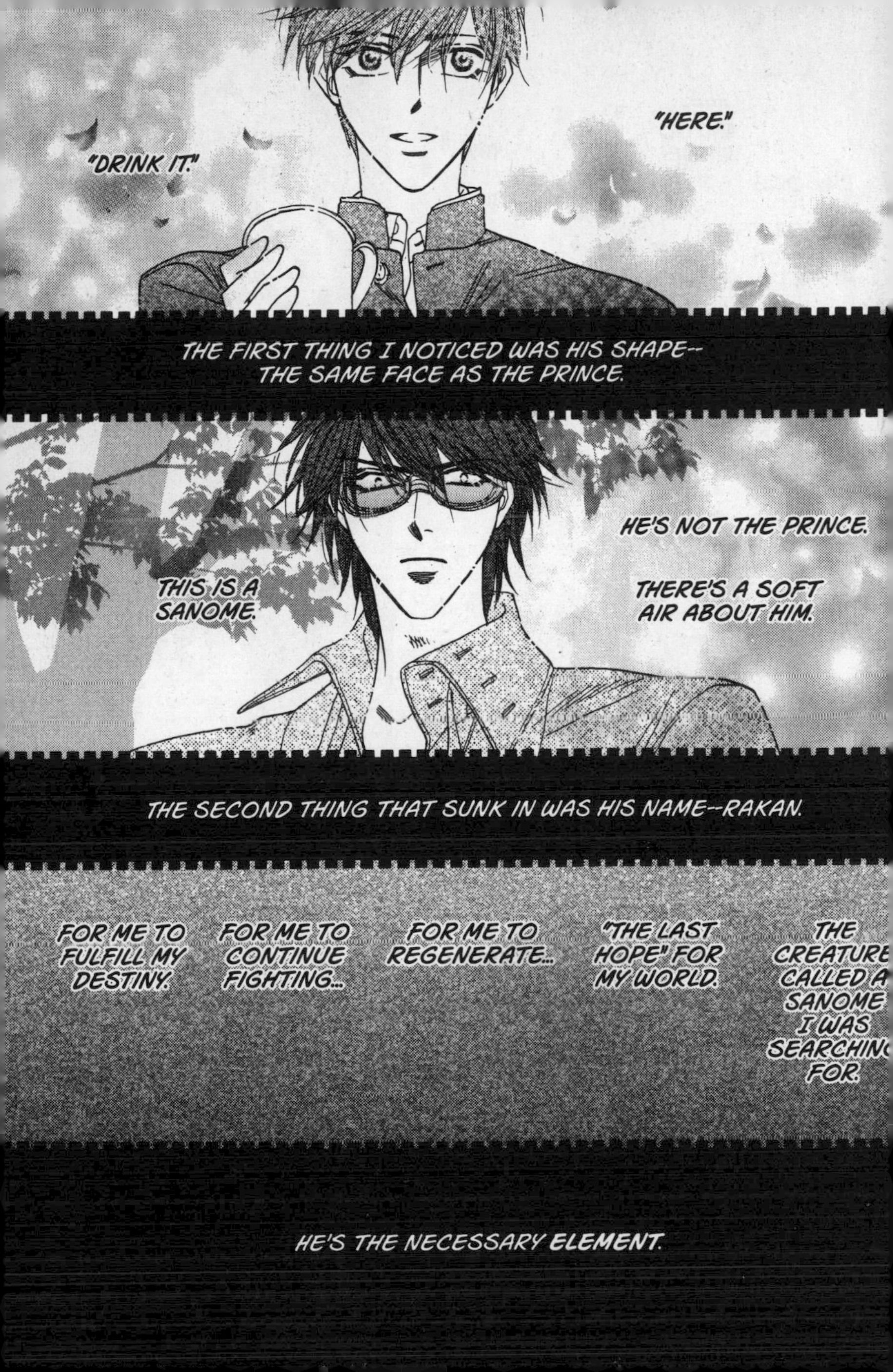
"HERE."
"DRINK IT."
THE FIRST THING I NOTICED WAS HIS SHAPE-- THE SAME FACE AS THE PRINCE.
HE'S NOT THE PRINCE.
THERE'S A SOFT AIR ABOUT HIM.
THIS IS A SANOME.
THE SECOND THING THAT SUNK IN WAS HIS NAME--RAKAN.
THE CREATURE CALLED A SANOME I WAS SEARCHING FOR.
"THE LAST HOPE" FOR MY WORLD.
FOR ME TO REGENERATE...
FOR ME TO CONTINUE FIGHTING...
FOR ME TO FULFILL MY DESTINY.
HE'S THE NECESSARY **ELEMENT**.

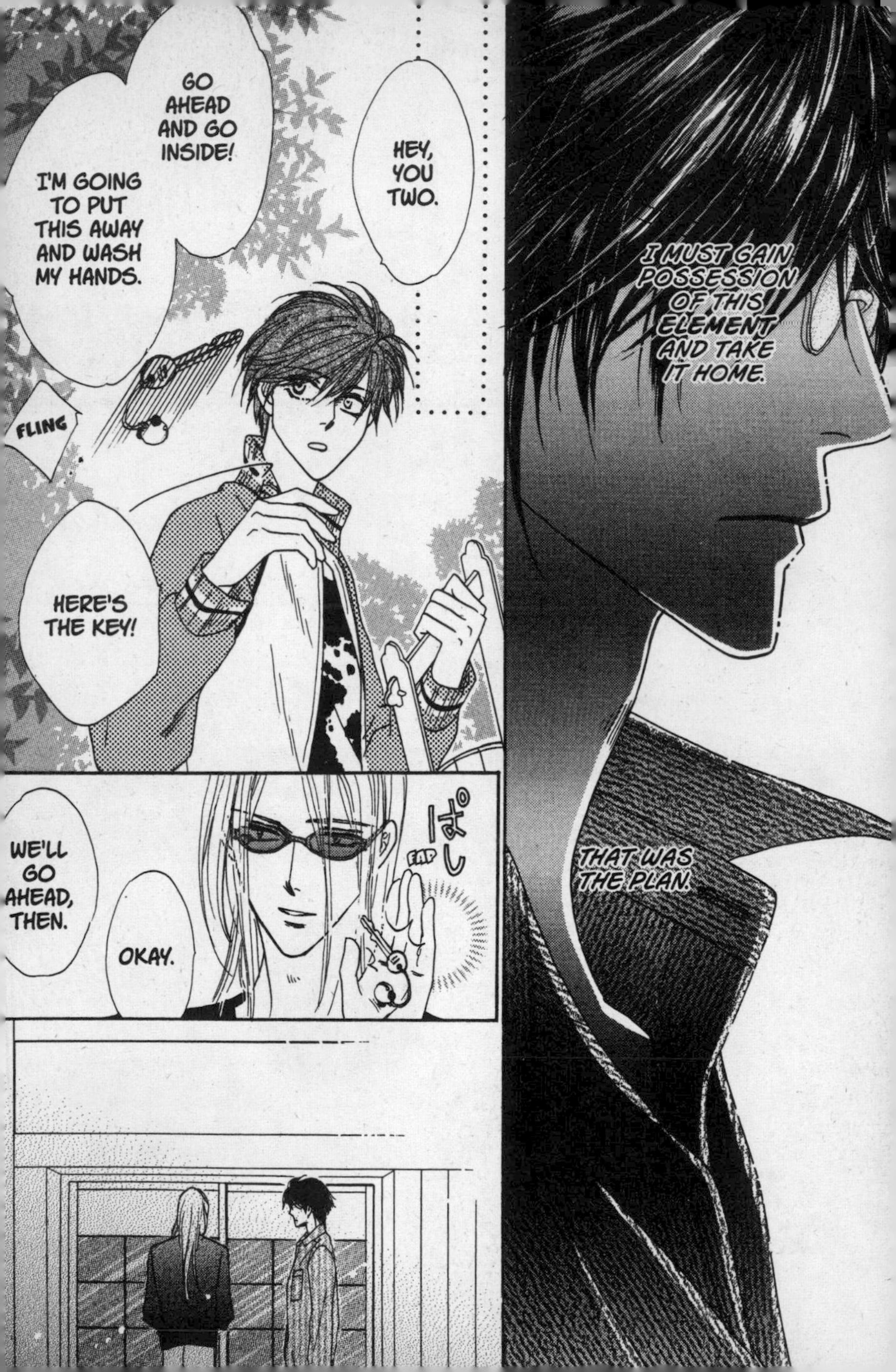
I MUST GAIN POSSESSION OF THIS ELEMENT AND TAKE IT HOME.
THAT WAS THE PLAN.
HEY, YOU TWO.
GO AHEAD AND GO INSIDE!
I'M GOING TO PUT THIS AWAY AND WASH MY HANDS.
FLING
HERE'S THE KEY!
ぱし
FAP
WE'LL GO AHEAD, THEN.
OKAY.

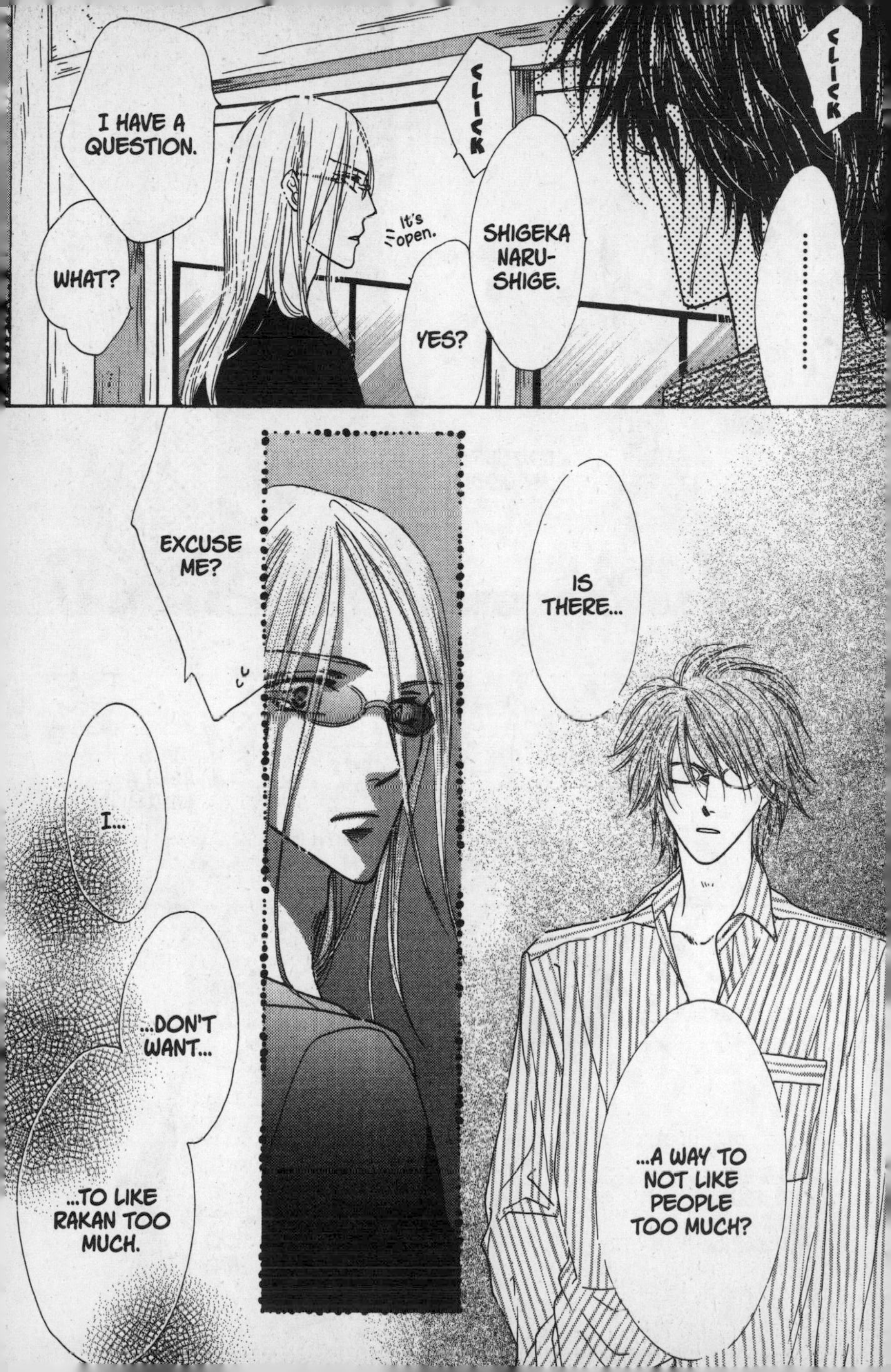
CLICK
......
CLICK
SHIGEKA NARU-SHIGE.
It's open.
YES?
I HAVE A QUESTION.
WHAT?
IS THERE...
...A WAY TO NOT LIKE PEOPLE TOO MUCH?
EXCUSE ME?
I...
...DON'T WANT...
...TO LIKE RAKAN TOO MUCH.

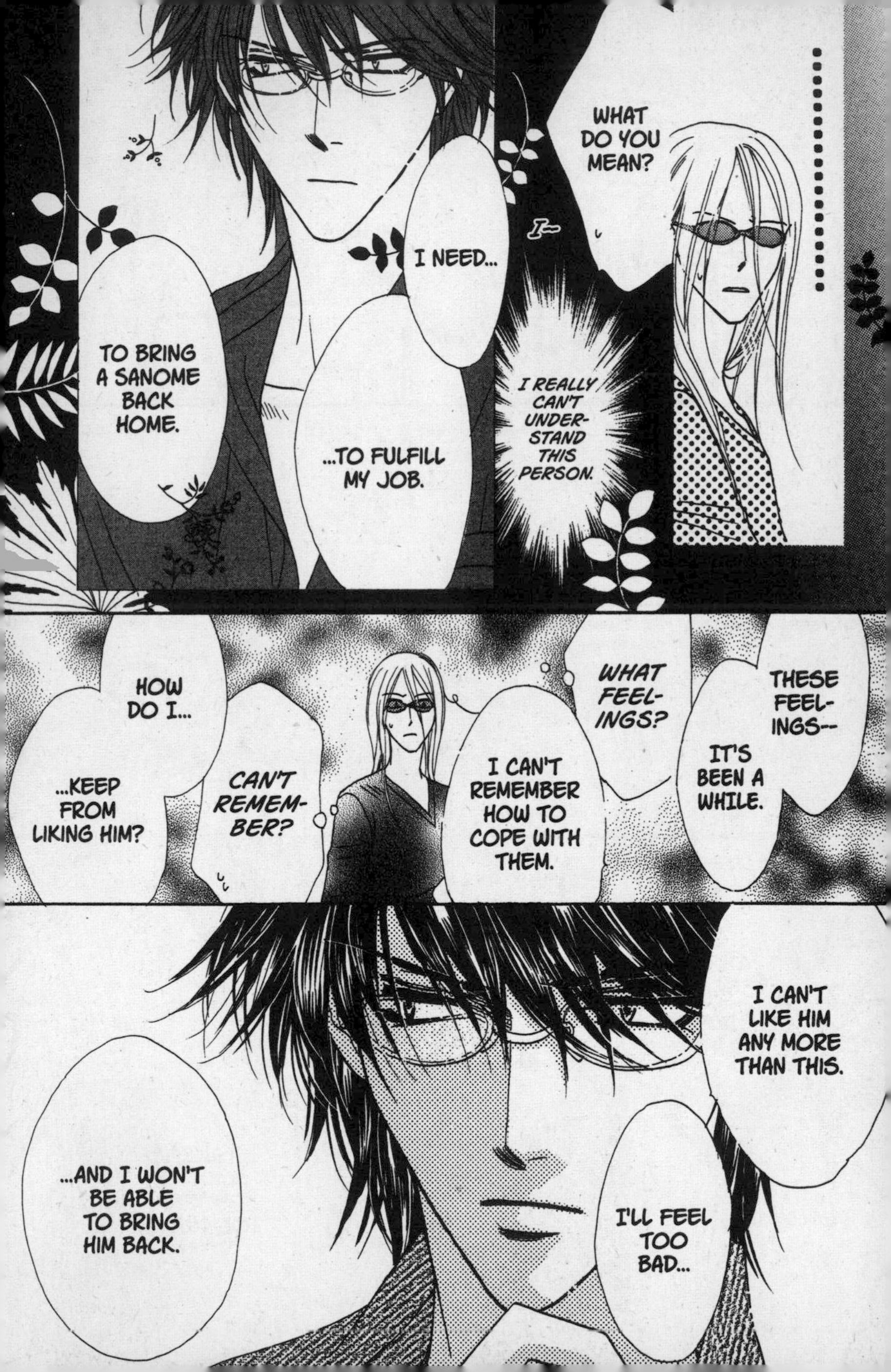

......
WHAT DO YOU MEAN?
I—
I REALLY CAN'T UNDERSTAND THIS PERSON.
I NEED...
...TO FULFILL MY JOB.
TO BRING A SANOME BACK HOME.
THESE FEEL-INGS--
IT'S BEEN A WHILE.
WHAT FEEL-INGS?
I CAN'T REMEMBER HOW TO COPE WITH THEM.
CAN'T REMEM-BER?
HOW DO I...
...KEEP FROM LIKING HIM?
I CAN'T LIKE HIM ANY MORE THAN THIS.
I'LL FEEL TOO BAD...
...AND I WON'T BE ABLE TO BRING HIM BACK.

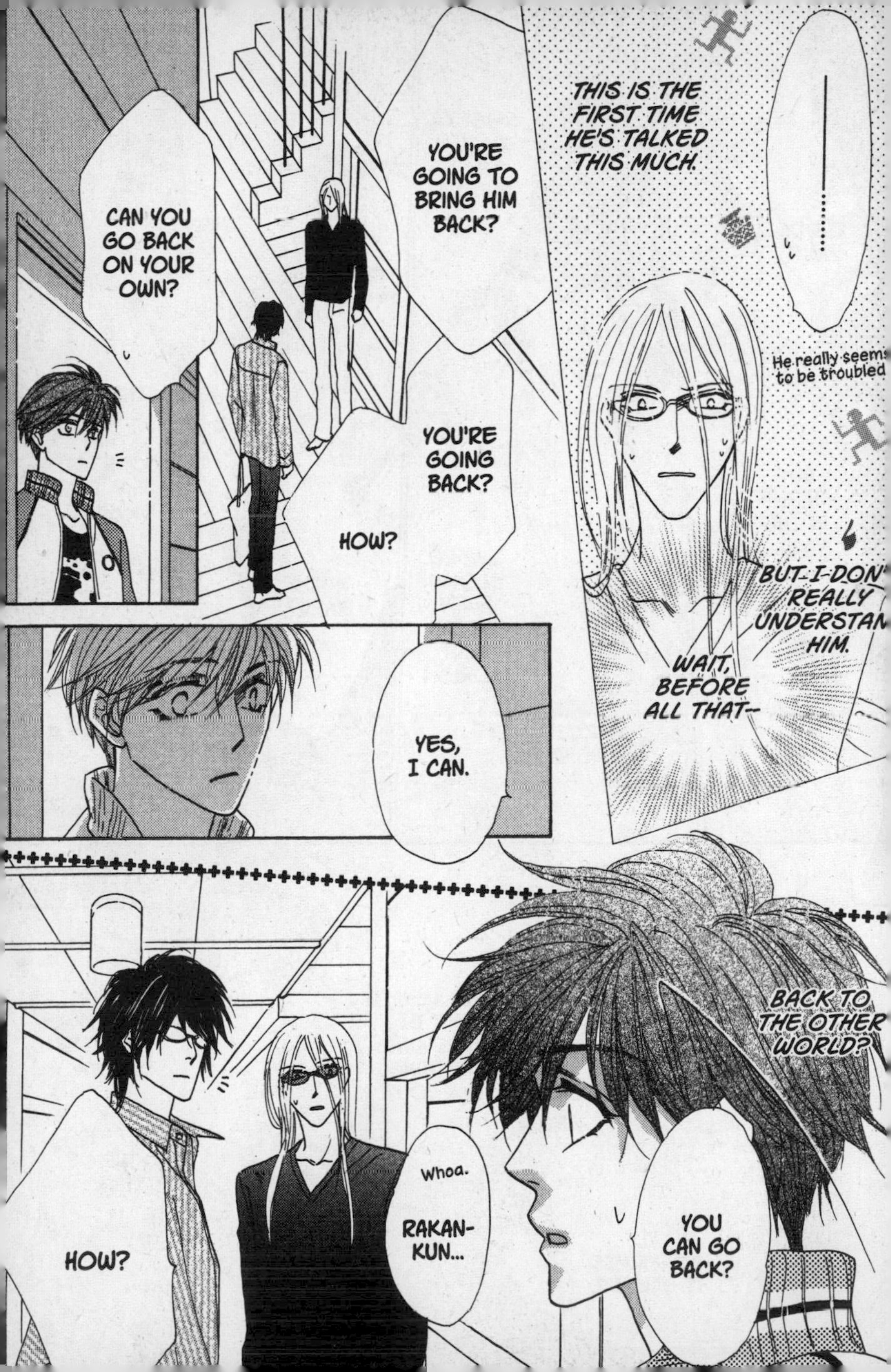
......
He really seems to be troubled
THIS IS THE FIRST TIME HE'S TALKED THIS MUCH.
BUT I DON' REALLY UNDERSTAN HIM.
WAIT, BEFORE ALL THAT-
YOU'RE GOING TO BRING HIM BACK?
CAN YOU GO BACK ON YOUR OWN?
YOU'RE GOING BACK?
HOW?
YES, I CAN.
BACK TO THE OTHER WORLD?
YOU CAN GO BACK?
Whoa.
RAKAN-KUN...
HOW?

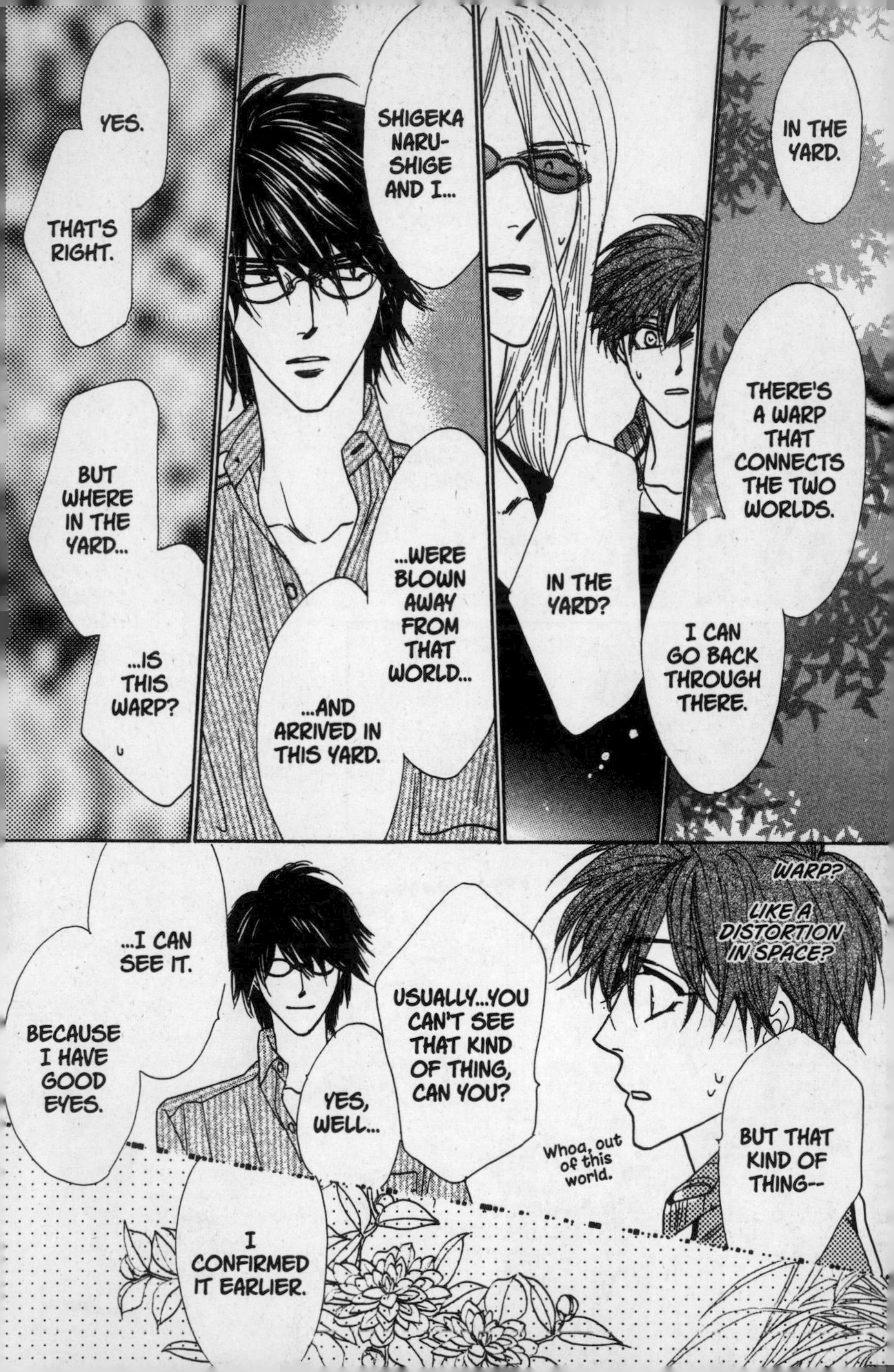
IN THE YARD.
THERE'S A WARP THAT CONNECTS THE TWO WORLDS.
I CAN GO BACK THROUGH THERE.
IN THE YARD?
SHIGEKA NARUSHIGE AND I...
...WERE BLOWN AWAY FROM THAT WORLD...
...AND ARRIVED IN THIS YARD.
YES.
THAT'S RIGHT.
BUT WHERE IN THE YARD...
...IS THIS WARP?
WARP? LIKE A DISTORTION IN SPACE?
BUT THAT KIND OF THING--
Whoa, out of this world.
USUALLY...YOU CAN'T SEE THAT KIND OF THING, CAN YOU?
YES, WELL...
...I CAN SEE IT.
BECAUSE I HAVE GOOD EYES.
I CONFIRMED IT EARLIER.

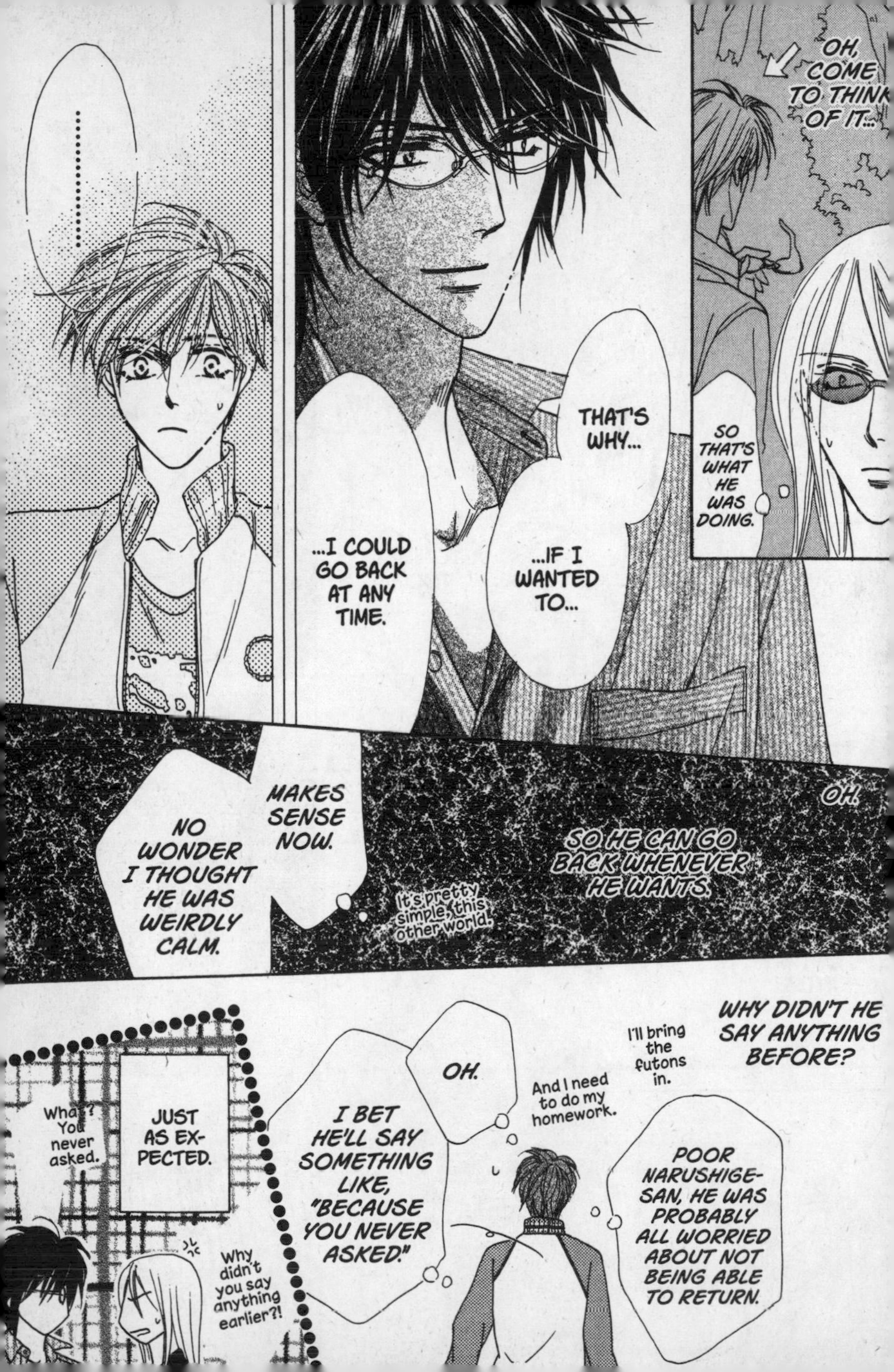
OH, COME TO THINK OF IT...
SO THAT'S WHAT HE WAS DOING.
THAT'S WHY...
...IF I WANTED TO...
...I COULD GO BACK AT ANY TIME.
......
OH.
SO HE CAN GO BACK WHENEVER HE WANTS.
It's pretty simple, this other world.
MAKES SENSE NOW.
NO WONDER I THOUGHT HE WAS WEIRDLY CALM.
WHY DIDN'T HE SAY ANYTHING BEFORE?
I'll bring the futons in.
POOR NARUSHIGE-SAN, HE WAS PROBABLY ALL WORRIED ABOUT NOT BEING ABLE TO RETURN.
And I need to do my homework.
OH.
I BET HE'LL SAY SOMETHING LIKE, "BECAUSE YOU NEVER ASKED."
JUST AS EX-PECTED.
Why didn't you say anything earlier?!
What? You never asked.

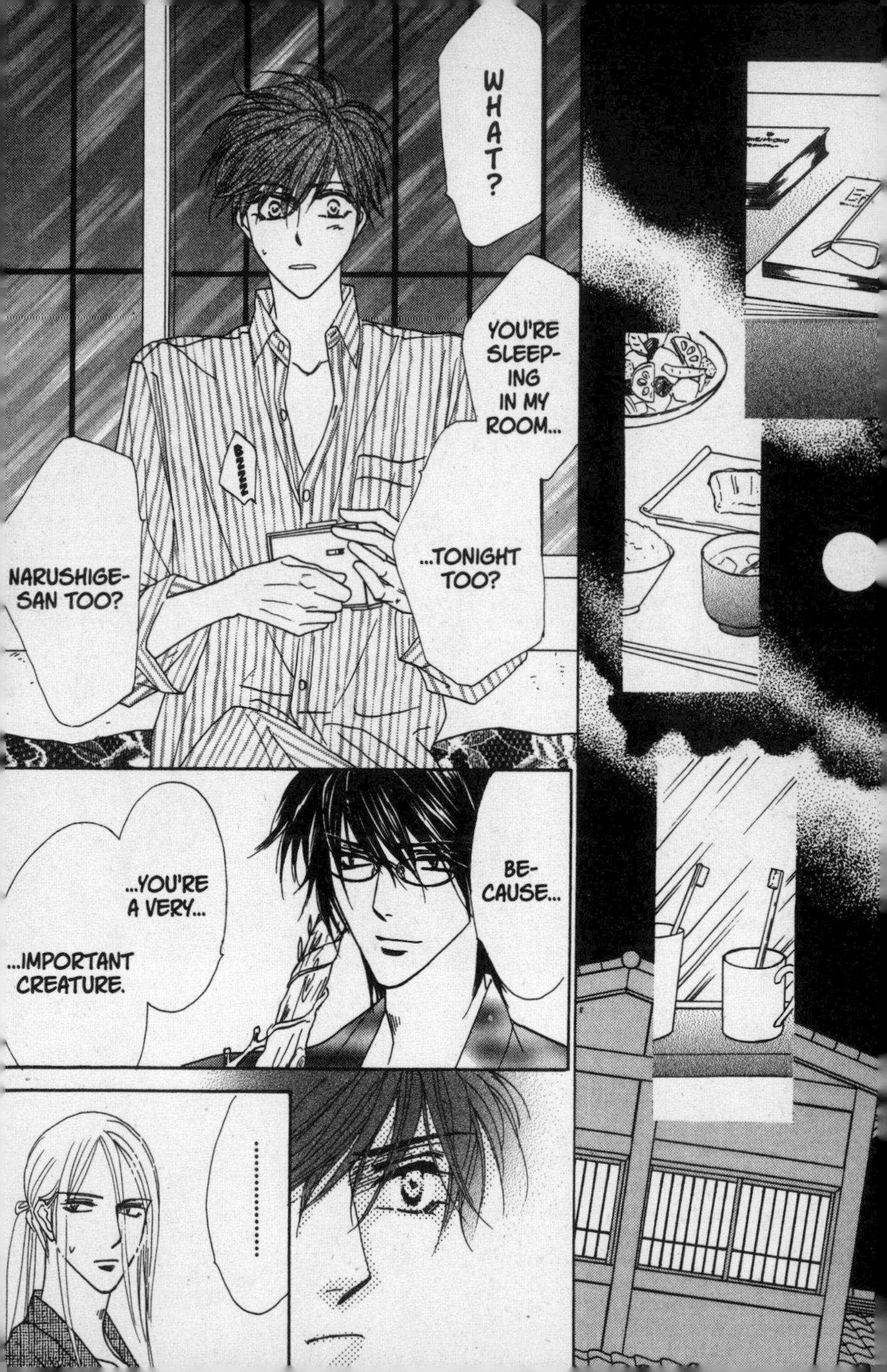
WHAT?
YOU'RE SLEEPING IN MY ROOM...
...TONIGHT TOO?
NARUSHIGE-SAN TOO?
BE-CAUSE...
...YOU'RE A VERY...
...IMPORTANT CREATURE.
......

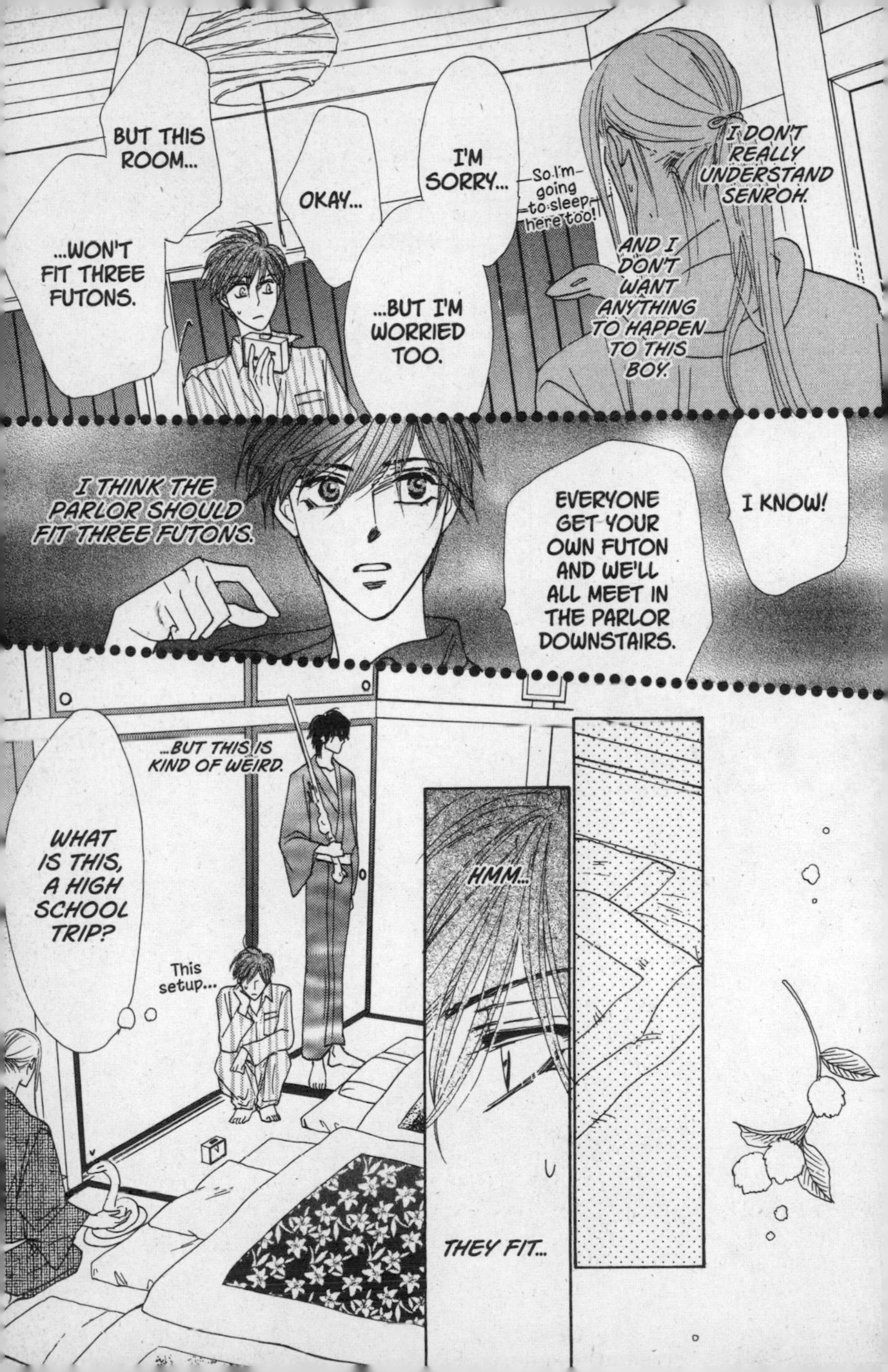
I DON'T REALLY UNDERSTAND SENROH.
AND I DON'T WANT ANYTHING TO HAPPEN TO THIS BOY.
I'M SORRY...
So I'm going to sleep here too!
...BUT I'M WORRIED TOO.
OKAY...
BUT THIS ROOM...
...WON'T FIT THREE FUTONS.
I KNOW!
EVERYONE GET YOUR OWN FUTON AND WE'LL ALL MEET IN THE PARLOR DOWNSTAIRS.
I THINK THE PARLOR SHOULD FIT THREE FUTONS.
HMM...
THEY FIT...
...BUT THIS IS KIND OF WEIRD.
WHAT IS THIS, A HIGH SCHOOL TRIP?
This setup...

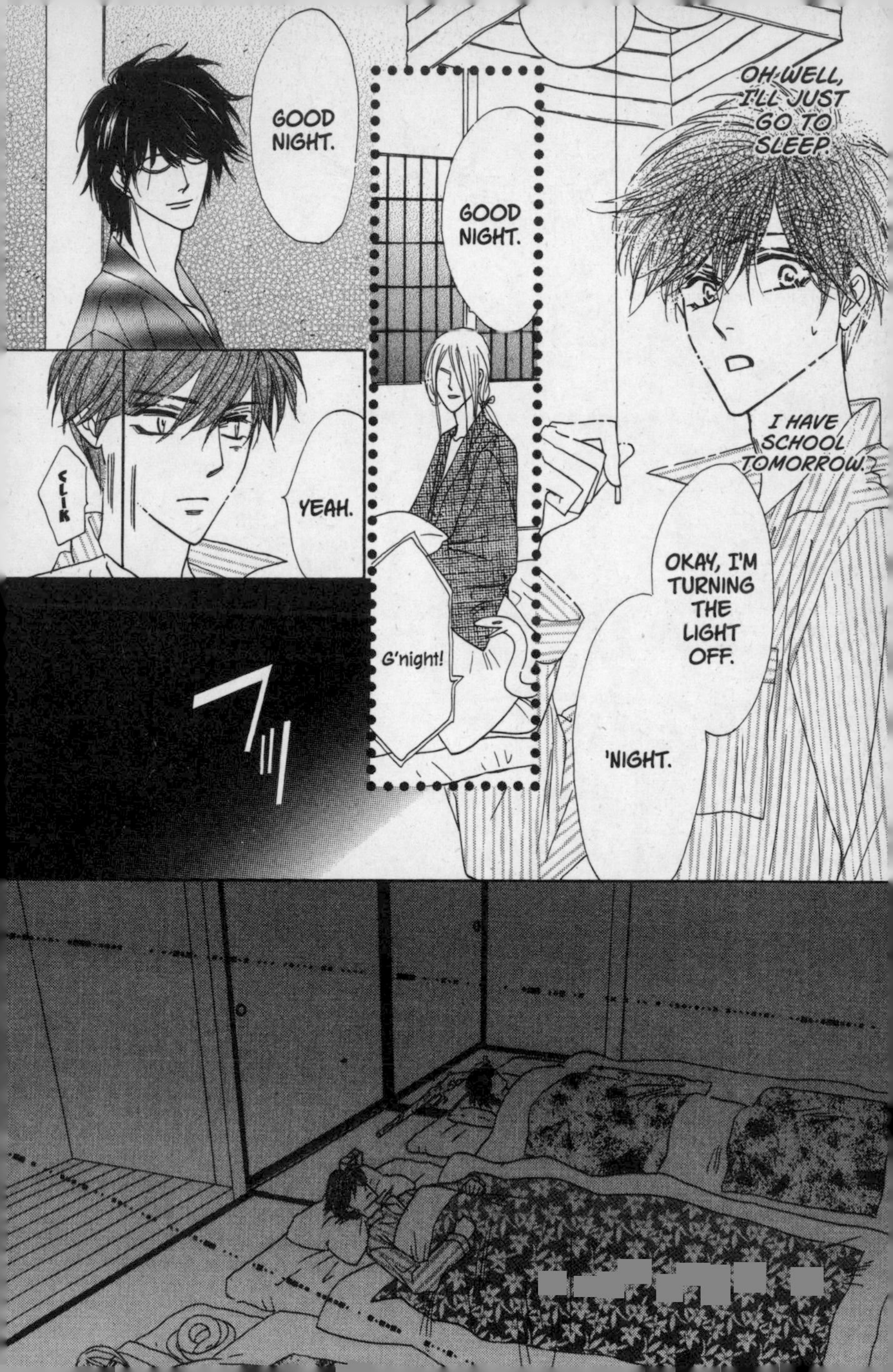

OH WELL, I'LL JUST GO TO SLEEP.
I HAVE SCHOOL TOMORROW.
OKAY, I'M TURNING THE LIGHT OFF.
'NIGHT.
GOOD NIGHT.
G'night!
GOOD NIGHT.
YEAH.
CLIK

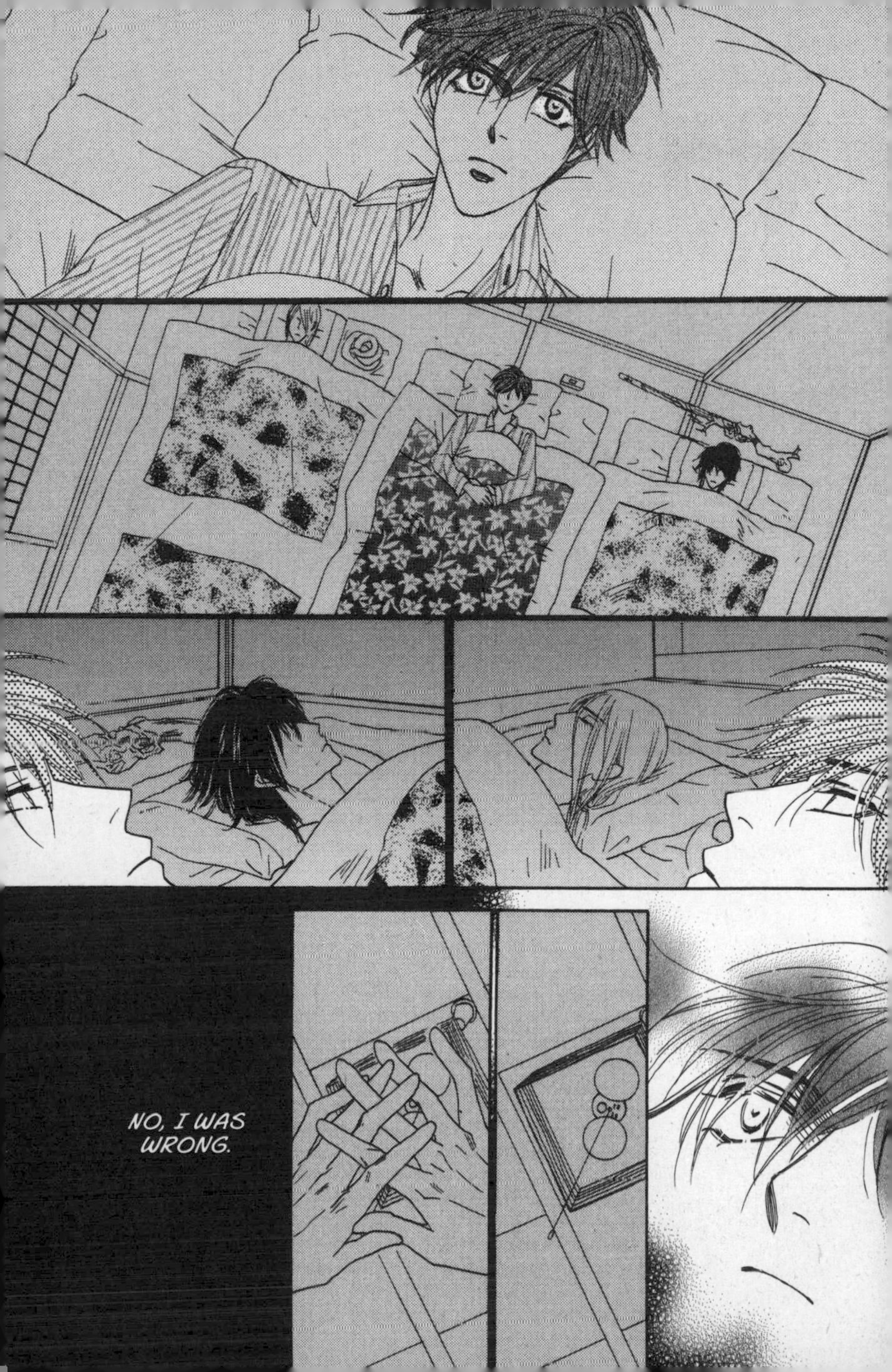
NO, I WAS WRONG.

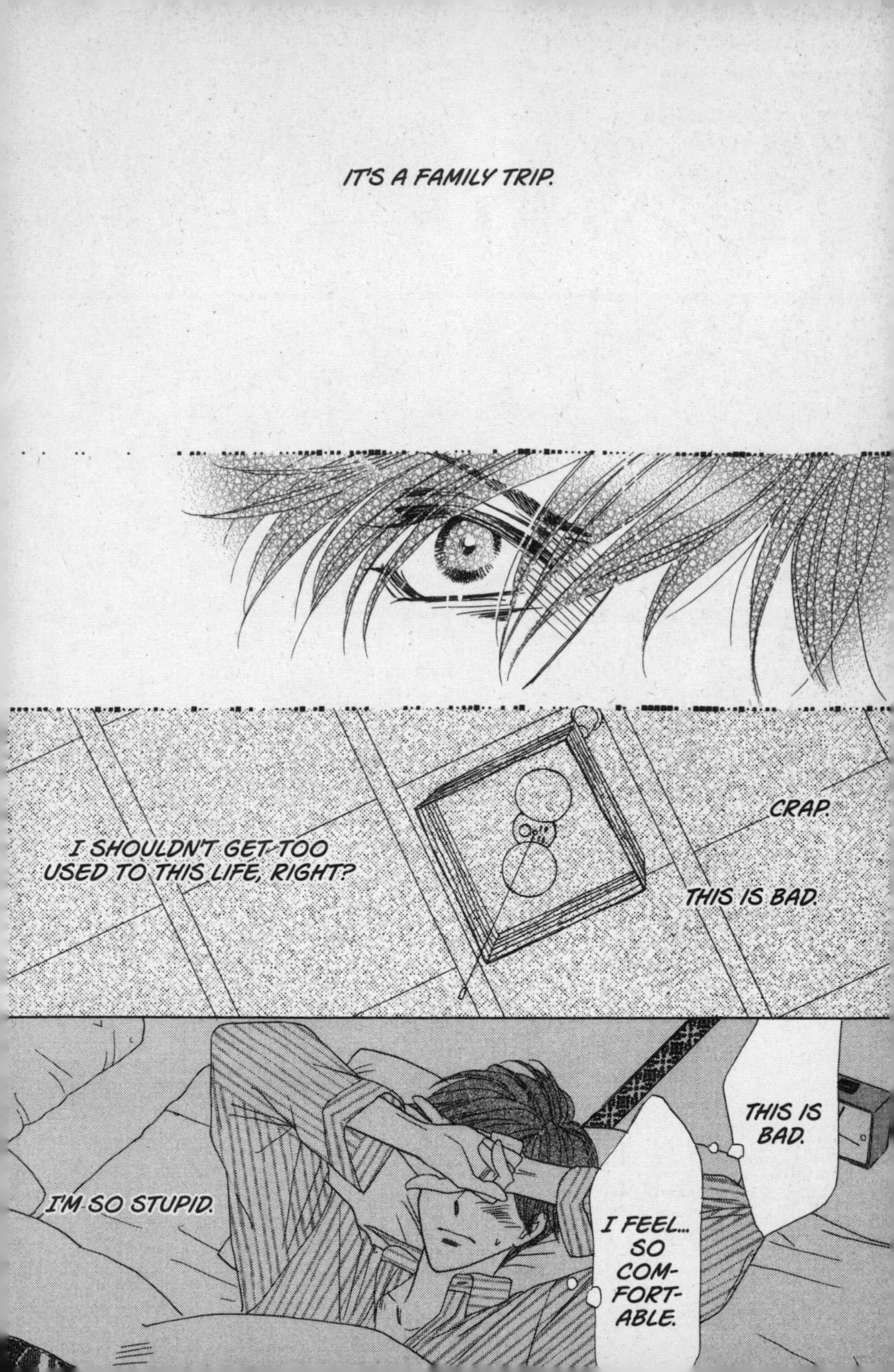
IT'S A FAMILY TRIP.
CRAP.
THIS IS BAD.
I SHOULDN'T GET TOO USED TO THIS LIFE, RIGHT?
THIS IS BAD.
I FEEL... SO COMFORTABLE.
I'M SO STUPID.

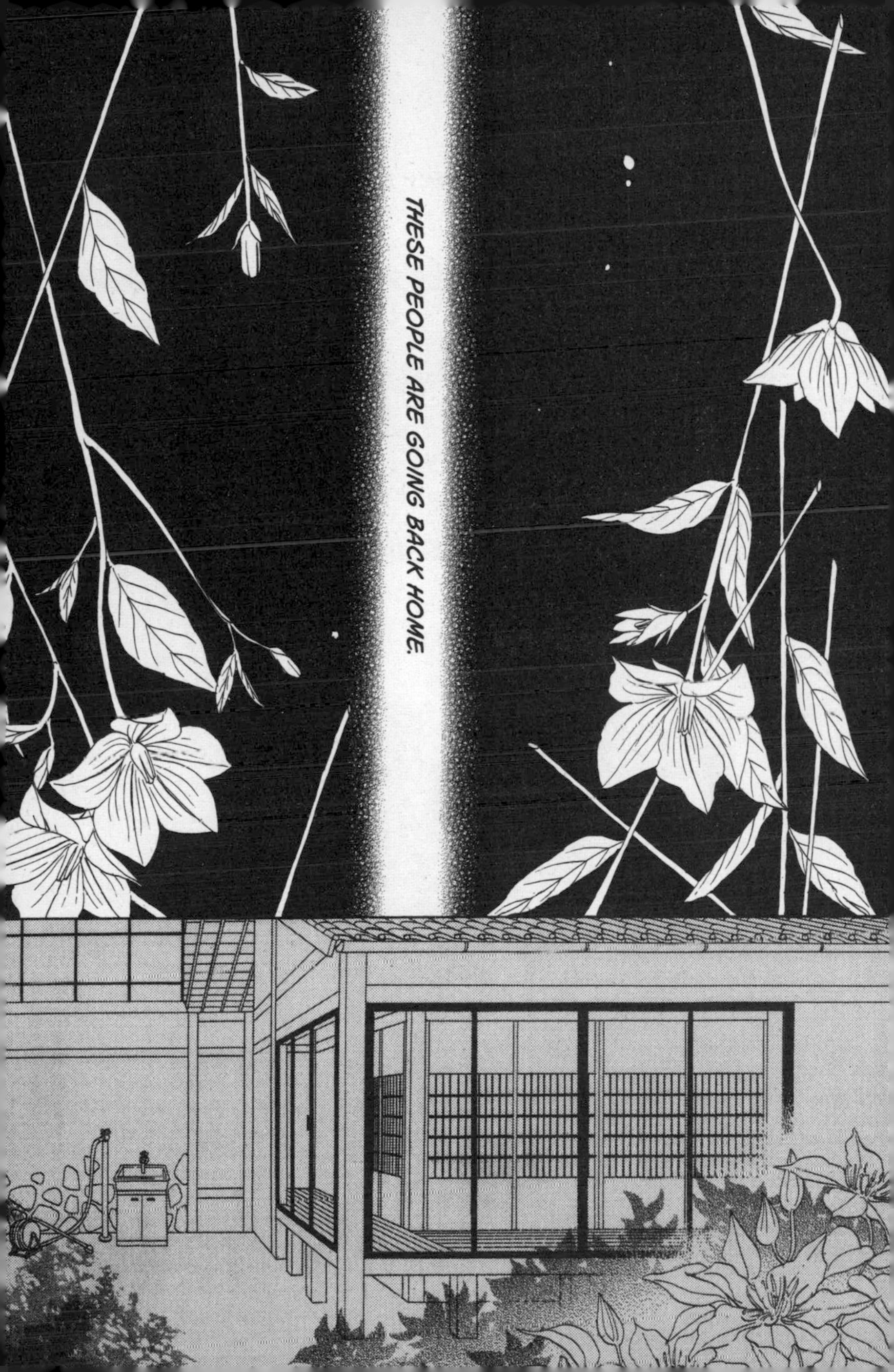
THESE PEOPLE ARE GOING BACK HOME.

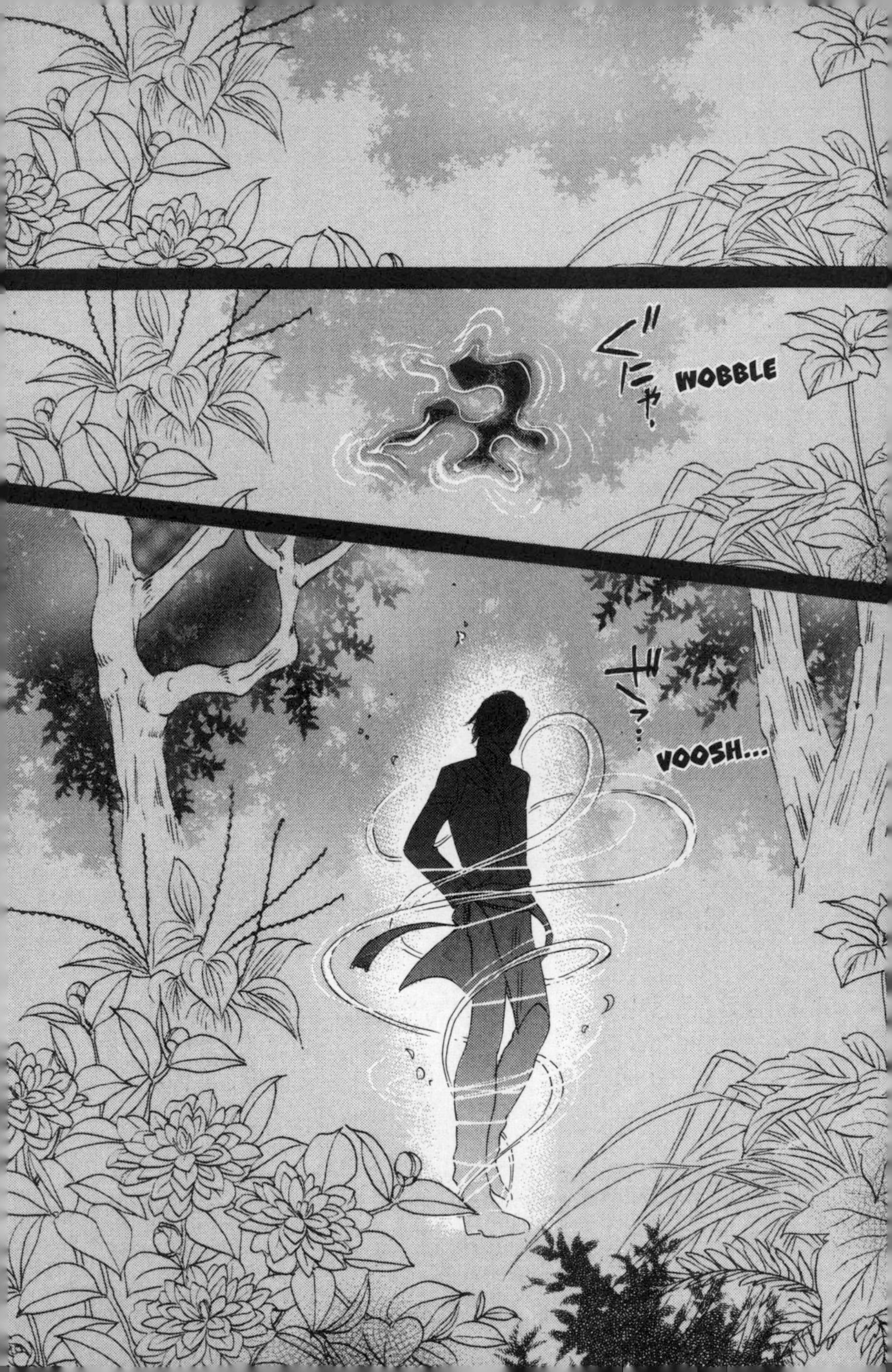
ぐにゃ
WOBBLE
VOOSH...

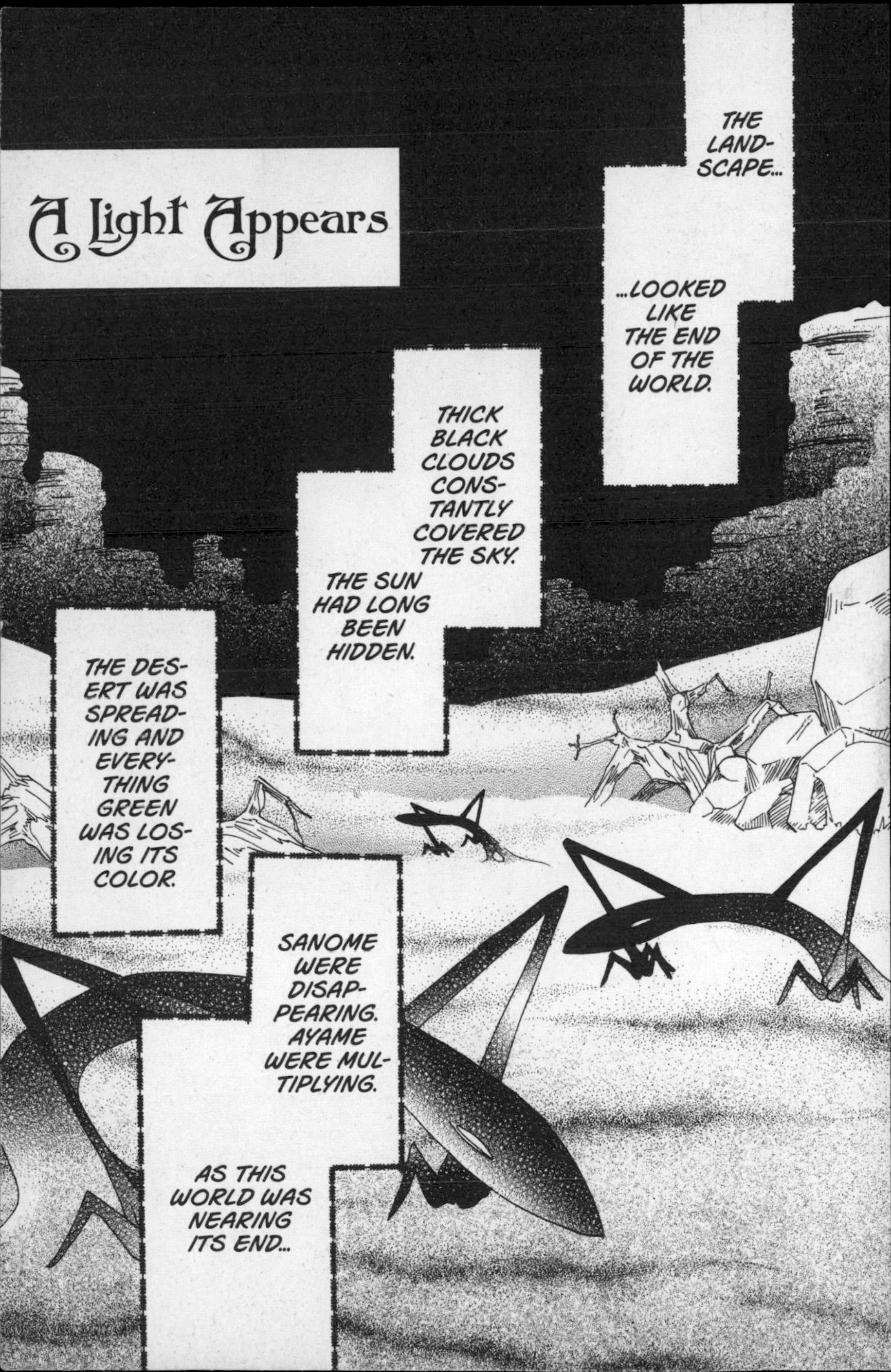
A Light Appears
THE LAND-SCAPE...
...LOOKED LIKE THE END OF THE WORLD.
THICK BLACK CLOUDS CONS-TANTLY COVERED THE SKY.
THE SUN HAD LONG BEEN HIDDEN.
THE DES-ERT WAS SPREAD-ING AND EVERY-THING GREEN WAS LOS-ING ITS COLOR.
SANOME WERE DISAP-PEARING. AYAME WERE MUL-TIPLYING.
AS THIS WORLD WAS NEARING ITS END...

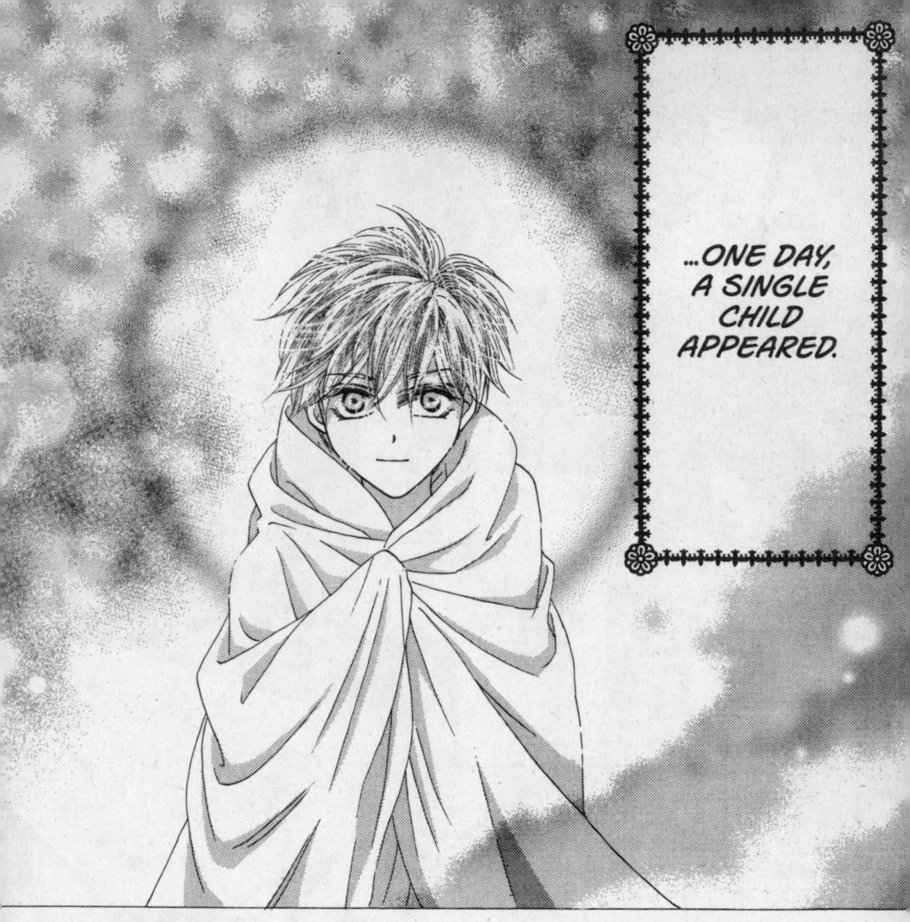
...ONE DAY, A SINGLE CHILD APPEARED.

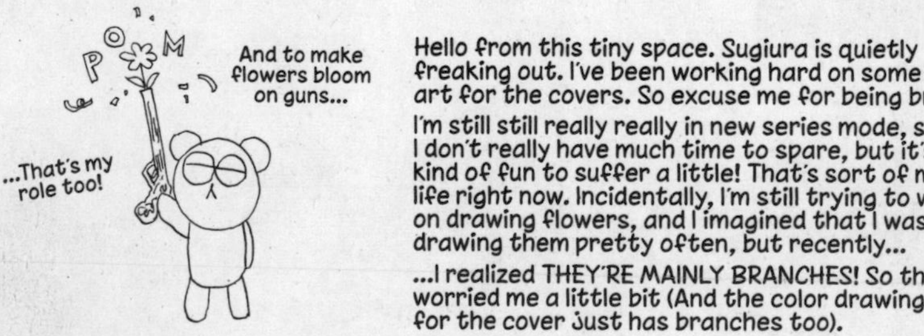
POM
And to make flowers bloom on guns...
...That's my role too!

Hello from this tiny space. Sugiura is quietly freaking out. I've been working hard on some color art for the covers. So excuse me for being brief.

I'm still still really really in new series mode, so I don't really have much time to spare, but it's kind of fun to suffer a little! That's sort of my life right now. Incidentally, I'm still trying to work on drawing flowers, and I imagined that I was drawing them pretty often, but recently...

...I realized THEY'RE MAINLY BRANCHES! So that worried me a little bit (And the color drawing for the cover just has branches too).

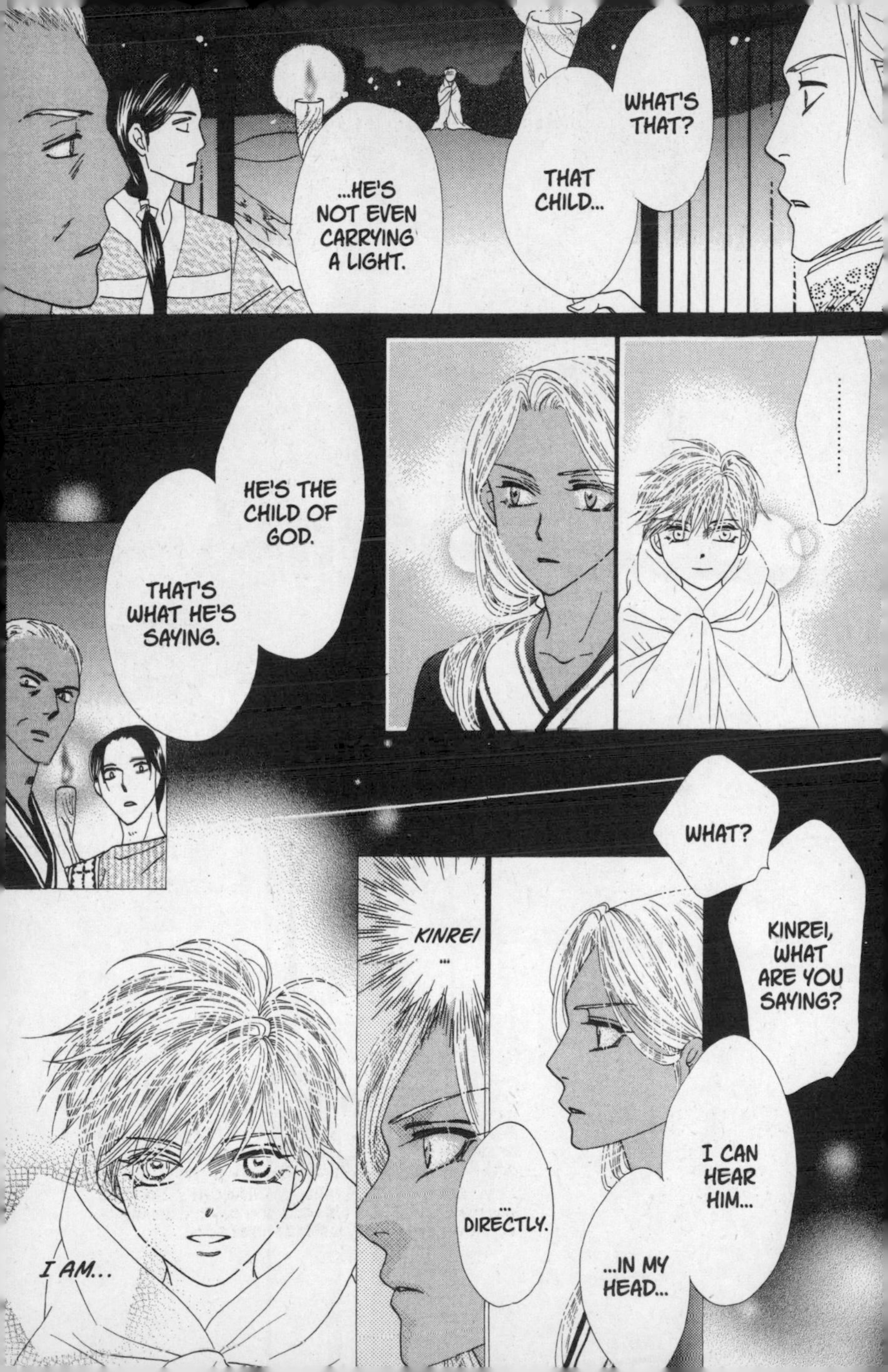
WHAT'S THAT?
THAT CHILD...
...HE'S NOT EVEN CARRYING A LIGHT.
......
HE'S THE CHILD OF GOD.
THAT'S WHAT HE'S SAYING.
WHAT?
KINREI, WHAT ARE YOU SAYING?
I CAN HEAR HIM...
...IN MY HEAD...
... DIRECTLY.
KINREI ...
I AM...

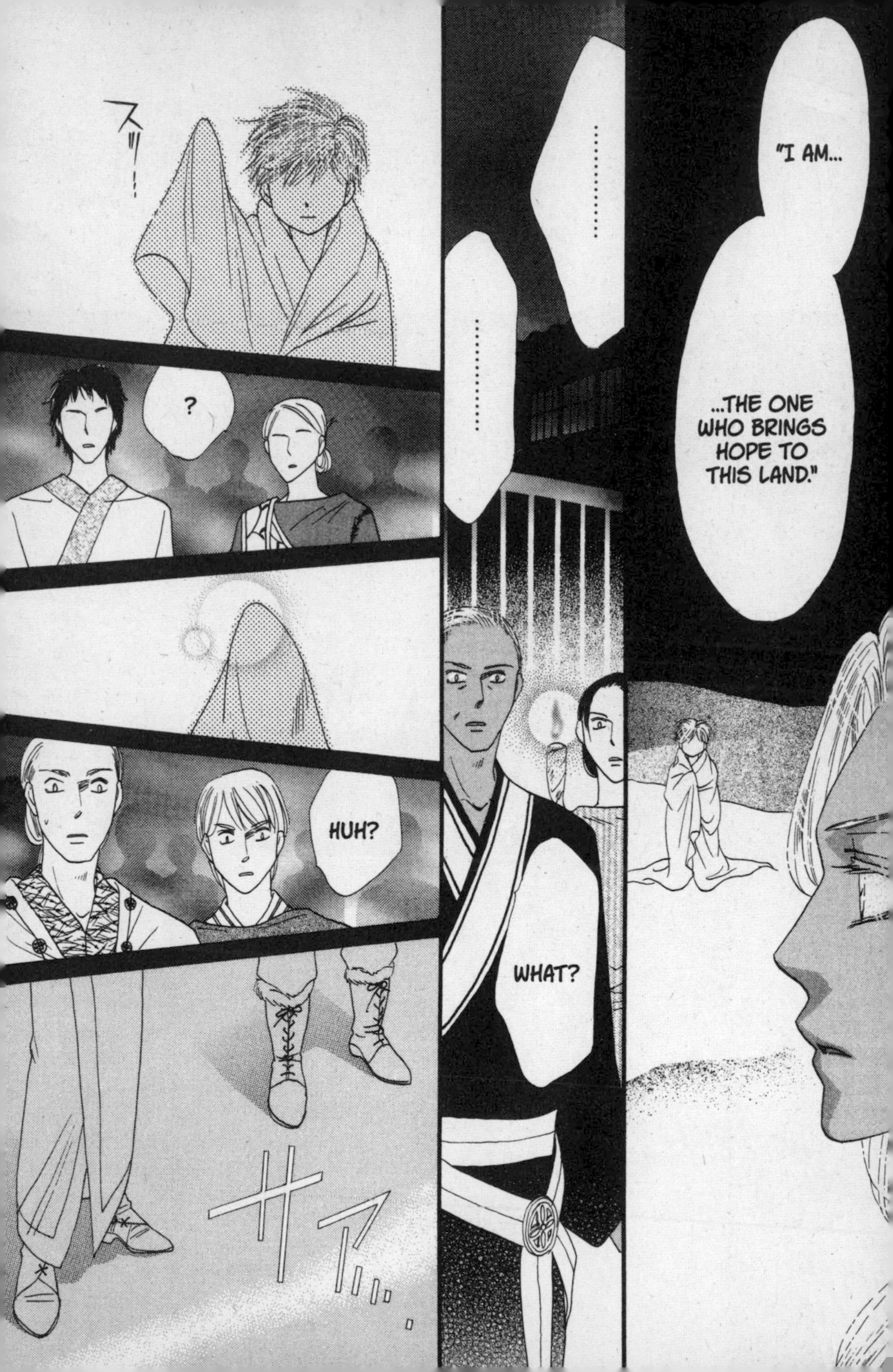
"I AM...
...THE ONE WHO BRINGS HOPE TO THIS LAND."
......
......
WHAT?
スッ!!
?
HUH?
サァ…

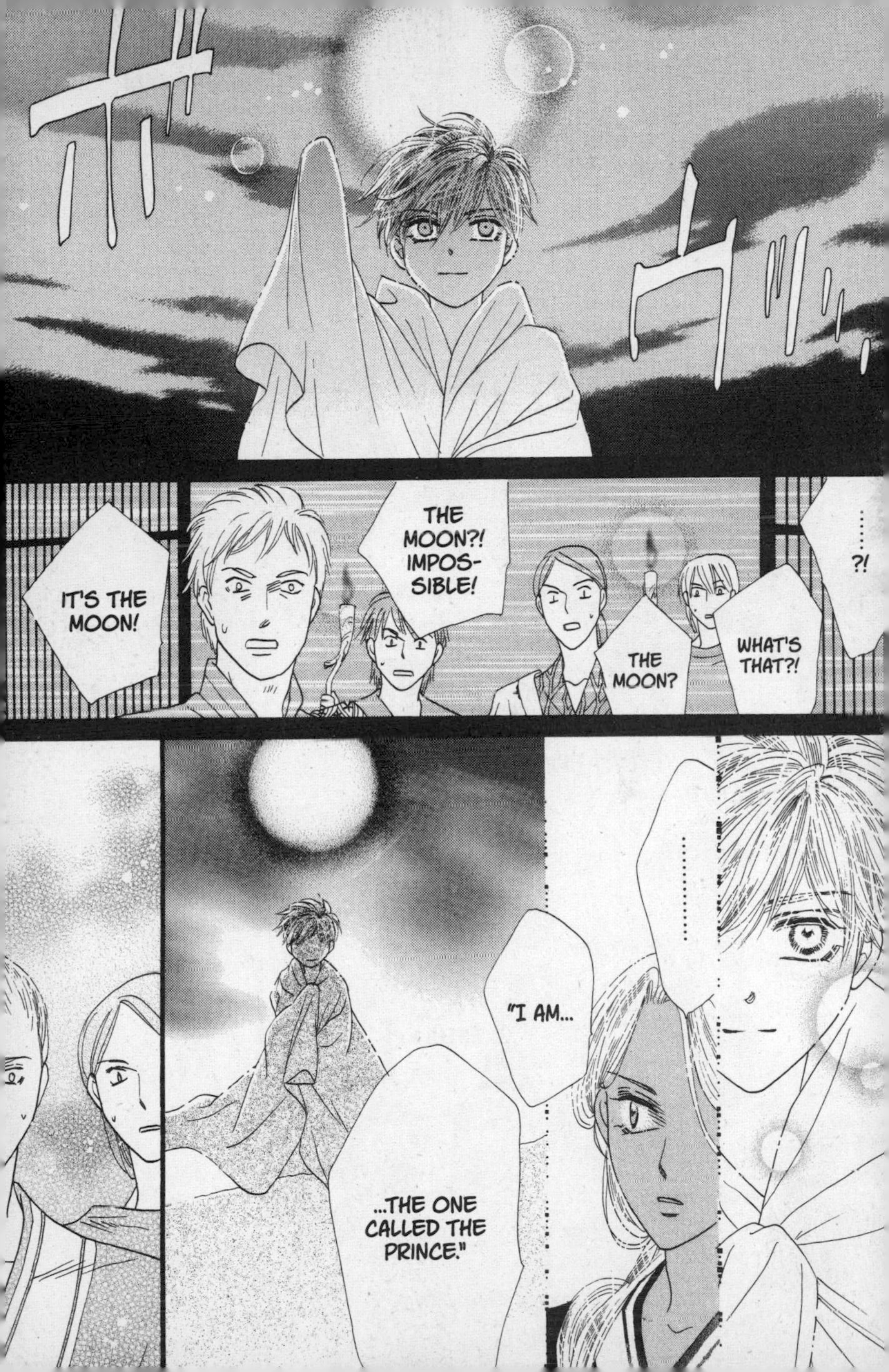

...?!
WHAT'S THAT?!
THE MOON?
THE MOON?! IMPOSSIBLE!
IT'S THE MOON!
......
"I AM...
...THE ONE CALLED THE PRINCE."

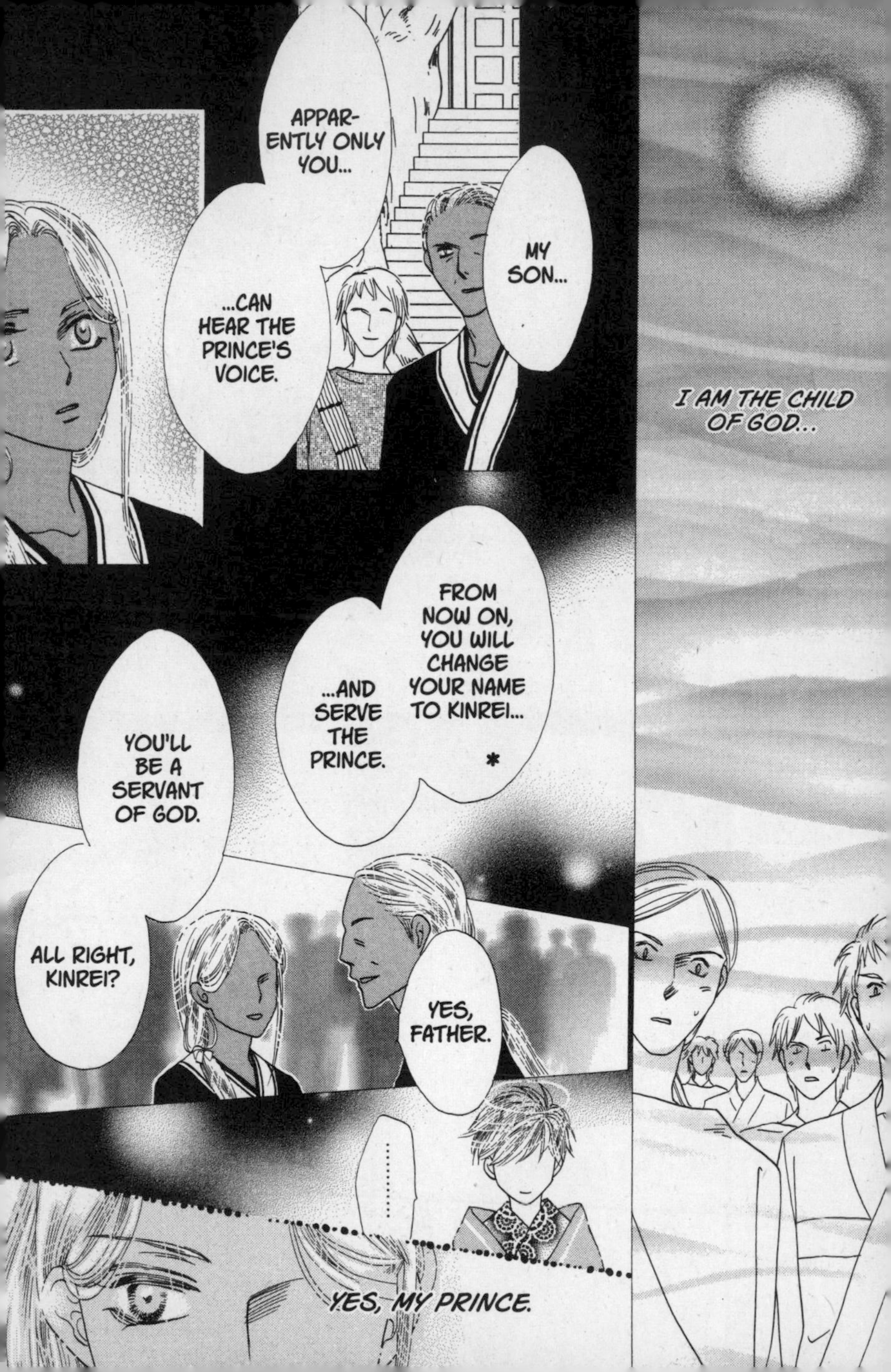
I AM THE CHILD OF GOD...
MY SON...
APPARENTLY ONLY YOU...
...CAN HEAR THE PRINCE'S VOICE.
FROM NOW ON, YOU WILL CHANGE YOUR NAME TO KINREI...
...AND SERVE THE PRINCE.
YOU'LL BE A SERVANT OF GOD.
ALL RIGHT, KINREI?
YES, FATHER.
......
YES, MY PRINCE.

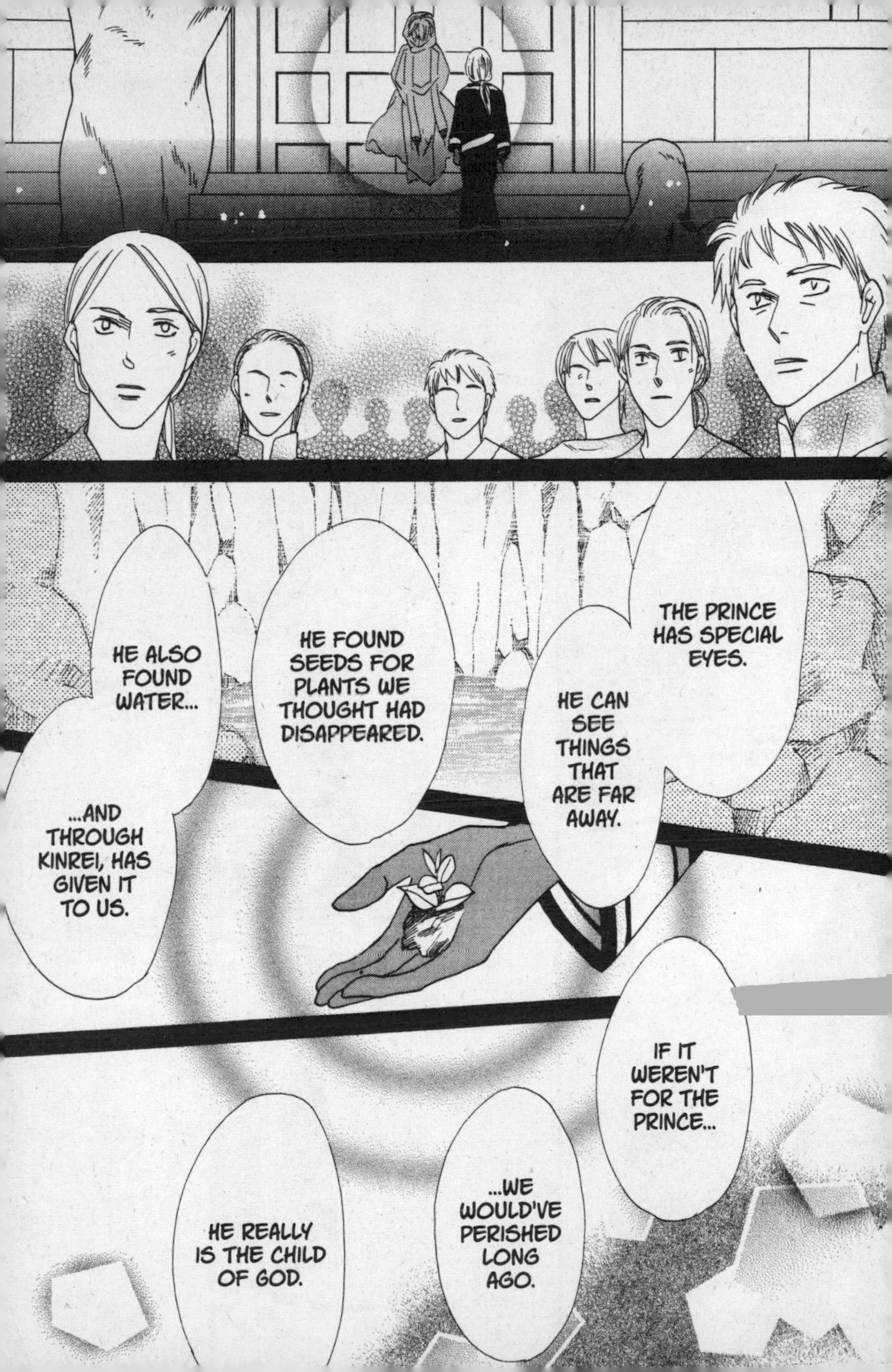
THE PRINCE HAS SPECIAL EYES.
HE CAN SEE THINGS THAT ARE FAR AWAY.
HE FOUND SEEDS FOR PLANTS WE THOUGHT HAD DISAPPEARED.
HE ALSO FOUND WATER...
...AND THROUGH KINREI, HAS GIVEN IT TO US.
IF IT WEREN'T FOR THE PRINCE...
...WE WOULD'VE PERISHED LONG AGO.
HE REALLY IS THE CHILD OF GOD.

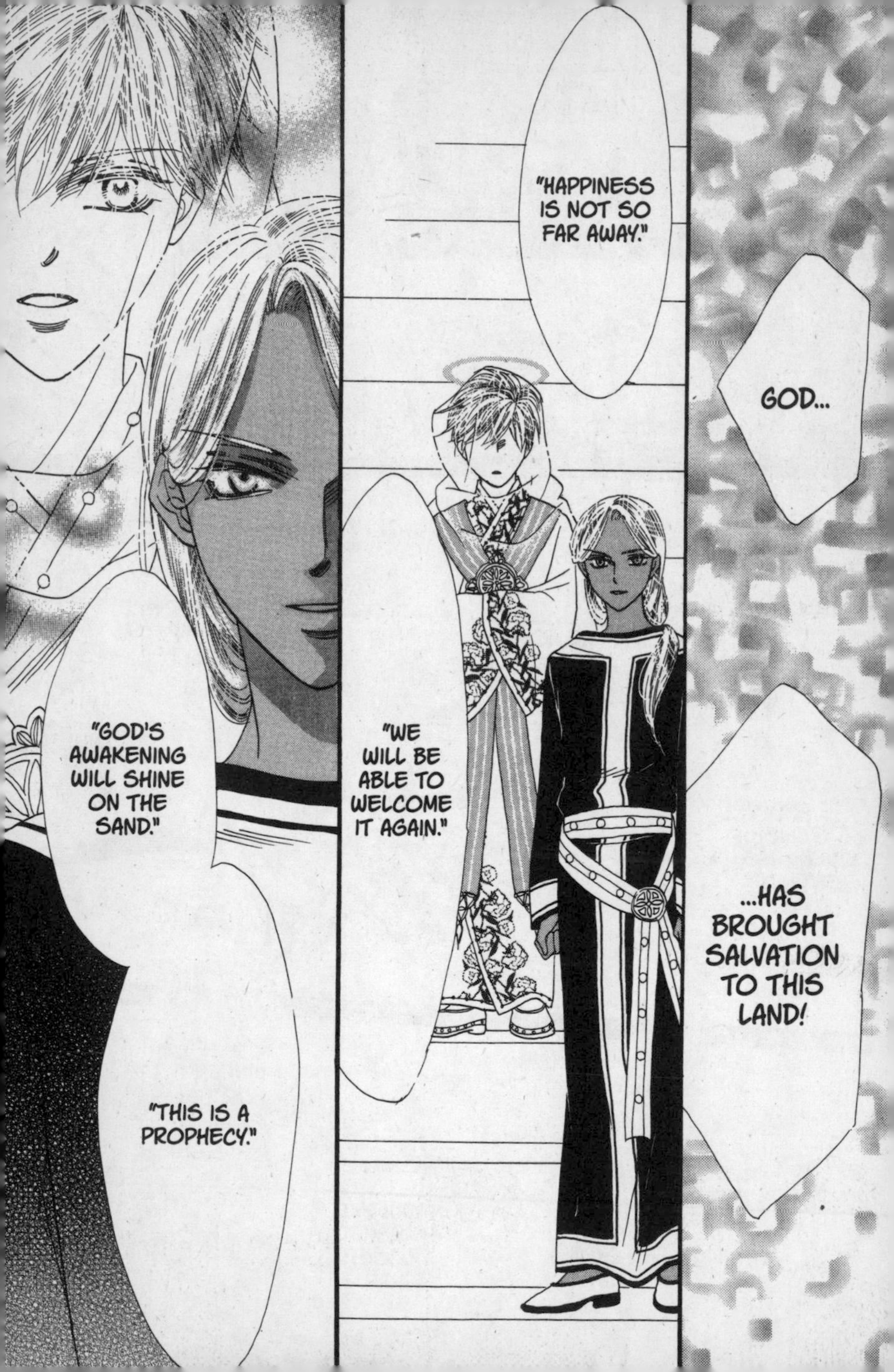
GOD...
...HAS BROUGHT SALVATION TO THIS LAND!
"HAPPINESS IS NOT SO FAR AWAY."
"WE WILL BE ABLE TO WELCOME IT AGAIN."
"GOD'S AWAKENING WILL SHINE ON THE SAND."
"THIS IS A PROPHECY."

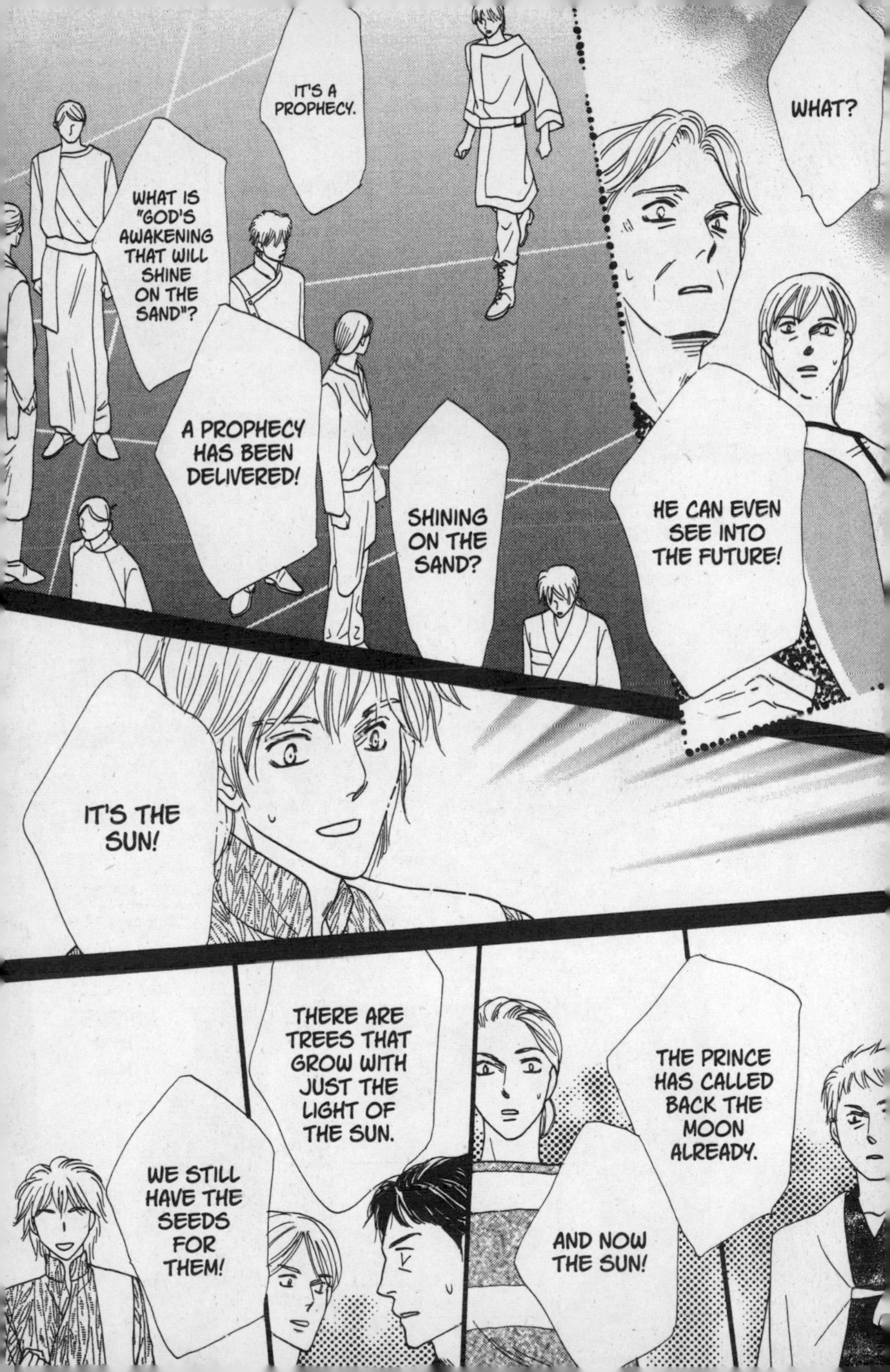
WHAT?
HE CAN EVEN SEE INTO THE FUTURE!
IT'S A PROPHECY.
WHAT IS "GOD'S AWAKENING THAT WILL SHINE ON THE SAND"?
A PROPHECY HAS BEEN DELIVERED!
SHINING ON THE SAND?
IT'S THE SUN!
THE PRINCE HAS CALLED BACK THE MOON ALREADY.
AND NOW THE SUN!
THERE ARE TREES THAT GROW WITH JUST THE LIGHT OF THE SUN.
WE STILL HAVE THE SEEDS FOR THEM!

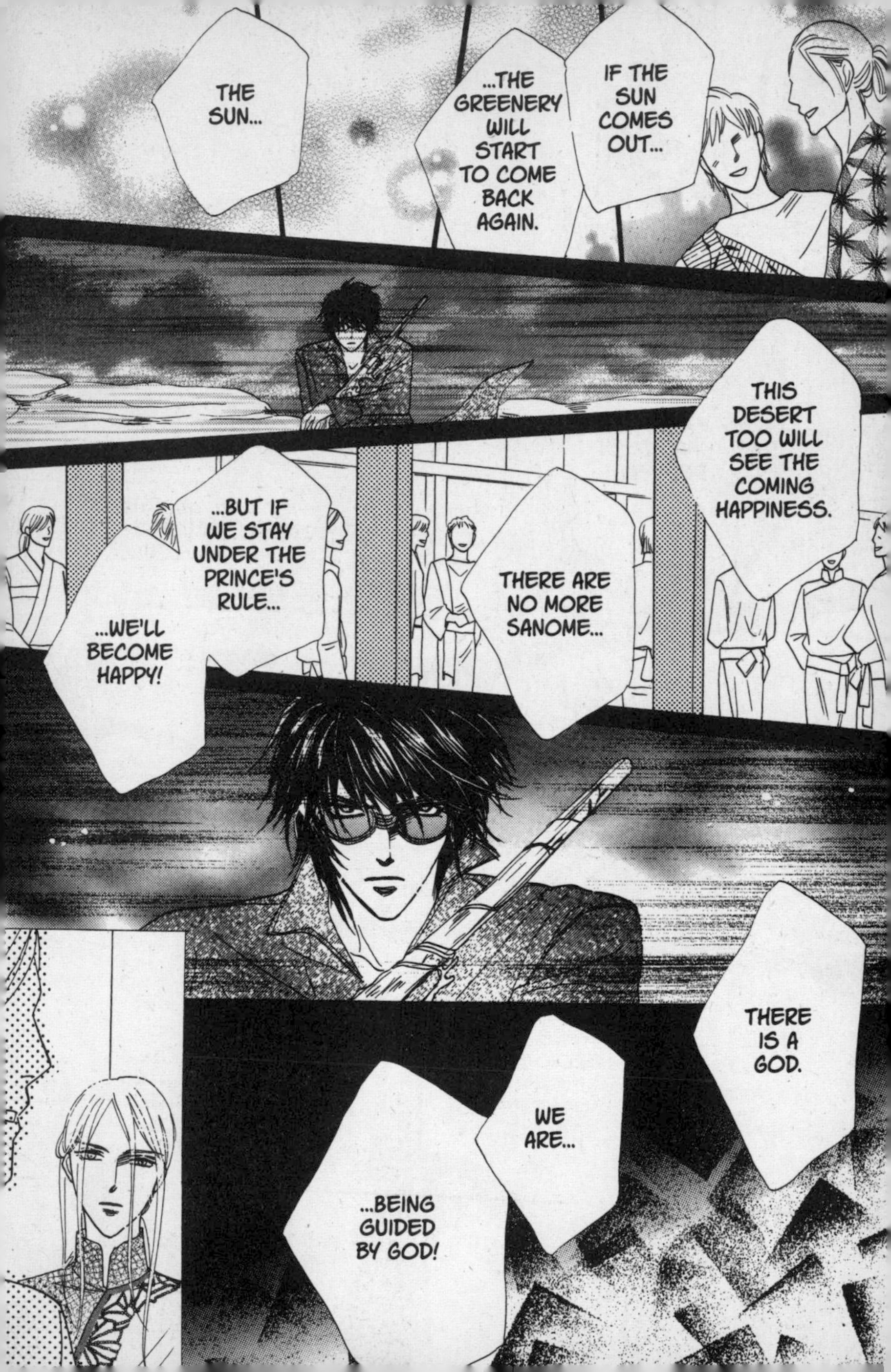
IF THE SUN COMES OUT...
...THE GREENERY WILL START TO COME BACK AGAIN.
THE SUN...
THIS DESERT TOO WILL SEE THE COMING HAPPINESS.
THERE ARE NO MORE SANOME...
...BUT IF WE STAY UNDER THE PRINCE'S RULE...
...WE'LL BECOME HAPPY!
THERE IS A GOD.
WE ARE...
...BEING GUIDED BY GOD!

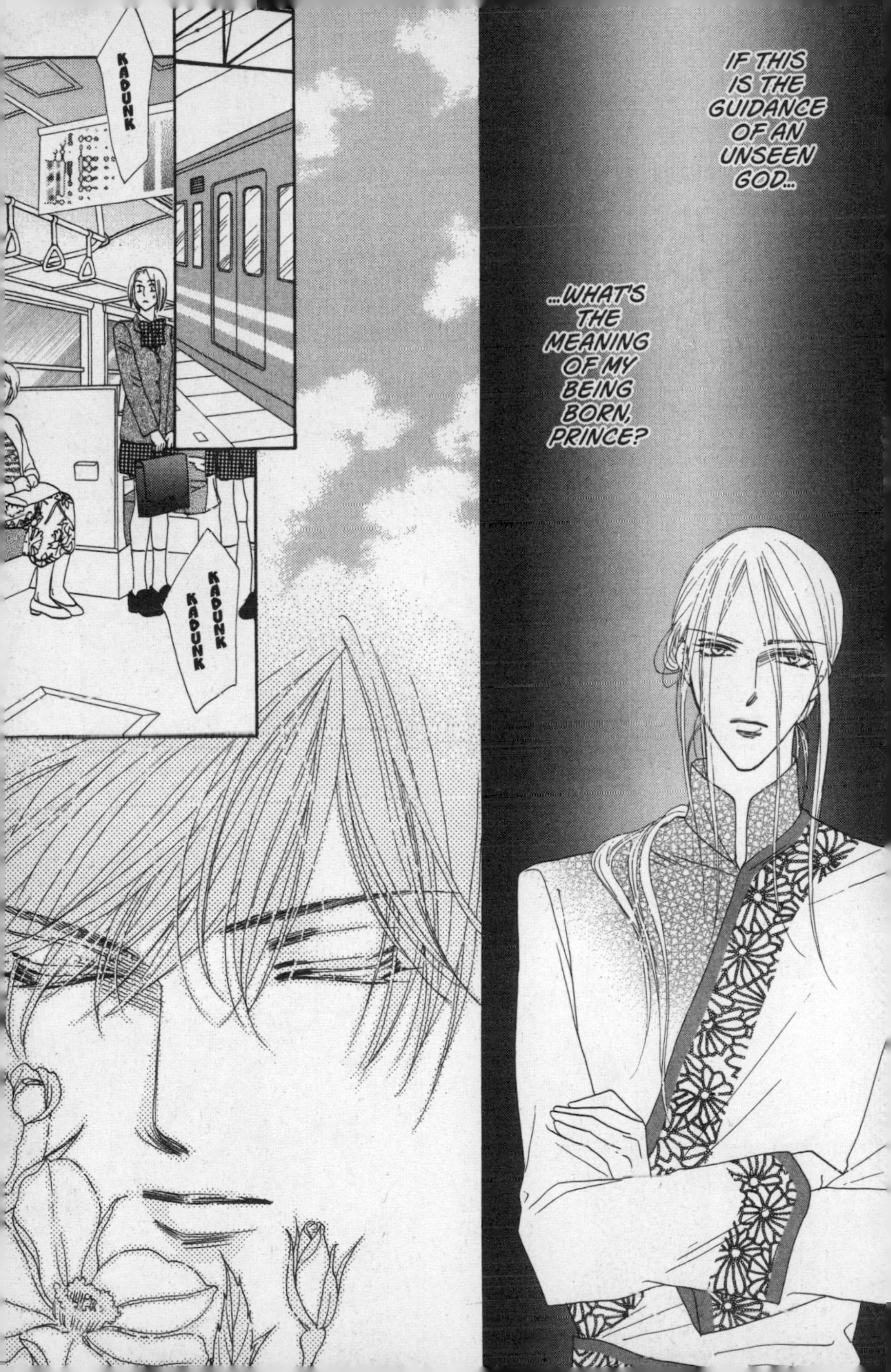
IF THIS IS THE GUIDANCE OF AN UNSEEN GOD...
...WHAT'S THE MEANING OF MY BEING BORN, PRINCE?
KADUNK
KADUNK
KADUNK

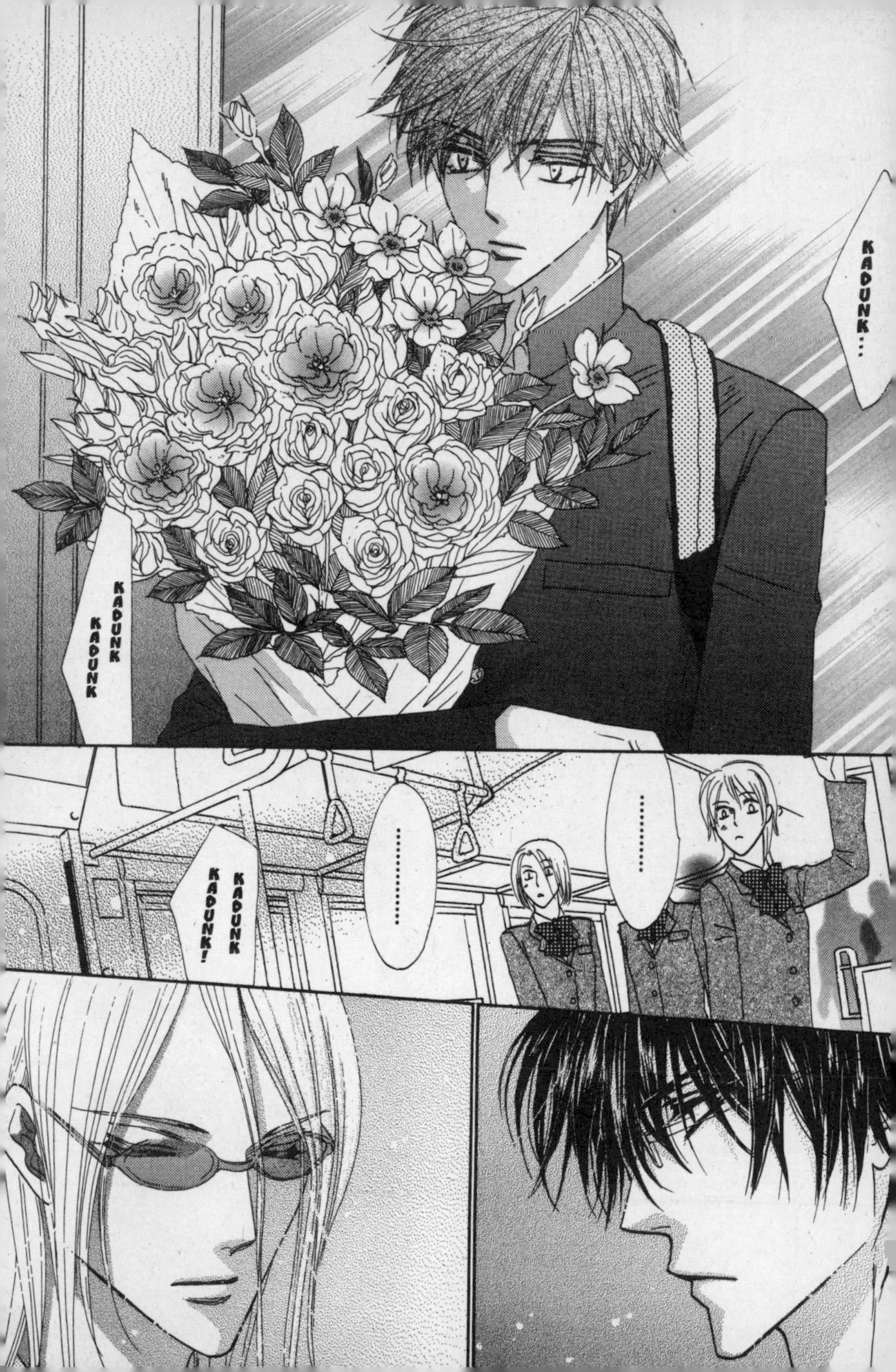
KADUNK...
KADUNK
KADUNK
....
....
KADUNK
KADUNK!

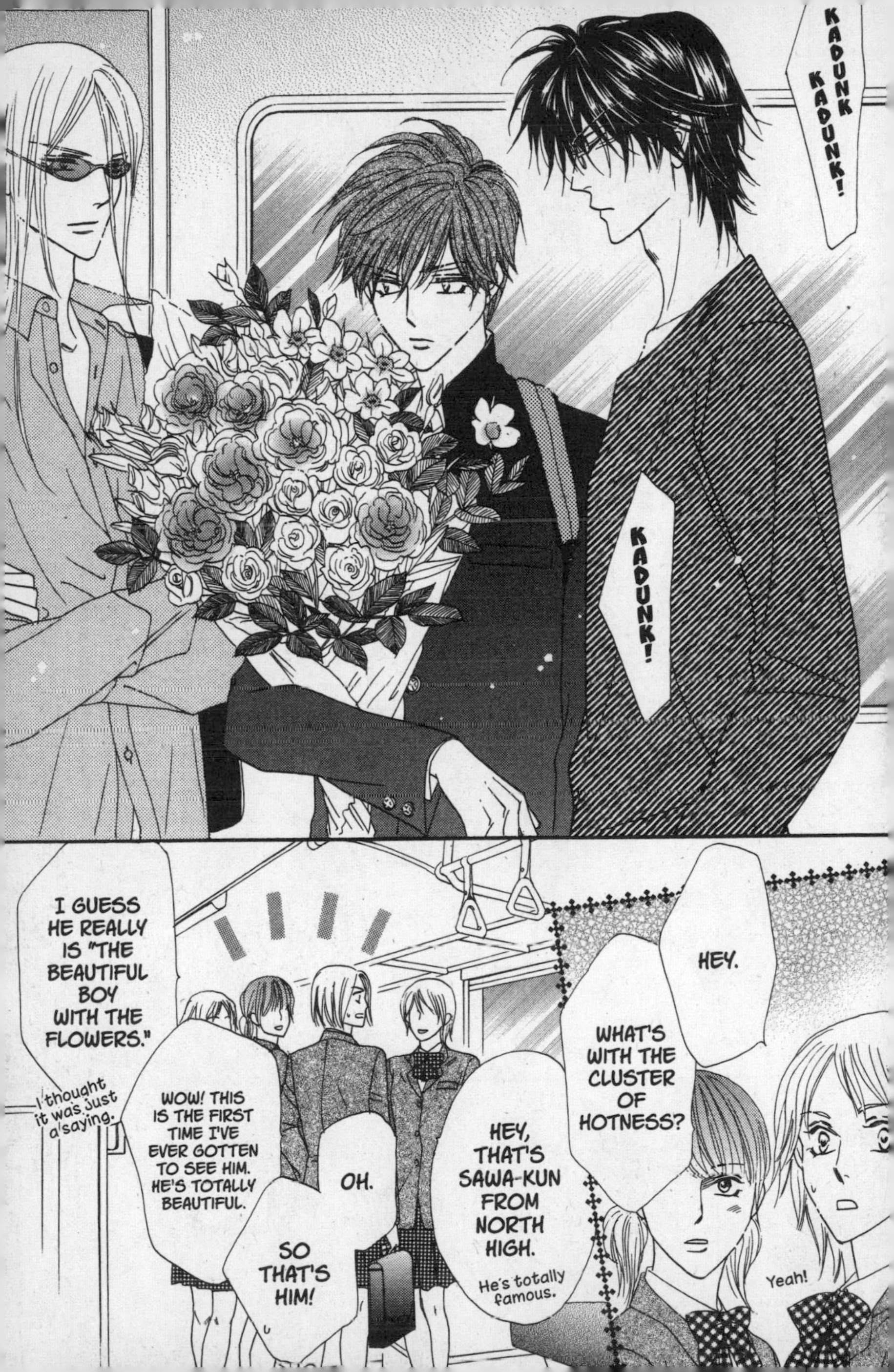
KADUNK KADUNK!
KADUNK!
HEY.
WHAT'S WITH THE CLUSTER OF HOTNESS?
Yeah!
HEY, THAT'S SAWA-KUN FROM NORTH HIGH.
He's totally famous.
OH.
SO THAT'S HIM!
WOW! THIS IS THE FIRST TIME I'VE EVER GOTTEN TO SEE HIM. HE'S TOTALLY BEAUTIFUL.
I GUESS HE REALLY IS "THE BEAUTIFUL BOY WITH THE FLOWERS."
I thought it was just a saying.

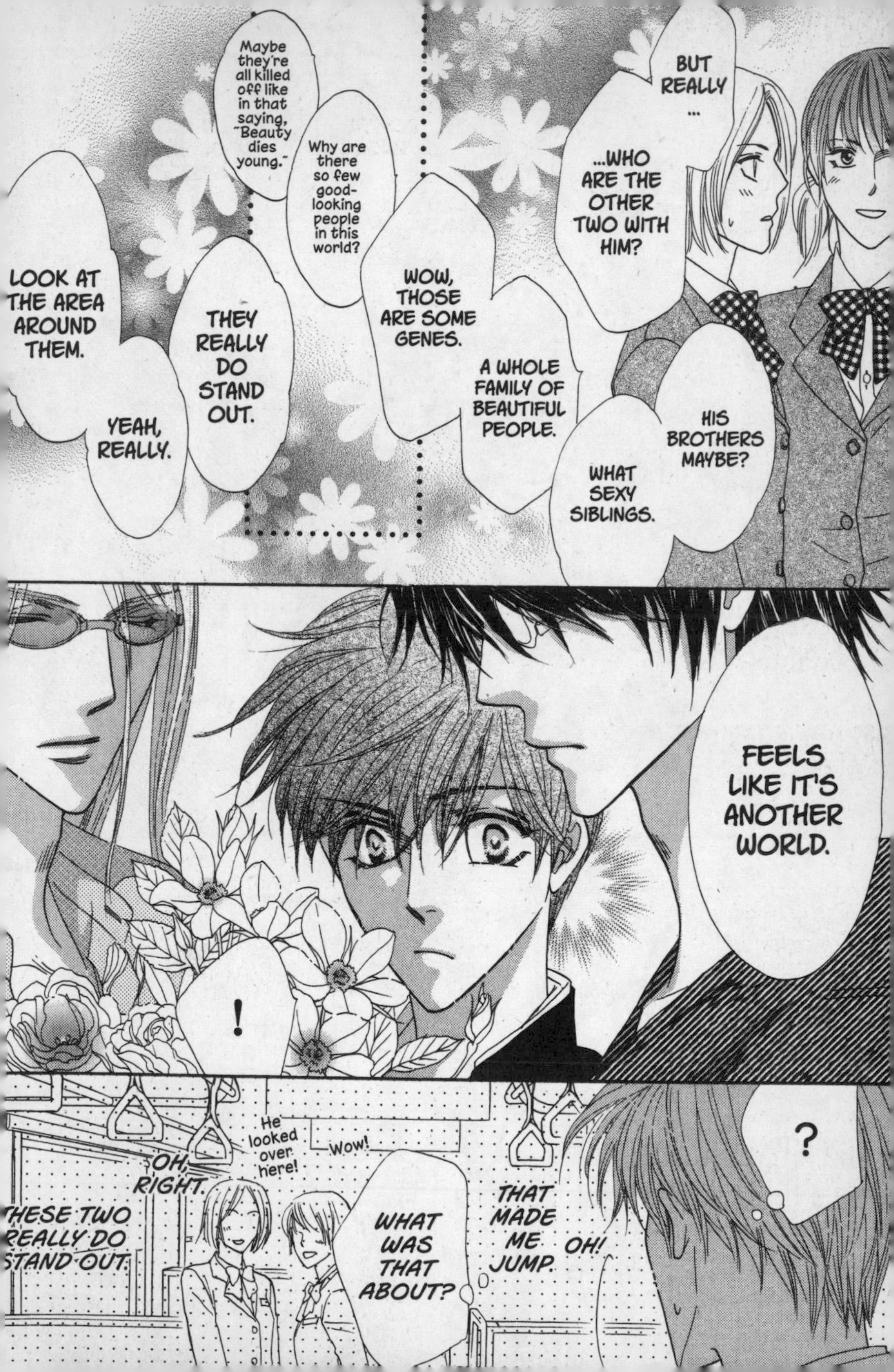
BUT REALLY ...
...WHO ARE THE OTHER TWO WITH HIM?
HIS BROTHERS MAYBE?
WHAT SEXY SIBLINGS.
A WHOLE FAMILY OF BEAUTIFUL PEOPLE.
WOW, THOSE ARE SOME GENES.
Why are there so few good-looking people in this world?
Maybe they're all killed off like in that saying, "Beauty dies young."
THEY REALLY DO STAND OUT.
LOOK AT THE AREA AROUND THEM.
YEAH, REALLY.
FEELS LIKE IT'S ANOTHER WORLD.
!
?
OH!
THAT MADE ME JUMP.
WHAT WAS THAT ABOUT?
Wow!
He looked over here!
OH, RIGHT.
THESE TWO REALLY DO STAND OUT.

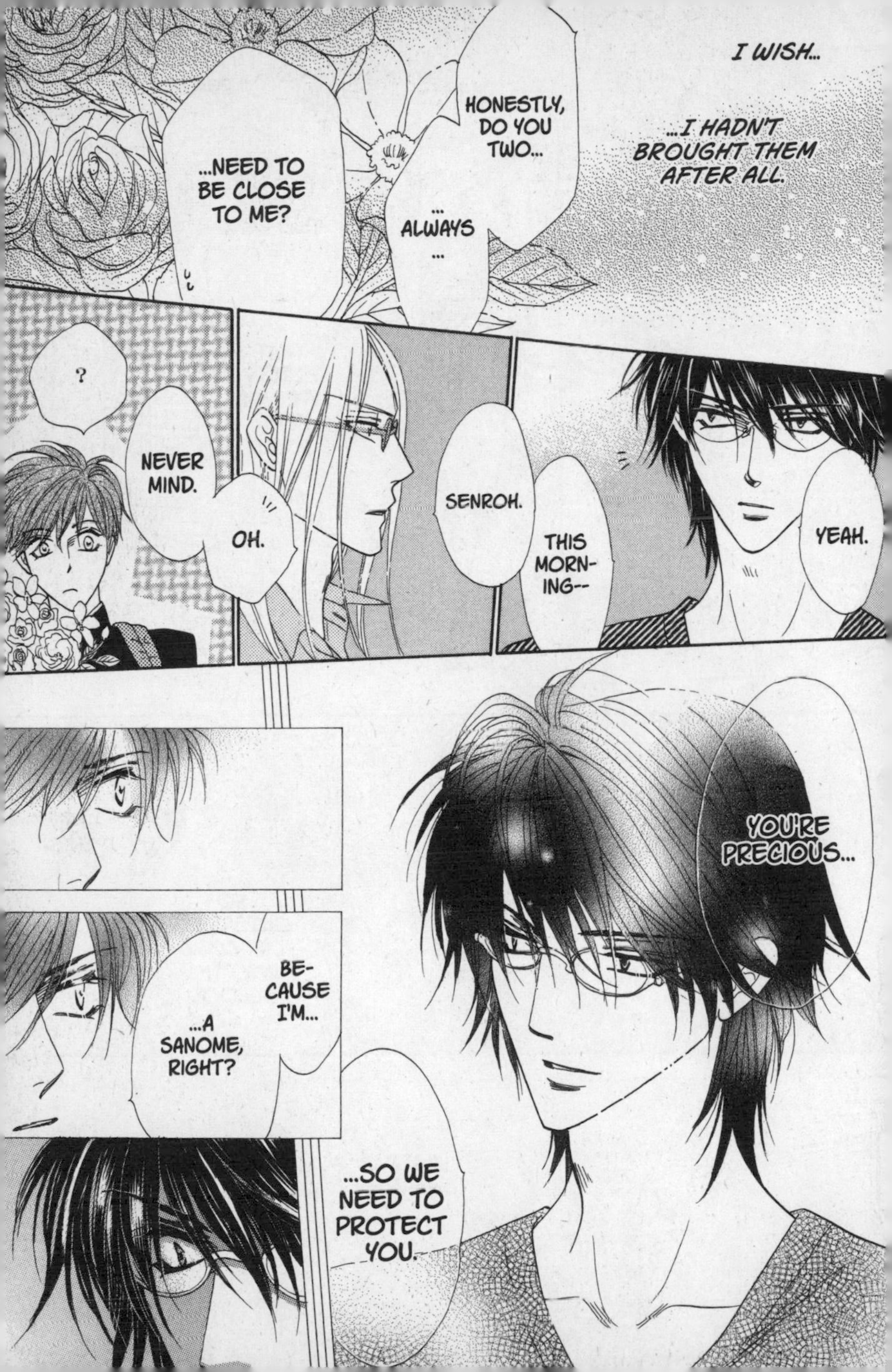
I WISH...
...I HADN'T BROUGHT THEM AFTER ALL.
HONESTLY, DO YOU TWO...
...ALWAYS...
...NEED TO BE CLOSE TO ME?
YEAH.
THIS MORNING--
SENROH.
OH.
NEVER MIND.
?
YOU'RE PRECIOUS...
...SO WE NEED TO PROTECT YOU.
BE-CAUSE I'M...
...A SANOME, RIGHT?

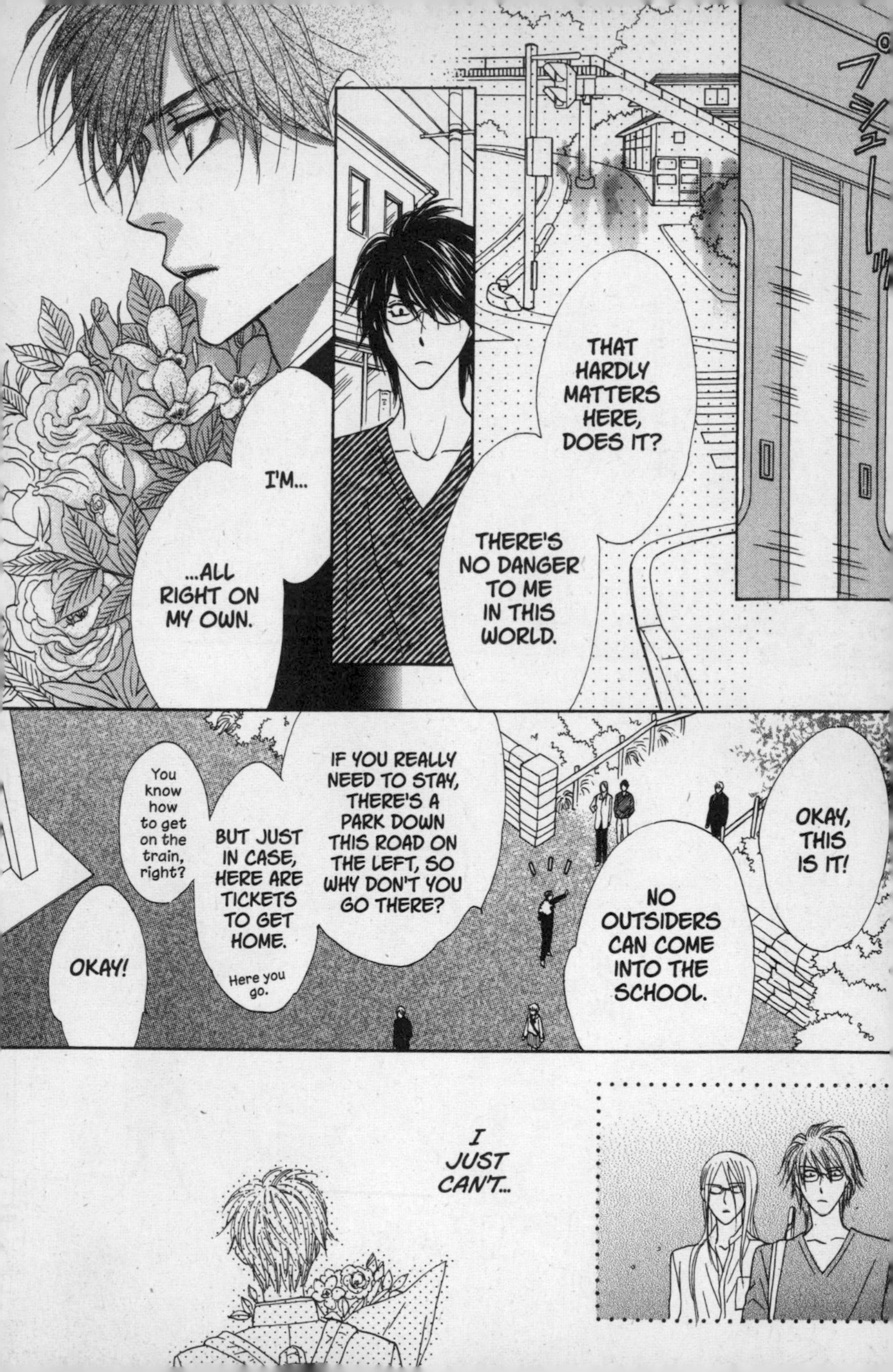
ペシューーッ
THAT HARDLY MATTERS HERE, DOES IT?
THERE'S NO DANGER TO ME IN THIS WORLD.
I'M...
...ALL RIGHT ON MY OWN.
OKAY, THIS IS IT!
NO OUTSIDERS CAN COME INTO THE SCHOOL.
IF YOU REALLY NEED TO STAY, THERE'S A PARK DOWN THIS ROAD ON THE LEFT, SO WHY DON'T YOU GO THERE?
BUT JUST IN CASE, HERE ARE TICKETS TO GET HOME.
Here you go.
You know how to get on the train, right?
OKAY!
I JUST CAN'T...

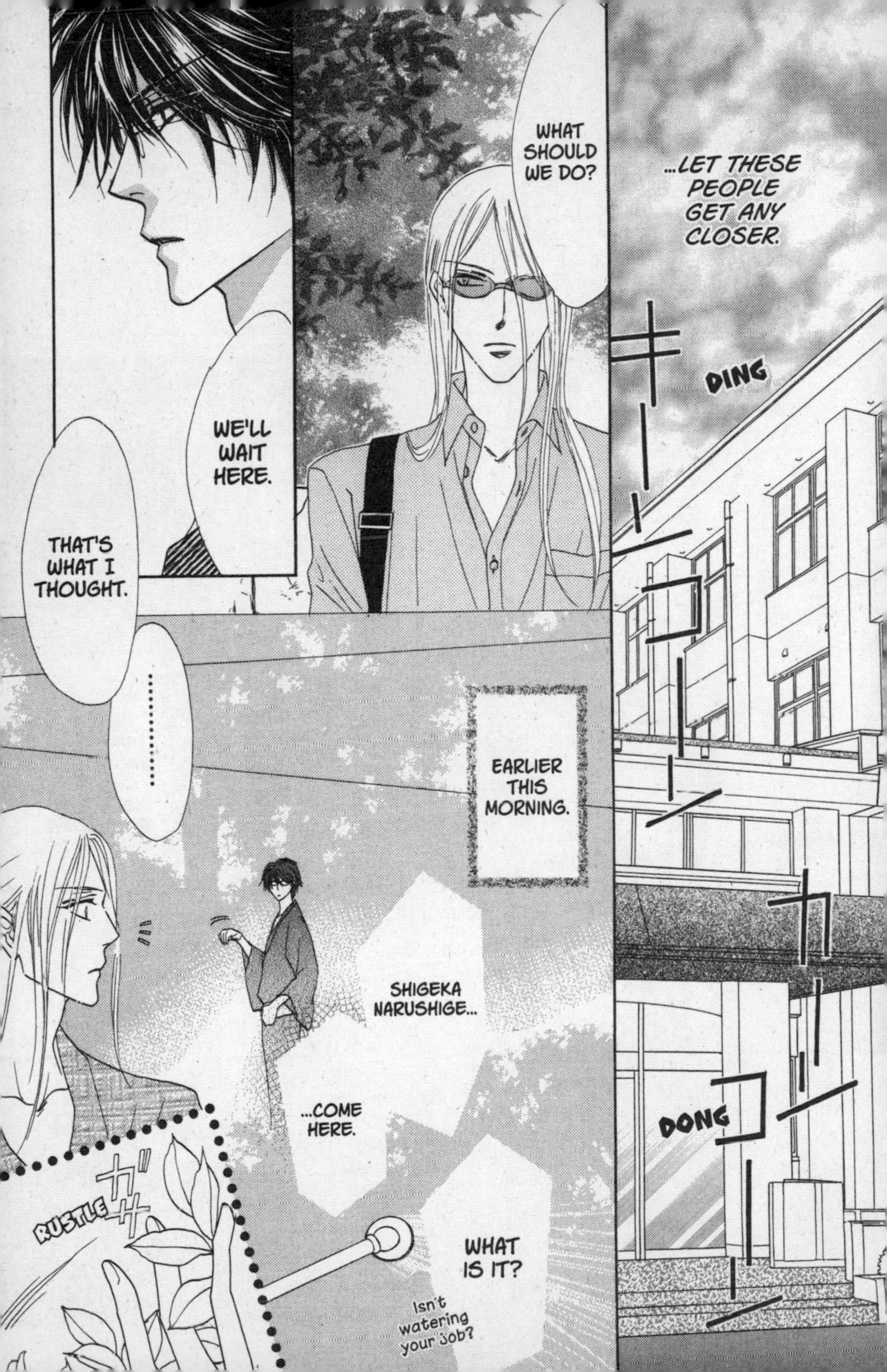
...LET THESE PEOPLE GET ANY CLOSER.
DING
DONG
WHAT SHOULD WE DO?
WE'LL WAIT HERE.
THAT'S WHAT I THOUGHT.
......
EARLIER THIS MORNING.
SHIGEKA NARUSHIGE...
...COME HERE.
WHAT IS IT?
Isn't watering your job?
RUSTLE

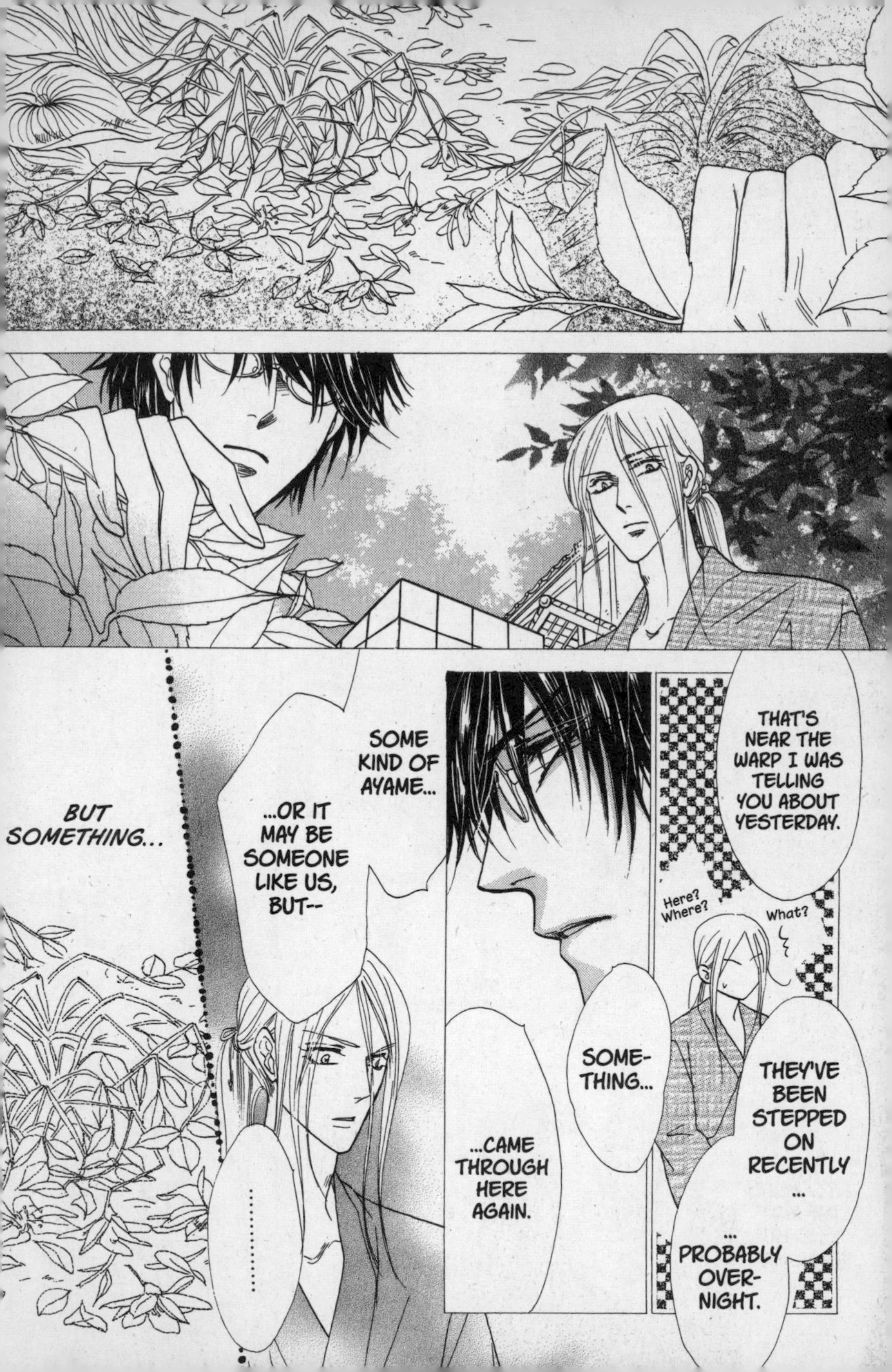
THAT'S NEAR THE WARP I WAS TELLING YOU ABOUT YESTERDAY.
What?
Here? Where?
THEY'VE BEEN STEPPED ON RECENTLY...
...PROBABLY OVER-NIGHT.
SOME-THING...
...CAME THROUGH HERE AGAIN.
SOME KIND OF AYAME...
...OR IT MAY BE SOMEONE LIKE US, BUT--
BUT SOMETHING...
......

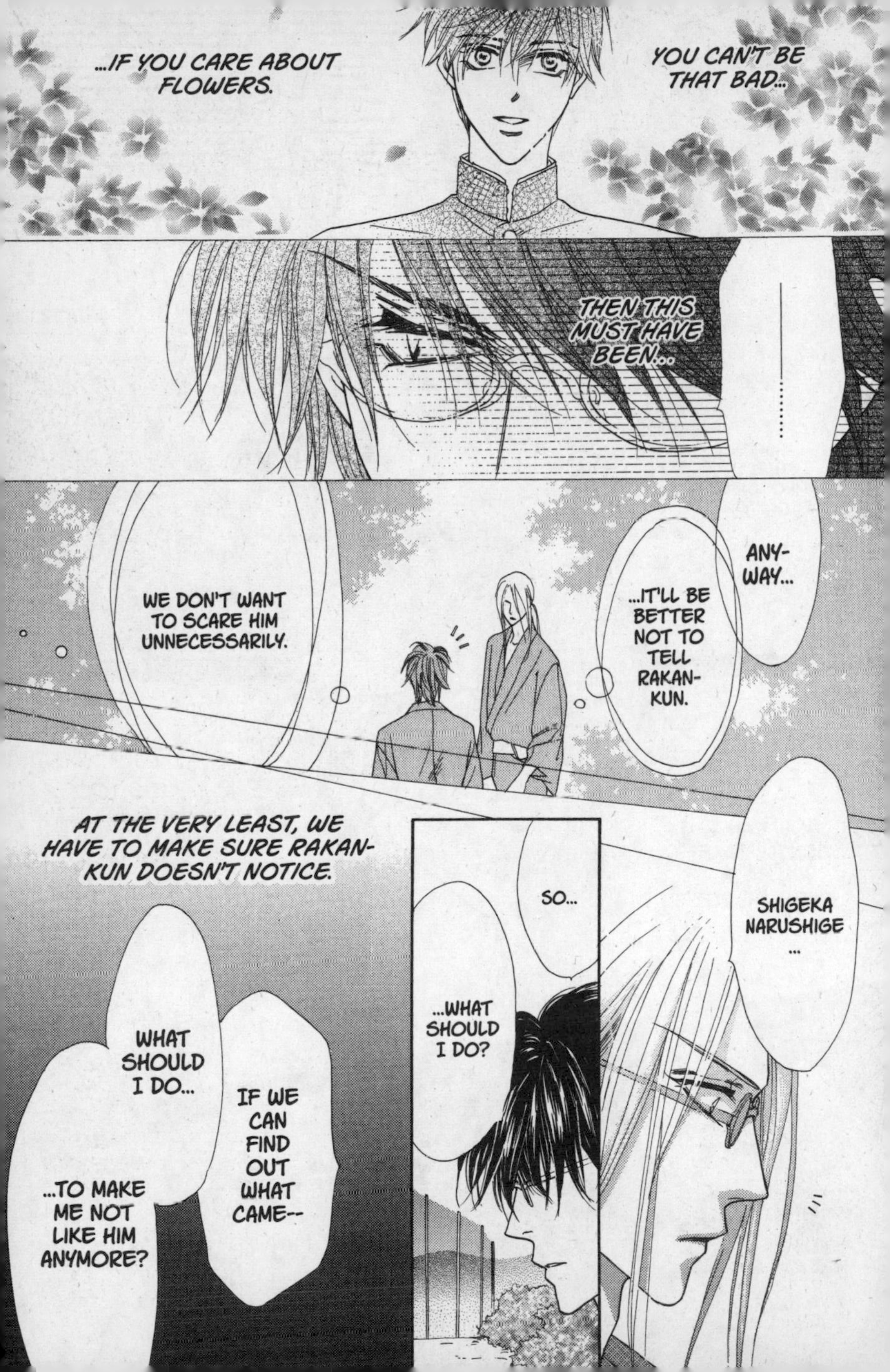
YOU CAN'T BE THAT BAD...
...IF YOU CARE ABOUT FLOWERS.
......
THEN THIS MUST HAVE BEEN...
ANY-WAY...
...IT'LL BE BETTER NOT TO TELL RAKAN-KUN.
WE DON'T WANT TO SCARE HIM UNNECESSARILY.
SHIGEKA NARUSHIGE ...
SO...
...WHAT SHOULD I DO?
AT THE VERY LEAST, WE HAVE TO MAKE SURE RAKAN-KUN DOESN'T NOTICE.
IF WE CAN FIND OUT WHAT CAME--
WHAT SHOULD I DO...
...TO MAKE ME NOT LIKE HIM ANYMORE?

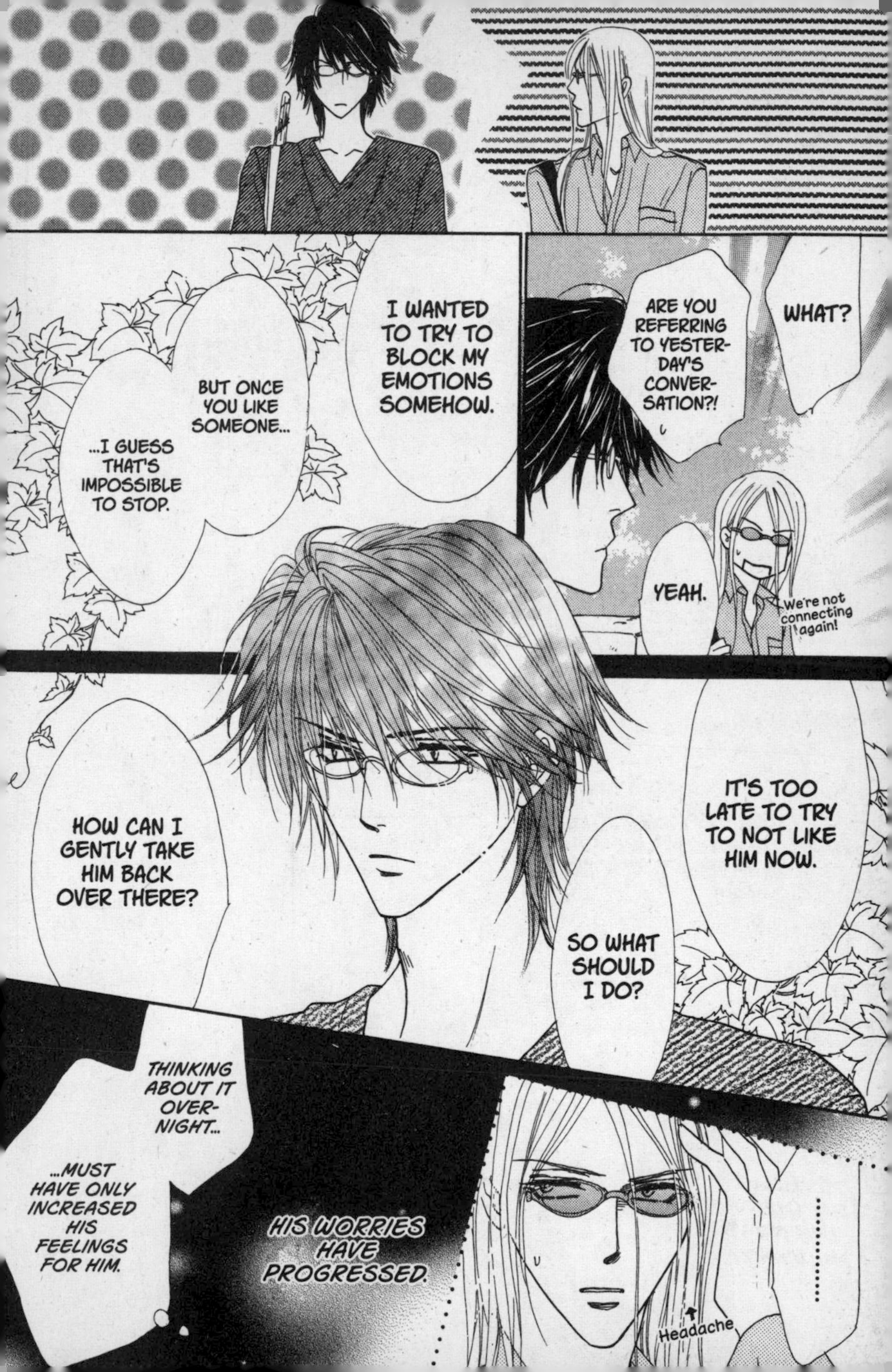
WHAT?
ARE YOU REFERRING TO YESTER-DAY'S CONVER-SATION?!
YEAH.
We're not connecting again!
I WANTED TO TRY TO BLOCK MY EMOTIONS SOMEHOW.
BUT ONCE YOU LIKE SOMEONE...
...I GUESS THAT'S IMPOSSIBLE TO STOP.
IT'S TOO LATE TO TRY TO NOT LIKE HIM NOW.
SO WHAT SHOULD I DO?
HOW CAN I GENTLY TAKE HIM BACK OVER THERE?
......
Headache
THINKING ABOUT IT OVER-NIGHT...
...MUST HAVE ONLY INCREASED HIS FEELINGS FOR HIM.
HIS WORRIES HAVE PROGRESSED.

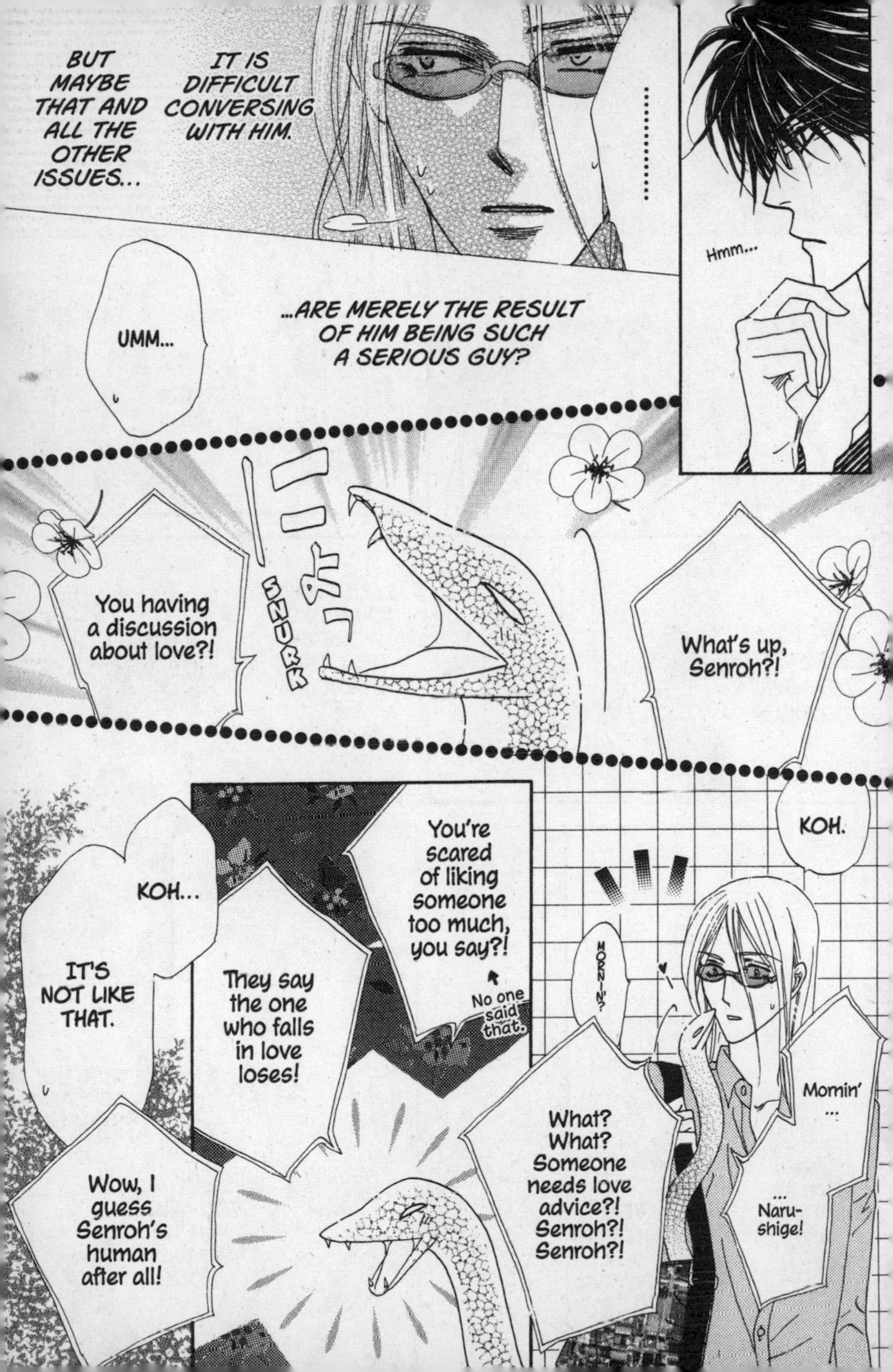
Hmm...
......
IT IS DIFFICULT CONVERSING WITH HIM.
BUT MAYBE THAT AND ALL THE OTHER ISSUES...
...ARE MERELY THE RESULT OF HIM BEING SUCH A SERIOUS GUY?
UMM...
What's up, Senroh?!
SNURK
You having a discussion about love?!
KOH.
MORNIN'?
Mornin' ...
... Narushige!
What? What? Someone needs love advice?! Senroh?! Senroh?!
You're scared of liking someone too much, you say?!
No one said that.
They say the one who falls in love loses!
Wow, I guess Senroh's human after all!
KOH...
IT'S NOT LIKE THAT.

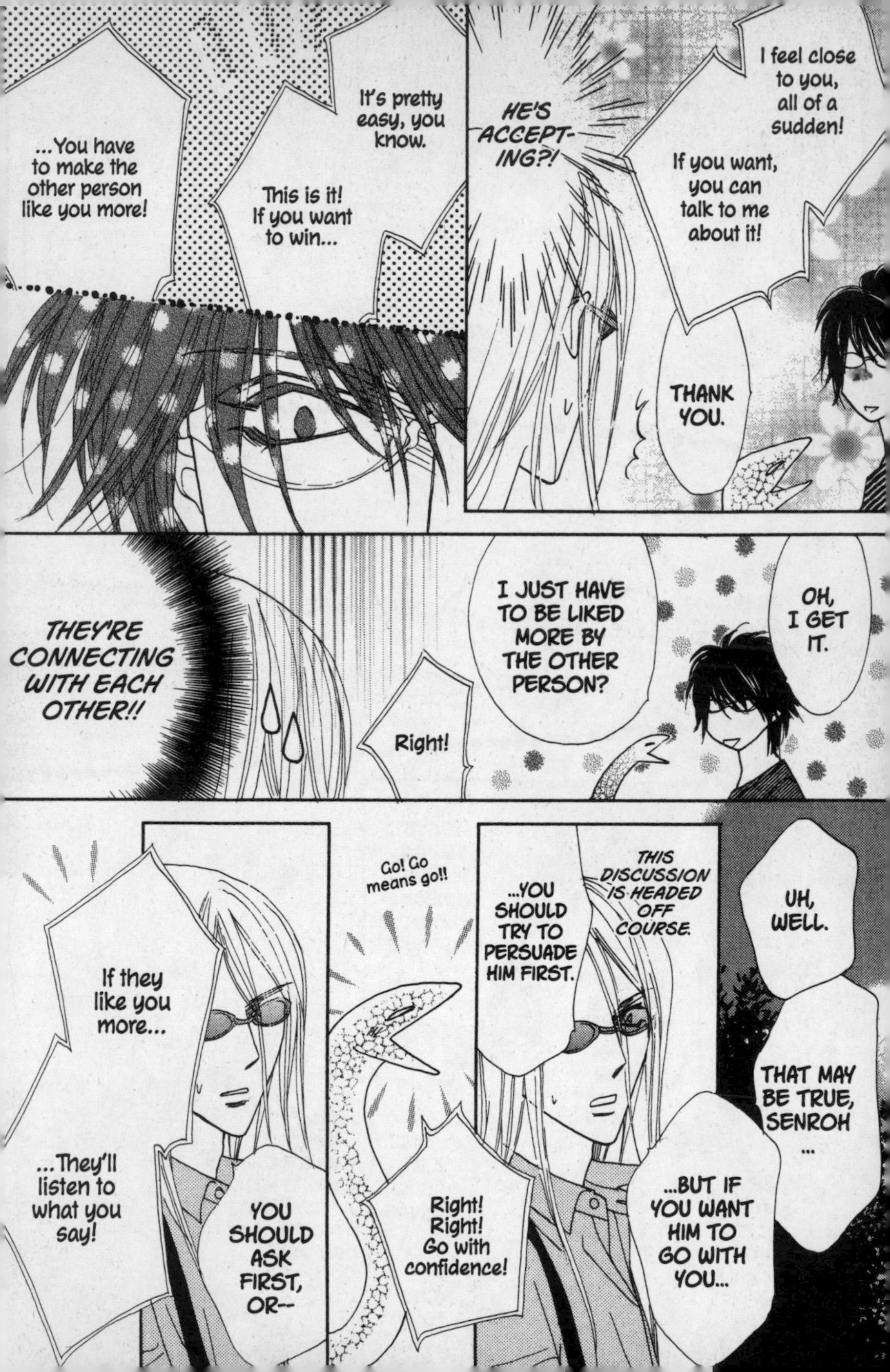
I feel close to you, all of a sudden!
If you want, you can talk to me about it!
HE'S ACCEPTING?!
THANK YOU.
It's pretty easy, you know.
This is it! If you want to win...
...You have to make the other person like you more!
OH, I GET IT.
I JUST HAVE TO BE LIKED MORE BY THE OTHER PERSON?
Right!
THEY'RE CONNECTING WITH EACH OTHER!!
UH, WELL.
THAT MAY BE TRUE, SENROH...
...BUT IF YOU WANT HIM TO GO WITH YOU...
THIS DISCUSSION IS HEADED OFF COURSE.
...YOU SHOULD TRY TO PERSUADE HIM FIRST.
Go! Go means go!!
Right! Right! Go with confidence!
YOU SHOULD ASK FIRST, OR--
If they like you more...
...They'll listen to what you say!

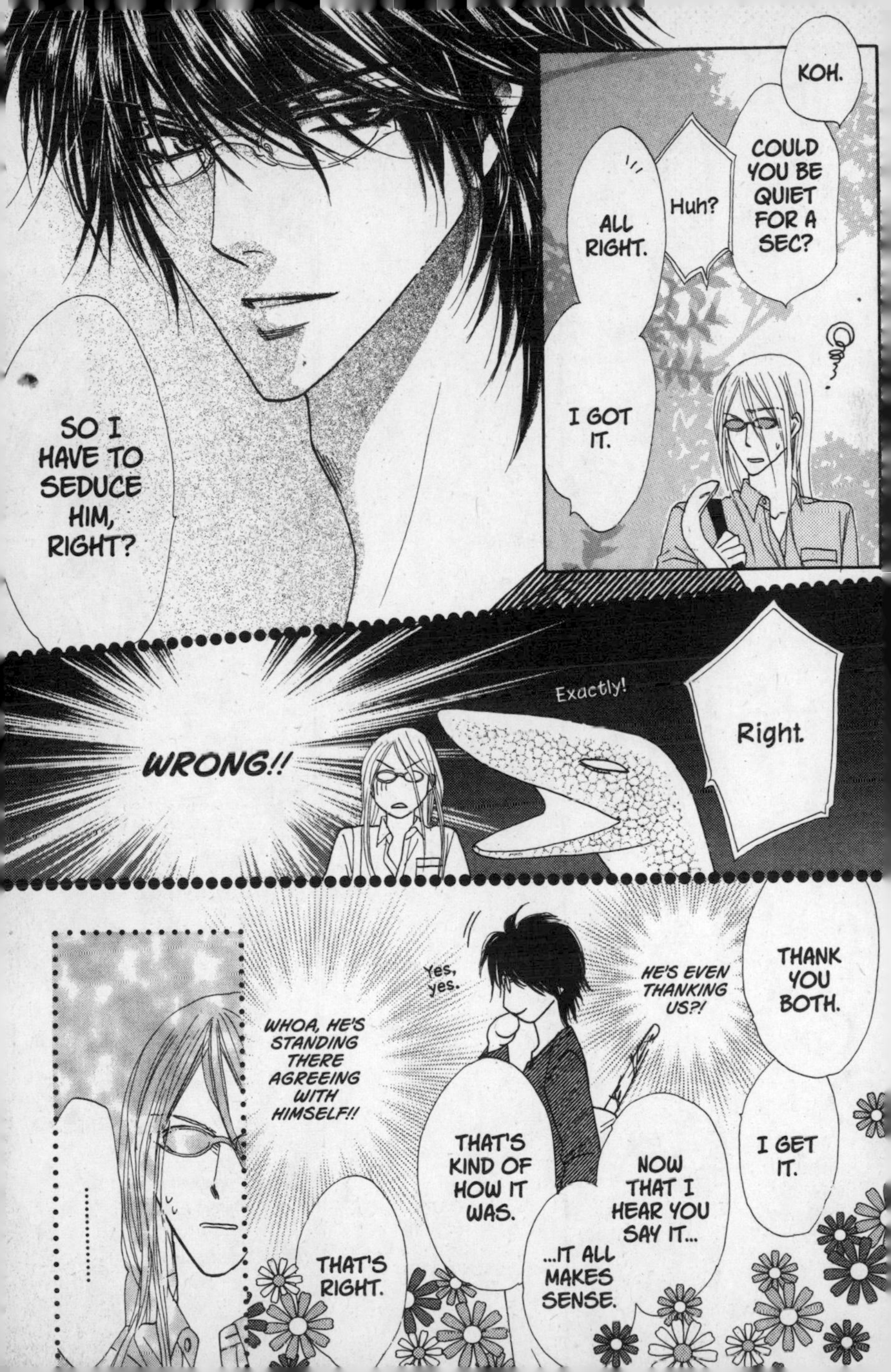
KOH.
COULD YOU BE QUIET FOR A SEC?
Huh?
ALL RIGHT.
I GOT IT.
SO I HAVE TO SEDUCE HIM, RIGHT?
Right.
Exactly!
WRONG!!
THANK YOU BOTH.
HE'S EVEN THANKING US?!
I GET IT.
NOW THAT I HEAR YOU SAY IT...
...IT ALL MAKES SENSE.
THAT'S KIND OF HOW IT WAS.
Yes, yes.
THAT'S RIGHT.
WHOA, HE'S STANDING THERE AGREEING WITH HIMSELF!!
......

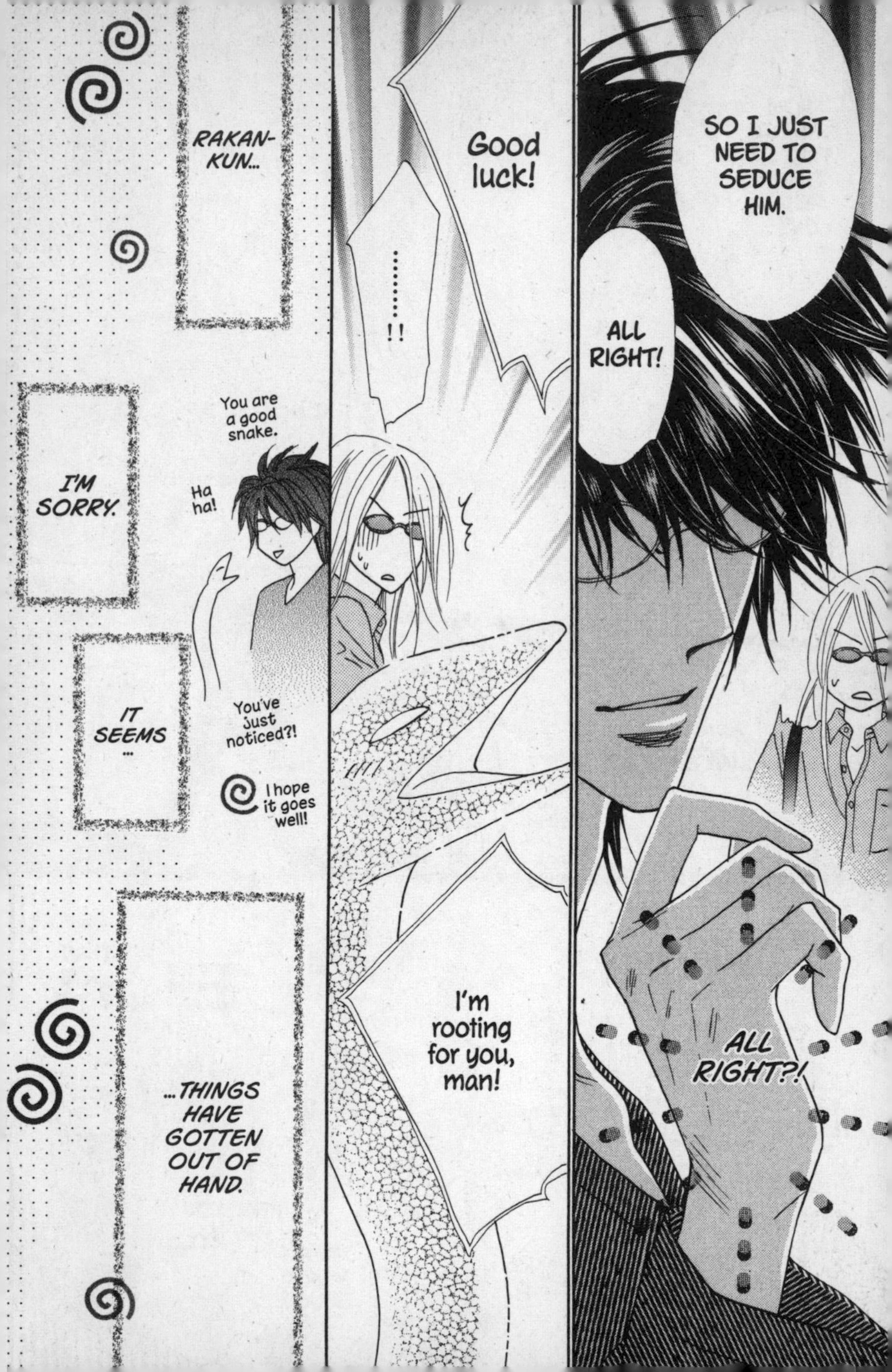
SO I JUST NEED TO SEDUCE HIM.
ALL RIGHT!
ALL RIGHT?!
Good luck!
......!!
I'm rooting for you, man!
RAKAN-KUN...
You are a good snake.
Ha ha!
I'M SORRY.
IT SEEMS...
You've just noticed?!
I hope it goes well!
...THINGS HAVE GOTTEN OUT OF HAND.

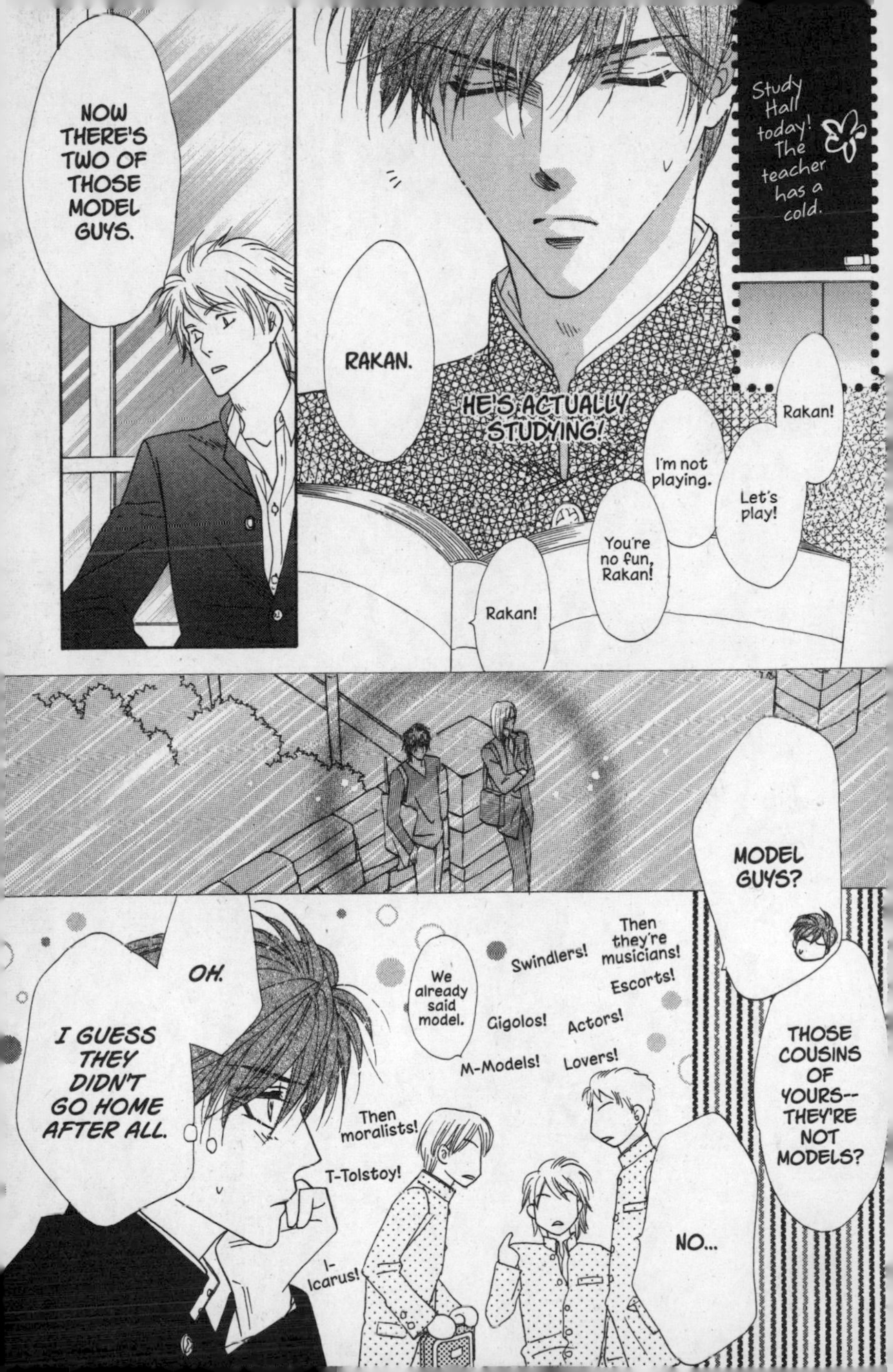
Study Hall today! The teacher has a cold.
Rakan!
Let's play!
I'm not playing.
You're no fun, Rakan!
Rakan!
HE'S ACTUALLY STUDYING!
RAKAN.
NOW THERE'S TWO OF THOSE MODEL GUYS.
MODEL GUYS?
THOSE COUSINS OF YOURS-- THEY'RE NOT MODELS?
NO...
Then they're musicians!
Swindlers!
Escorts!
Actors!
Gigolos!
We already said model.
Lovers!
M-Models!
Then moralists!
T-Tolstoy!
I-Icarus!
OH.
I GUESS THEY DIDN'T GO HOME AFTER ALL.

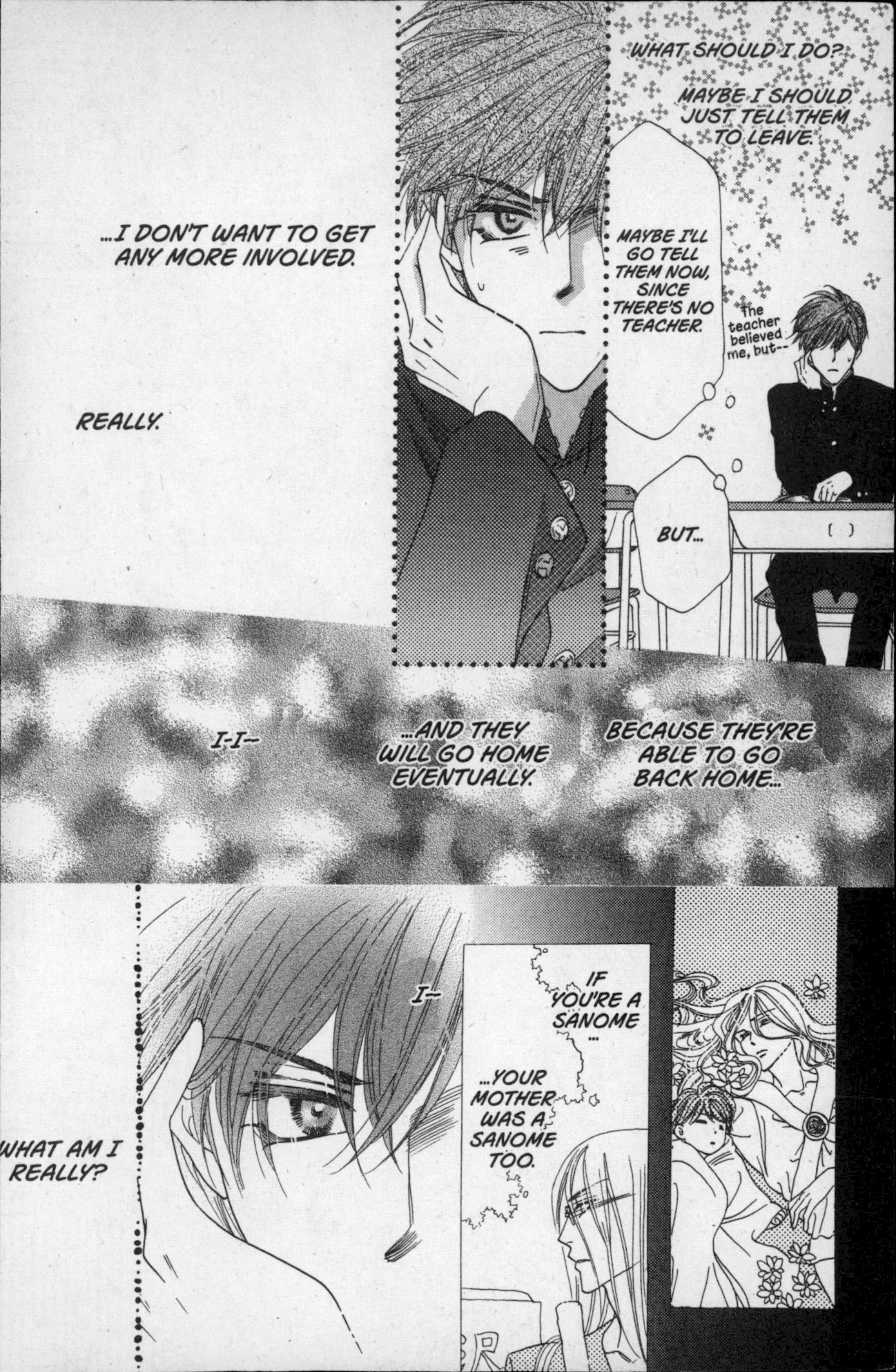
WHAT SHOULD I DO?
MAYBE I SHOULD JUST TELL THEM TO LEAVE.
The teacher believed me, but--
MAYBE I'LL GO TELL THEM NOW, SINCE THERE'S NO TEACHER.
BUT...
...I DON'T WANT TO GET ANY MORE INVOLVED.
REALLY.
BECAUSE THEY'RE ABLE TO GO BACK HOME...
...AND THEY WILL GO HOME EVENTUALLY.
I-I--
IF YOU'RE A SANOME...
...YOUR MOTHER WAS A SANOME TOO.
I--
WHAT AM I REALLY?

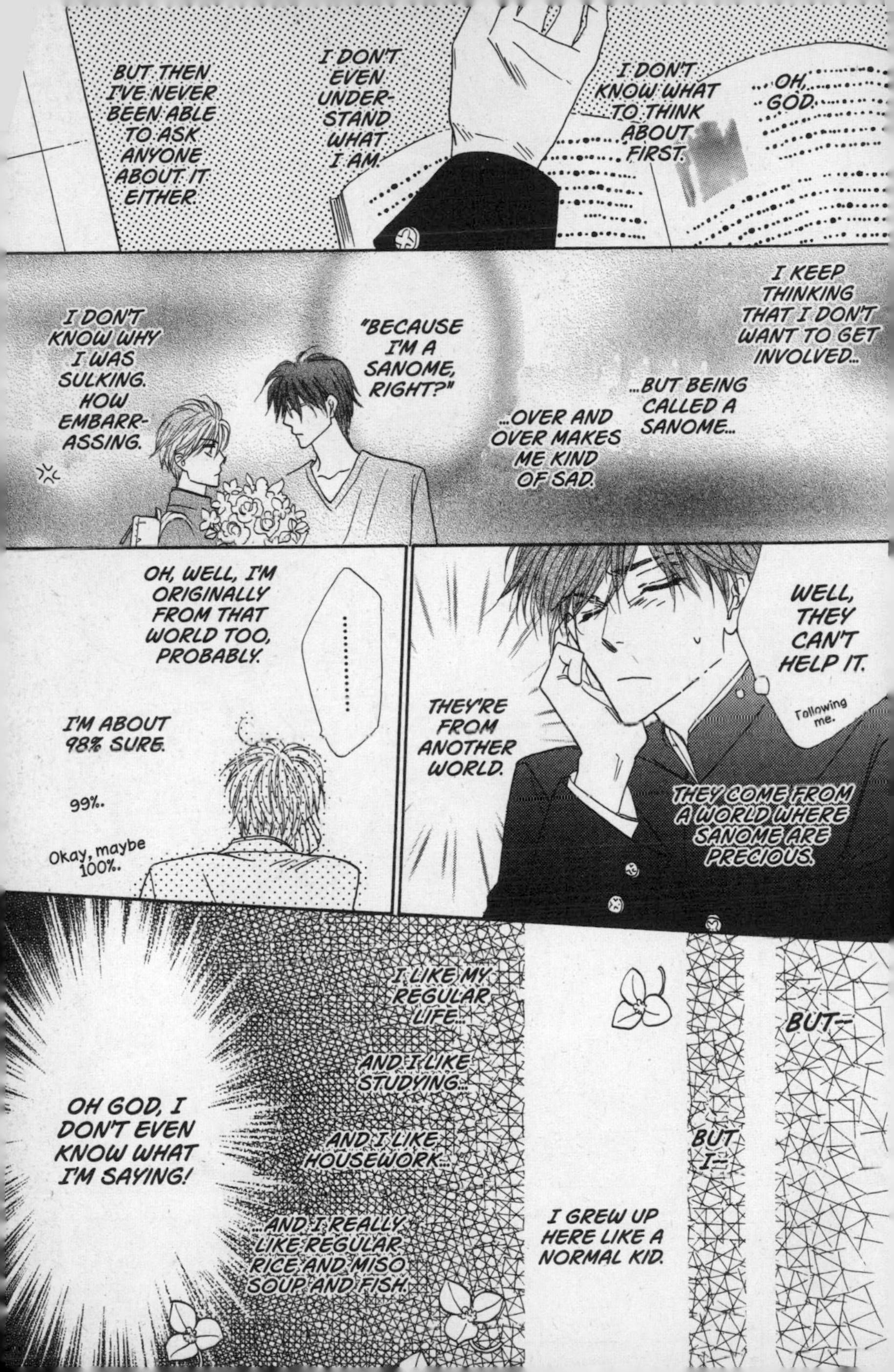
...OH, GOD.
I DON'T KNOW WHAT TO THINK ABOUT FIRST.
I DON'T EVEN UNDERSTAND WHAT I AM.
BUT THEN I'VE NEVER BEEN ABLE TO ASK ANYONE ABOUT IT EITHER.
I KEEP THINKING THAT I DON'T WANT TO GET INVOLVED...
...BUT BEING CALLED A SANOME...
...OVER AND OVER MAKES ME KIND OF SAD.
"BECAUSE I'M A SANOME, RIGHT?"
I DON'T KNOW WHY I WAS SULKING. HOW EMBARRASSING.
WELL, THEY CAN'T HELP IT.
Following me.
THEY'RE FROM ANOTHER WORLD.
THEY COME FROM A WORLD WHERE SANOME ARE PRECIOUS.
......
OH, WELL, I'M ORIGINALLY FROM THAT WORLD TOO, PROBABLY.
I'M ABOUT 98% SURE.
99%.
Okay, maybe 100%.
BUT—
BUT I—
I GREW UP HERE LIKE A NORMAL KID.
I LIKE MY REGULAR LIFE...
AND I LIKE STUDYING...
AND I LIKE HOUSEWORK...
...AND I REALLY LIKE REGULAR RICE AND MISO SOUP AND FISH.
OH GOD, I DON'T EVEN KNOW WHAT I'M SAYING!

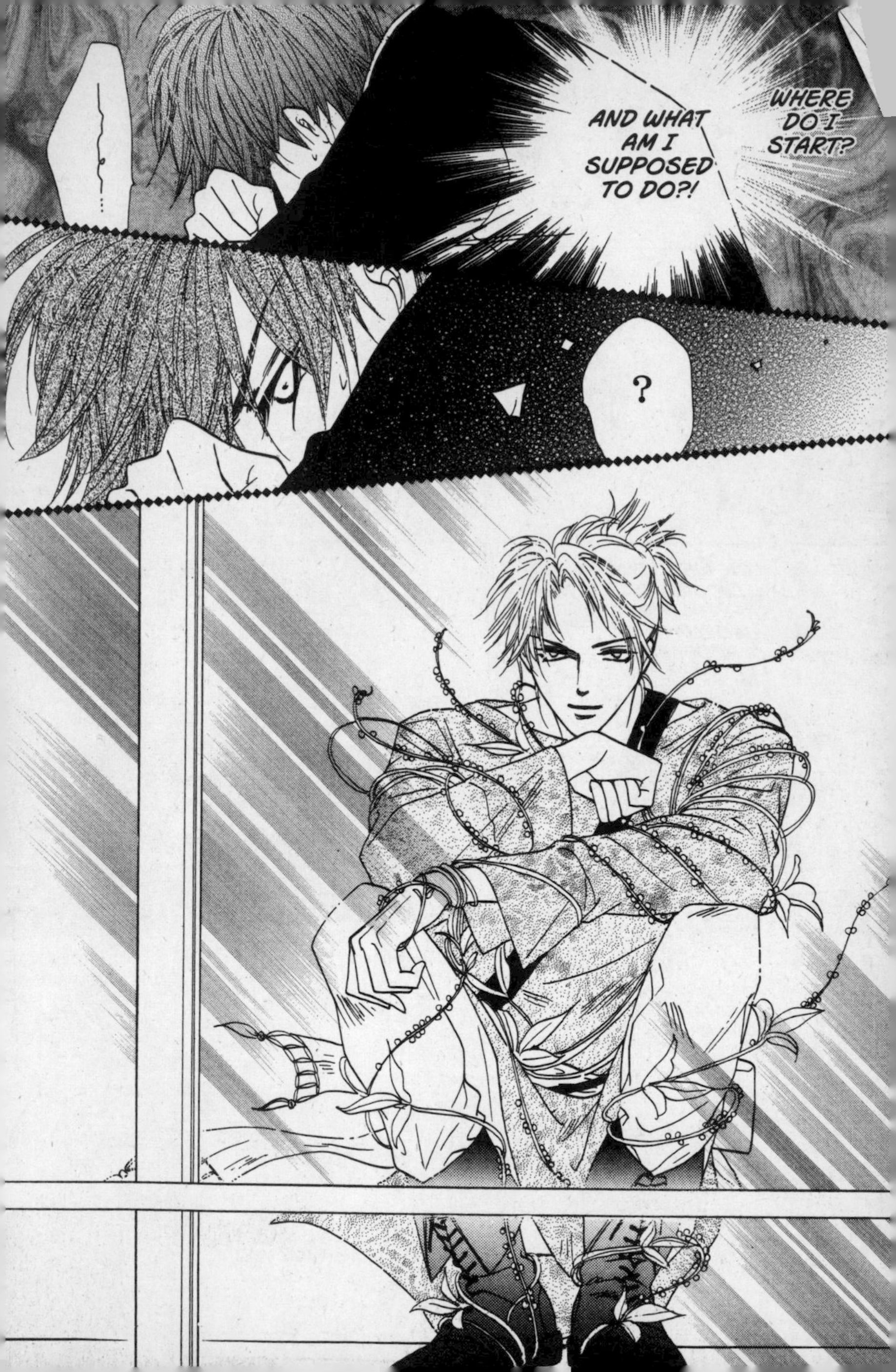
WHERE DO I START?
AND WHAT AM I SUPPOSED TO DO?!
...
?

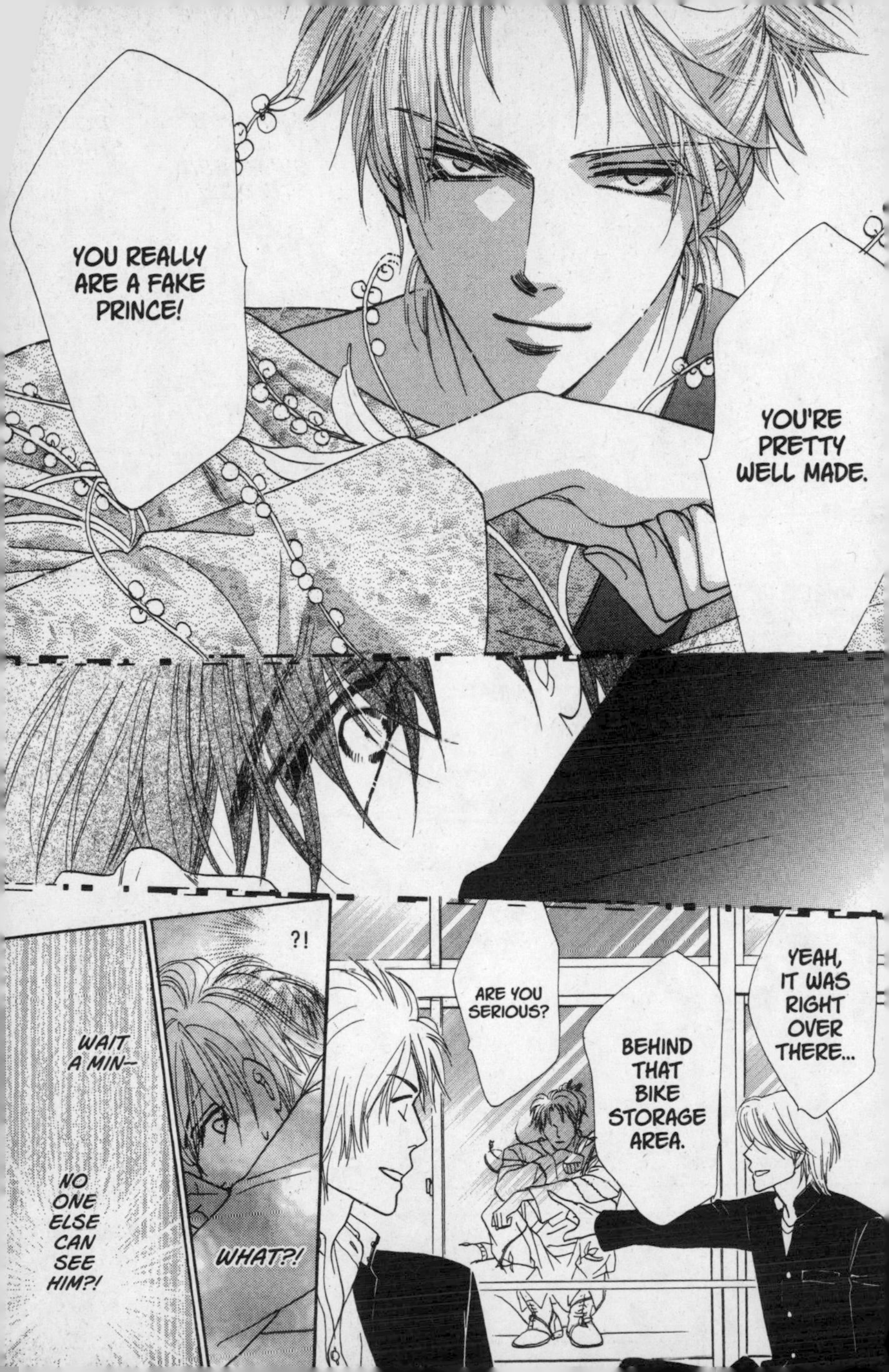
YOU'RE PRETTY WELL MADE.
YOU REALLY ARE A FAKE PRINCE!
YEAH, IT WAS RIGHT OVER THERE...
BEHIND THAT BIKE STORAGE AREA.
ARE YOU SERIOUS?
?!
WHAT?!
WAIT A MIN—
NO ONE ELSE CAN SEE HIM?!

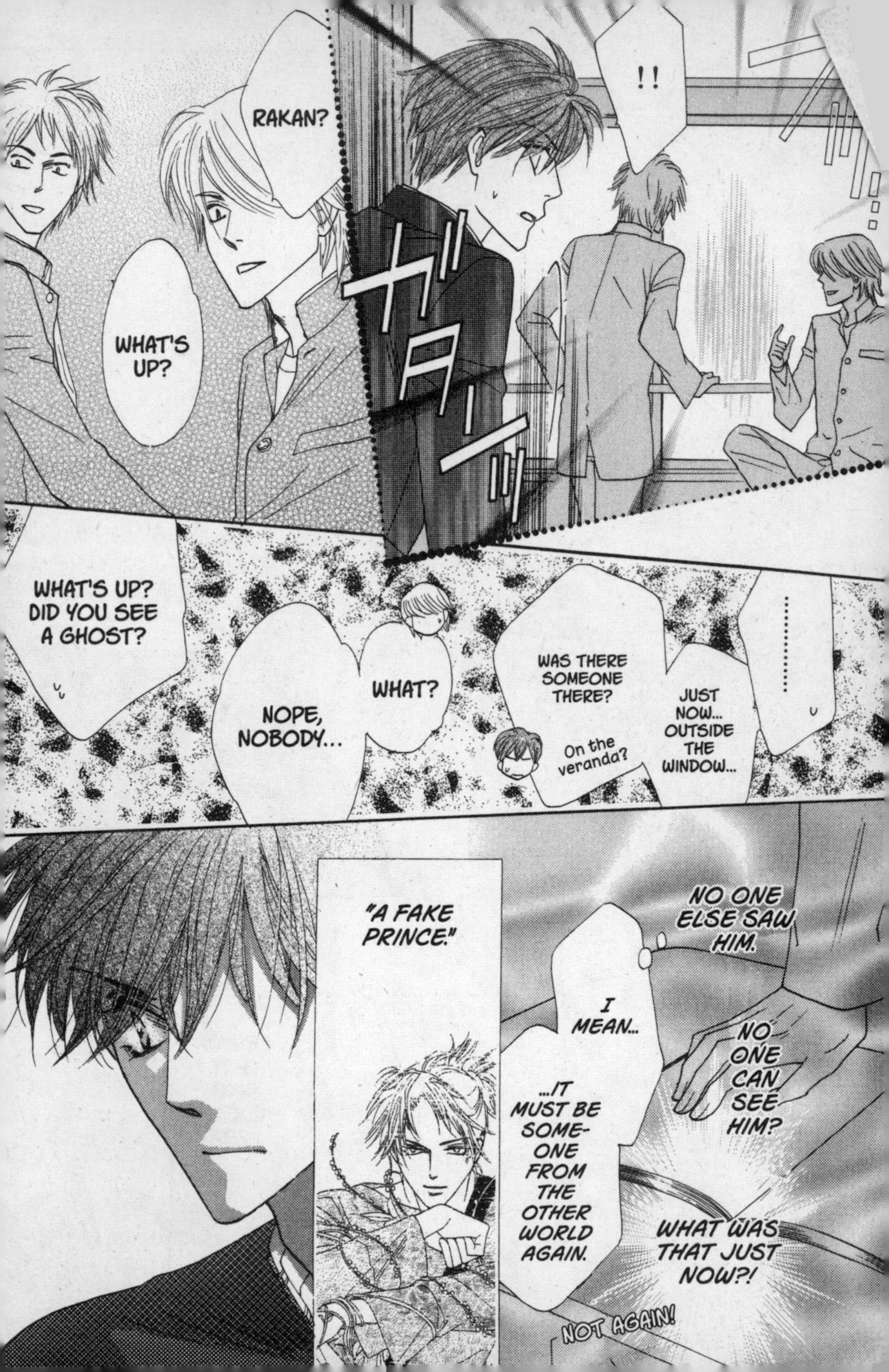
!!
ガタ―ッ
RAKAN?
WHAT'S UP?
......
JUST NOW... OUTSIDE THE WINDOW...
WAS THERE SOMEONE THERE?
On the veranda?
WHAT?
NOPE, NOBODY...
WHAT'S UP? DID YOU SEE A GHOST?
NO ONE ELSE SAW HIM.
NO ONE CAN SEE HIM?
WHAT WAS THAT JUST NOW?!
I MEAN...
...IT MUST BE SOME-ONE FROM THE OTHER WORLD AGAIN.
NOT AGAIN!
"A FAKE PRINCE."

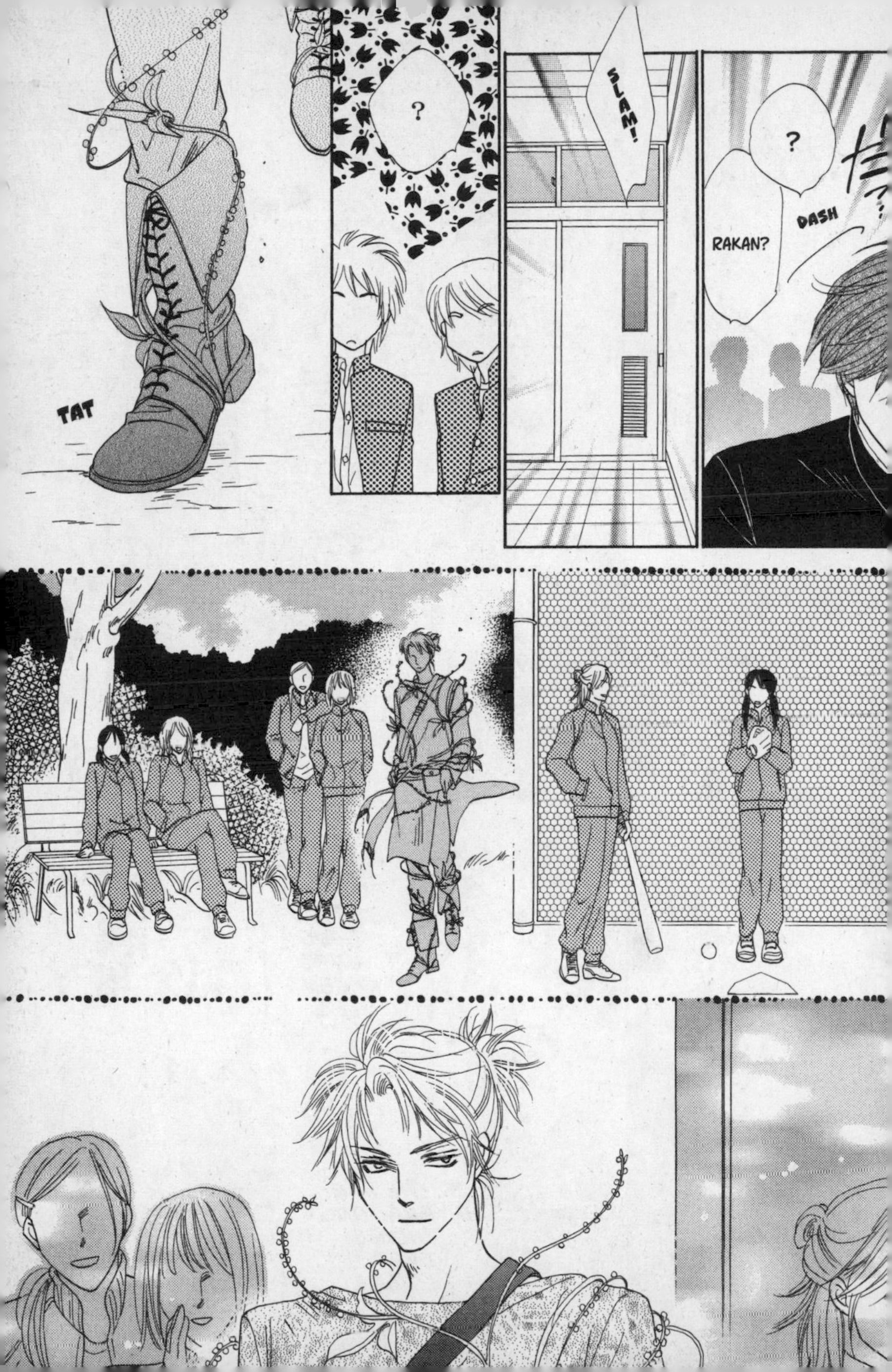
?
DASH
RAKAN?
SLAM!
?
TAT

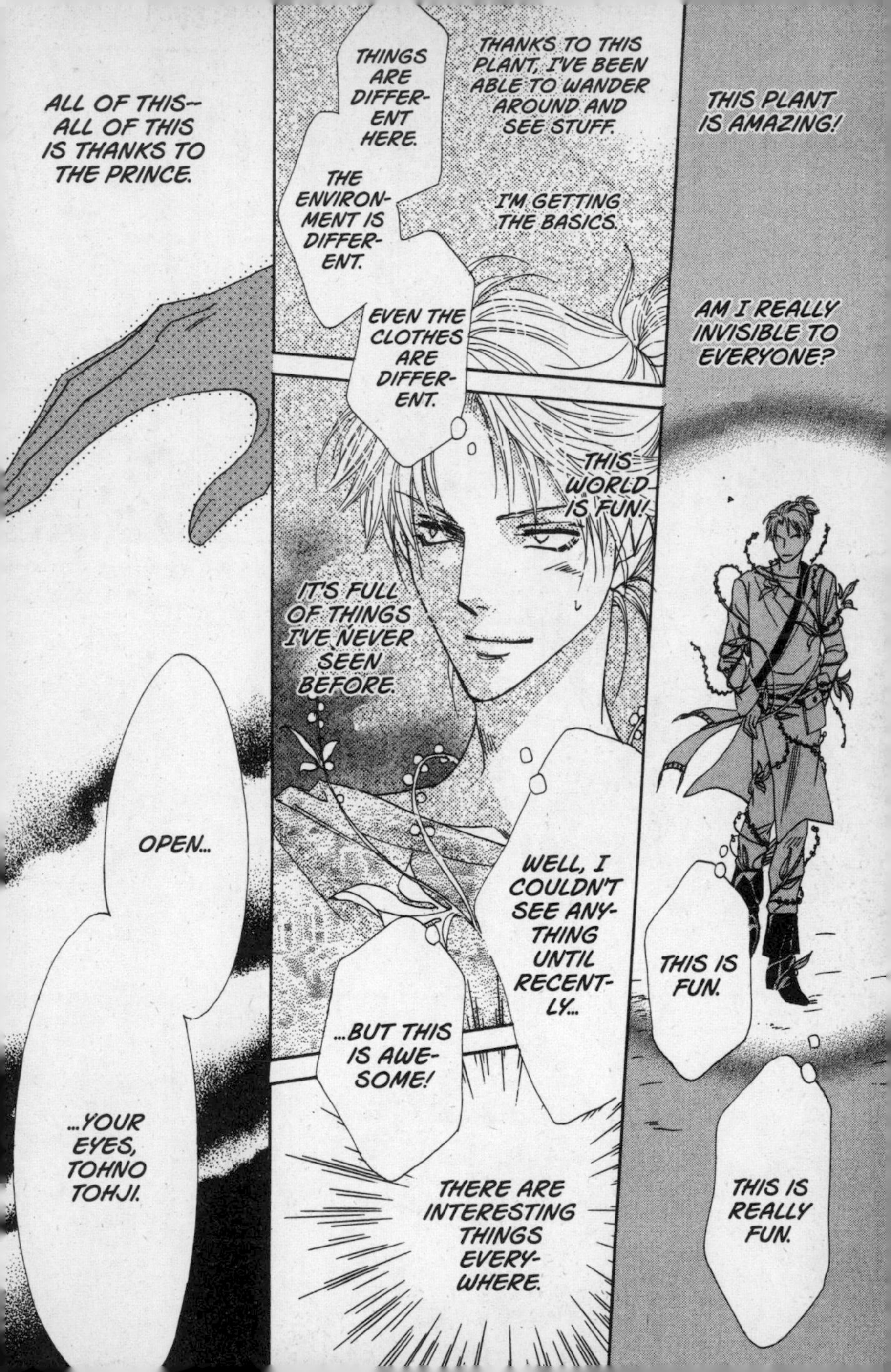
THIS PLANT IS AMAZING!
AM I REALLY INVISIBLE TO EVERYONE?
THIS IS FUN.
THIS IS REALLY FUN.
THANKS TO THIS PLANT, I'VE BEEN ABLE TO WANDER AROUND AND SEE STUFF.
I'M GETTING THE BASICS.
THINGS ARE DIFFERENT HERE.
THE ENVIRONMENT IS DIFFERENT.
EVEN THE CLOTHES ARE DIFFERENT.
THIS WORLD IS FUN!
IT'S FULL OF THINGS I'VE NEVER SEEN BEFORE.
WELL, I COULDN'T SEE ANYTHING UNTIL RECENTLY...
...BUT THIS IS AWESOME!
THERE ARE INTERESTING THINGS EVERYWHERE.
ALL OF THIS-- ALL OF THIS IS THANKS TO THE PRINCE.
OPEN...
...YOUR EYES, TOHNO TOHJI.

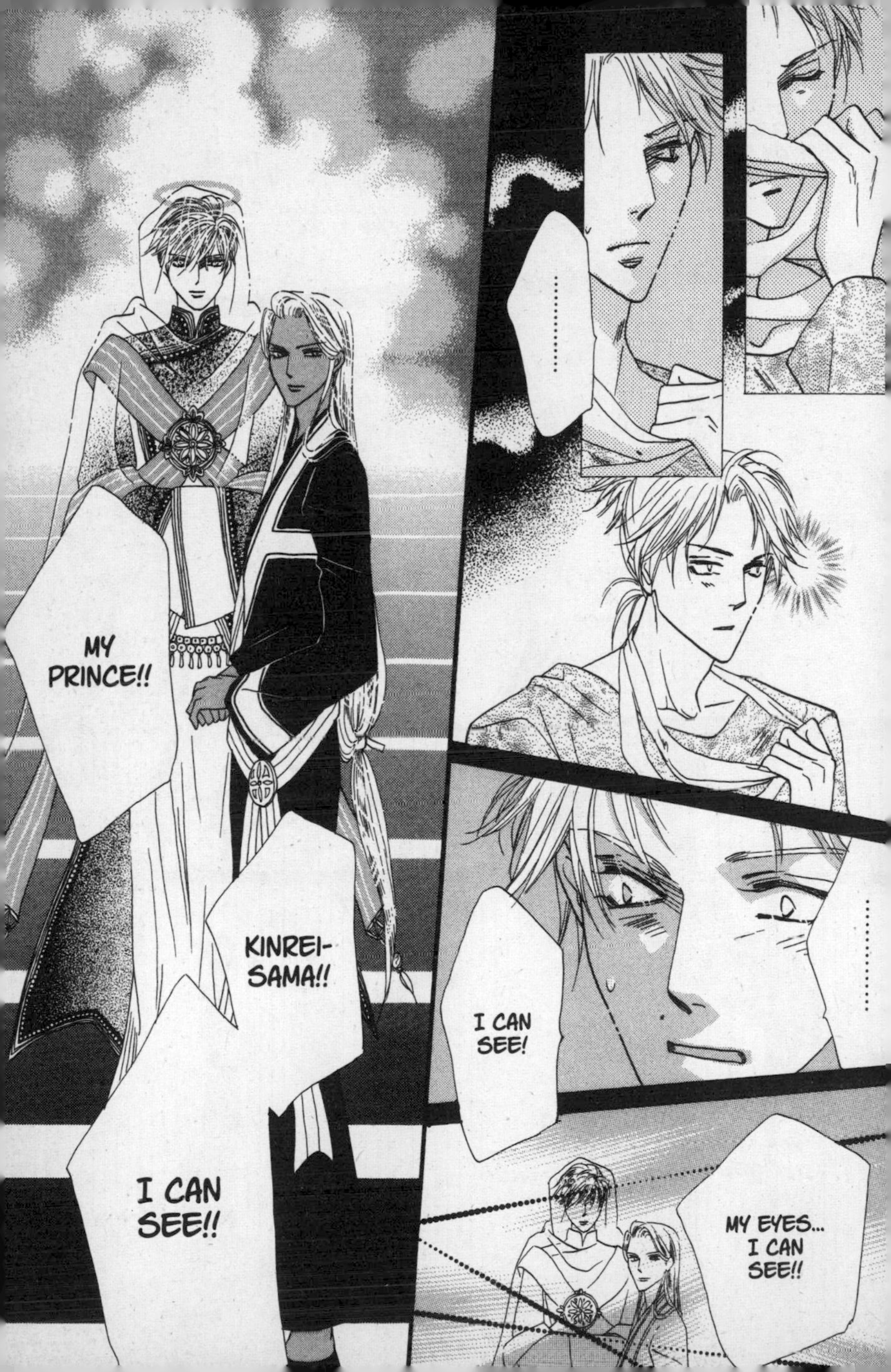
......
......
I CAN SEE!
MY EYES... I CAN SEE!!
MY PRINCE!!
KINREI-SAMA!!
I CAN SEE!!

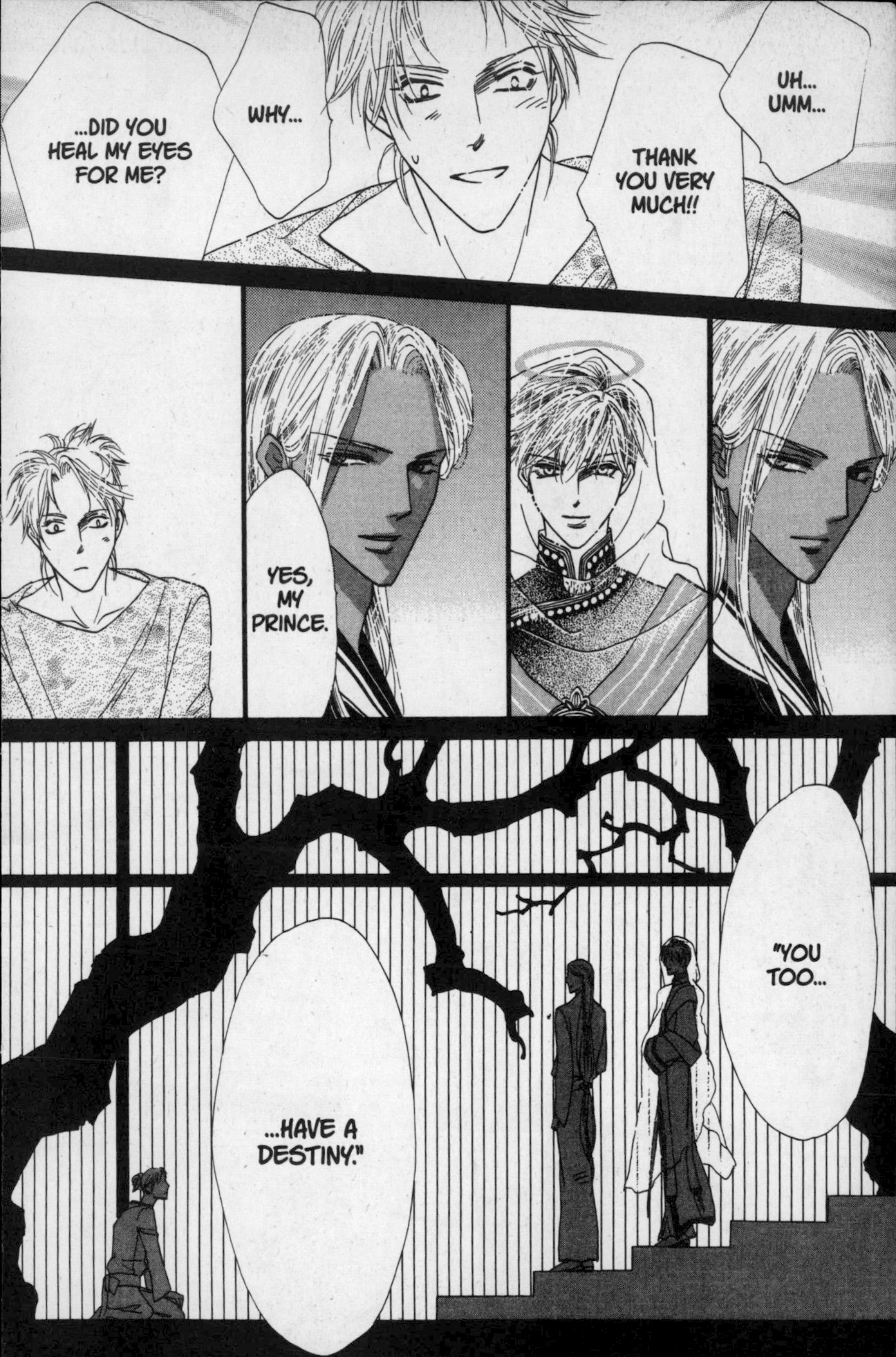
UH... UMM...
THANK YOU VERY MUCH!!
WHY...
...DID YOU HEAL MY EYES FOR ME?
YES, MY PRINCE.
"YOU TOO...
...HAVE A DESTINY."

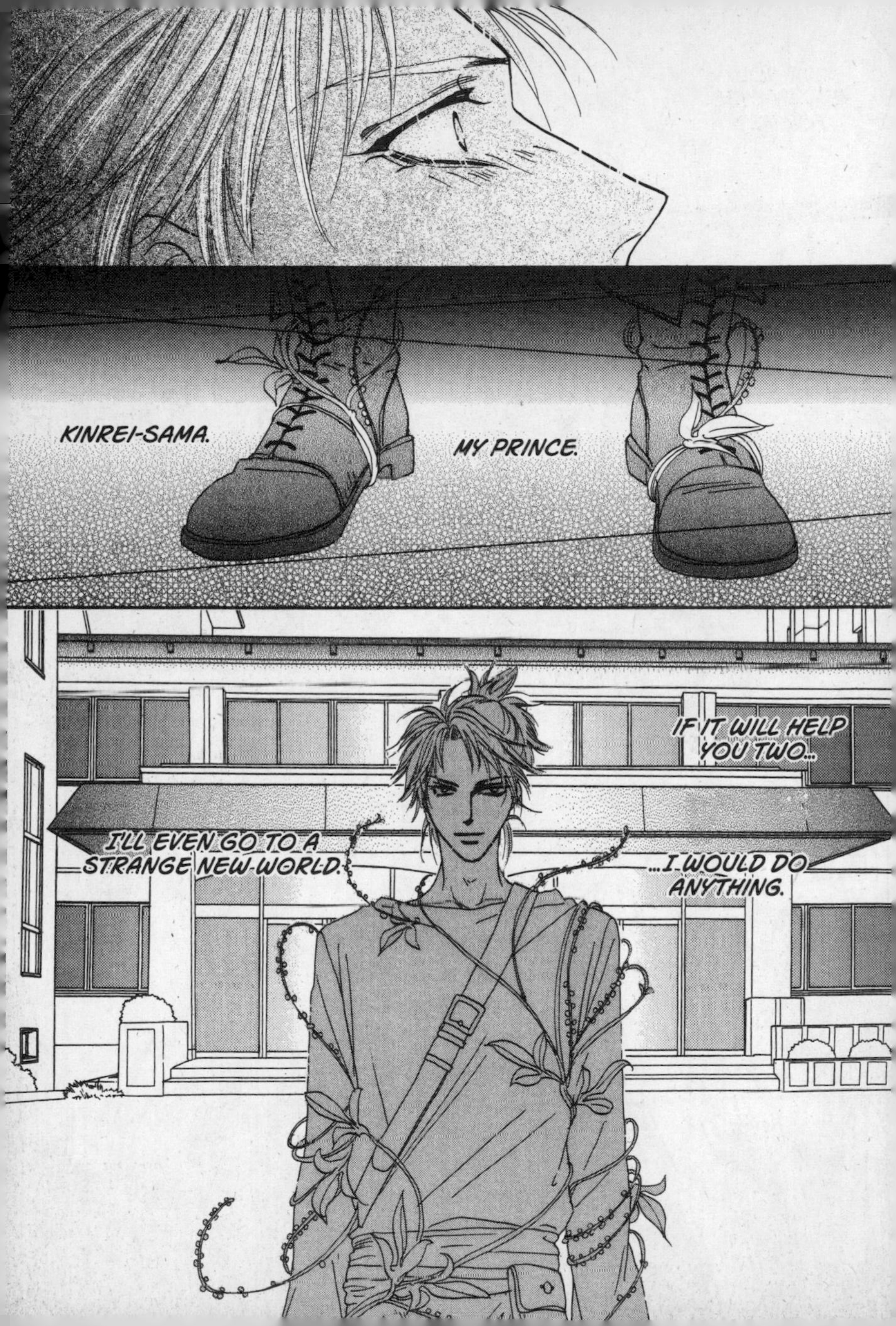
MY PRINCE.
KINREI-SAMA.
IF IT WILL HELP YOU TWO...
...I WOULD DO ANYTHING.
I'LL EVEN GO TO A STRANGE NEW WORLD.

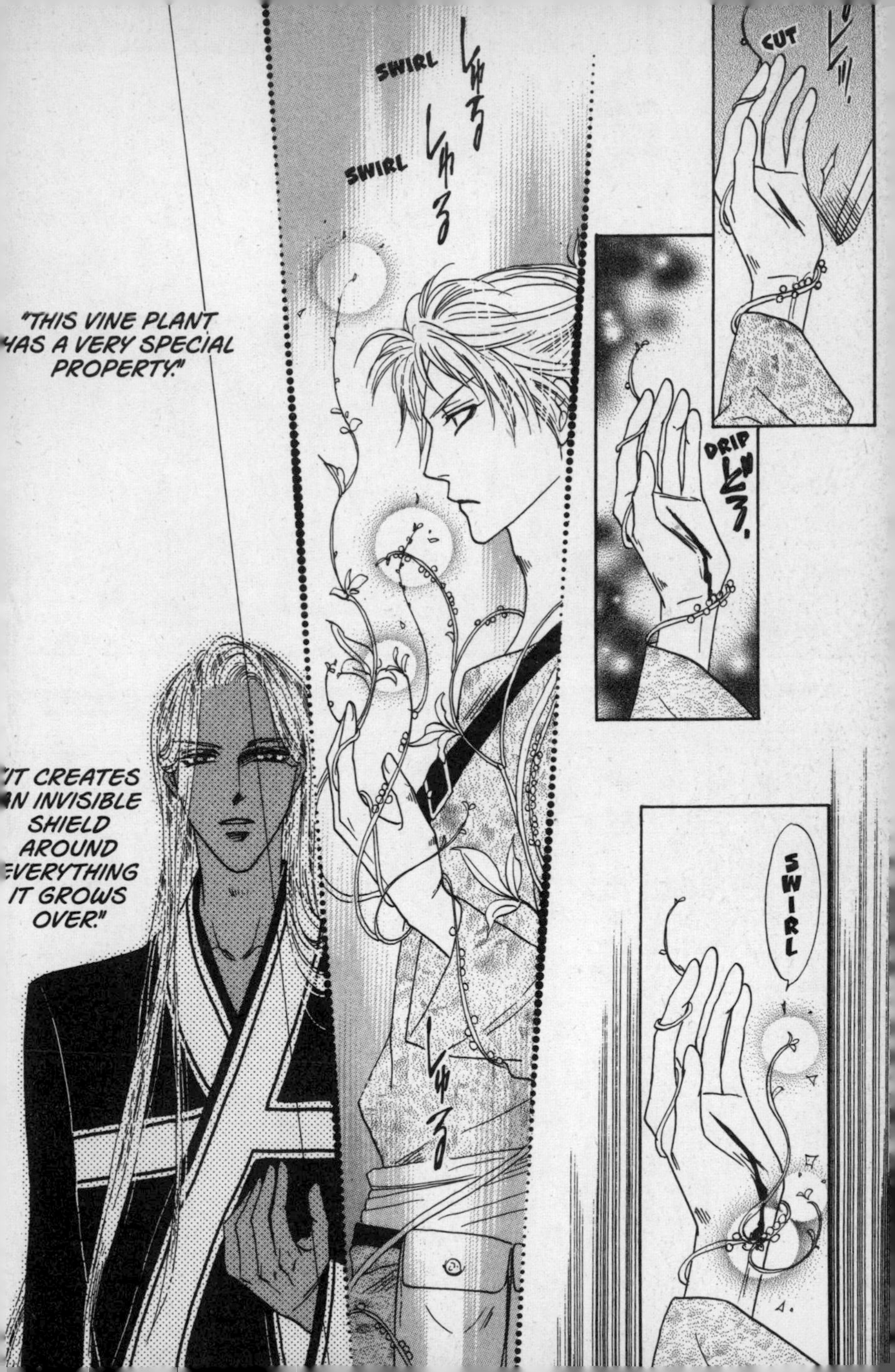
CUT
DRIP
SWIRL
SWIRL
しゅる
SWIRL
しゅる
しゅる
"THIS VINE PLANT HAS A VERY SPECIAL PROPERTY."
"IT CREATES AN INVISIBLE SHIELD AROUND EVERYTHING IT GROWS OVER."

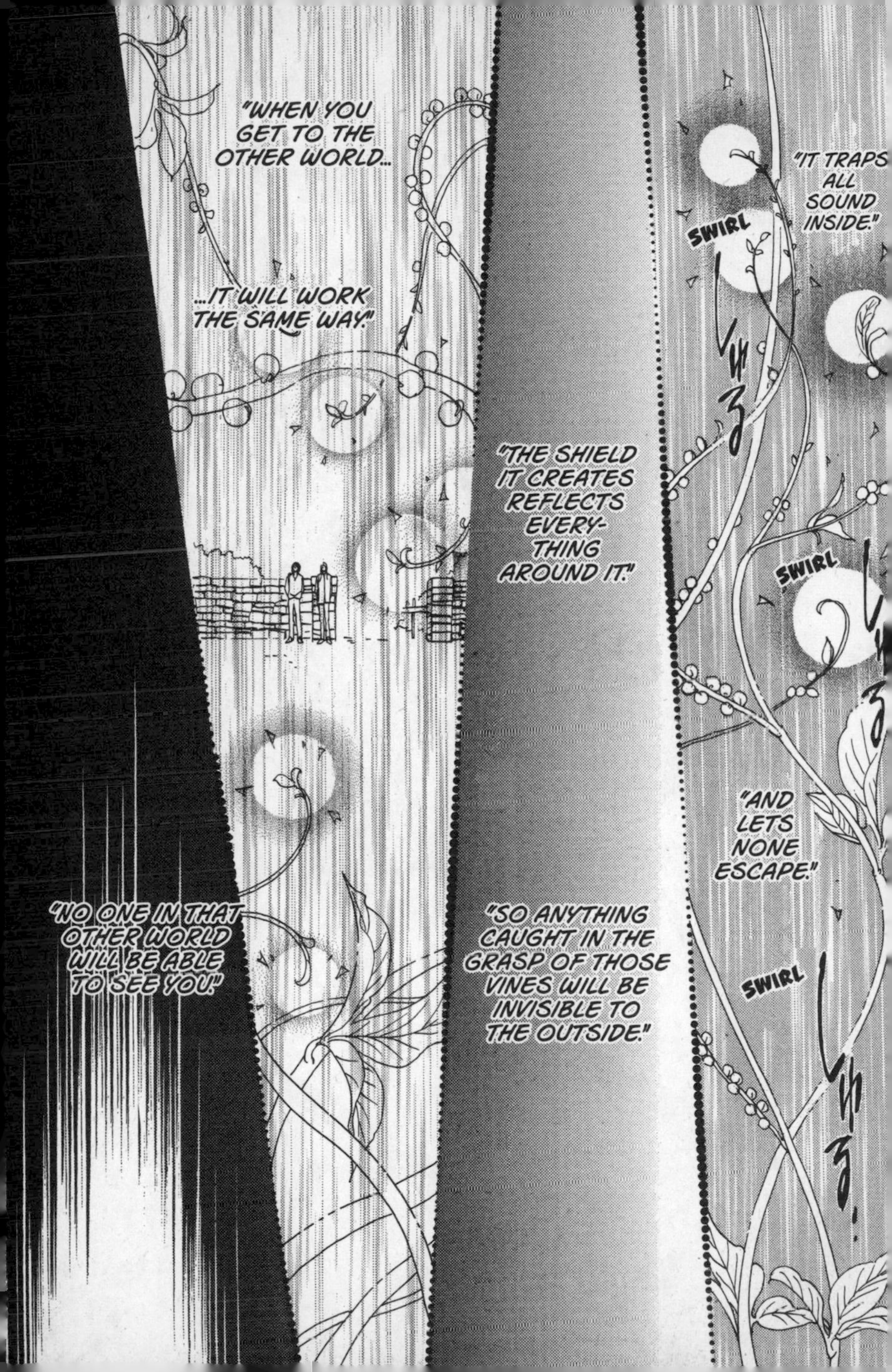
"IT TRAPS ALL SOUND INSIDE."
SWIRL
SWIRL
"AND LETS NONE ESCAPE."
SWIRL
"THE SHIELD IT CREATES REFLECTS EVERY-THING AROUND IT."
"SO ANYTHING CAUGHT IN THE GRASP OF THOSE VINES WILL BE INVISIBLE TO THE OUTSIDE."
"WHEN YOU GET TO THE OTHER WORLD...
...IT WILL WORK THE SAME WAY."
"NO ONE IN THAT OTHER WORLD WILL BE ABLE TO SEE YOU."

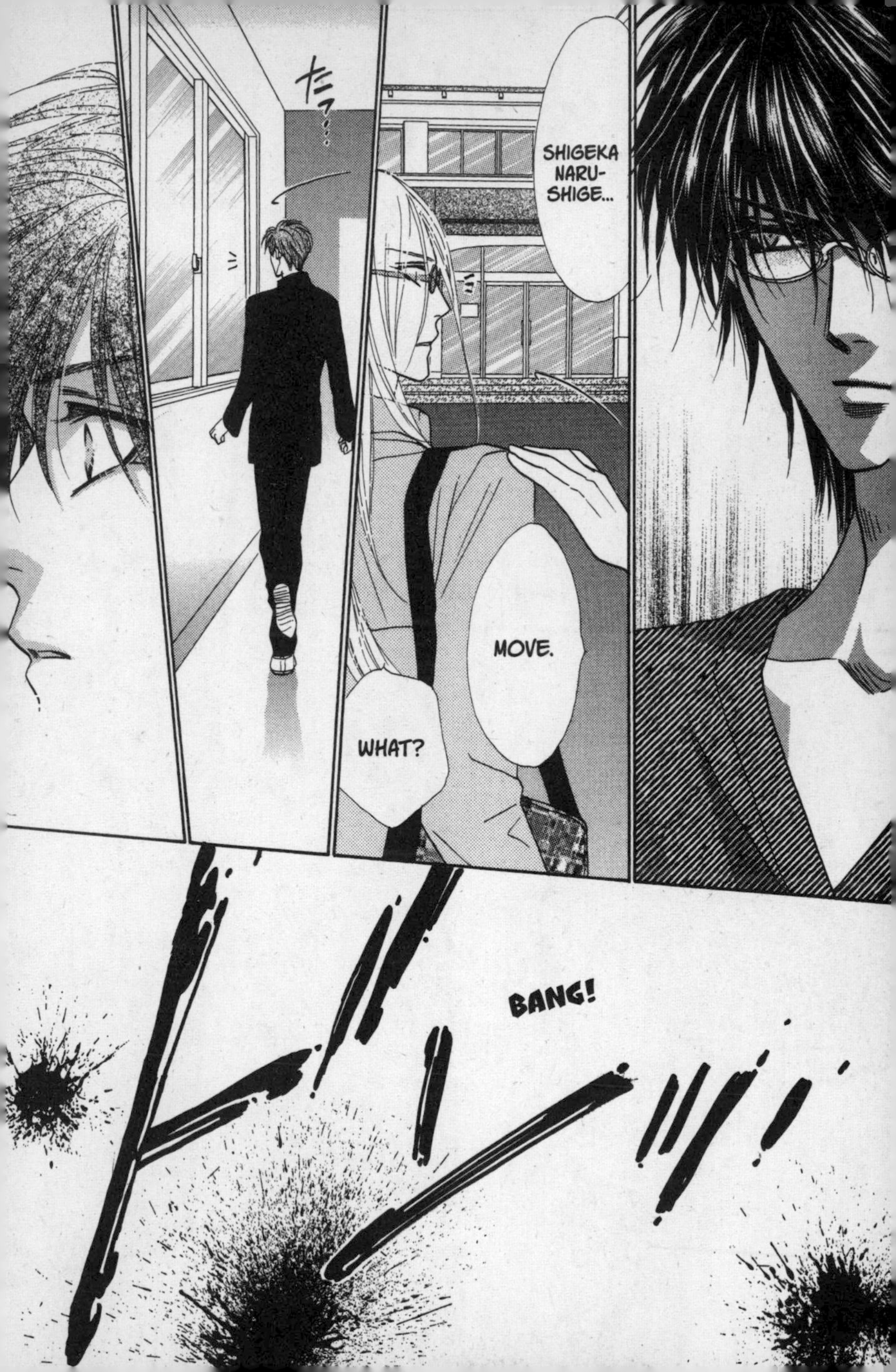
SHIGEKA NARU-SHIGE...
MOVE.
WHAT?
BANG!

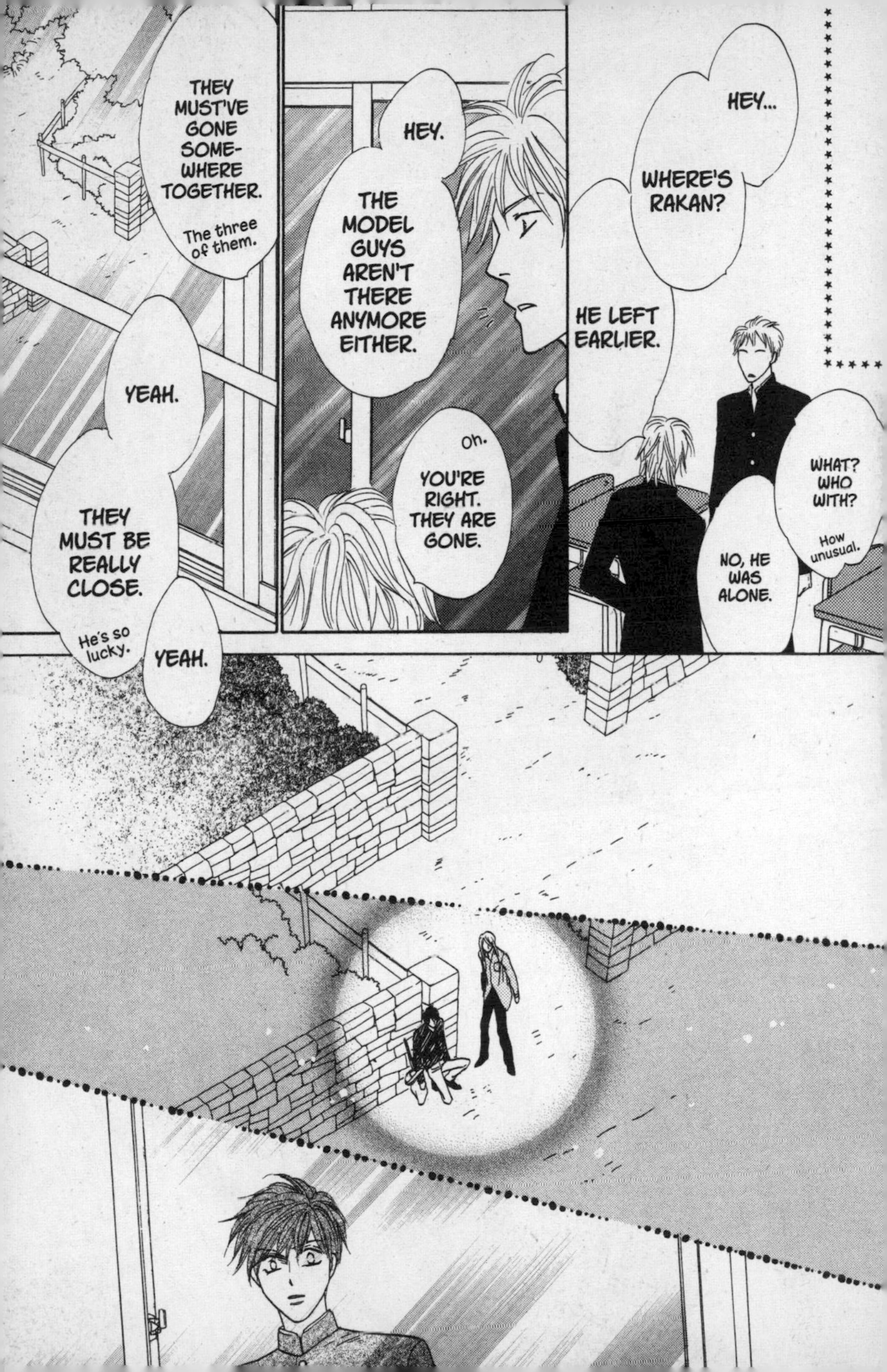
HEY...
WHERE'S RAKAN?
HE LEFT EARLIER.
WHAT? WHO WITH?
How unusual.
NO, HE WAS ALONE.
HEY.
THE MODEL GUYS AREN'T THERE ANYMORE EITHER.
Oh.
YOU'RE RIGHT. THEY ARE GONE.
THEY MUST'VE GONE SOME-WHERE TOGETHER.
The three of them.
YEAH.
THEY MUST BE REALLY CLOSE.
He's so lucky.
YEAH.

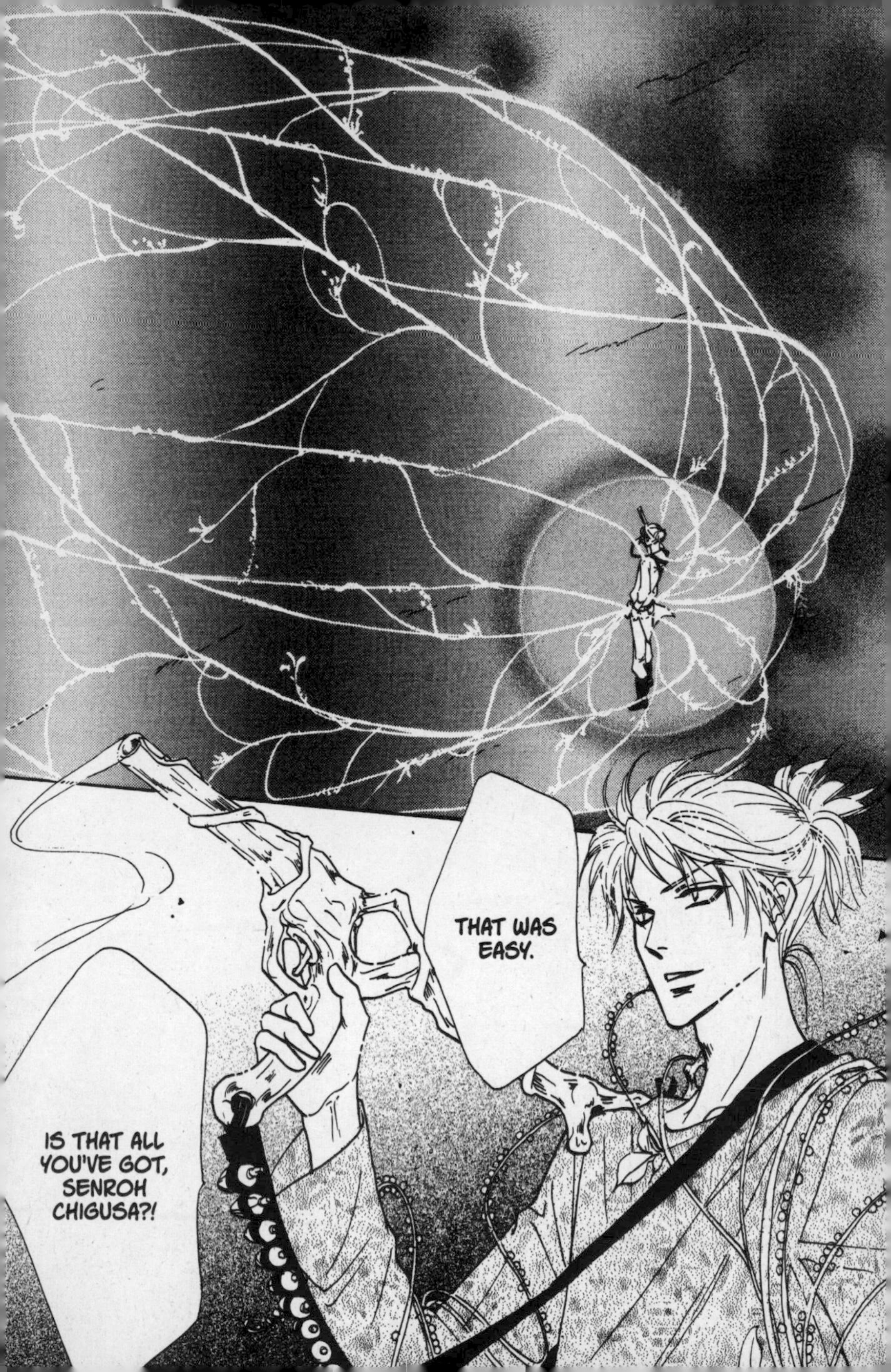
THAT WAS EASY.
IS THAT ALL YOU'VE GOT, SENROH CHIGUSA?!

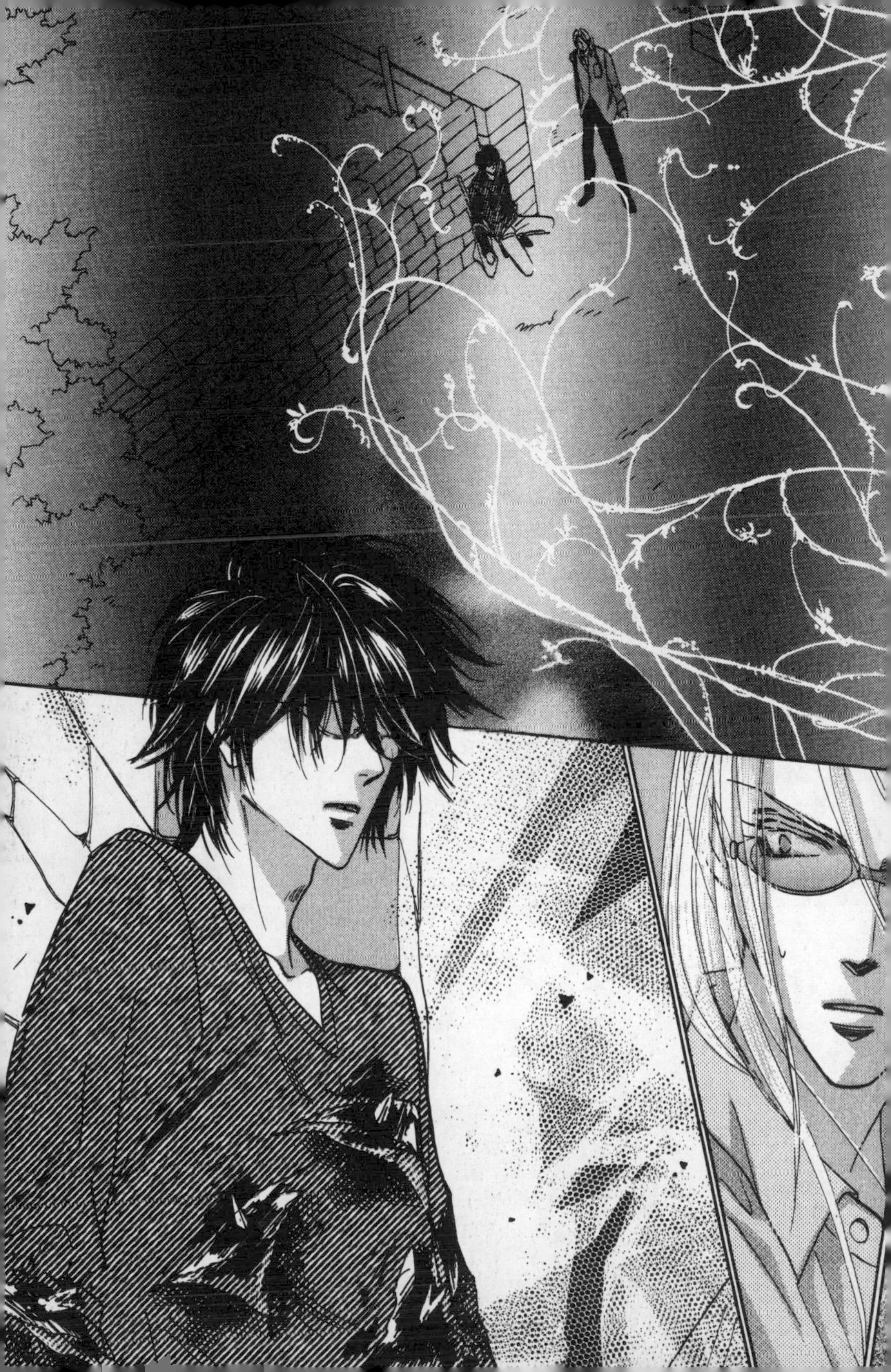

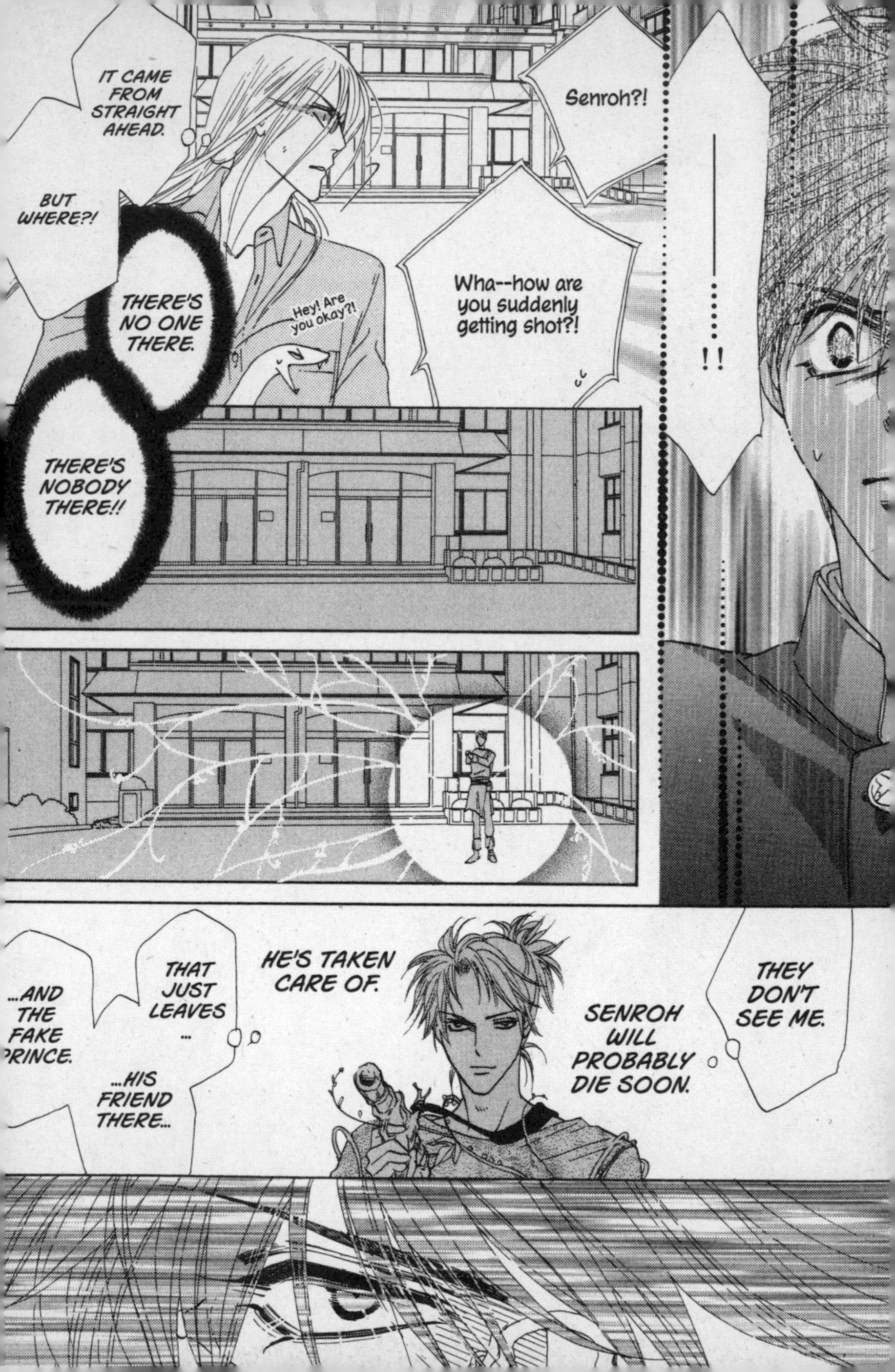

——......
!!
Senroh?!
Wha--how are you suddenly getting shot?!
Hey! Are you okay?!
IT CAME FROM STRAIGHT AHEAD.
BUT WHERE?!
THERE'S NO ONE THERE.
THERE'S NOBODY THERE!!
THEY DON'T SEE ME.
SENROH WILL PROBABLY DIE SOON.
HE'S TAKEN CARE OF.
THAT JUST LEAVES ...
...HIS FRIEND THERE...
...AND THE FAKE PRINCE.

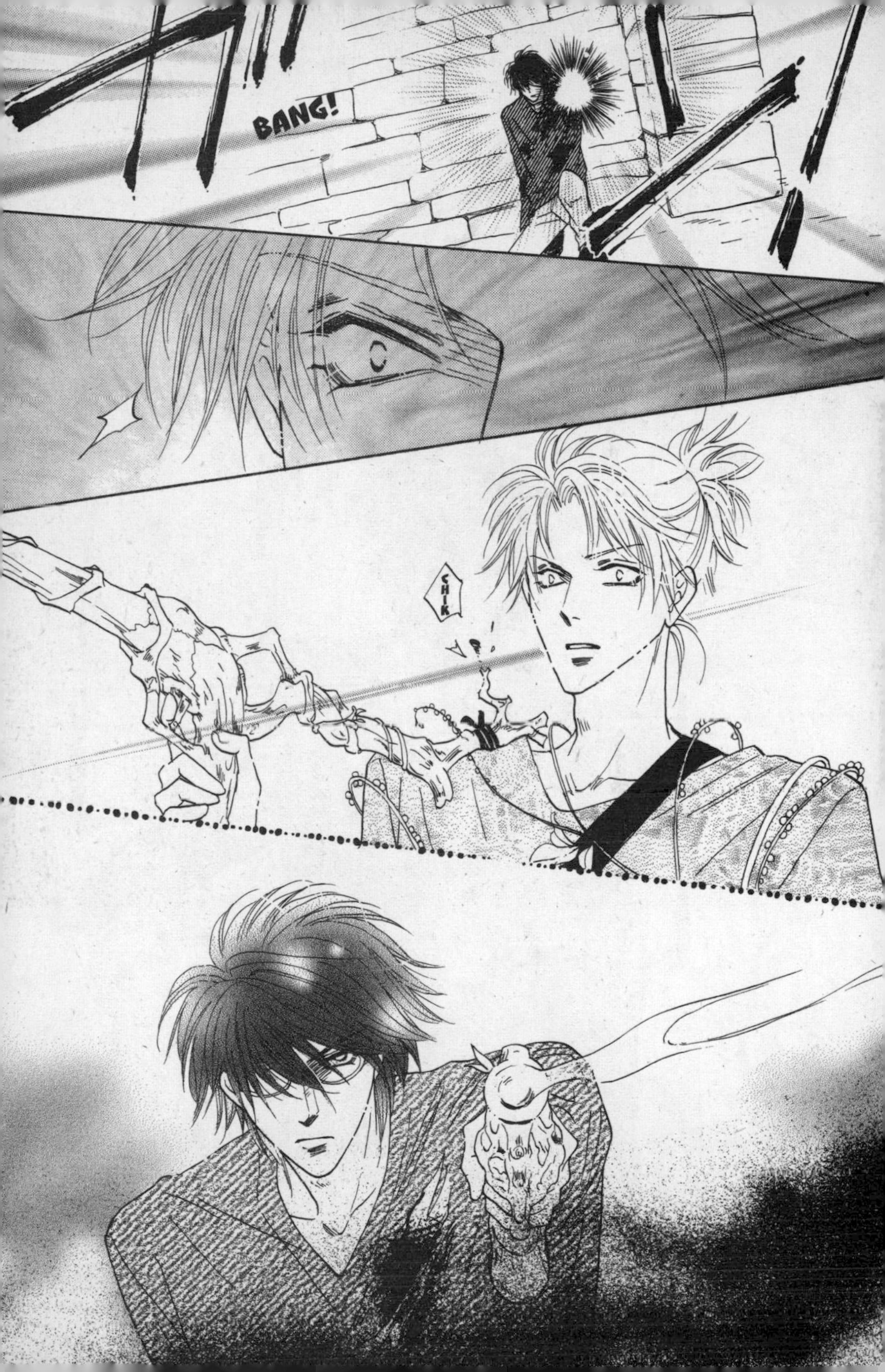
BANG!
CHIK

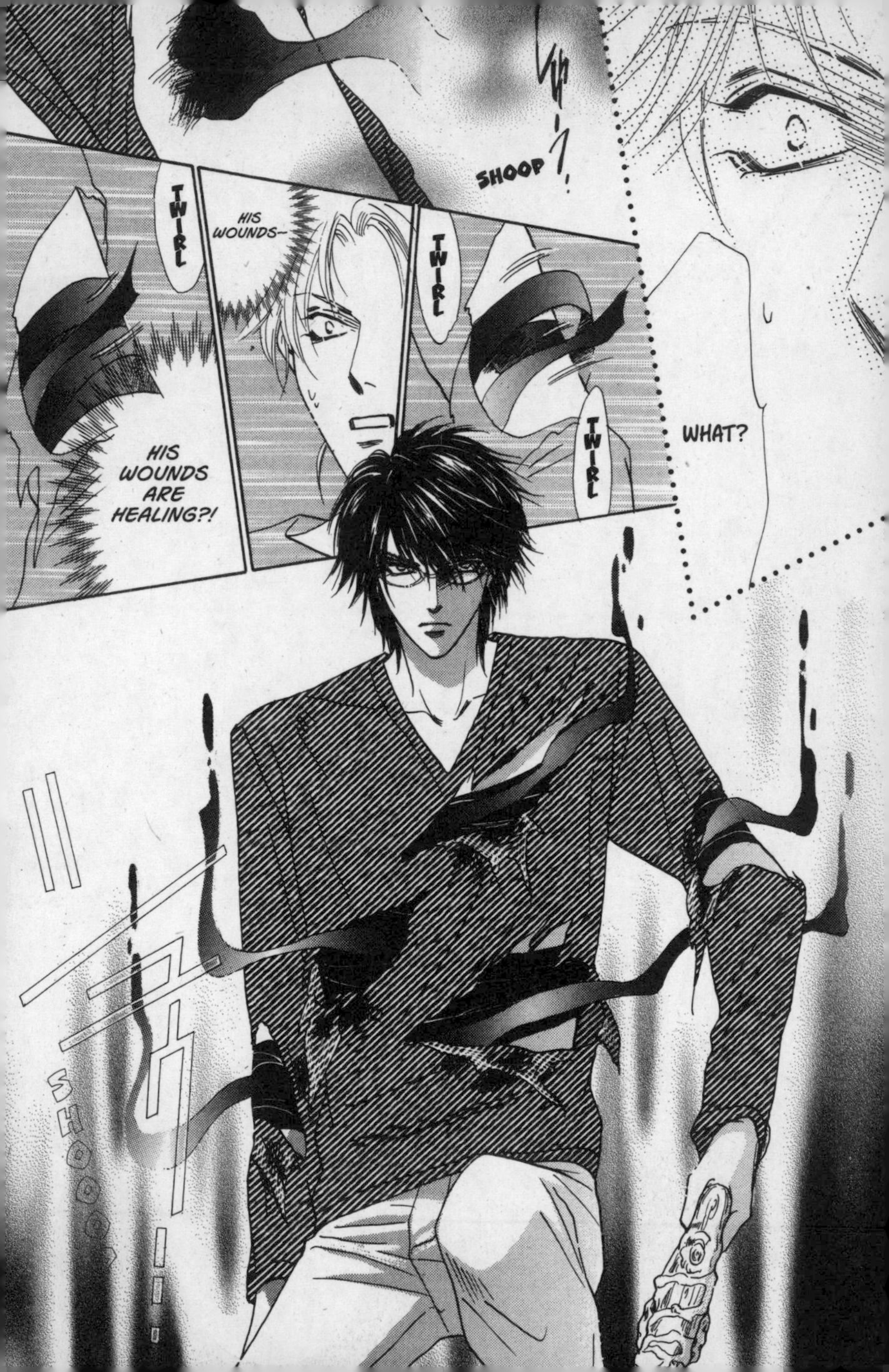

SHOOP
WHAT?
TWIRL
TWIRL
HIS WOUNDS--
TWIRL
HIS WOUNDS ARE HEALING?!
SHOOOO

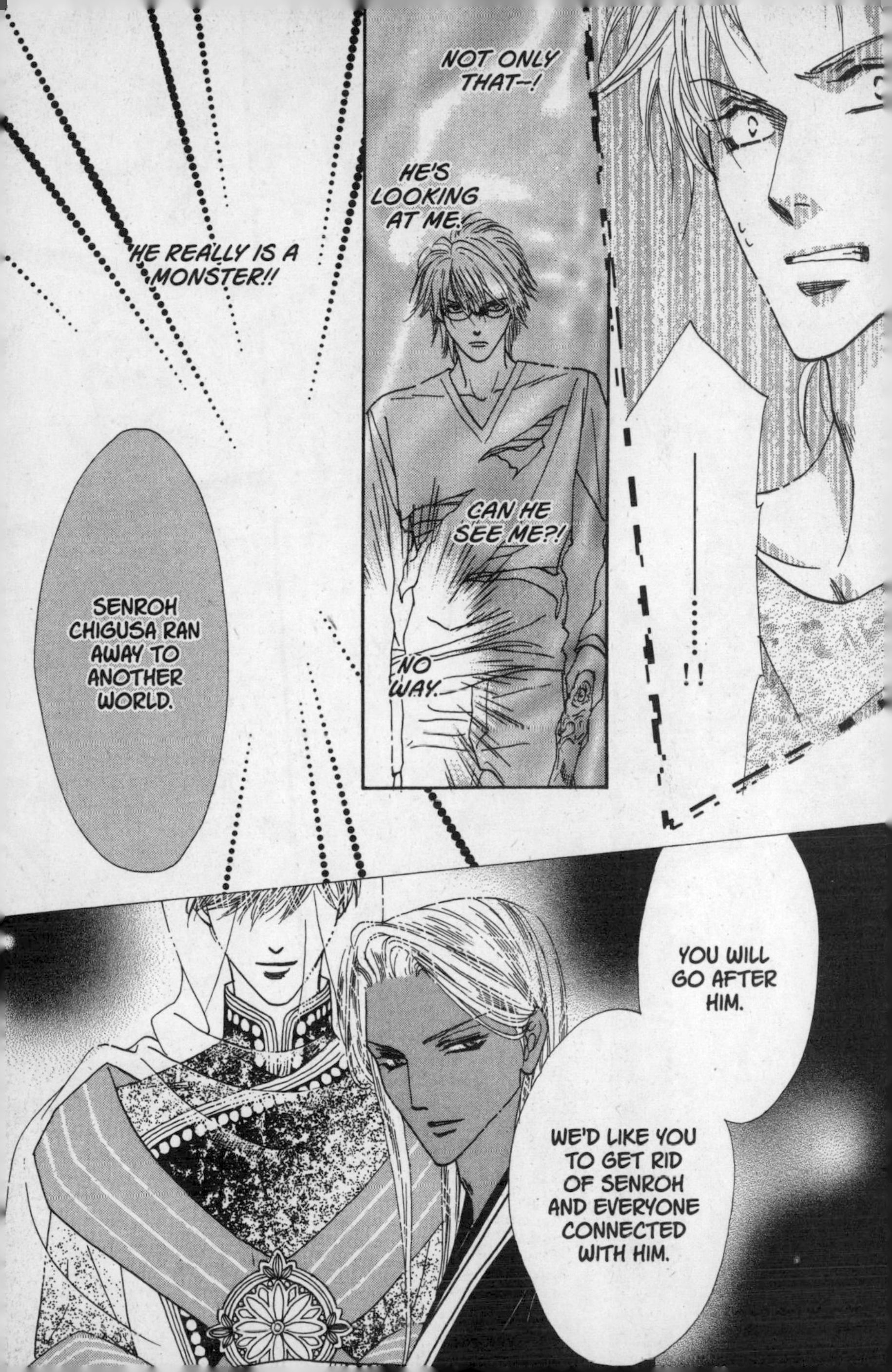
!!
NOT ONLY THAT--!
HE'S LOOKING AT ME.
CAN HE SEE ME?!
NO WAY.
HE REALLY IS A MONSTER!!
SENROH CHIGUSA RAN AWAY TO ANOTHER WORLD.
YOU WILL GO AFTER HIM.
WE'D LIKE YOU TO GET RID OF SENROH AND EVERYONE CONNECTED WITH HIM.

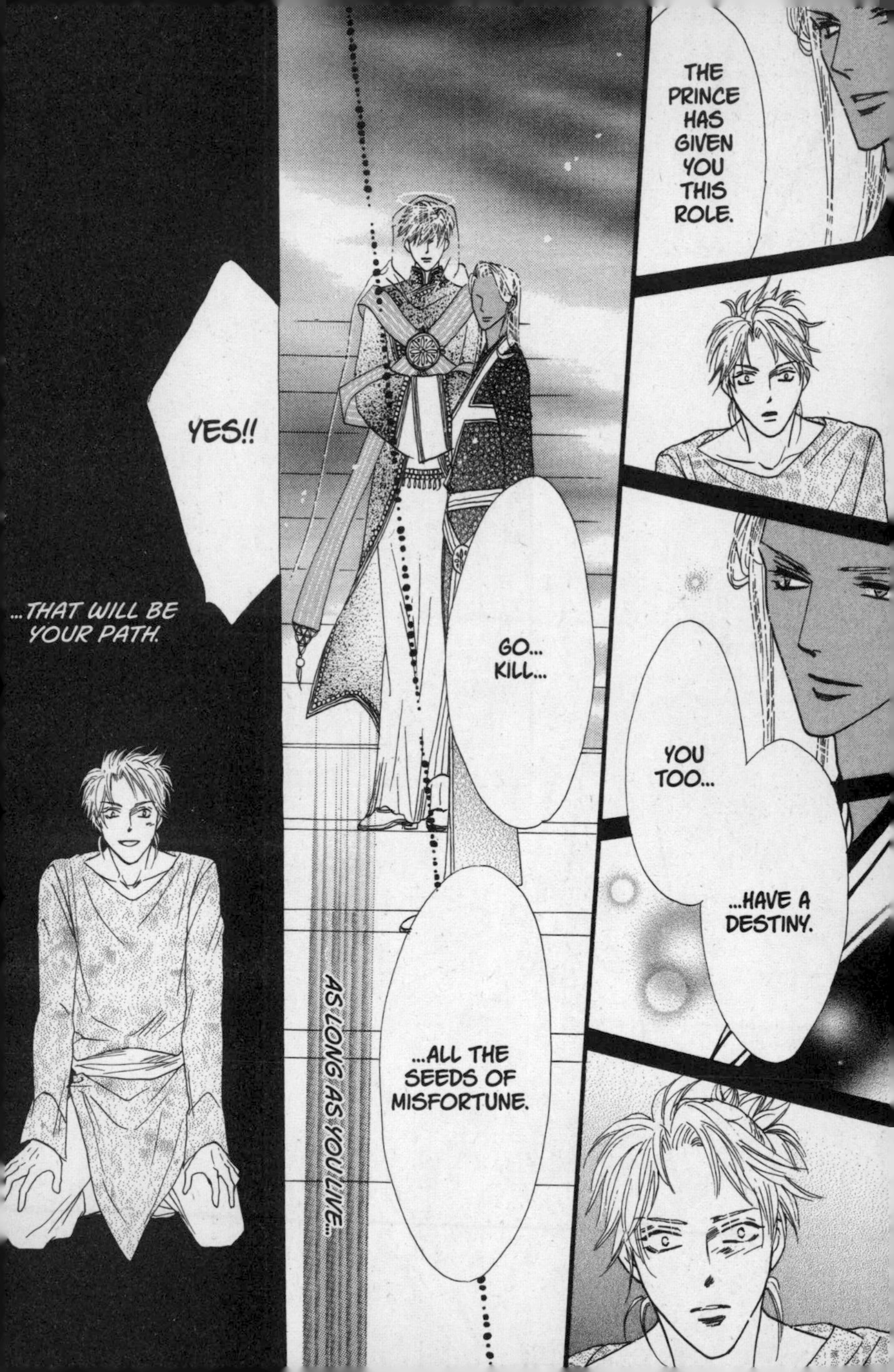
THE PRINCE HAS GIVEN YOU THIS ROLE.
YOU TOO...
...HAVE A DESTINY.
GO... KILL...
...ALL THE SEEDS OF MISFORTUNE.
AS LONG AS YOU LIVE...
YES!!
...THAT WILL BE YOUR PATH.

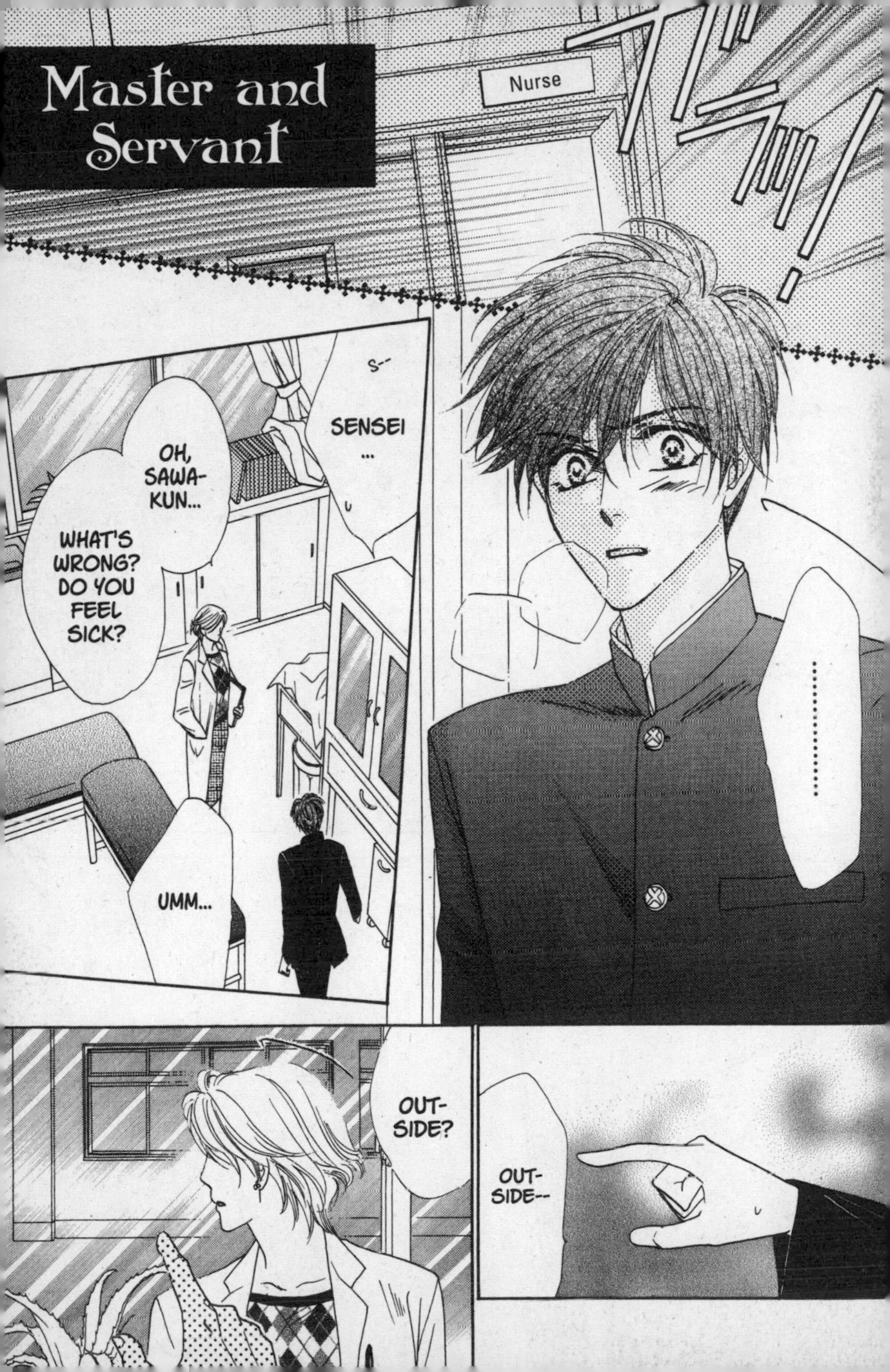

Master and Servant
Nurse
......
S-- SENSEI ...
OH, SAWA-KUN... WHAT'S WRONG? DO YOU FEEL SICK?
UMM...
OUT-SIDE--
OUT-SIDE?

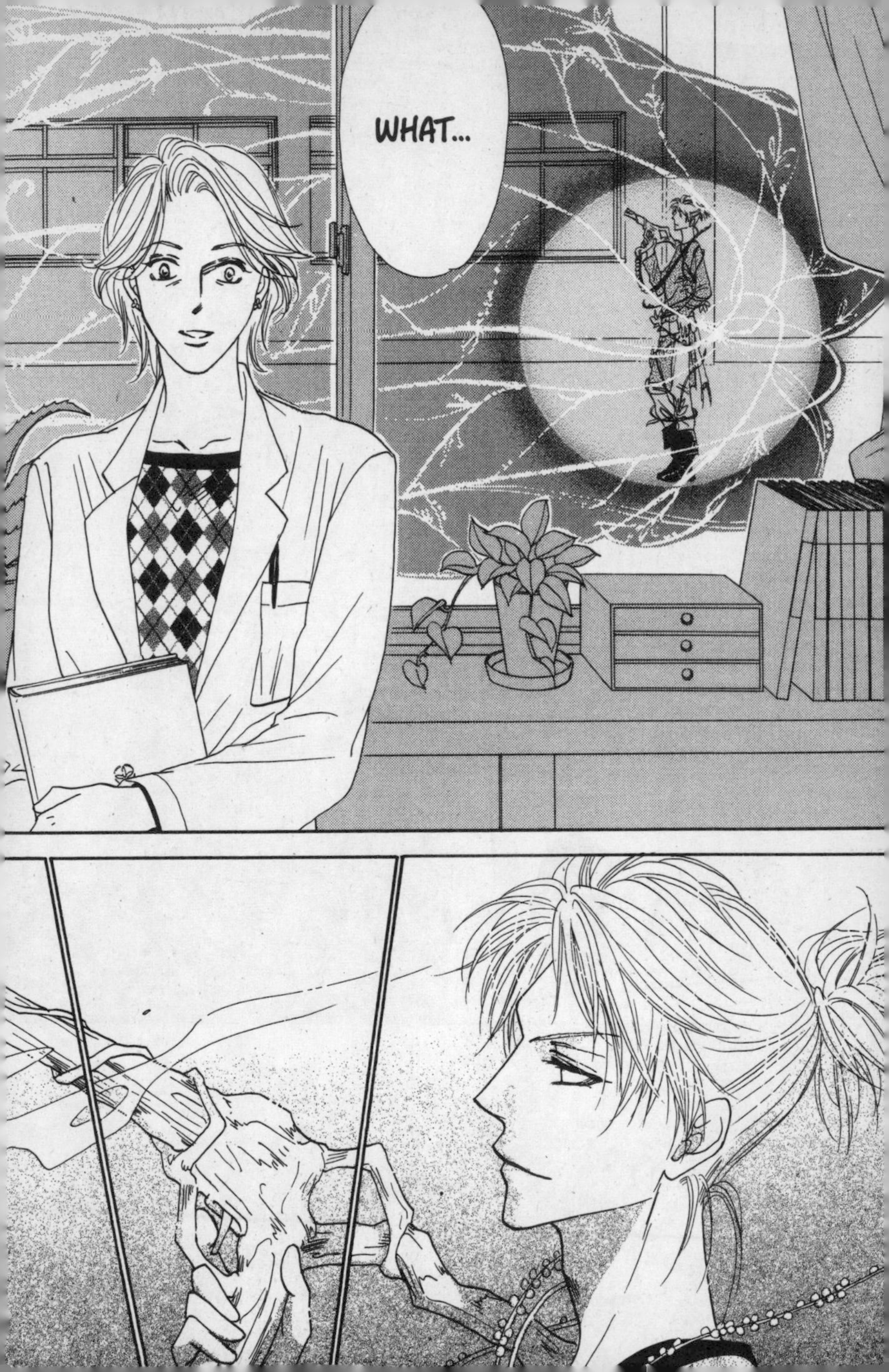
WHAT...

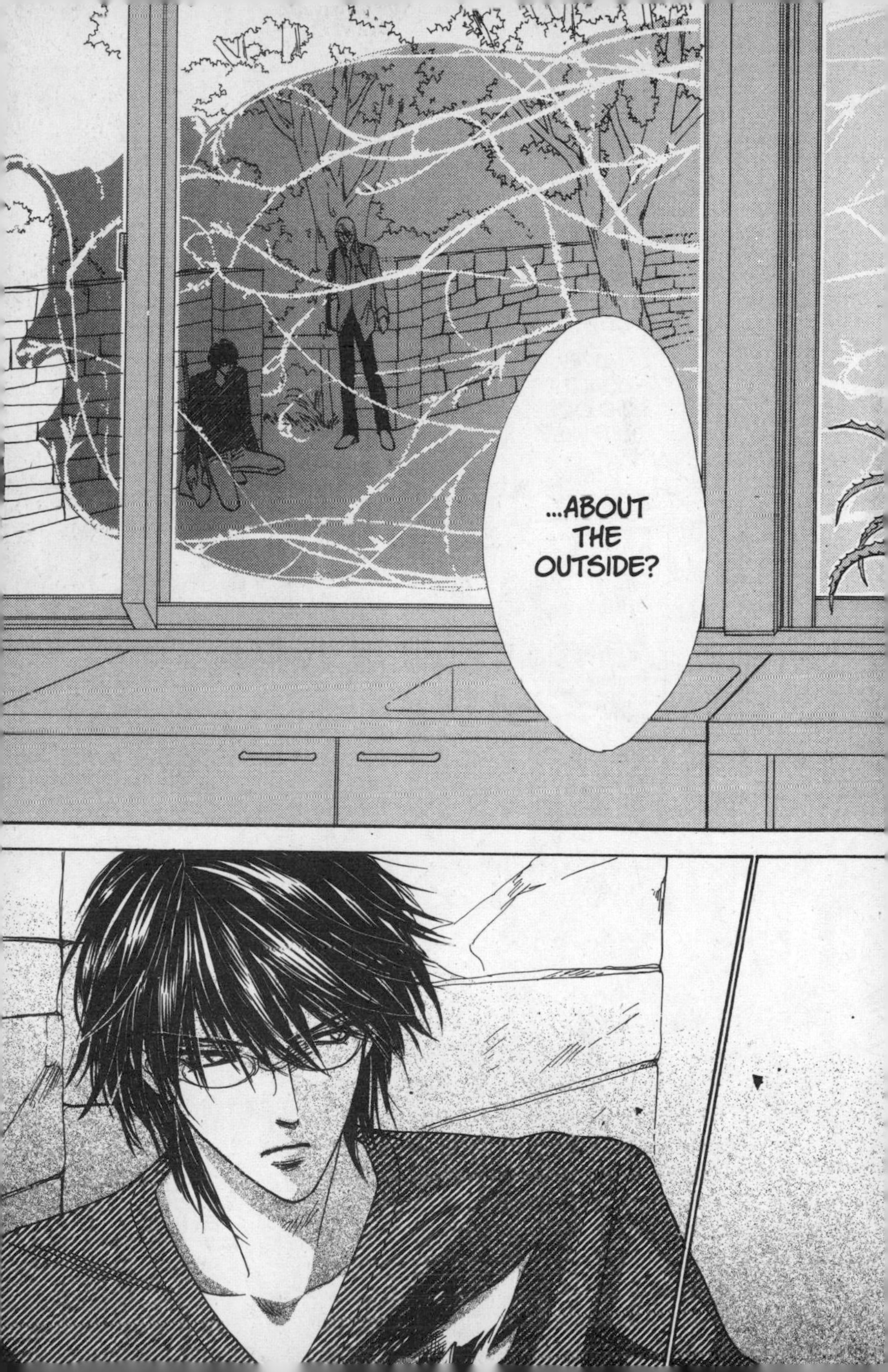
...ABOUT THE OUTSIDE?

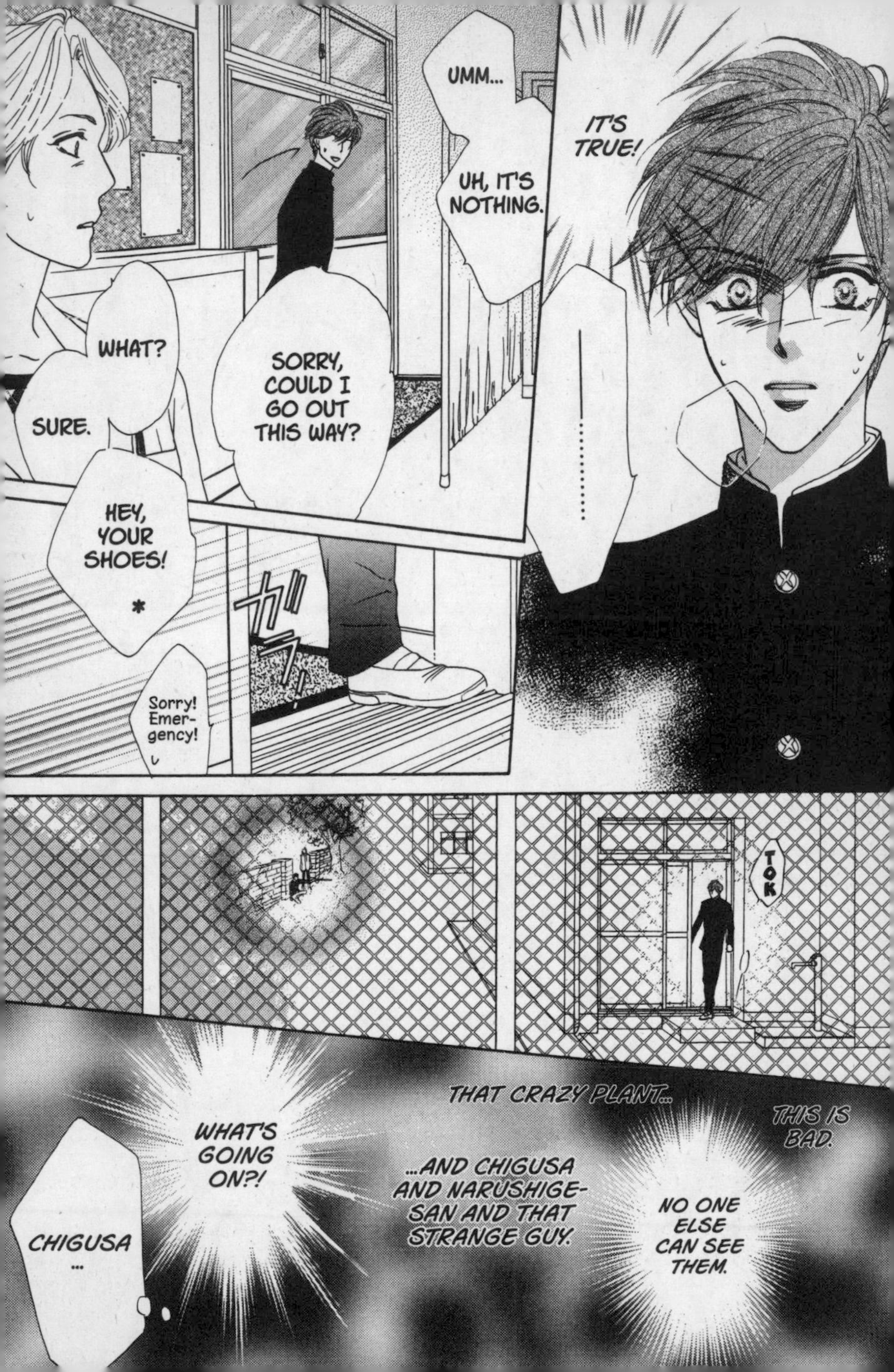
IT'S TRUE!
......
UMM...
UH, IT'S NOTHING.
SORRY, COULD I GO OUT THIS WAY?
WHAT?
SURE.
HEY, YOUR SHOES!
Sorry! Emergency!
TOK
THAT CRAZY PLANT...
THIS IS BAD.
...AND CHIGUSA AND NARUSHIGE-SAN AND THAT STRANGE GUY.
NO ONE ELSE CAN SEE THEM.
WHAT'S GOING ON?!
CHIGUSA ...

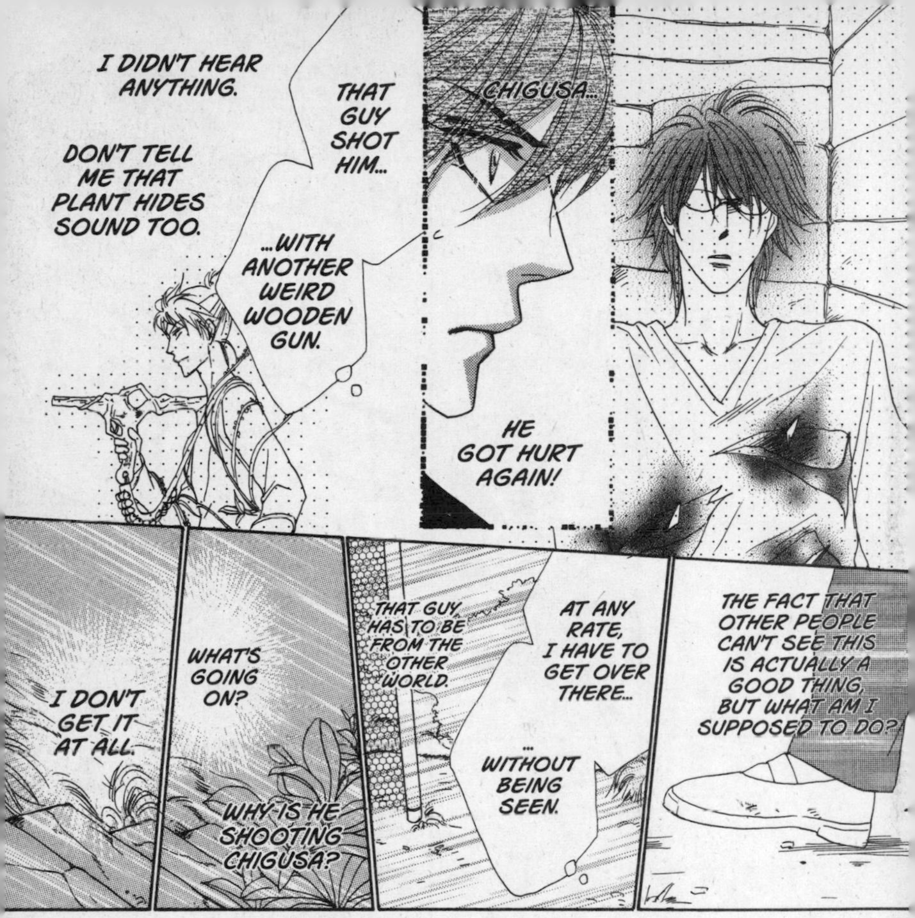
CHIGUSA...
HE GOT HURT AGAIN!
THAT GUY SHOT HIM...
...WITH ANOTHER WEIRD WOODEN GUN.
I DIDN'T HEAR ANYTHING.
DON'T TELL ME THAT PLANT HIDES SOUND TOO.
THE FACT THAT OTHER PEOPLE CAN'T SEE THIS IS ACTUALLY A GOOD THING, BUT WHAT AM I SUPPOSED TO DO?
AT ANY RATE, I HAVE TO GET OVER THERE...
...WITHOUT BEING SEEN.
THAT GUY HAS TO BE FROM THE OTHER WORLD.
WHAT'S GOING ON?
WHY IS HE SHOOTING CHIGUSA?
I DON'T GET IT AT ALL.

Thank you as always for the letters, etc. ✿ I can't tell if my work is good or bad myself, so I'm really happy to get your thoughts. Oh! And thank you for the New Year's greetings and the birthday presents!
Oh, wait, first of all, Happy New Year!! May this year be a good year!! Oh wait, what month is it now?

Oh, and thank you to the person who sent the bottle of sake with Chigusa's name engraved (and his full name, no less). And just imagine, somebody sent me the actress, Kumiko Okae's, autograph! Thank you very much!! Wow, what a surprise!! Thank you for such precious things! I'll take very good care of them. ✿
I'm even drinking the sake (I'm a wimp so it's good because I get drunk really fast). ✿

Well, that's it for now. Anyway, I'm working really hard on the manga, so I'm very grateful that you're reading it. ✿ Well, later then!

Uh, I mean that I'm happy drinking small amounts.

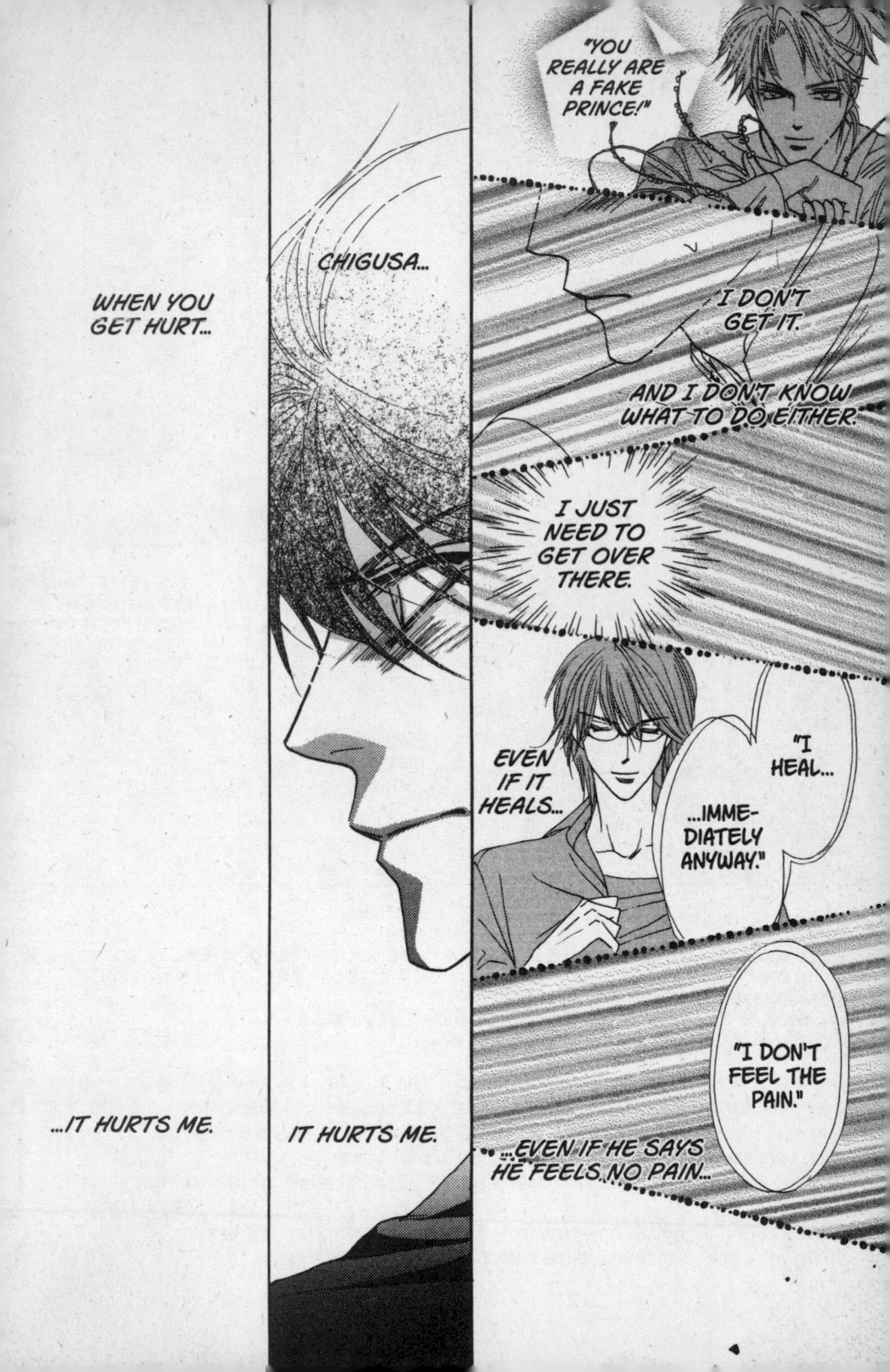
"YOU REALLY ARE A FAKE PRINCE!"
I DON'T GET IT.
AND I DON'T KNOW WHAT TO DO EITHER.
I JUST NEED TO GET OVER THERE.
"I HEAL...
...IMME-DIATELY ANYWAY."
EVEN IF IT HEALS...
"I DON'T FEEL THE PAIN."
...EVEN IF HE SAYS HE FEELS NO PAIN...
CHIGUSA...
IT HURTS ME.
WHEN YOU GET HURT...
...IT HURTS ME.

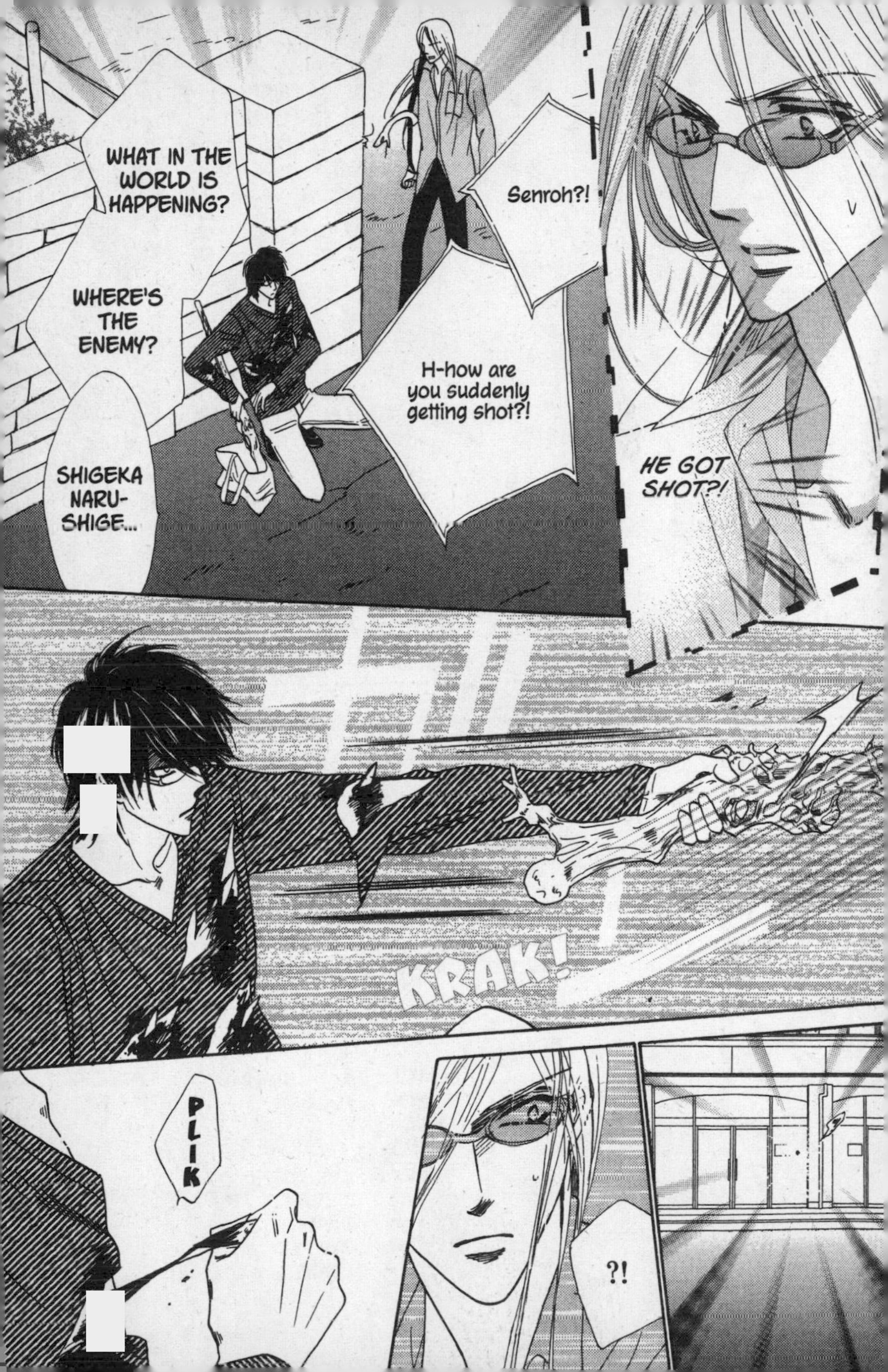
HE GOT SHOT?!
Senroh?!
WHAT IN THE WORLD IS HAPPENING?
H-how are you suddenly getting shot?!
WHERE'S THE ENEMY?
SHIGEKA NARU-SHIGE...
KRAK!
?!
PLIK

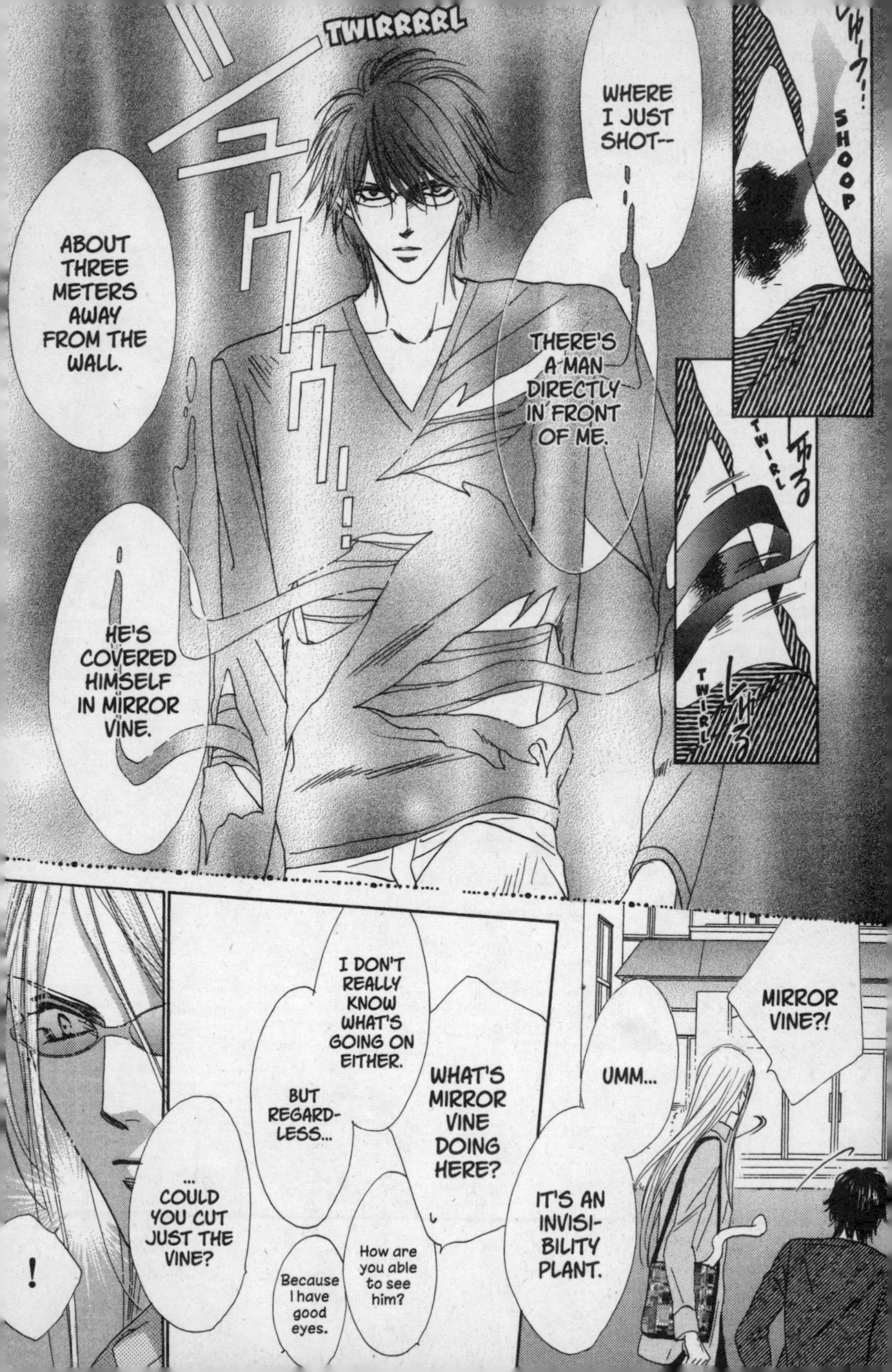
SHOOP
TWIRL
TWIRL
WHERE I JUST SHOT--
THERE'S A MAN DIRECTLY IN FRONT OF ME.
TWIRRRRL
ABOUT THREE METERS AWAY FROM THE WALL.
HE'S COVERED HIMSELF IN MIRROR VINE.
MIRROR VINE?!
UMM...
IT'S AN INVISIBILITY PLANT.
WHAT'S MIRROR VINE DOING HERE?
I DON'T REALLY KNOW WHAT'S GOING ON EITHER.
BUT REGARDLESS...
How are you able to see him?
Because I have good eyes.
... COULD YOU CUT JUST THE VINE?
!

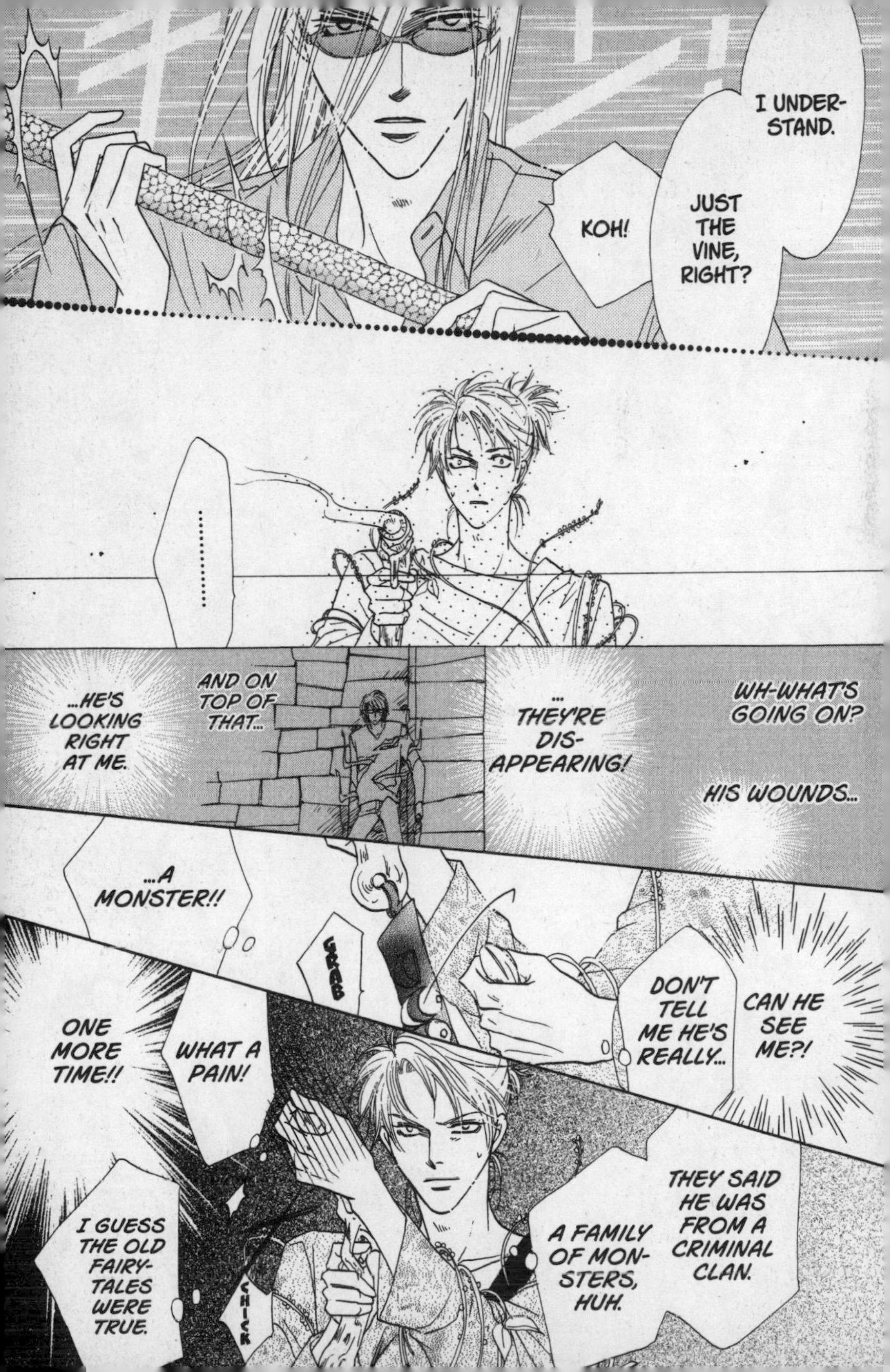
I UNDER-STAND.
JUST THE VINE, RIGHT?
KOH!
......
WH-WHAT'S GOING ON?
HIS WOUNDS...
...THEY'RE DIS-APPEARING!
AND ON TOP OF THAT...
...HE'S LOOKING RIGHT AT ME.
CAN HE SEE ME?!
DON'T TELL ME HE'S REALLY...
...A MONSTER!!
GRAB
THEY SAID HE WAS FROM A CRIMINAL CLAN.
A FAMILY OF MON-STERS, HUH.
WHAT A PAIN!
ONE MORE TIME!!
I GUESS THE OLD FAIRY-TALES WERE TRUE.
CHICK

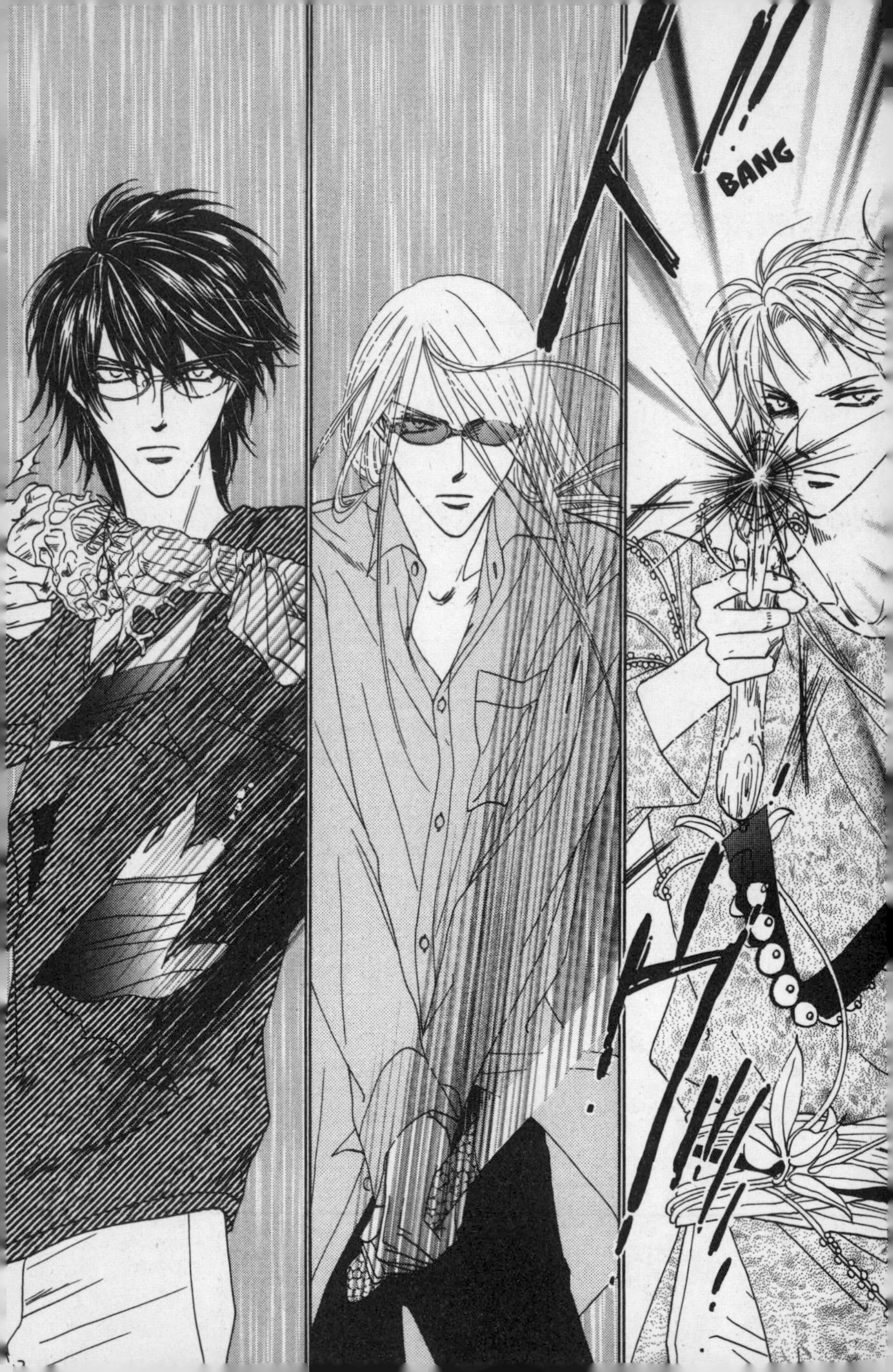
BANG

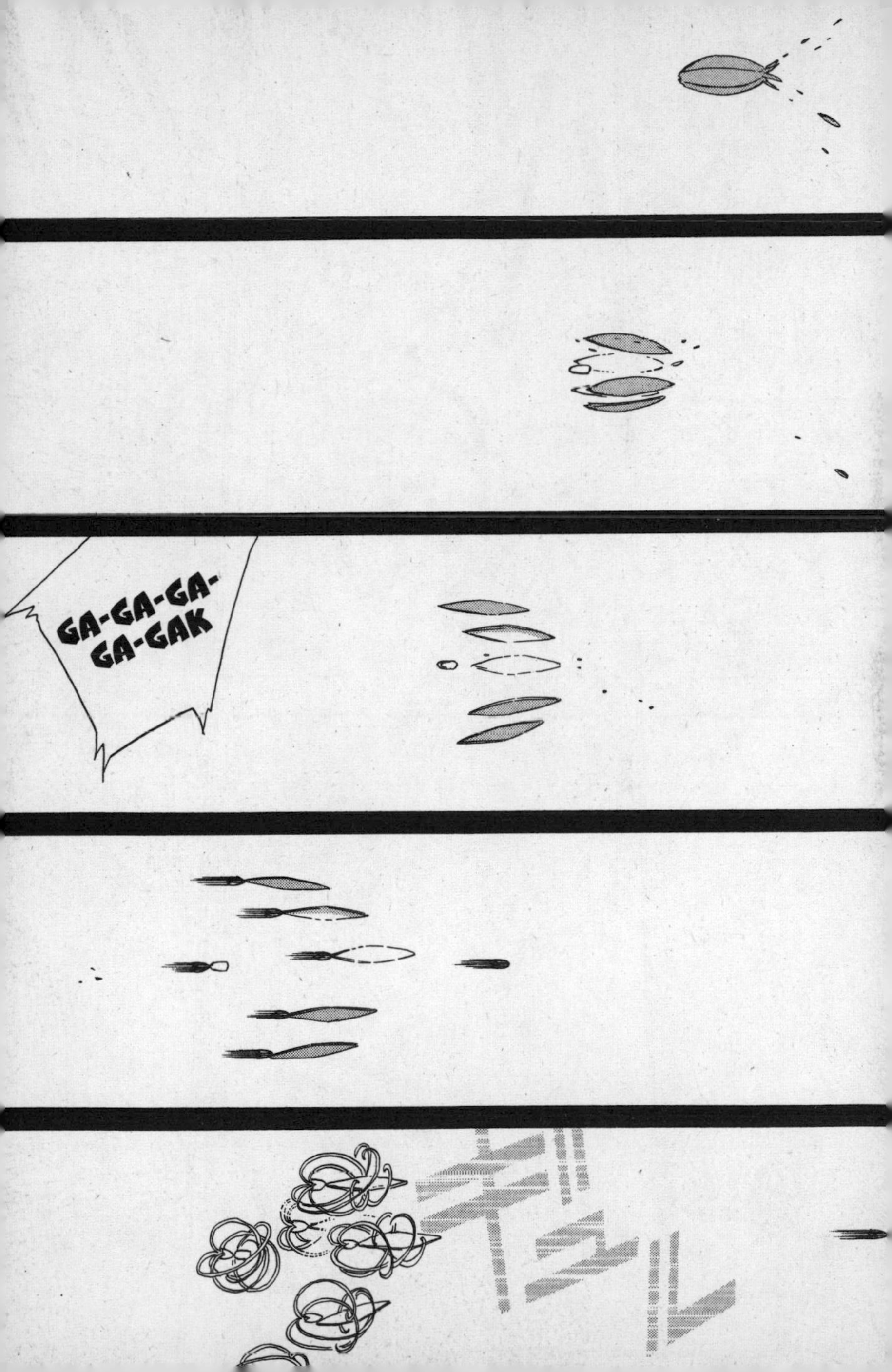
GA-GA-GA-GA-GAK

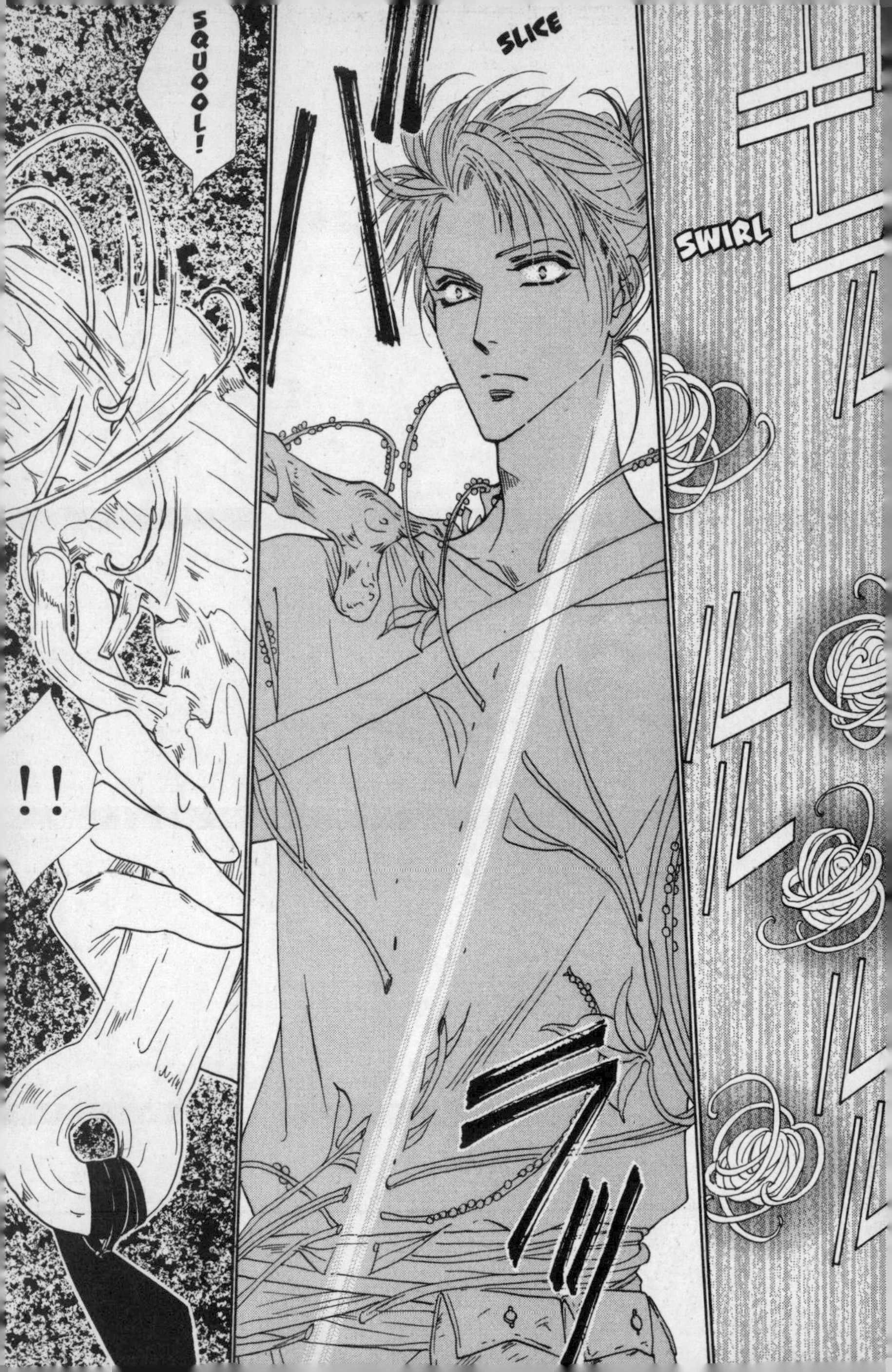
SWIRL
SLICE
SQUOOOL!
!!

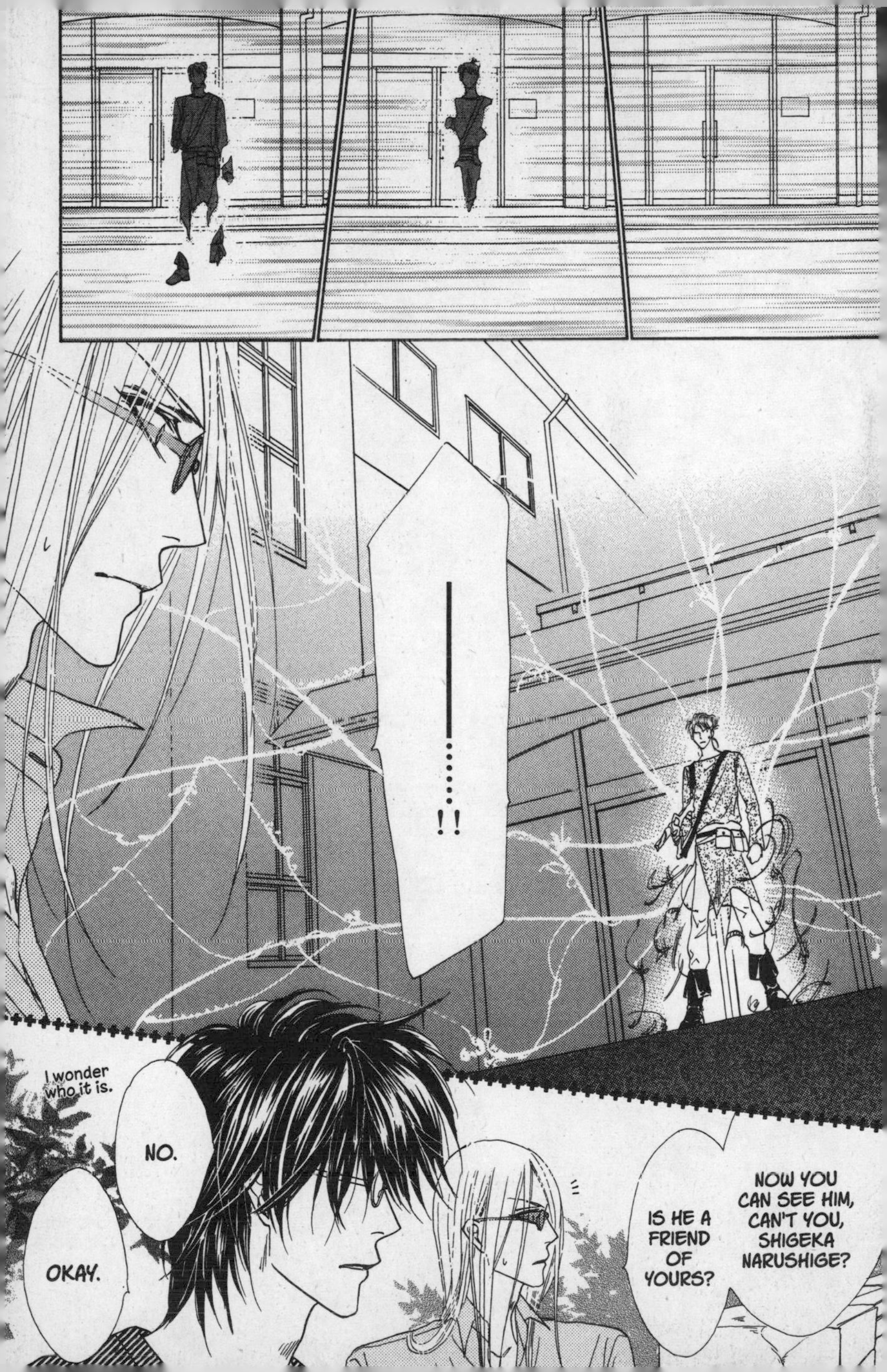
——......!!
NOW YOU CAN SEE HIM, CAN'T YOU, SHIGEKA NARUSHIGE?
IS HE A FRIEND OF YOURS?
NO.
I wonder who it is.
OKAY.

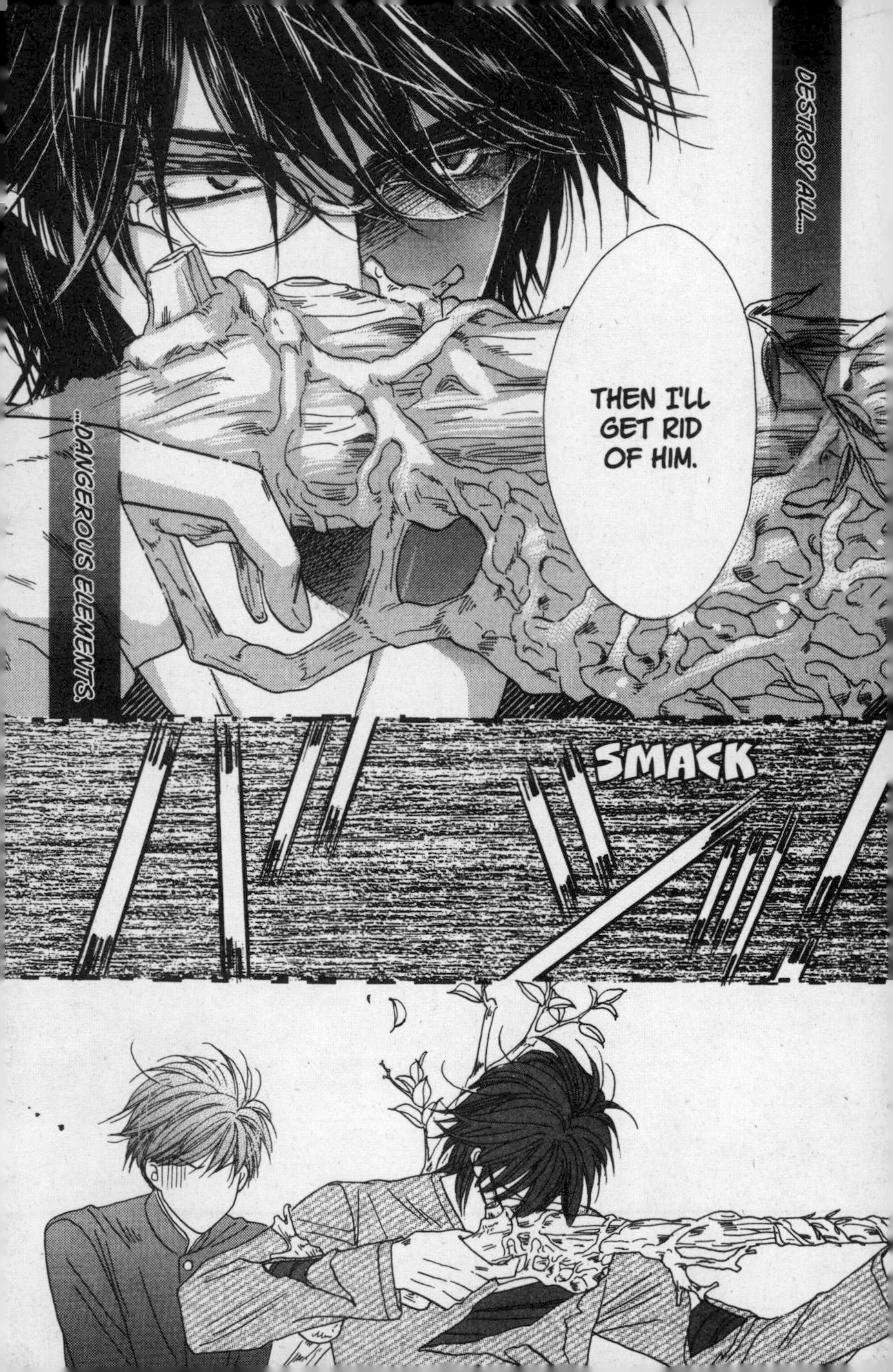
DESTROY ALL...
THEN I'LL GET RID OF HIM.
...DANGEROUS ELEMENTS.
SMACK

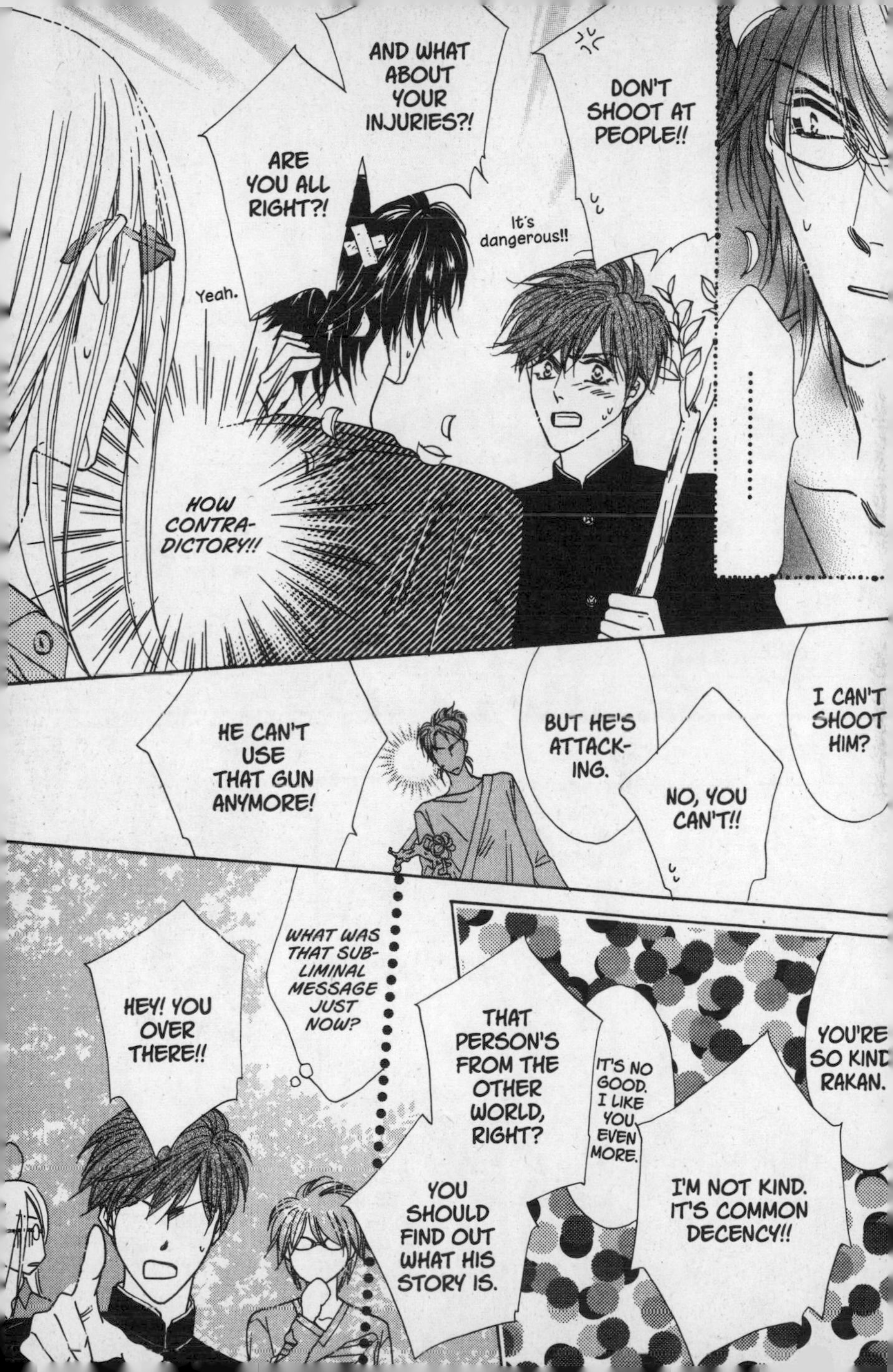
DON'T SHOOT AT PEOPLE!!
It's dangerous!!
AND WHAT ABOUT YOUR INJURIES?!
ARE YOU ALL RIGHT?!
Yeah.
HOW CONTRA-DICTORY!!
I CAN'T SHOOT HIM?
NO, YOU CAN'T!!
BUT HE'S ATTACK-ING.
HE CAN'T USE THAT GUN ANYMORE!
YOU'RE SO KIND RAKAN.
I'M NOT KIND. IT'S COMMON DECENCY!!
IT'S NO GOOD. I LIKE YOU EVEN MORE.
THAT PERSON'S FROM THE OTHER WORLD, RIGHT?
YOU SHOULD FIND OUT WHAT HIS STORY IS.
WHAT WAS THAT SUB-LIMINAL MESSAGE JUST NOW?
HEY! YOU OVER THERE!!

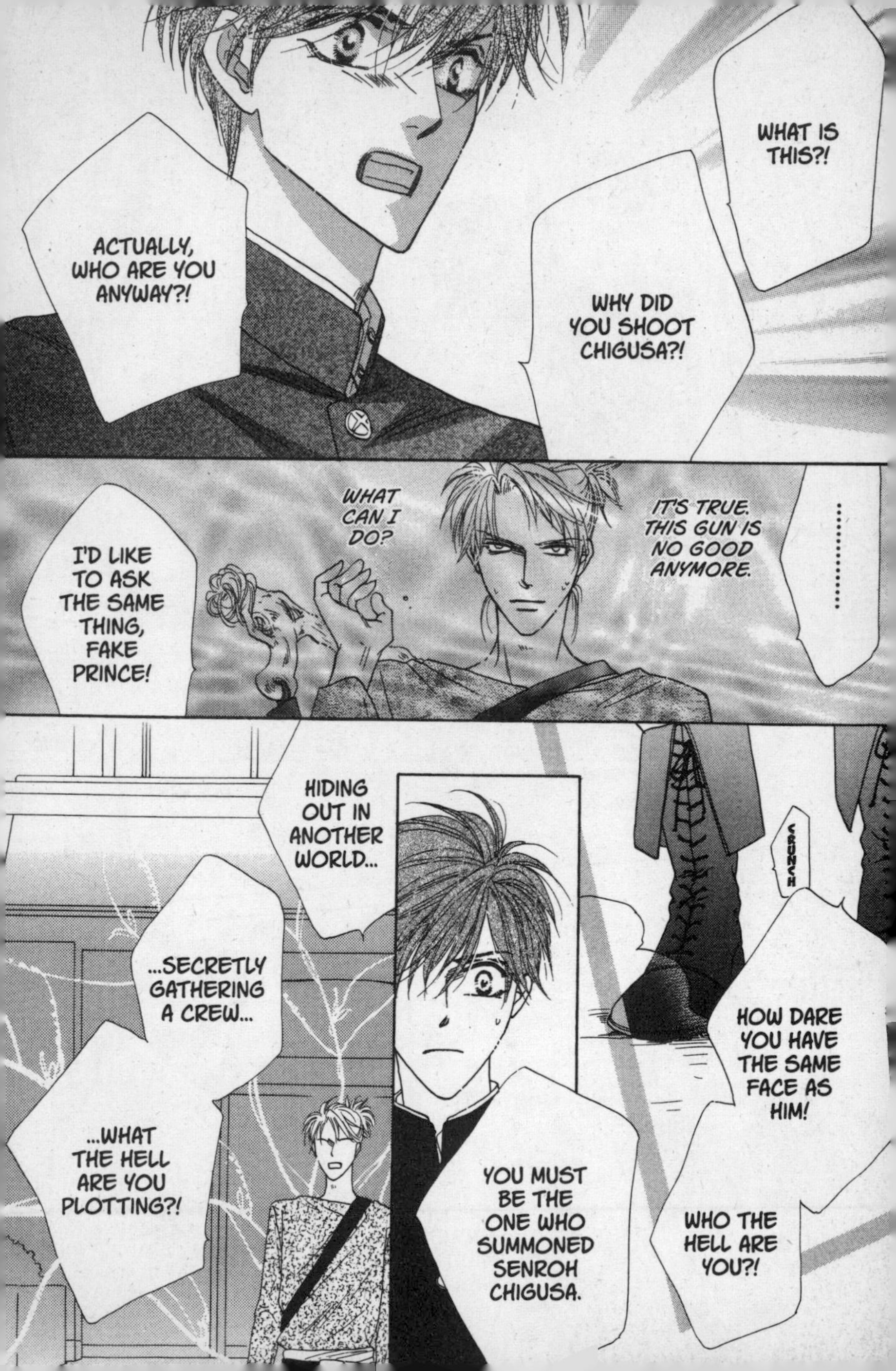
WHAT IS THIS?!
WHY DID YOU SHOOT CHIGUSA?!
ACTUALLY, WHO ARE YOU ANYWAY?!
......
IT'S TRUE. THIS GUN IS NO GOOD ANYMORE.
WHAT CAN I DO?
I'D LIKE TO ASK THE SAME THING, FAKE PRINCE!
CRUNCH
HOW DARE YOU HAVE THE SAME FACE AS HIM!
WHO THE HELL ARE YOU?!
YOU MUST BE THE ONE WHO SUMMONED SENROH CHIGUSA.
HIDING OUT IN ANOTHER WORLD...
...SECRETLY GATHERING A CREW...
...WHAT THE HELL ARE YOU PLOTTING?!

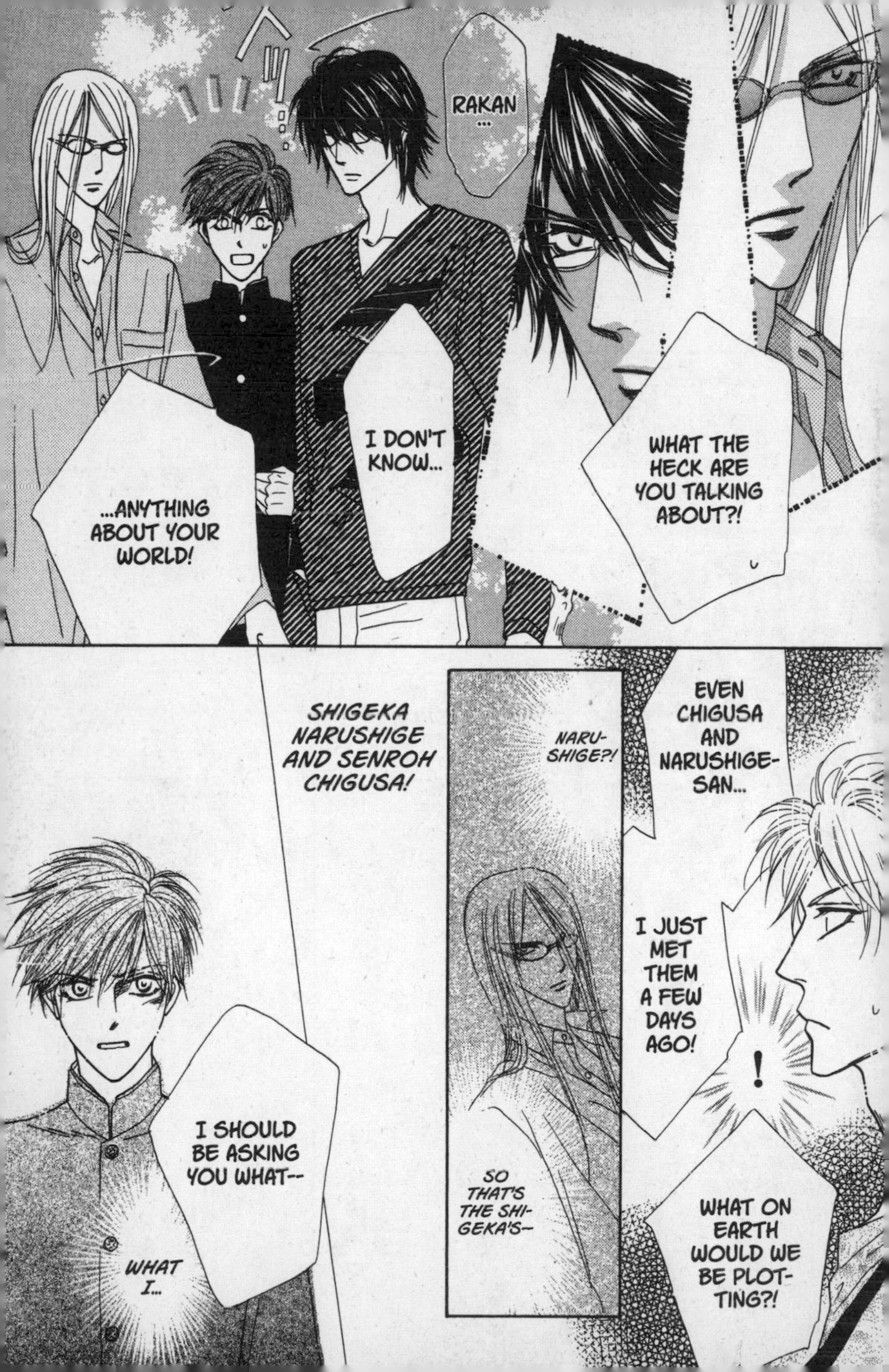
WHAT THE HECK ARE YOU TALKING ABOUT?!
RAKAN ...
I DON'T KNOW...
...ANYTHING ABOUT YOUR WORLD!
EVEN CHIGUSA AND NARUSHIGE-SAN...
I JUST MET THEM A FEW DAYS AGO!
!
WHAT ON EARTH WOULD WE BE PLOTTING?!
NARUSHIGE?!
SO THAT'S THE SHIGEKA'S--
SHIGEKA NARUSHIGE AND SENROH CHIGUSA!
I SHOULD BE ASKING YOU WHAT--
WHAT I...

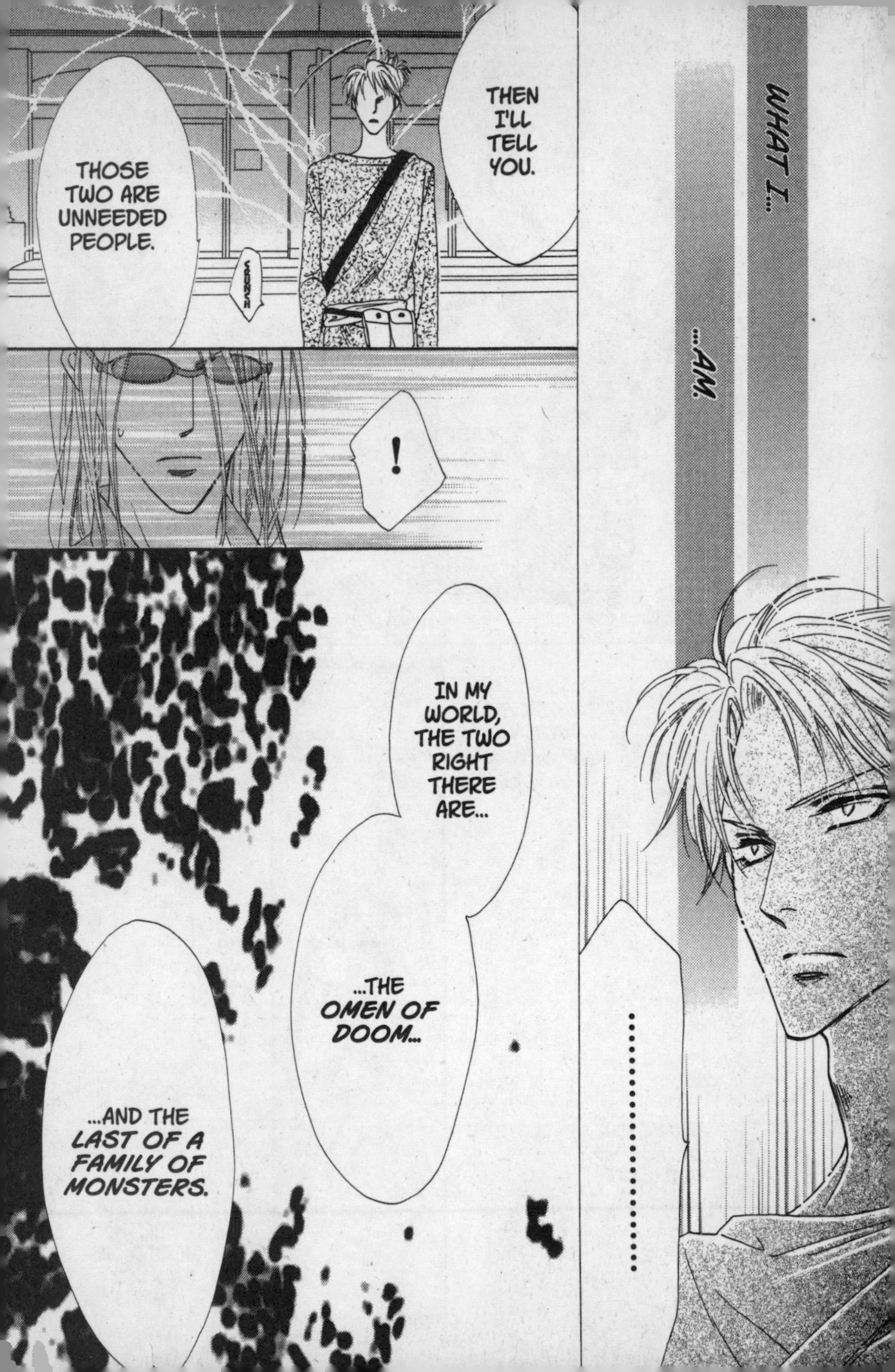
WHAT I...
...AM.
....
THEN I'LL TELL YOU.
THOSE TWO ARE UNNEEDED PEOPLE.
!
IN MY WORLD, THE TWO RIGHT THERE ARE...
...THE *OMEN OF DOOM*...
...AND THE *LAST OF A FAMILY OF MONSTERS.*

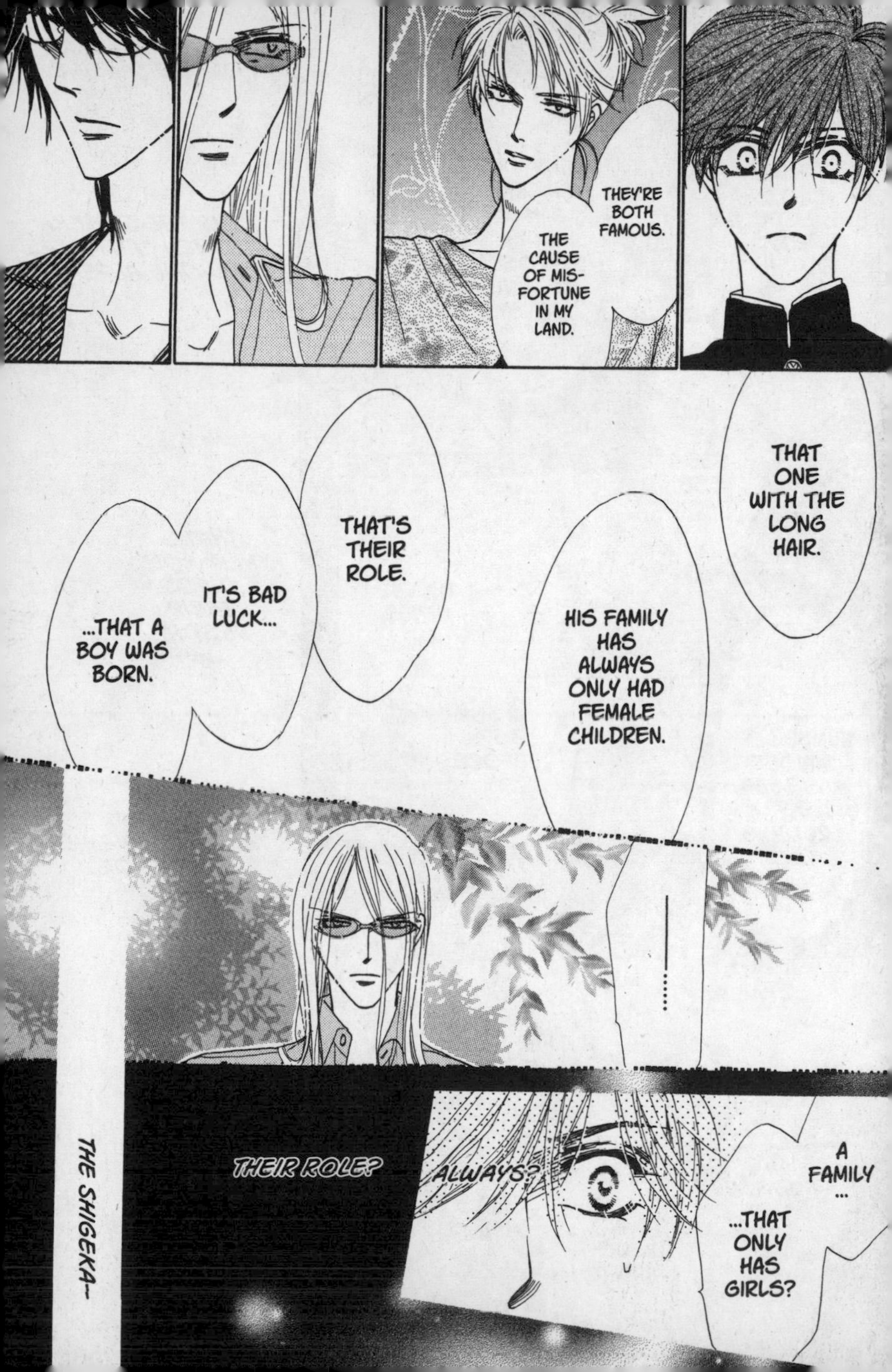
THEY'RE BOTH FAMOUS.
THE CAUSE OF MIS-FORTUNE IN MY LAND.
THAT ONE WITH THE LONG HAIR.
HIS FAMILY HAS ALWAYS ONLY HAD FEMALE CHILDREN.
THAT'S THEIR ROLE.
IT'S BAD LUCK...
...THAT A BOY WAS BORN.
......
A FAMILY...
...THAT ONLY HAS GIRLS?
ALWAYS?
THEIR ROLE?
THE SHIGEKA–

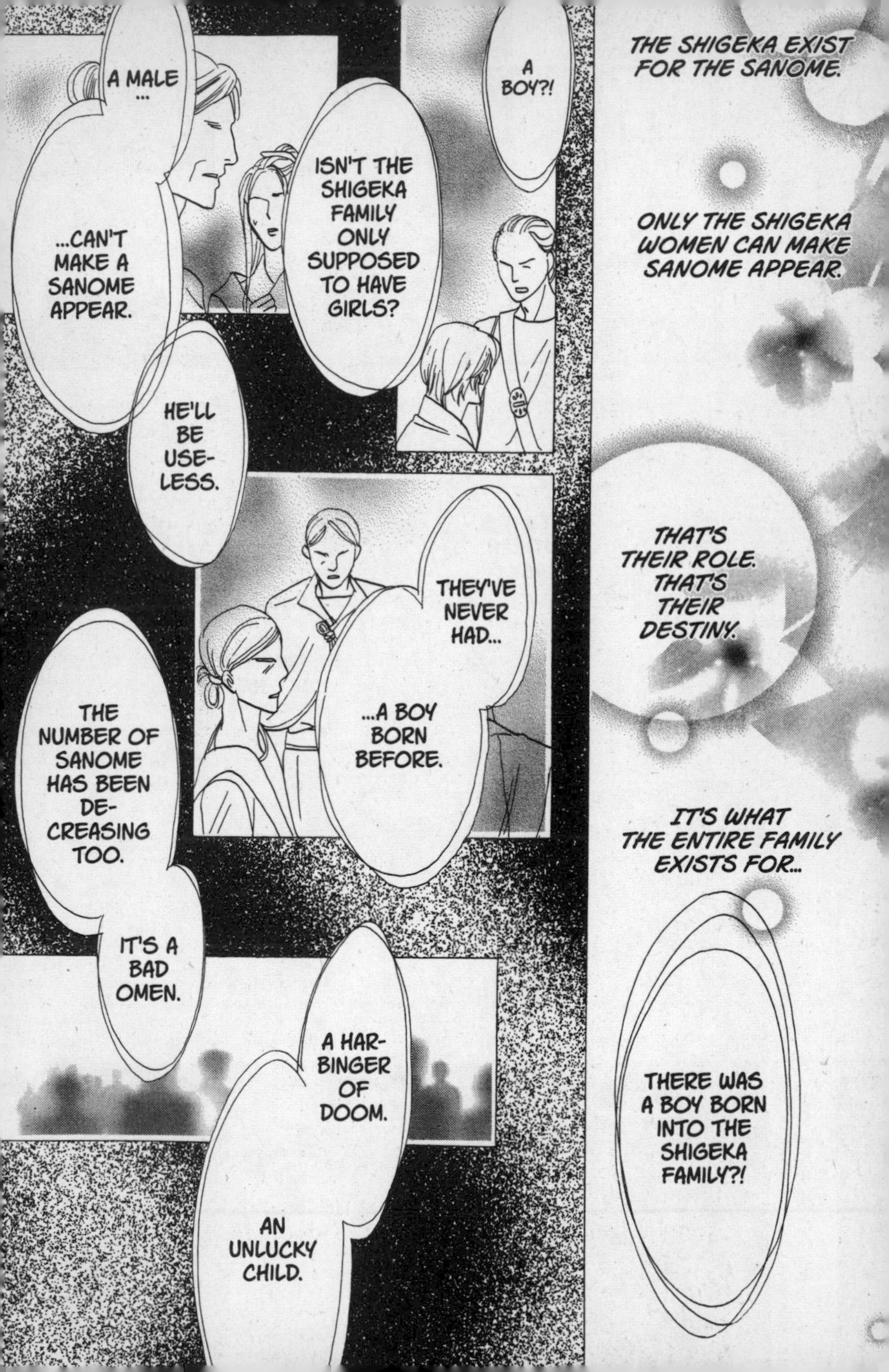
THE SHIGEKA EXIST FOR THE SANOME.
ONLY THE SHIGEKA WOMEN CAN MAKE SANOME APPEAR.
THAT'S THEIR ROLE. THAT'S THEIR DESTINY.
IT'S WHAT THE ENTIRE FAMILY EXISTS FOR...
THERE WAS A BOY BORN INTO THE SHIGEKA FAMILY?!
A BOY?!
ISN'T THE SHIGEKA FAMILY ONLY SUPPOSED TO HAVE GIRLS?
A MALE...
...CAN'T MAKE A SANOME APPEAR.
HE'LL BE USE-LESS.
THEY'VE NEVER HAD...
...A BOY BORN BEFORE.
THE NUMBER OF SANOME HAS BEEN DE-CREASING TOO.
IT'S A BAD OMEN.
A HAR-BINGER OF DOOM.
AN UNLUCKY CHILD.

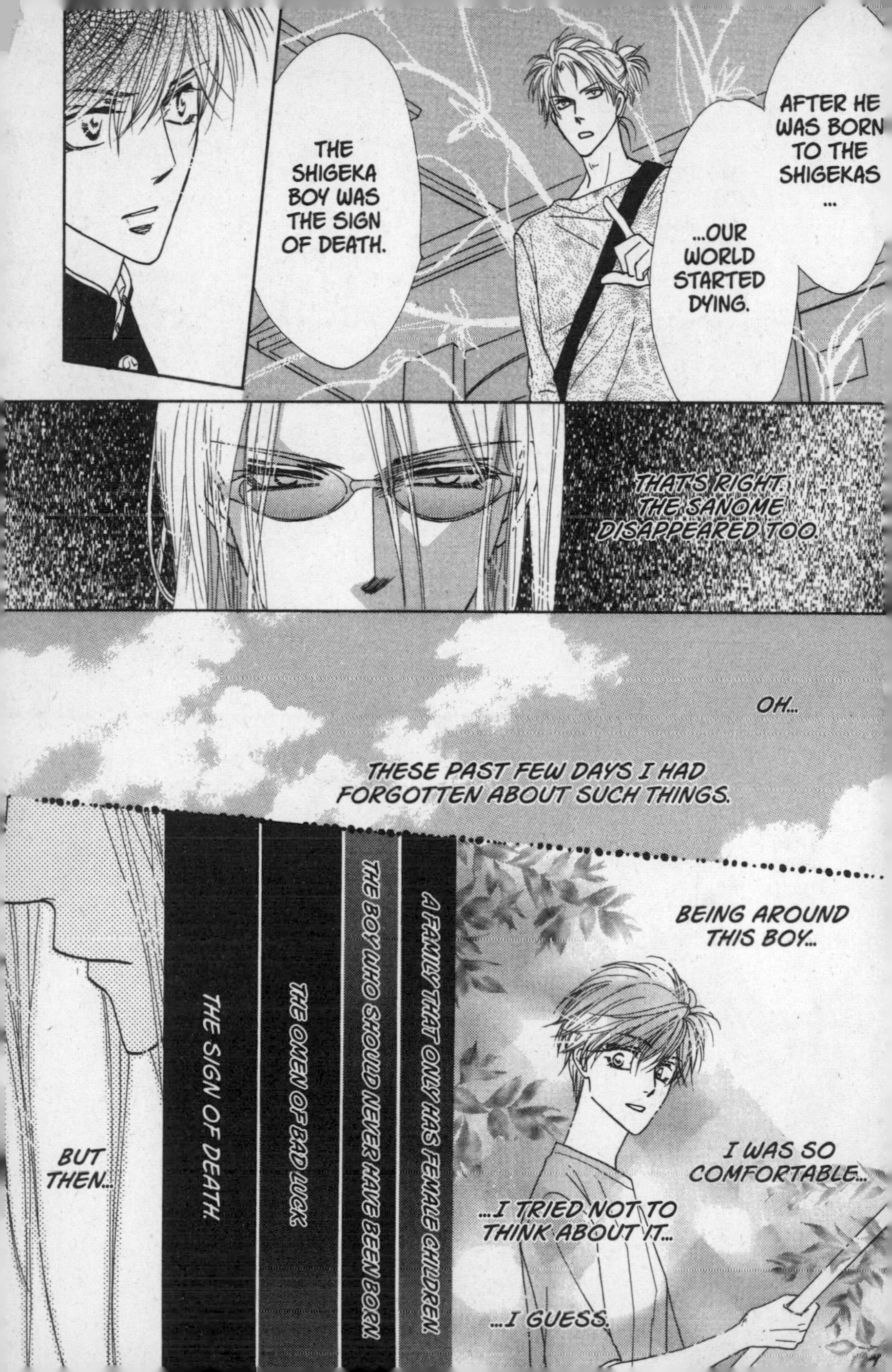
AFTER HE WAS BORN TO THE SHIGEKAS ...
...OUR WORLD STARTED DYING.
THE SHIGEKA BOY WAS THE SIGN OF DEATH.
THAT'S RIGHT. THE SANOME DISAPPEARED TOO.
OH...
THESE PAST FEW DAYS I HAD FORGOTTEN ABOUT SUCH THINGS.
BEING AROUND THIS BOY...
I WAS SO COMFORTABLE...
...I TRIED NOT TO THINK ABOUT IT...
...I GUESS.
A FAMILY THAT ONLY HAS FEMALE CHILDREN.
THE BOY WHO SHOULD NEVER HAVE BEEN BORN.
THE OMEN OF BAD LUCK.
THE SIGN OF DEATH.
BUT THEN...

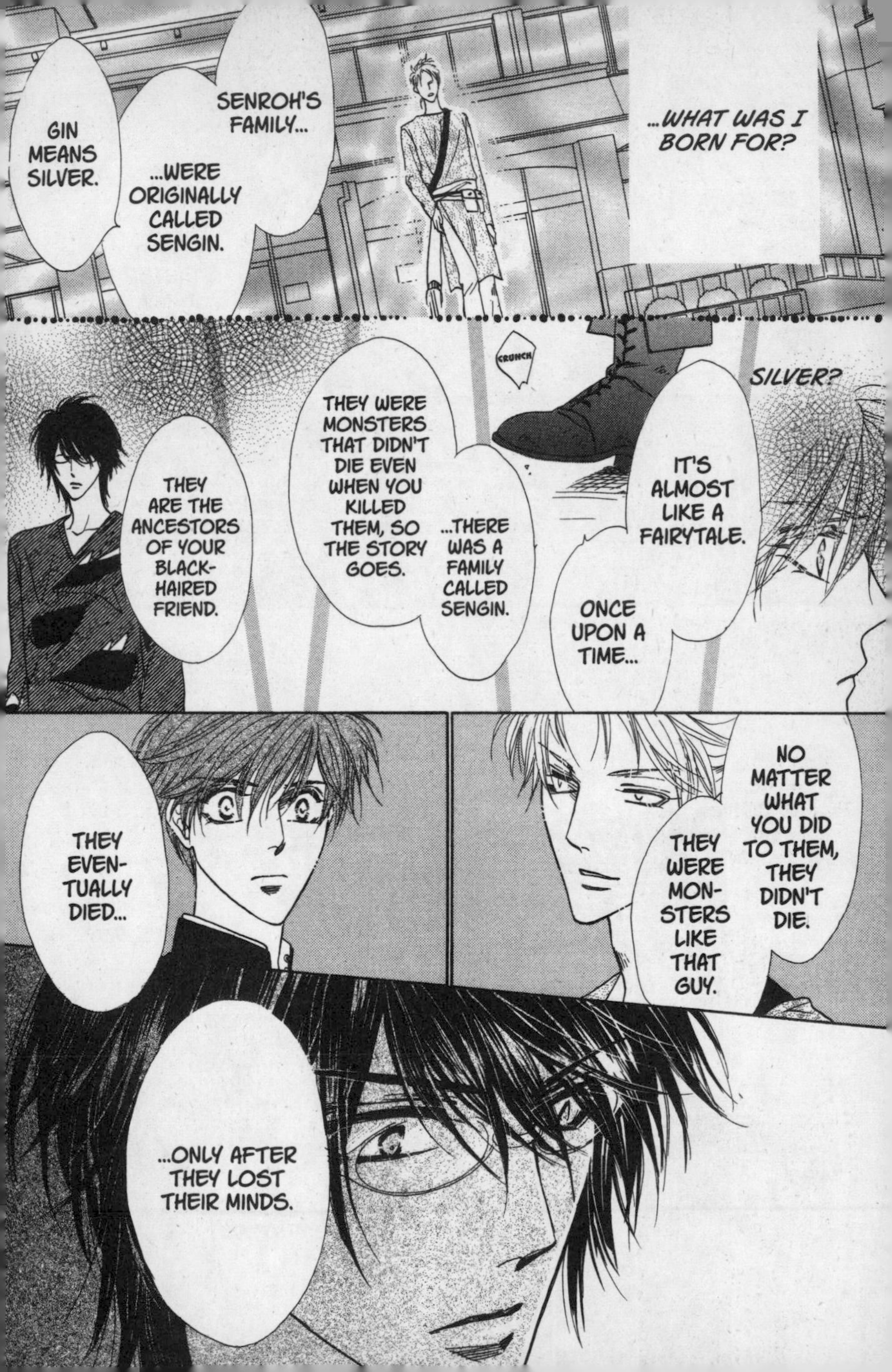
...WHAT WAS I BORN FOR?
SENROH'S FAMILY...
...WERE ORIGINALLY CALLED SENGIN.
GIN MEANS SILVER.
SILVER?
CRUNCH
IT'S ALMOST LIKE A FAIRYTALE.
ONCE UPON A TIME...
...THERE WAS A FAMILY CALLED SENGIN.
THEY WERE MONSTERS THAT DIDN'T DIE EVEN WHEN YOU KILLED THEM, SO THE STORY GOES.
THEY ARE THE ANCESTORS OF YOUR BLACK-HAIRED FRIEND.
NO MATTER WHAT YOU DID TO THEM, THEY DIDN'T DIE.
THEY WERE MON-STERS LIKE THAT GUY.
THEY EVEN-TUALLY DIED...
...ONLY AFTER THEY LOST THEIR MINDS.

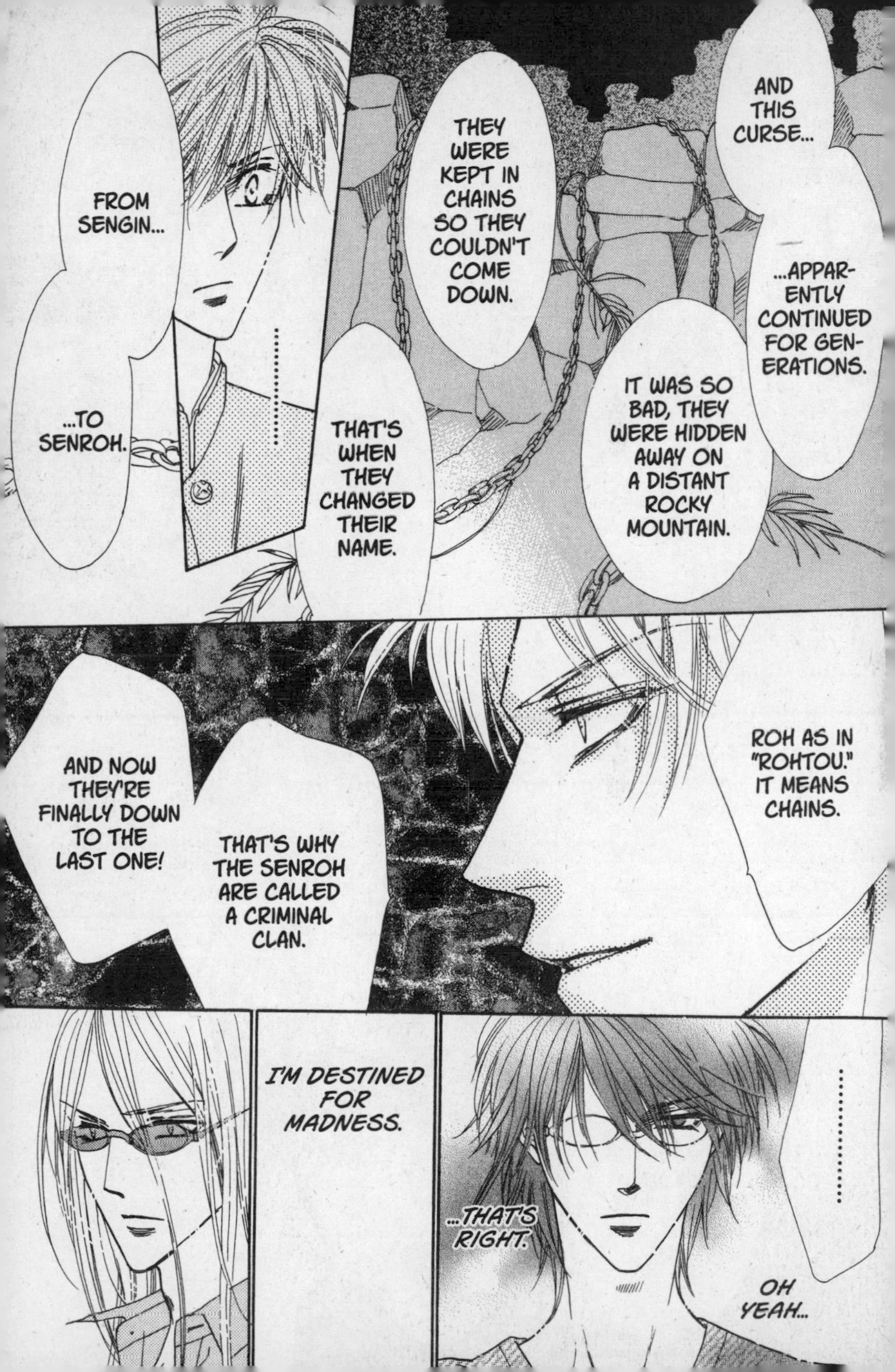
AND THIS CURSE...
...APPARENTLY CONTINUED FOR GENERATIONS.
IT WAS SO BAD, THEY WERE HIDDEN AWAY ON A DISTANT ROCKY MOUNTAIN.
THEY WERE KEPT IN CHAINS SO THEY COULDN'T COME DOWN.
THAT'S WHEN THEY CHANGED THEIR NAME.
......
FROM SENGIN...
...TO SENROH.
ROH AS IN "ROHTOU." IT MEANS CHAINS.
THAT'S WHY THE SENROH ARE CALLED A CRIMINAL CLAN.
AND NOW THEY'RE FINALLY DOWN TO THE LAST ONE!
......
OH YEAH...
...THAT'S RIGHT.
I'M DESTINED FOR MADNESS.

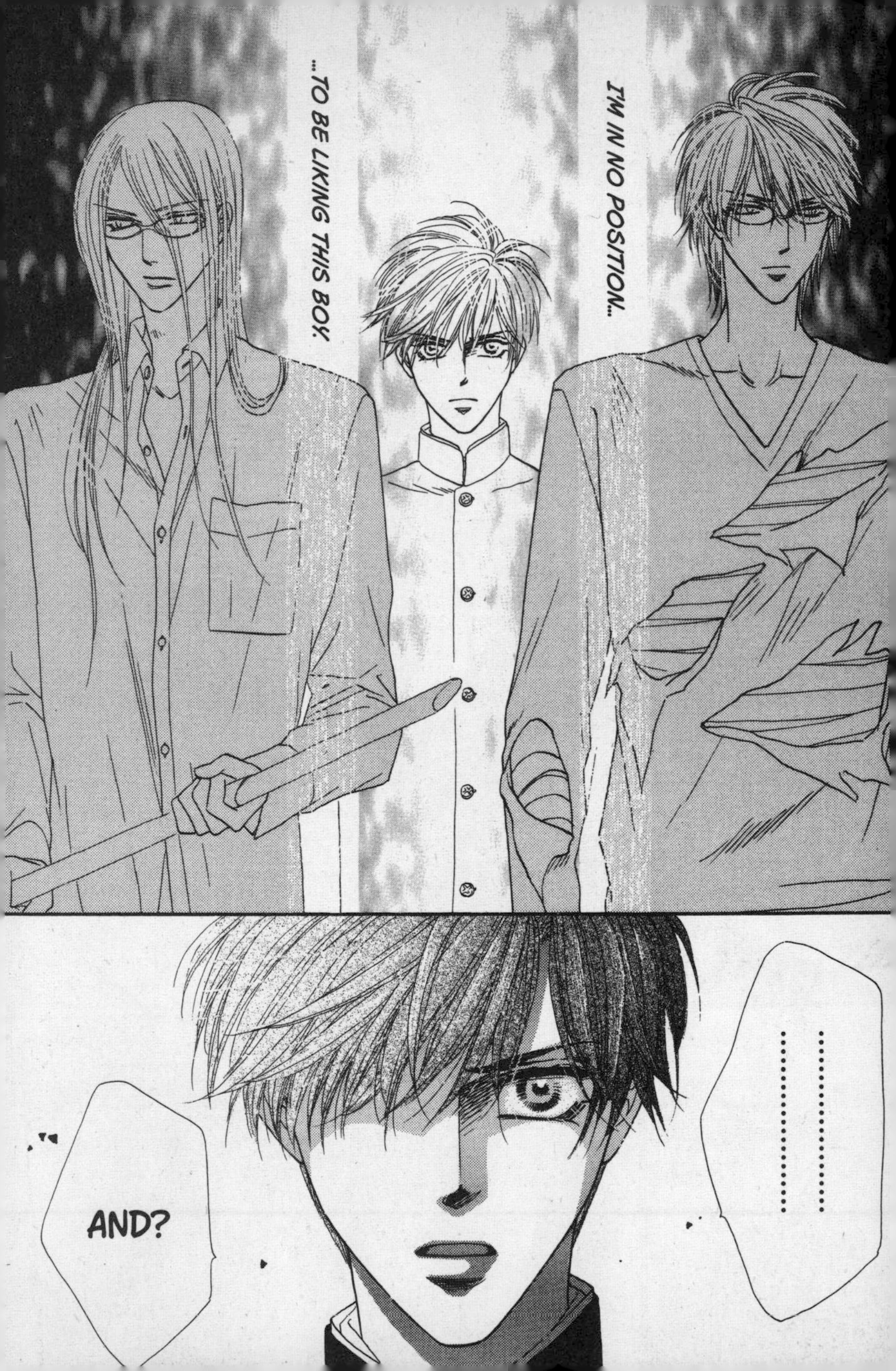
I'M IN NO POSITION...
...TO BE LIKING THIS BOY.
......
AND?

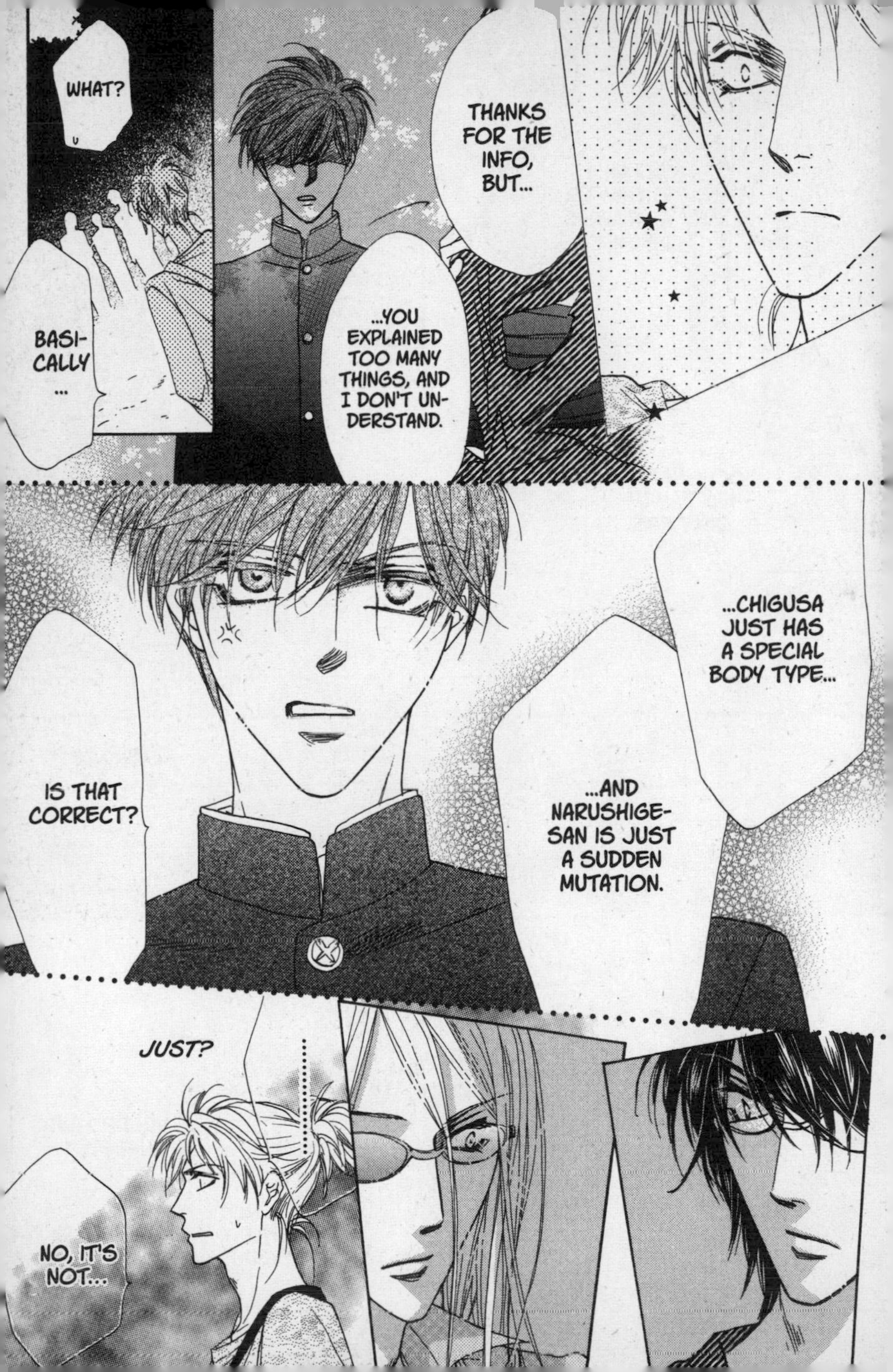
THANKS FOR THE INFO, BUT...
...YOU EXPLAINED TOO MANY THINGS, AND I DON'T UNDERSTAND.
WHAT?
BASICALLY...
...CHIGUSA JUST HAS A SPECIAL BODY TYPE...
...AND NARUSHIGE-SAN IS JUST A SUDDEN MUTATION.
IS THAT CORRECT?
JUST?
NO, IT'S NOT...

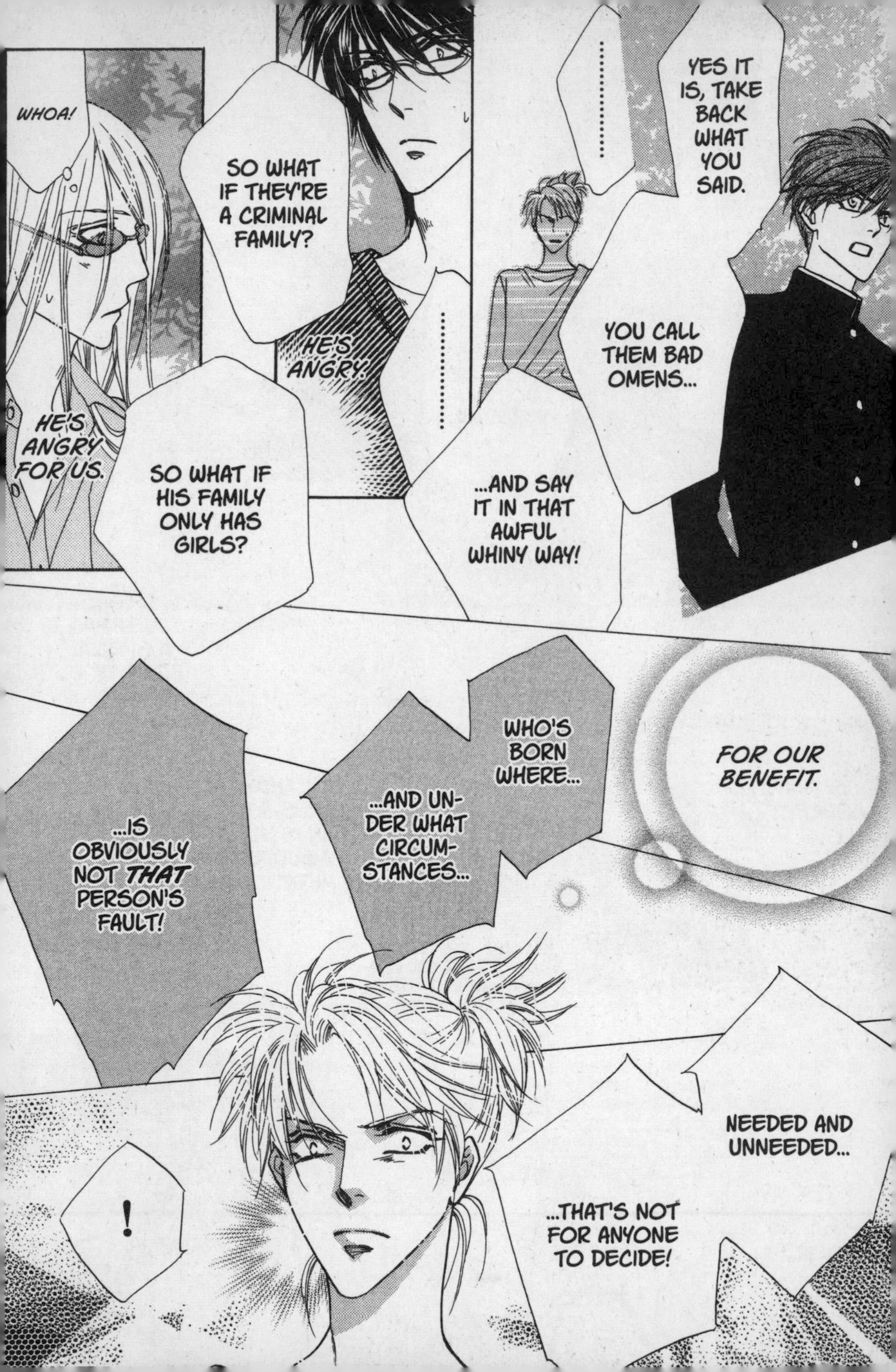
YES IT IS, TAKE BACK WHAT YOU SAID.
......
YOU CALL THEM BAD OMENS...
...AND SAY IT IN THAT AWFUL WHINY WAY!
SO WHAT IF THEY'RE A CRIMINAL FAMILY?
......
HE'S ANGRY.
SO WHAT IF HIS FAMILY ONLY HAS GIRLS?
WHOA!
HE'S ANGRY FOR US.
FOR OUR BENEFIT.
WHO'S BORN WHERE...
...AND UNDER WHAT CIRCUMSTANCES...
...IS OBVIOUSLY NOT *THAT* PERSON'S FAULT!
NEEDED AND UNNEEDED...
...THAT'S NOT FOR ANYONE TO DECIDE!
!

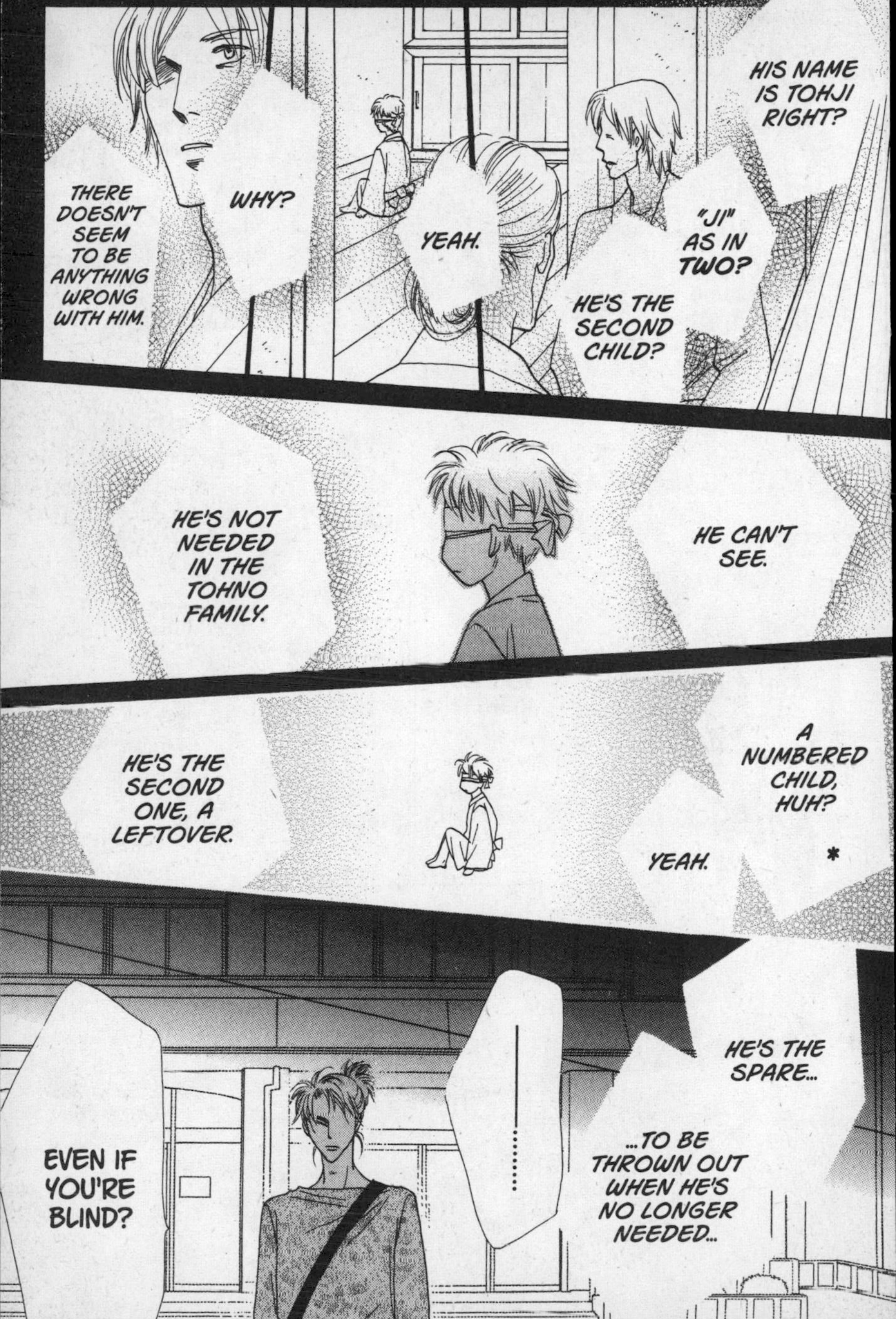
HIS NAME IS TOHJI RIGHT?
"JI" AS IN TWO?
HE'S THE SECOND CHILD?
YEAH.
WHY?
THERE DOESN'T SEEM TO BE ANYTHING WRONG WITH HIM.
HE CAN'T SEE.
HE'S NOT NEEDED IN THE TOHNO FAMILY.
A NUMBERED CHILD, HUH?
*
YEAH.
HE'S THE SECOND ONE, A LEFTOVER.
HE'S THE SPARE...
...TO BE THROWN OUT WHEN HE'S NO LONGER NEEDED...
......
EVEN IF YOU'RE BLIND?

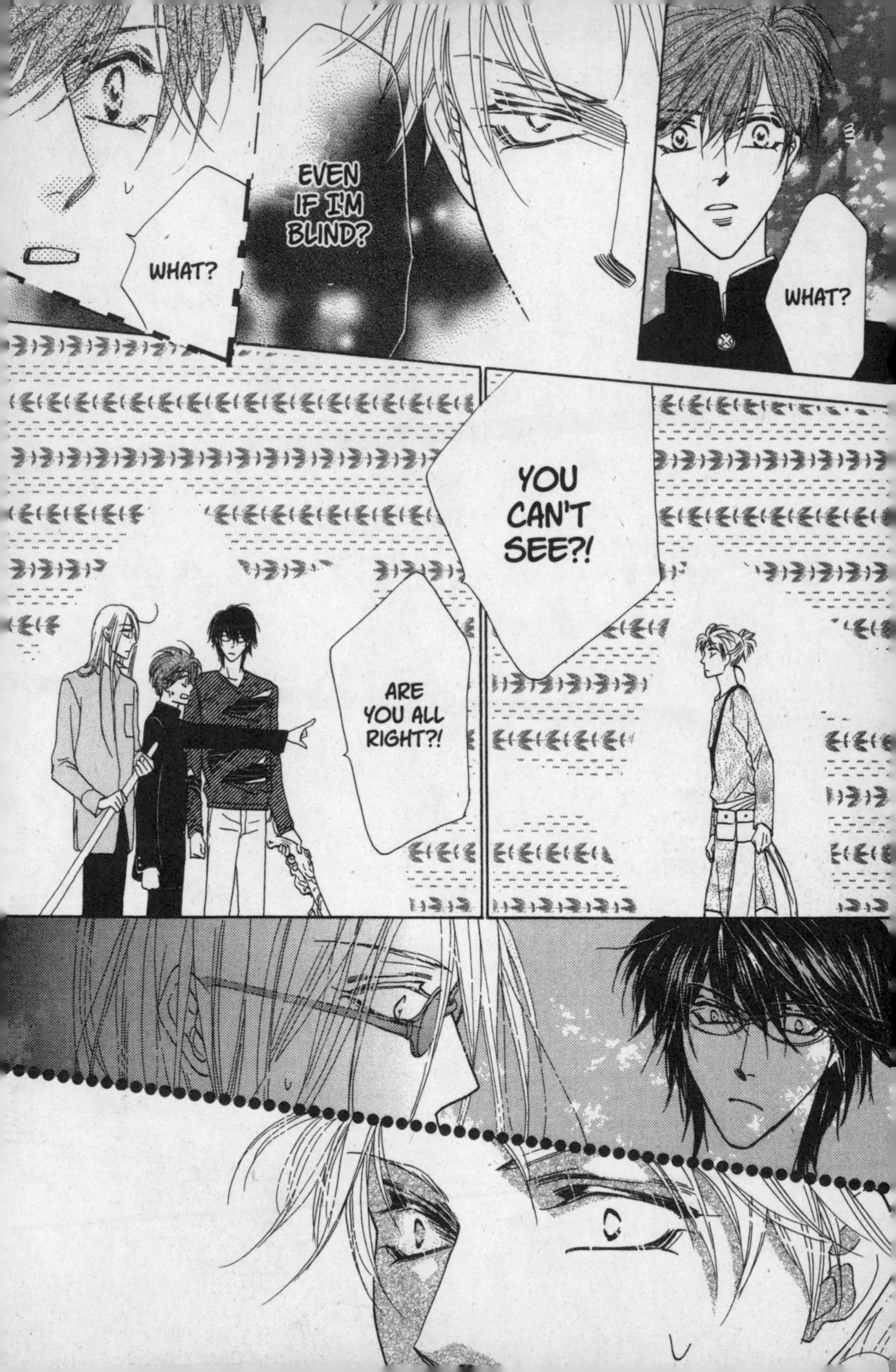
WHAT?
EVEN IF I'M BLIND?
WHAT?
YOU CAN'T SEE?!
ARE YOU ALL RIGHT?!

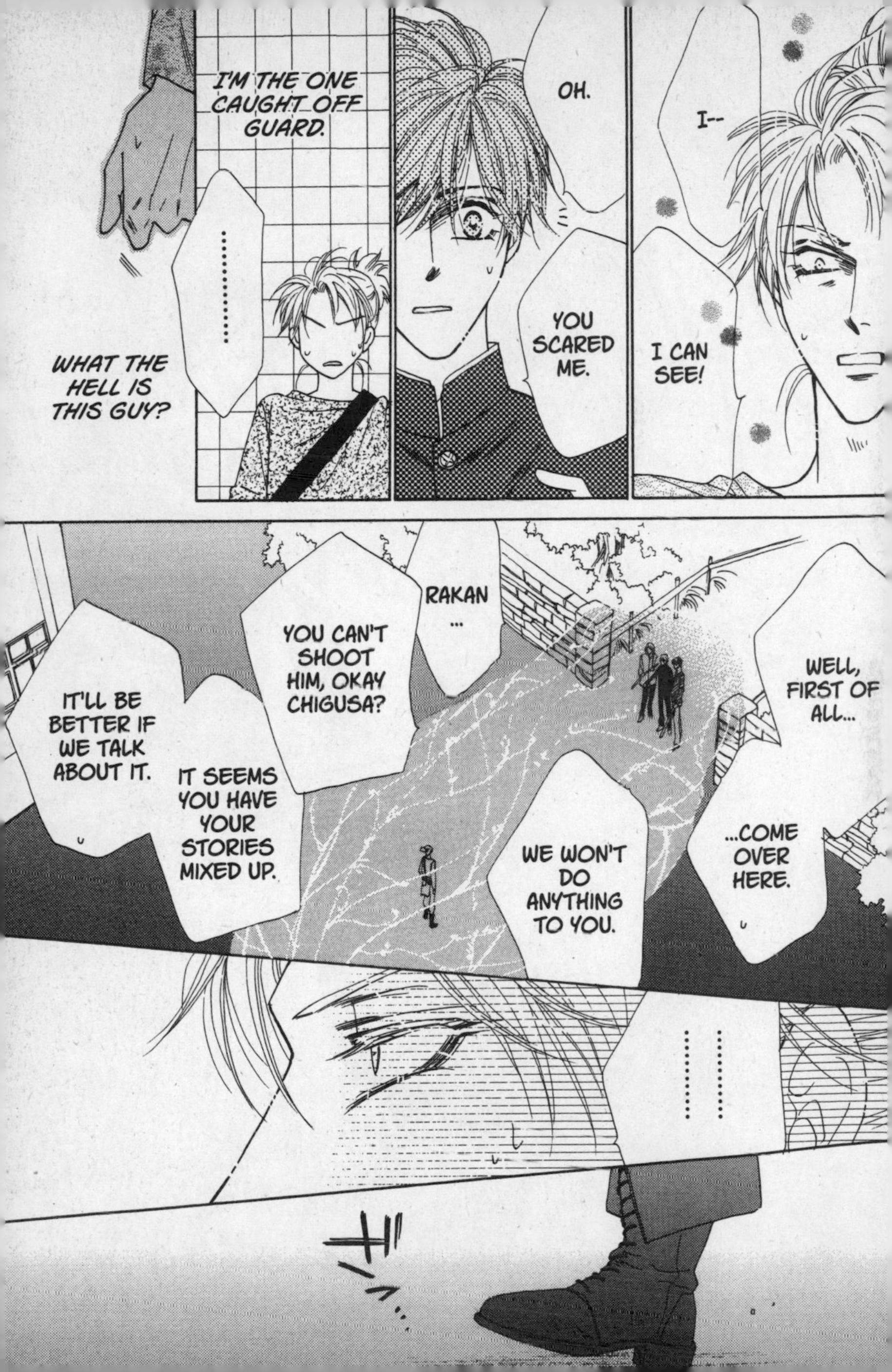
I--
I CAN SEE!
OH.
YOU SCARED ME.
I'M THE ONE CAUGHT OFF GUARD.
......
WHAT THE HELL IS THIS GUY?
WELL, FIRST OF ALL...
...COME OVER HERE.
WE WON'T DO ANYTHING TO YOU.
RAKAN...
YOU CAN'T SHOOT HIM, OKAY CHIGUSA?
IT'LL BE BETTER IF WE TALK ABOUT IT.
IT SEEMS YOU HAVE YOUR STORIES MIXED UP.
....

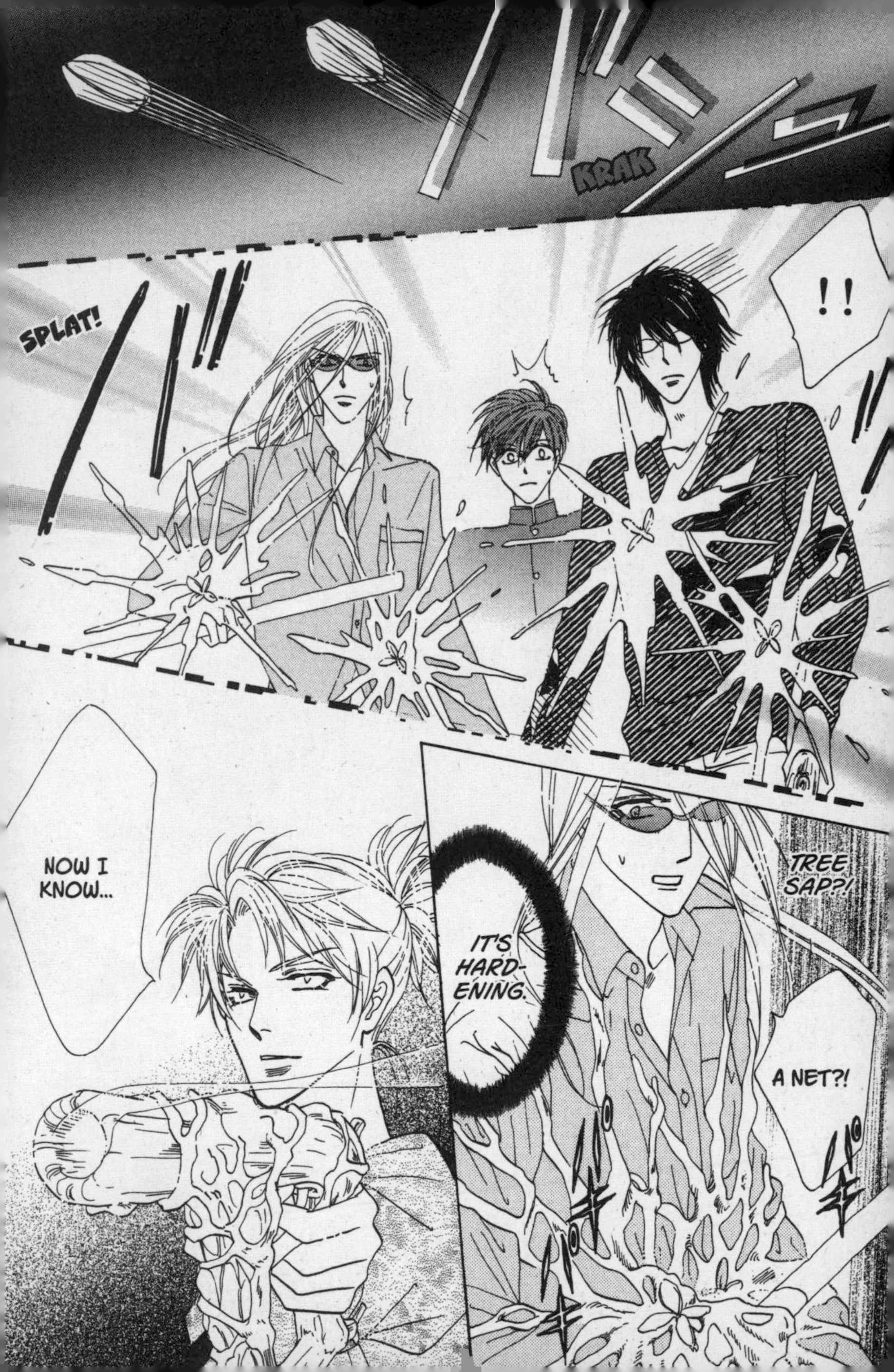
KRAK
!!
SPLAT!
TREE SAP?!
IT'S HARDENING.
A NET?!
NOW I KNOW...

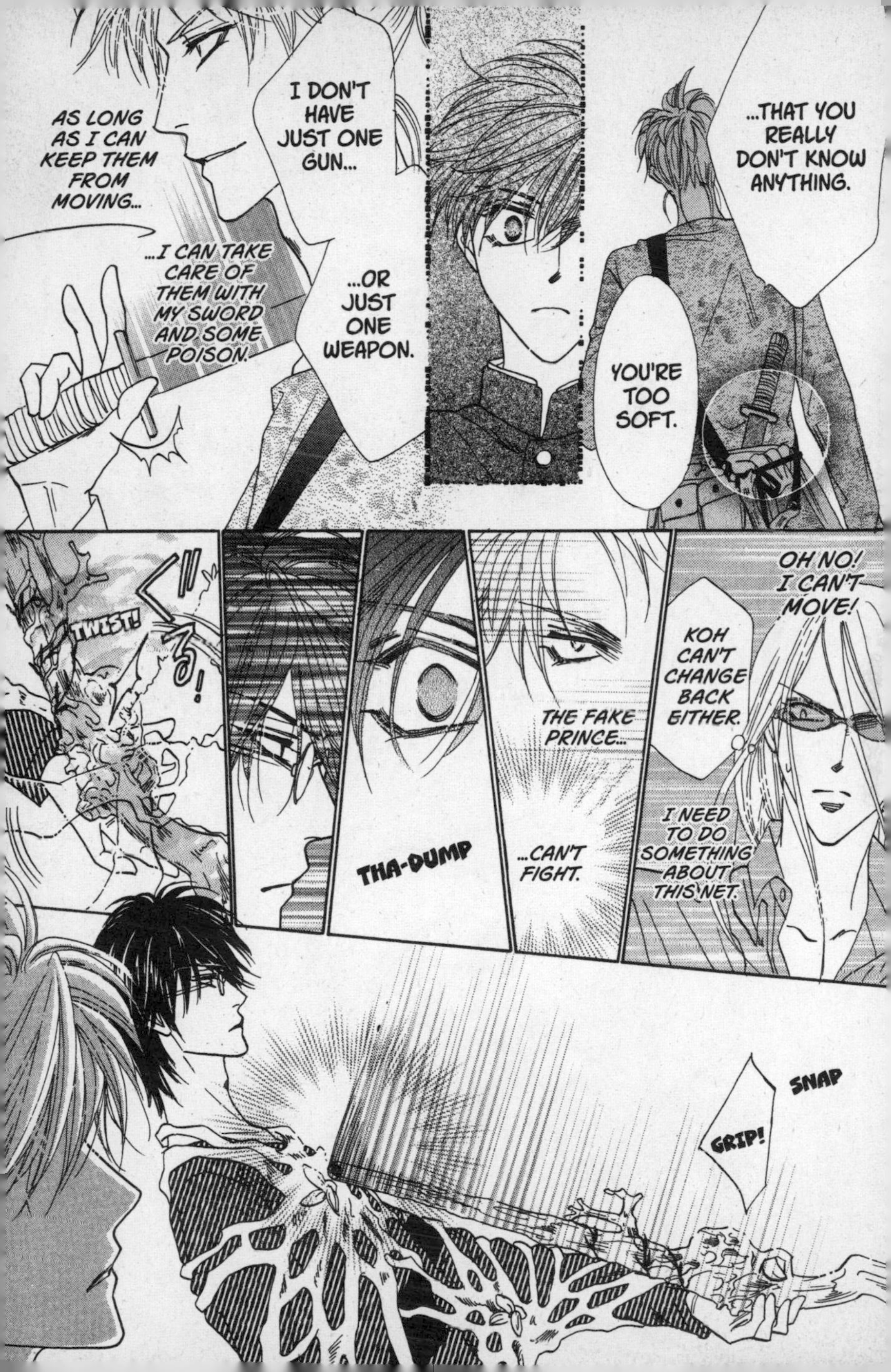
...THAT YOU REALLY DON'T KNOW ANYTHING.
YOU'RE TOO SOFT.
I DON'T HAVE JUST ONE GUN...
...OR JUST ONE WEAPON.
AS LONG AS I CAN KEEP THEM FROM MOVING...
...I CAN TAKE CARE OF THEM WITH MY SWORD AND SOME POISON.
OH NO! I CAN'T MOVE!
KOH CAN'T CHANGE BACK EITHER.
I NEED TO DO SOMETHING ABOUT THIS NET.
THE FAKE PRINCE...
...CAN'T FIGHT.
THA-DUMP
TWIST!
SNAP
GRIP!

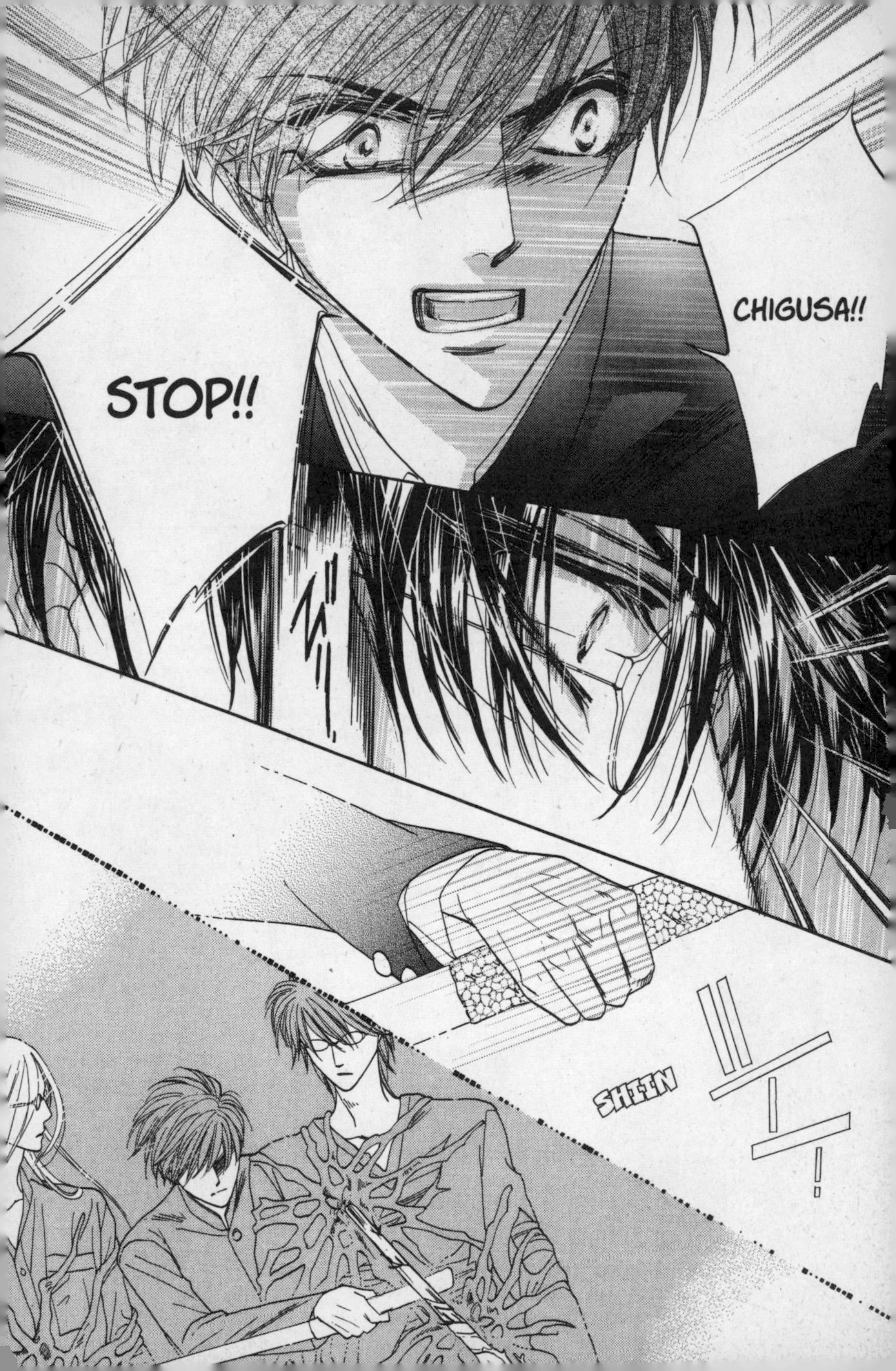
CHIGUSA!!
STOP!!
SHIIN

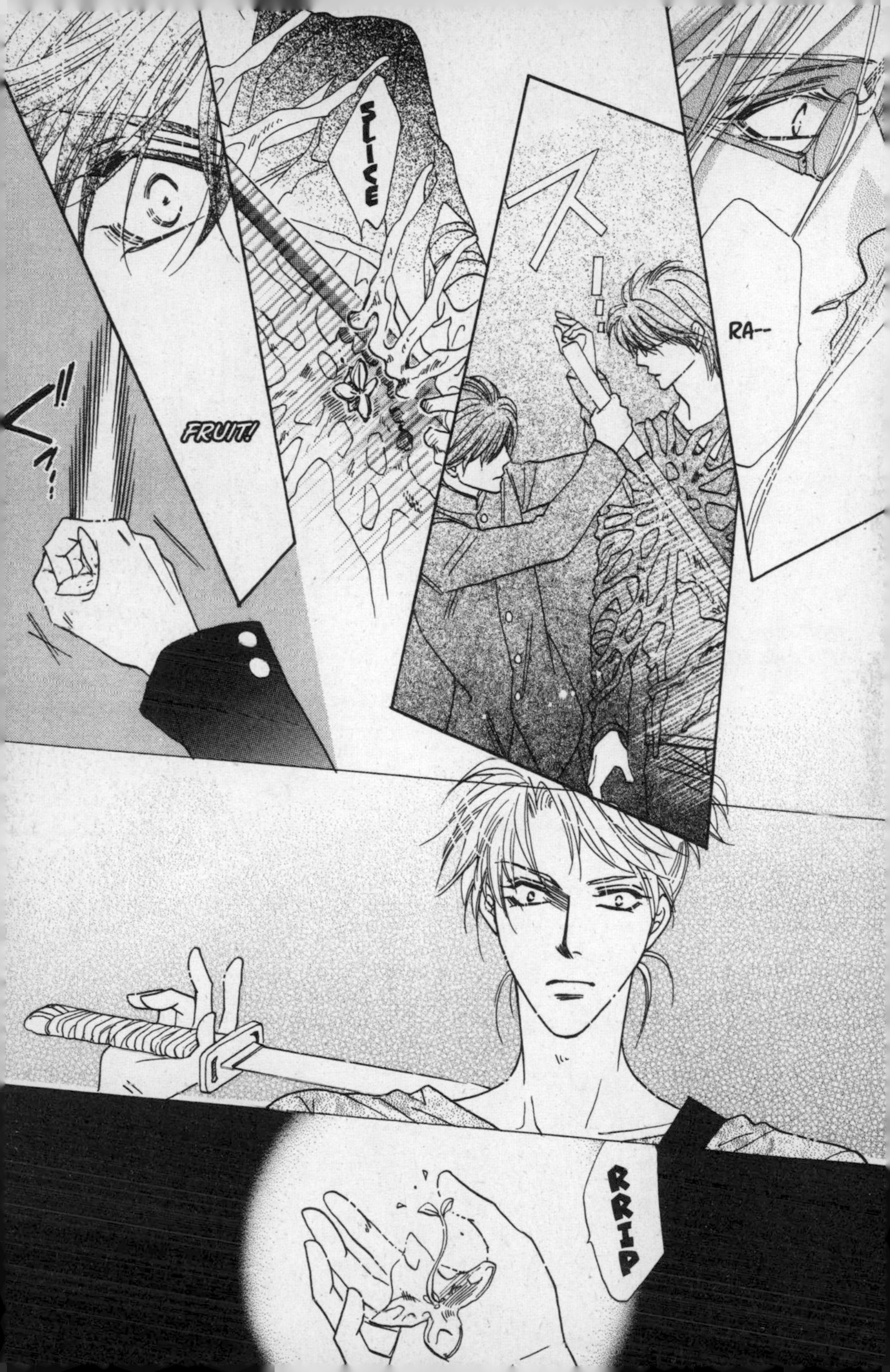
RA--
SLICE
FRUIT!
RRIP

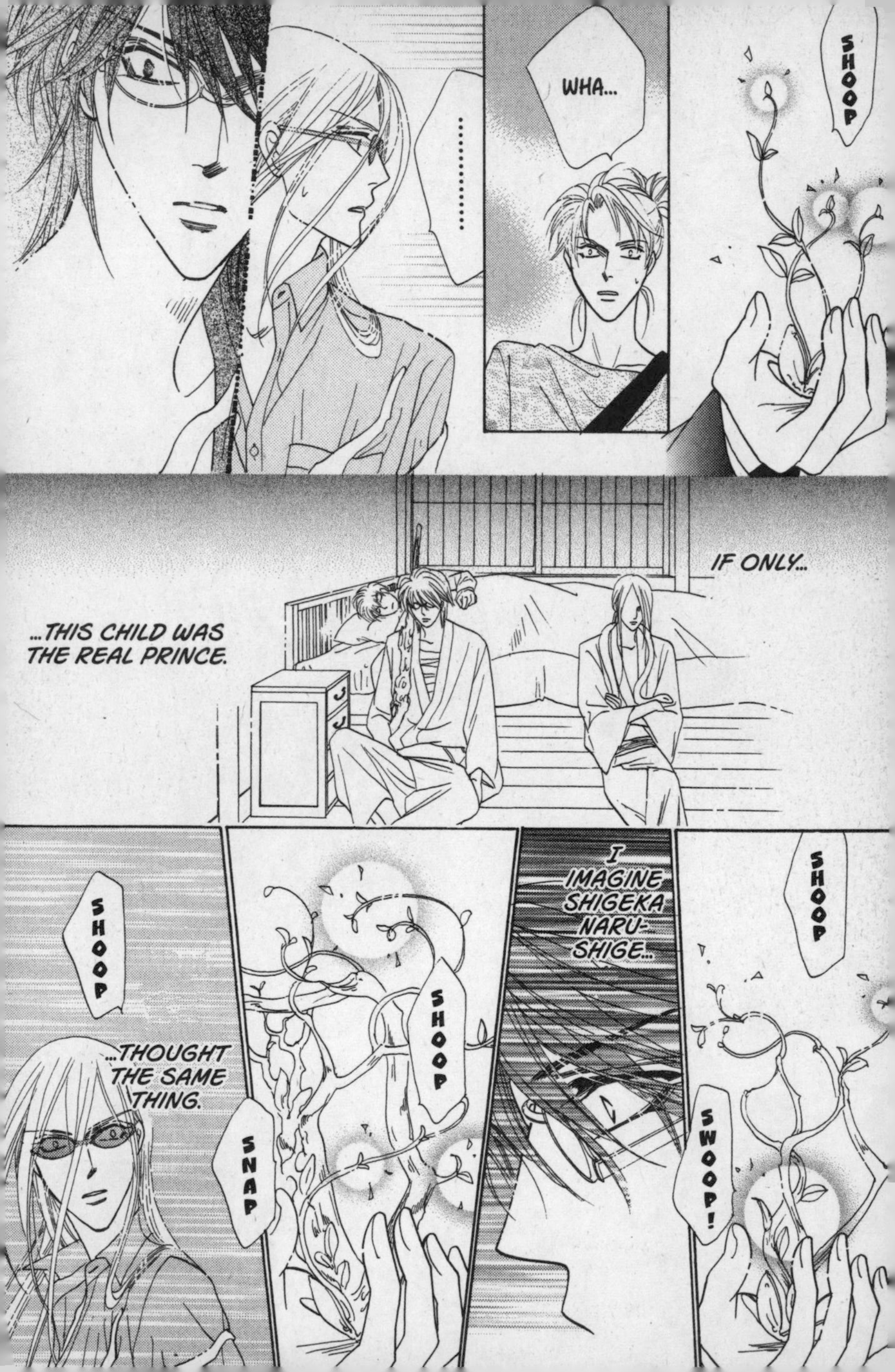
SHOOP
WHA...
......
IF ONLY...
...THIS CHILD WAS THE REAL PRINCE.
SHOOP
SWOOP!
I IMAGINE SHIGEKA NARU-SHIGE...
SHOOP
SNAP
SHOOP
...THOUGHT THE SAME THING.

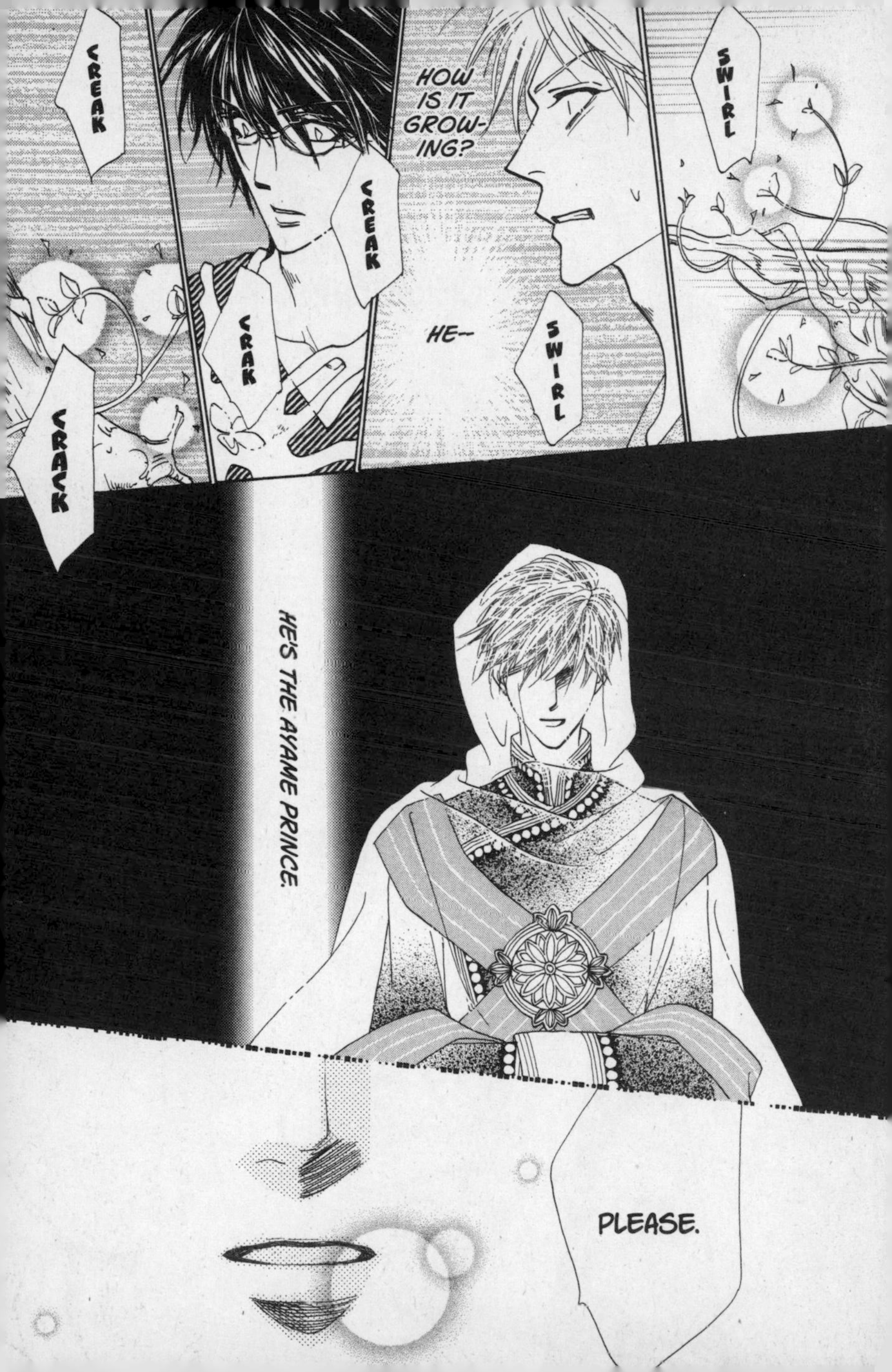
SWIRL
HOW IS IT GROWING?
SWIRL
HE--
CREAK
CRAK
CREAK
CRACK
HE'S THE AYAME PRINCE.
PLEASE.

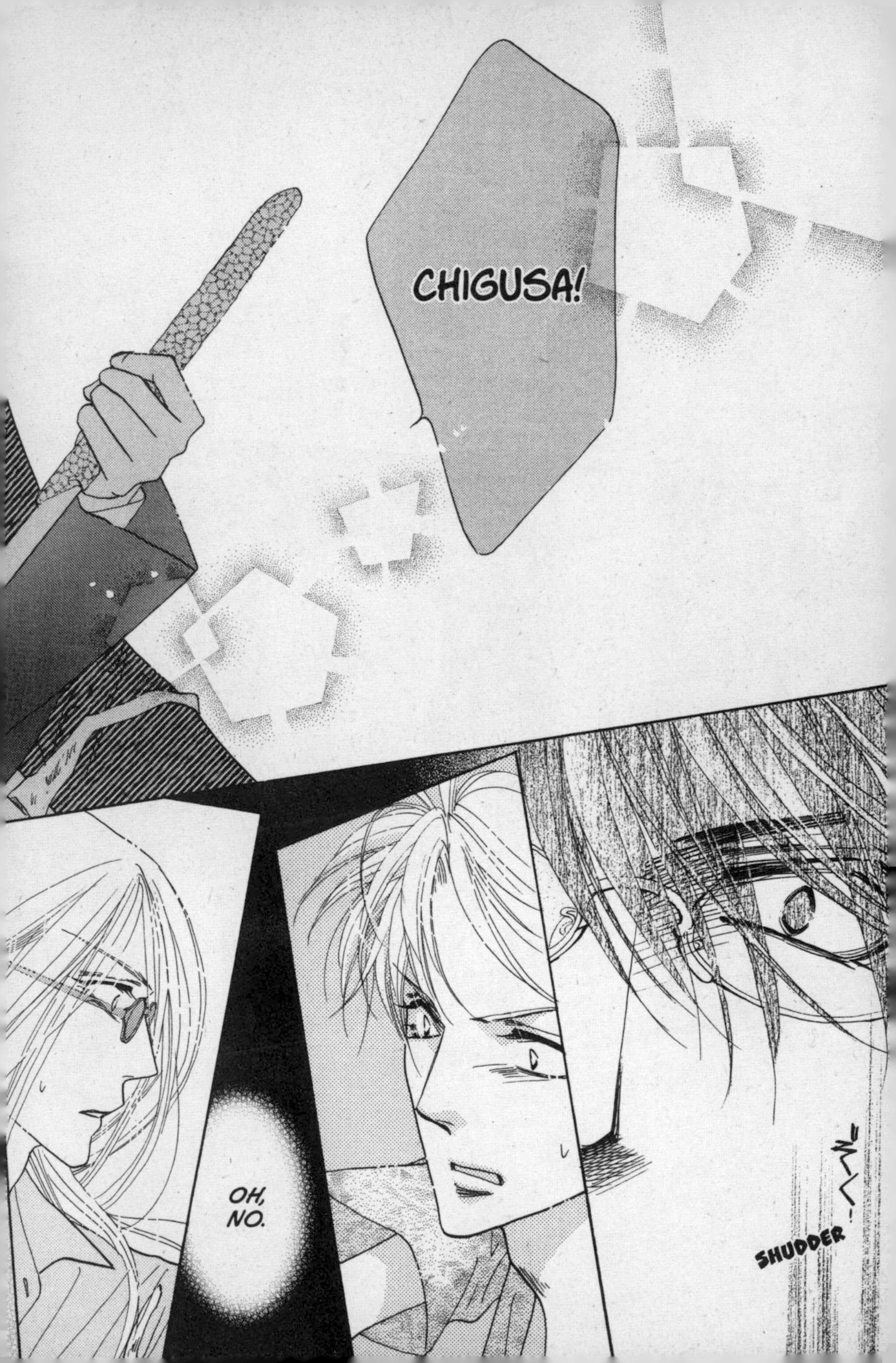
CHIGUSA!
SHUDDER
OH, NO.

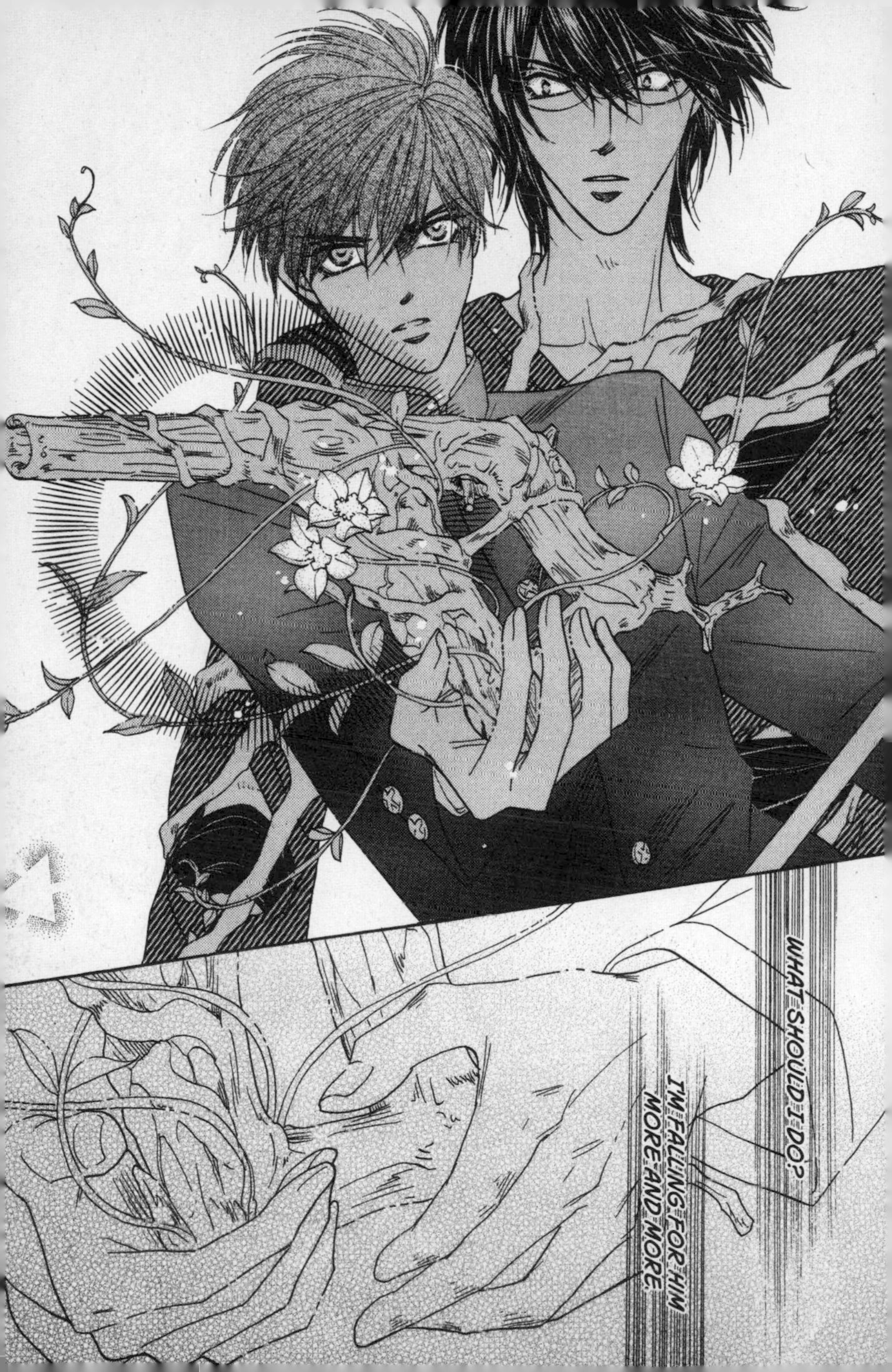
WHAT SHOULD I DO?
I'M FALLING FOR HIM MORE AND MORE.

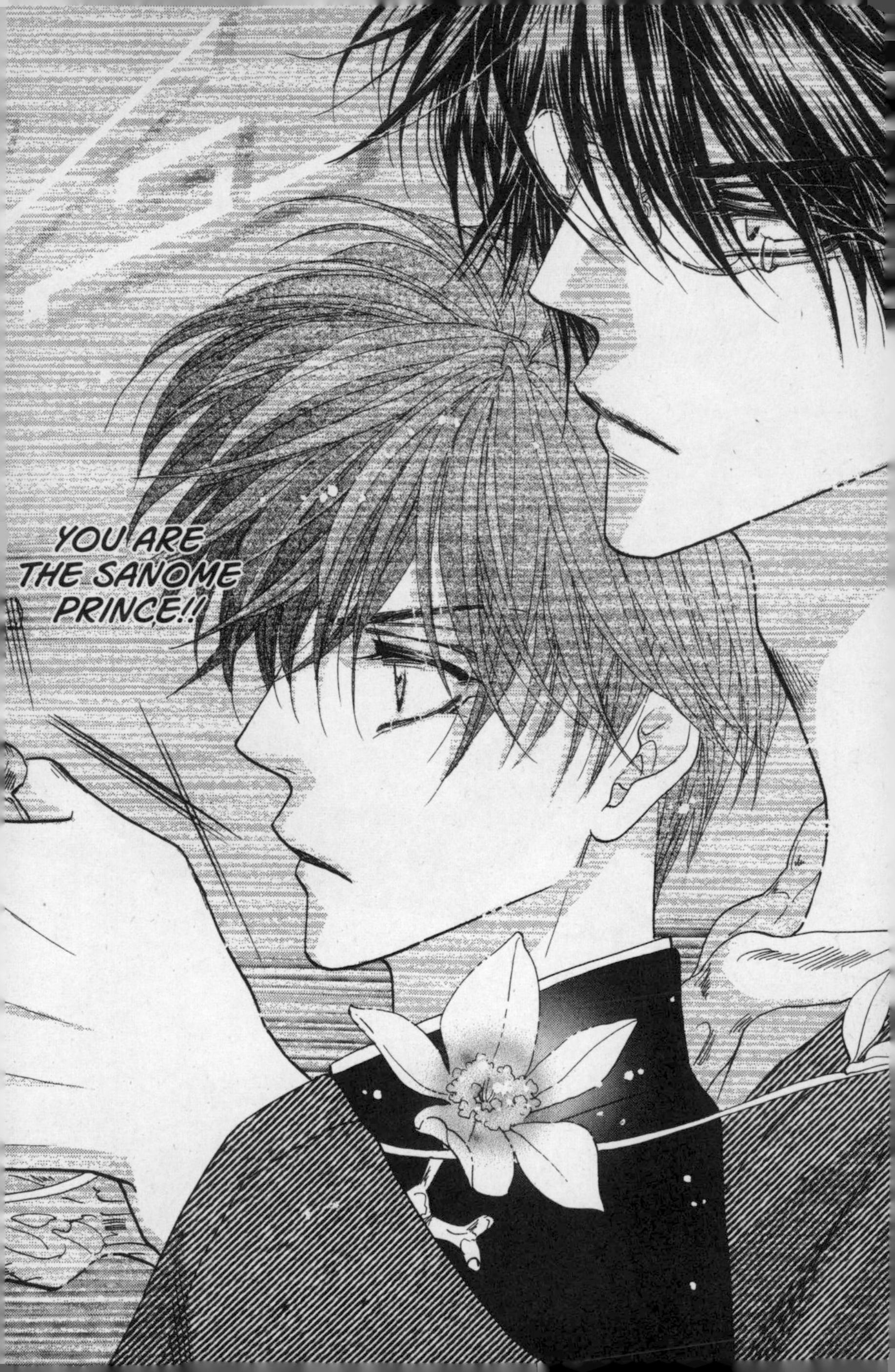
YOU ARE THE SANOME PRINCE!!

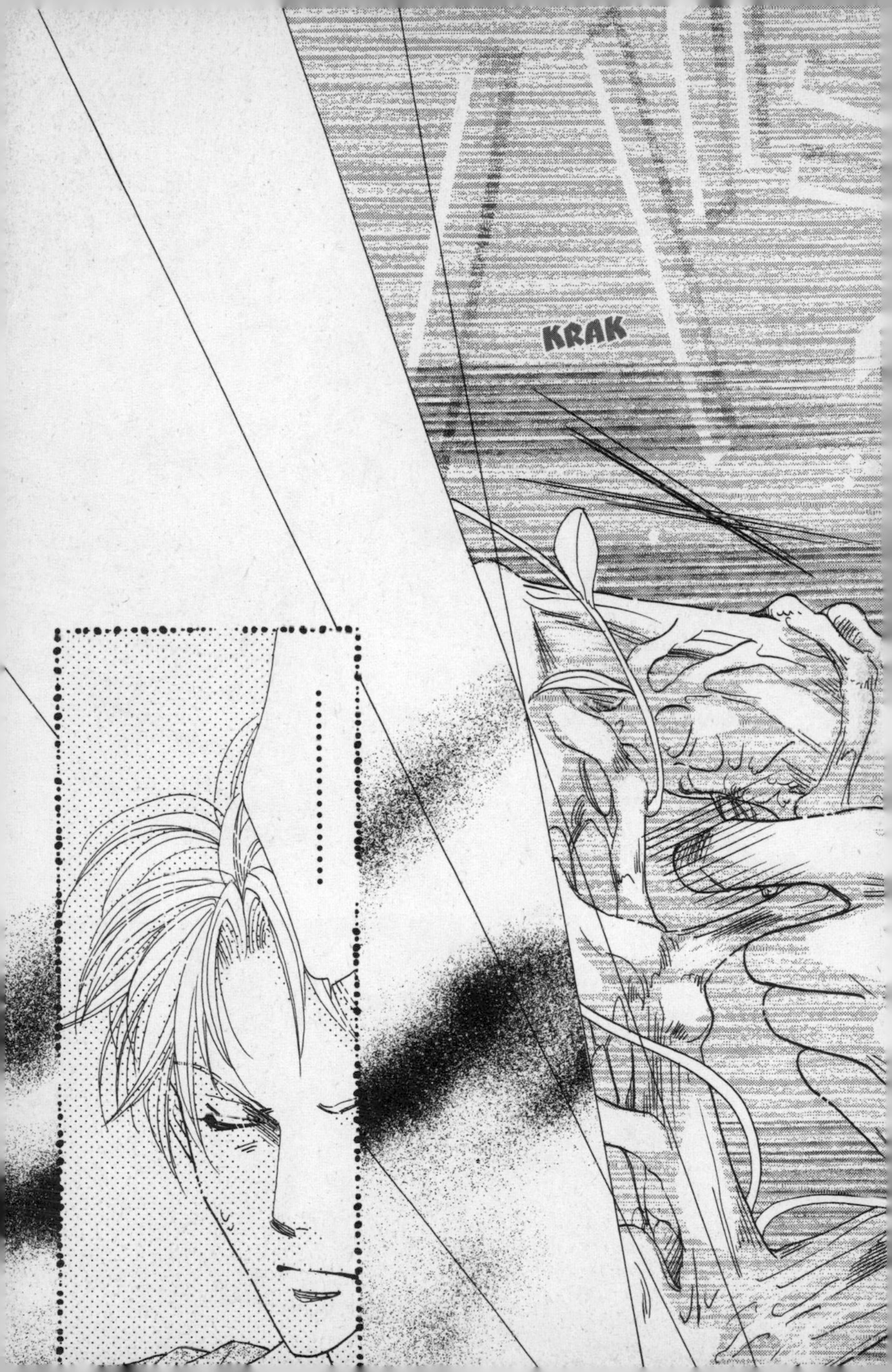
KRAK

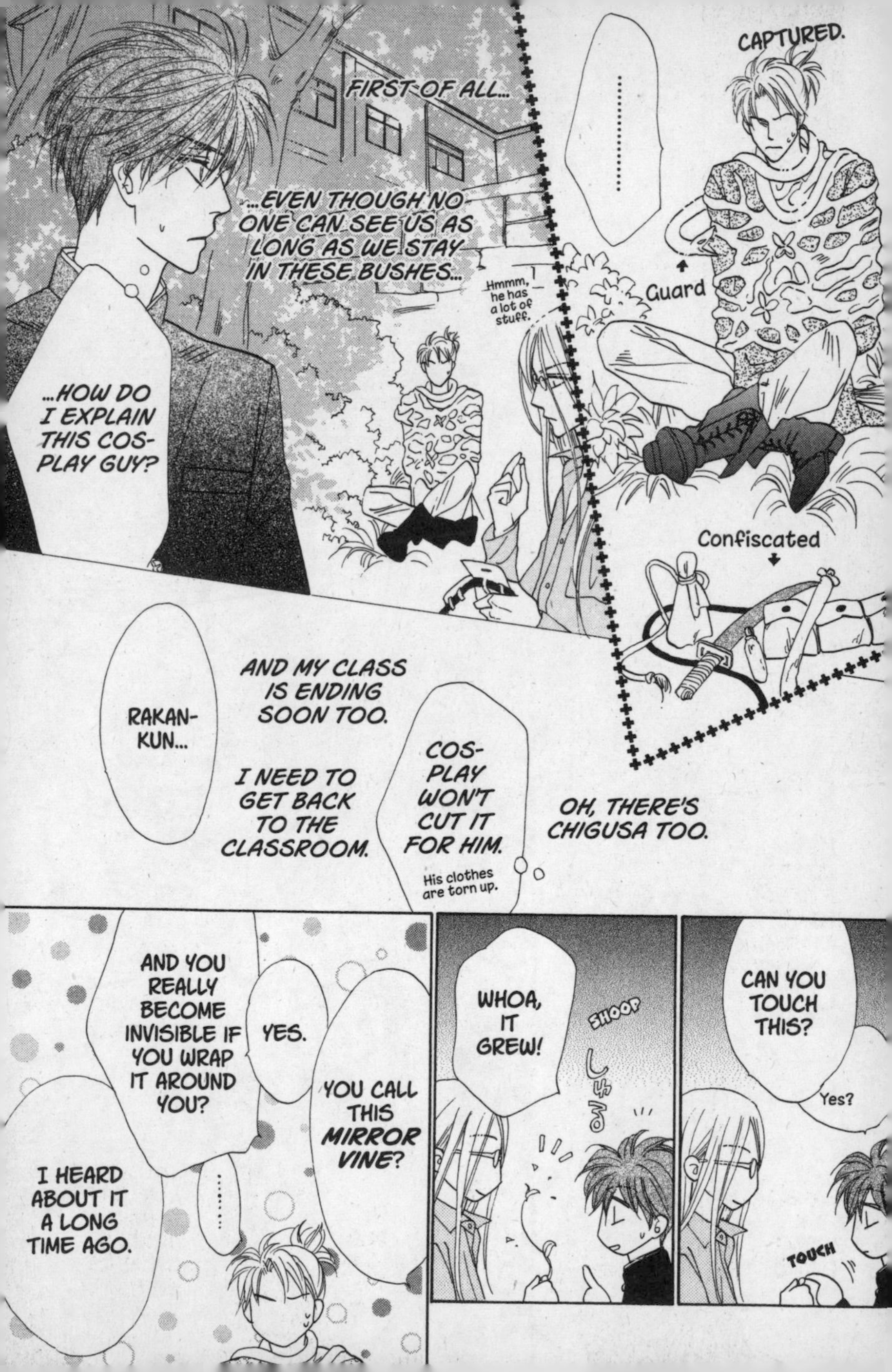
......
CAPTURED.
Guard
Confiscated
FIRST OF ALL...
...EVEN THOUGH NO-ONE CAN SEE US AS LONG AS WE STAY IN THESE BUSHES...
Hmmm, he has a lot of stuff.
...HOW DO I EXPLAIN THIS COS-PLAY GUY?
OH, THERE'S CHIGUSA TOO.
COS-PLAY WON'T CUT IT FOR HIM.
His clothes are torn up.
AND MY CLASS IS ENDING SOON TOO.
I NEED TO GET BACK TO THE CLASSROOM.
RAKAN-KUN...
CAN YOU TOUCH THIS?
Yes?
TOUCH
WHOA, IT GREW!
SHOOP
しゅる
AND YOU REALLY BECOME INVISIBLE IF YOU WRAP IT AROUND YOU?
YES.
YOU CALL THIS MIRROR VINE?
I HEARD ABOUT IT A LONG TIME AGO.
......

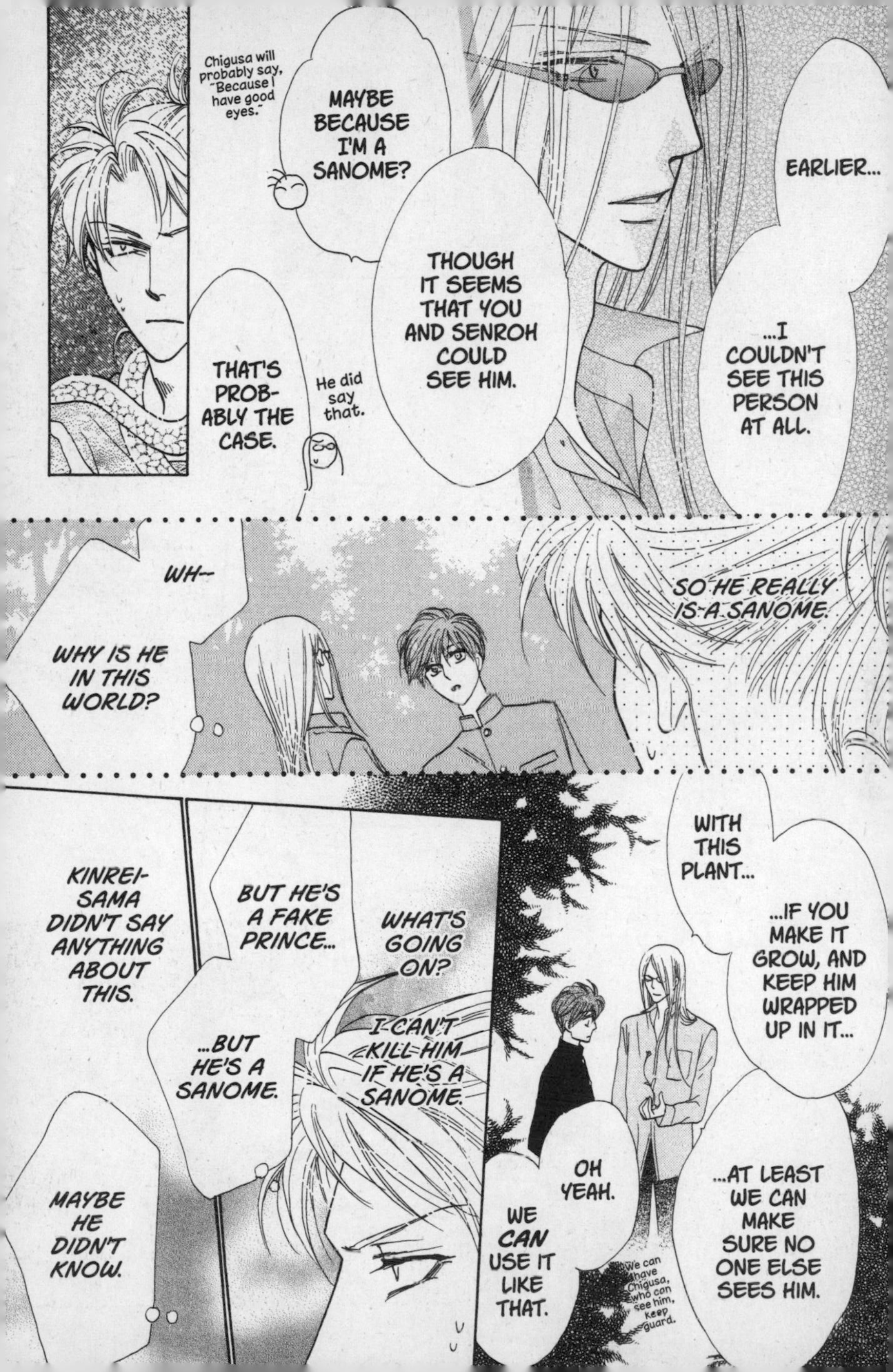

EARLIER...
...I COULDN'T SEE THIS PERSON AT ALL.
THOUGH IT SEEMS THAT YOU AND SENROH COULD SEE HIM.
MAYBE BECAUSE I'M A SANOME?
Chigusa will probably say, "Because I have good eyes."
THAT'S PROBABLY THE CASE.
He did say that.
SO HE REALLY IS A SANOME.
WH--
WHY IS HE IN THIS WORLD?
WITH THIS PLANT...
...IF YOU MAKE IT GROW, AND KEEP HIM WRAPPED UP IN IT...
...AT LEAST WE CAN MAKE SURE NO ONE ELSE SEES HIM.
OH YEAH.
WE CAN USE IT LIKE THAT.
We can have Chigusa, who can see him, keep guard.
WHAT'S GOING ON?
I CAN'T KILL HIM IF HE'S A SANOME.
BUT HE'S A FAKE PRINCE...
...BUT HE'S A SANOME.
KINREI-SAMA DIDN'T SAY ANYTHING ABOUT THIS.
MAYBE HE DIDN'T KNOW.

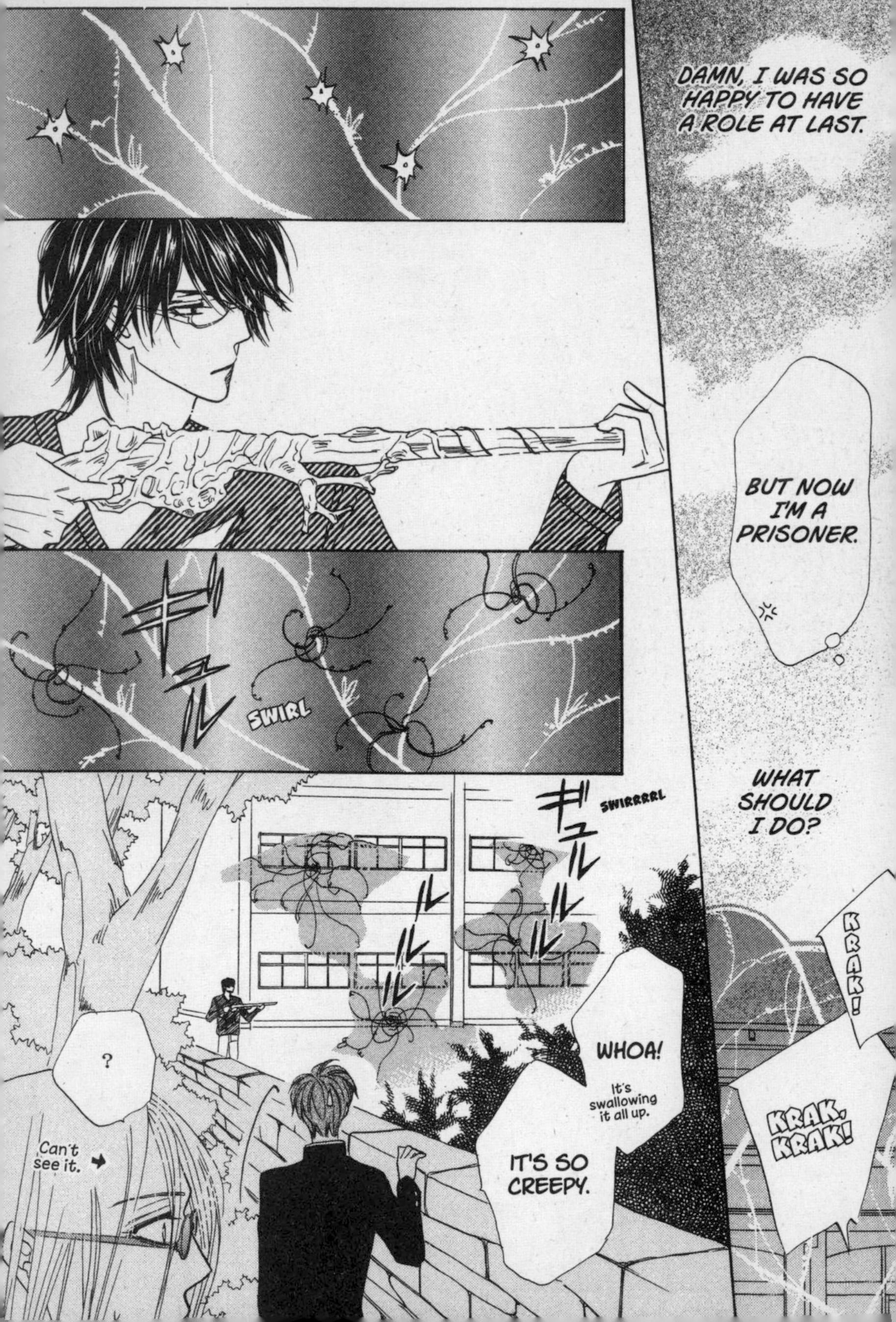

DAMN, I WAS SO HAPPY TO HAVE A ROLE AT LAST.
BUT NOW I'M A PRISONER.
WHAT SHOULD I DO?
ギュル
SWIRL
KRAK!
KRAK, KRAK!
SWIRRRRL
WHOA!
It's swallowing it all up.
IT'S SO CREEPY.
?
Can't see it.

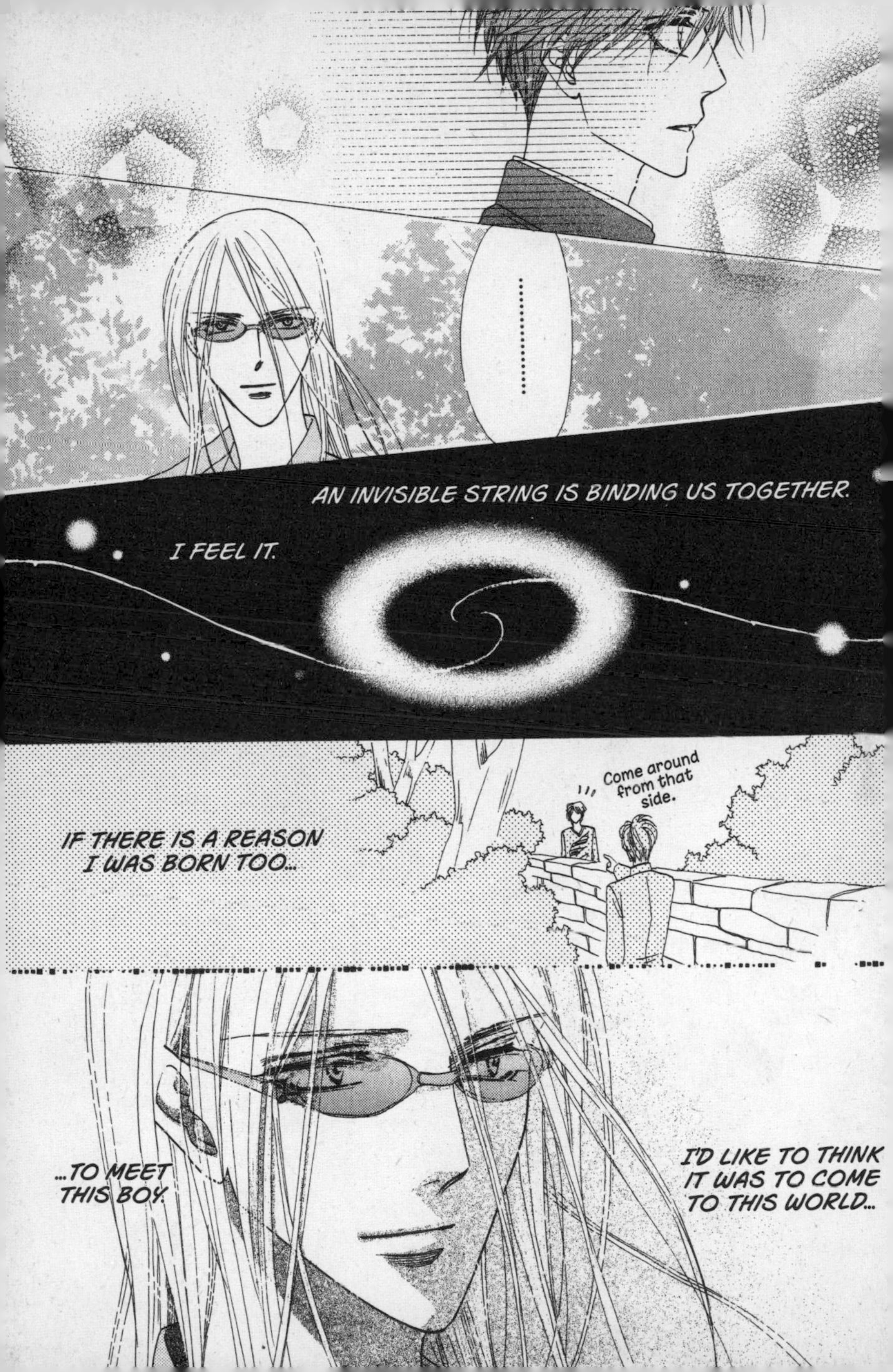
......
AN INVISIBLE STRING IS BINDING US TOGETHER.
I FEEL IT.
Come around from that side.
IF THERE IS A REASON I WAS BORN TOO...
I'D LIKE TO THINK IT WAS TO COME TO THIS WORLD...
...TO MEET THIS BOY.

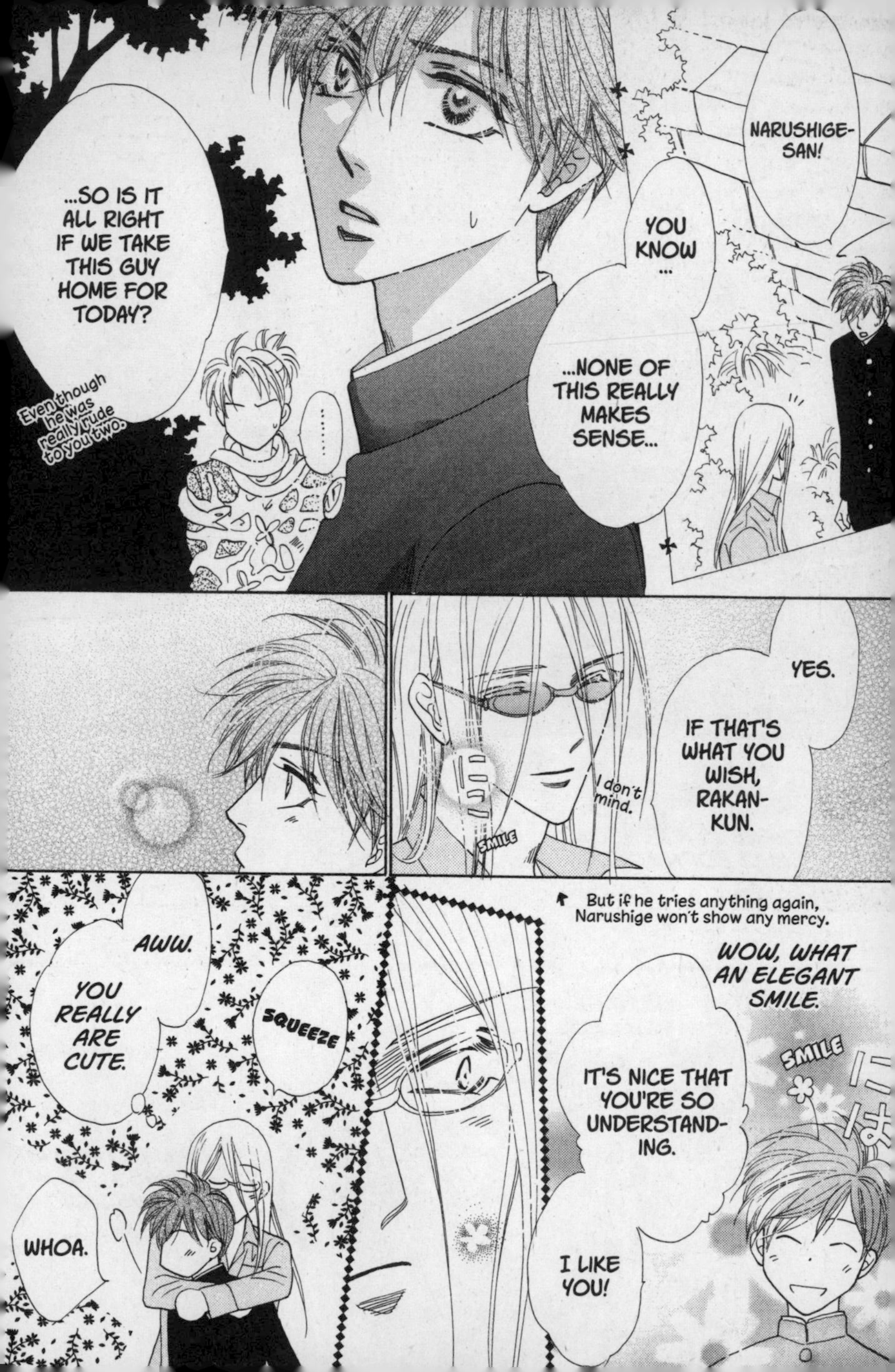
NARUSHIGE-SAN!
YOU KNOW ...
...NONE OF THIS REALLY MAKES SENSE...
...SO IS IT ALL RIGHT IF WE TAKE THIS GUY HOME FOR TODAY?
......
Even though he was really rude to you two.
YES.
IF THAT'S WHAT YOU WISH, RAKAN-KUN.
I don't mind.
SMILE
But if he tries anything again, Narushige won't show any mercy.
WOW, WHAT AN ELEGANT SMILE.
SMILE
IT'S NICE THAT YOU'RE SO UNDERSTANDING.
I LIKE YOU!
AWW.
YOU REALLY ARE CUTE.
SQUEEZE
WHOA.

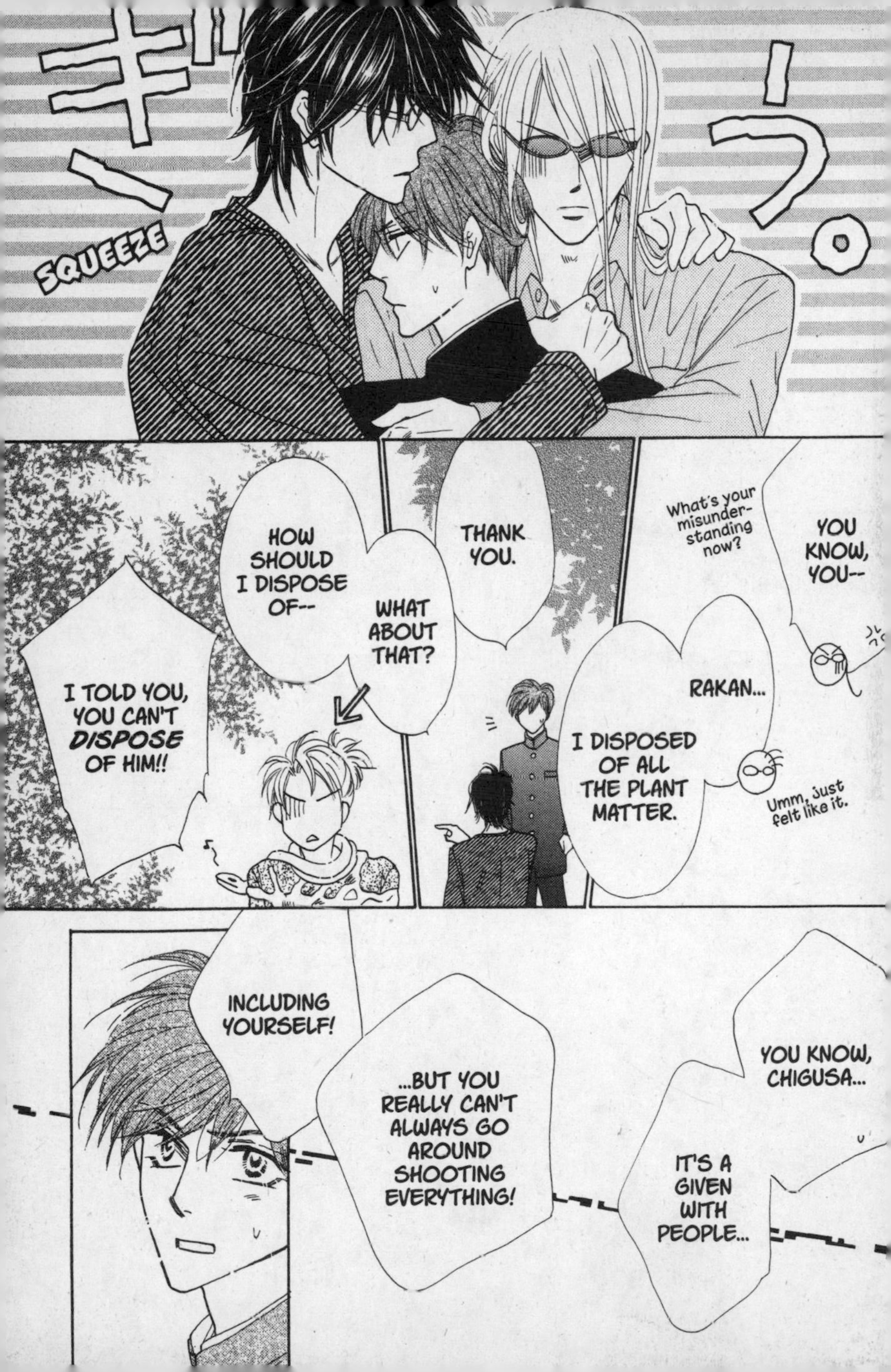
SQUEEZE
YOU KNOW, YOU--
What's your misunderstanding now?
RAKAN...
I DISPOSED OF ALL THE PLANT MATTER.
Umm, just felt like it.
THANK YOU.
HOW SHOULD I DISPOSE OF--
WHAT ABOUT THAT?
I TOLD YOU, YOU CAN'T *DISPOSE* OF HIM!!
YOU KNOW, CHIGUSA...
IT'S A GIVEN WITH PEOPLE...
...BUT YOU REALLY CAN'T ALWAYS GO AROUND SHOOTING EVERYTHING!
INCLUDING YOURSELF!

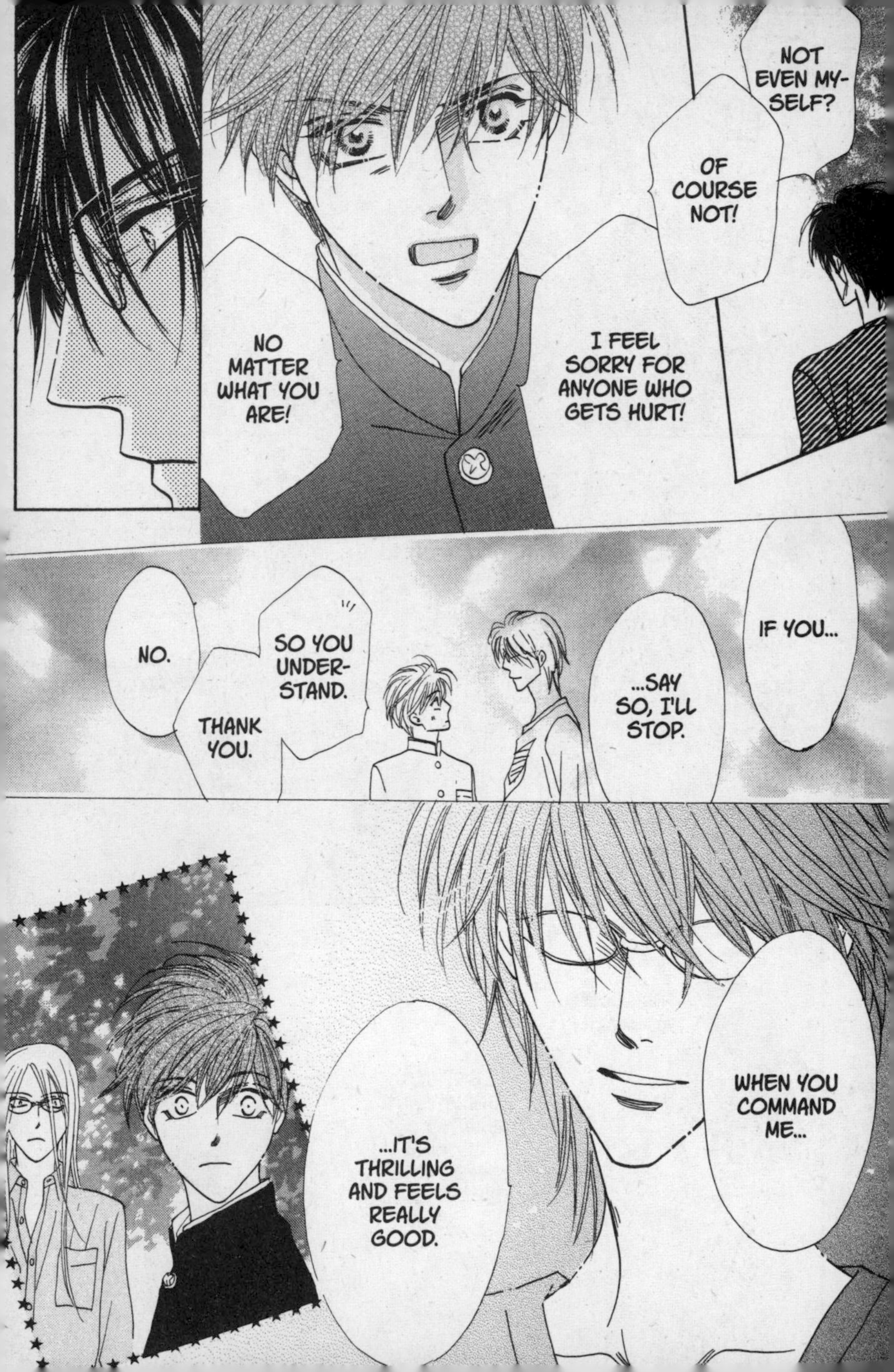
NOT EVEN MY-SELF?
OF COURSE NOT!
I FEEL SORRY FOR ANYONE WHO GETS HURT!
NO MATTER WHAT YOU ARE!
IF YOU...
...SAY SO, I'LL STOP.
SO YOU UNDERSTAND.
THANK YOU.
NO.
WHEN YOU COMMAND ME...
...IT'S THRILLING AND FEELS REALLY GOOD.

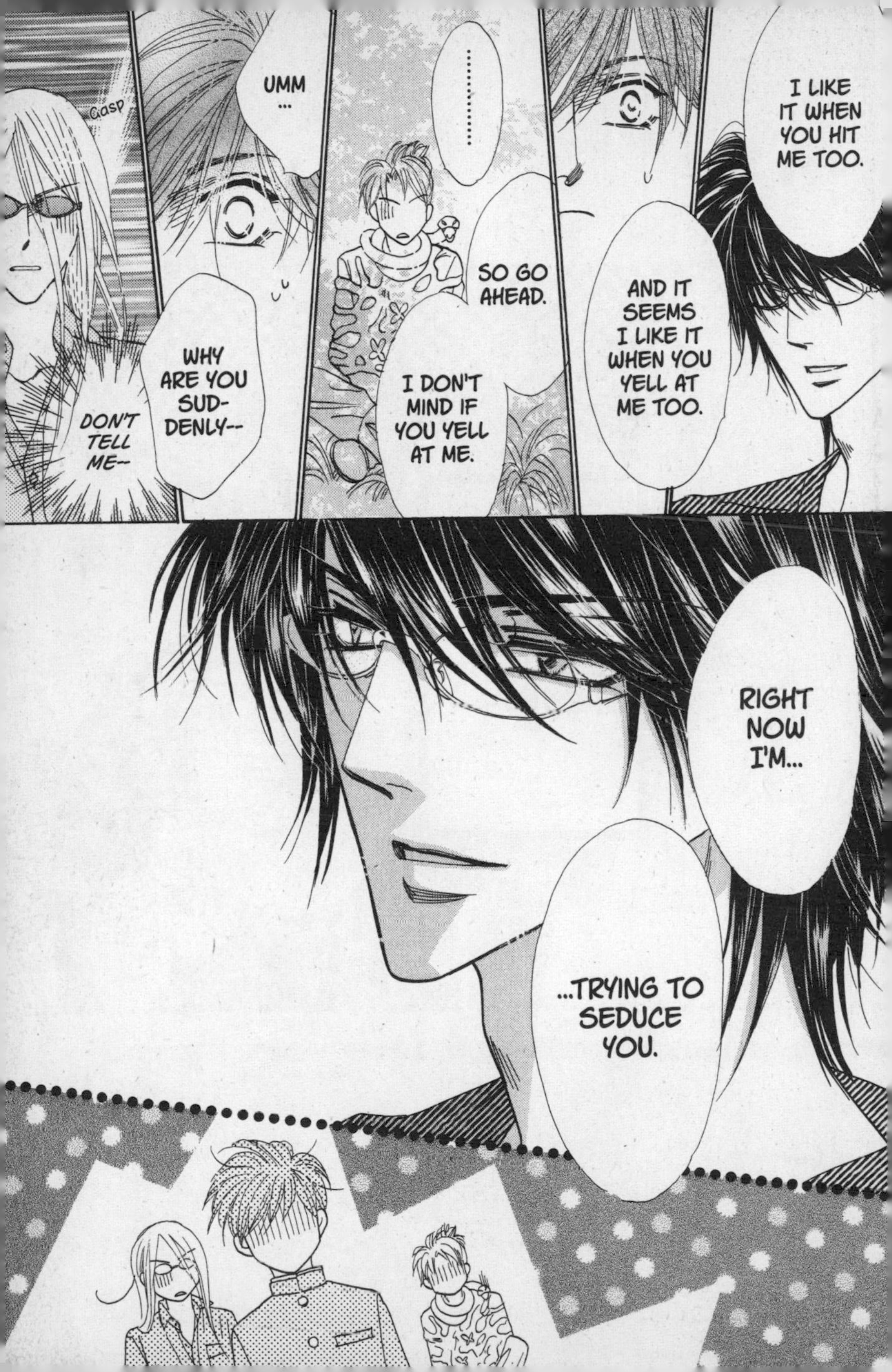
I LIKE IT WHEN YOU HIT ME TOO.
AND IT SEEMS I LIKE IT WHEN YOU YELL AT ME TOO.
....
SO GO AHEAD.
I DON'T MIND IF YOU YELL AT ME.
UMM ...
WHY ARE YOU SUD-DENLY--
Gasp
DON'T TELL ME--
RIGHT NOW I'M...
...TRYING TO SEDUCE YOU.

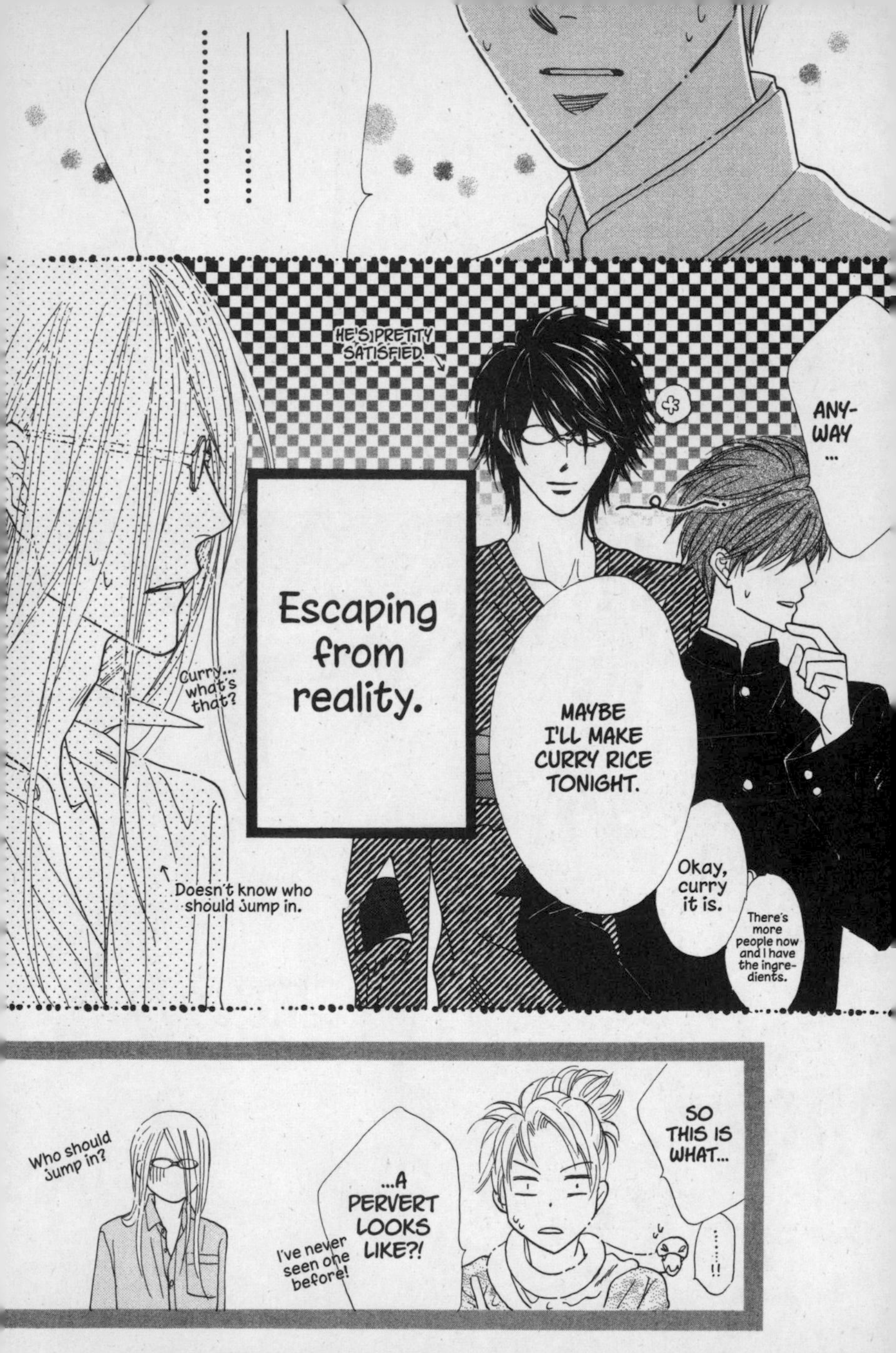

ANY-WAY ...
MAYBE I'LL MAKE CURRY RICE TONIGHT.
Okay, curry it is.
There's more people now and I have the ingre-dients.
HE'S PRETTY SATISFIED.
Escaping from reality.
Curry... what's that?
Doesn't know who should jump in.
SO THIS IS WHAT...
...!!
...A PERVERT LOOKS LIKE?!
I've never seen one before!
Who should jump in?

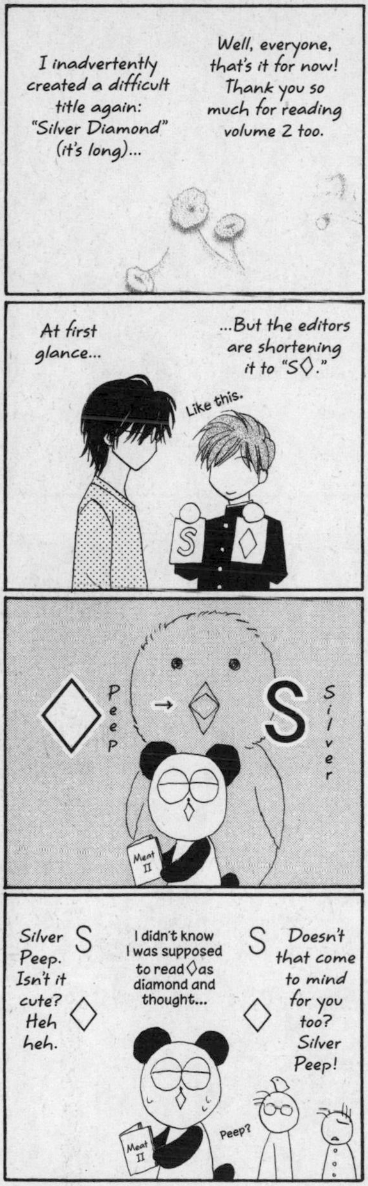
Well, everyone, that's it for now! Thank you so much for reading volume 2 too.
I inadvertently created a difficult title again: "Silver Diamond" (it's long)...
...But the editors are shortening it to "S◊."
Like this.
At first glance...
S
◊
Silver
S
Peep
◊
Meat II
Doesn't that come to mind for you too? Silver Peep!
S
◊
I didn't know I was supposed to read ◊ as diamond and thought...
Silver Peep. Isn't it cute? Heh heh.
S
◊
Peep?
Meat II

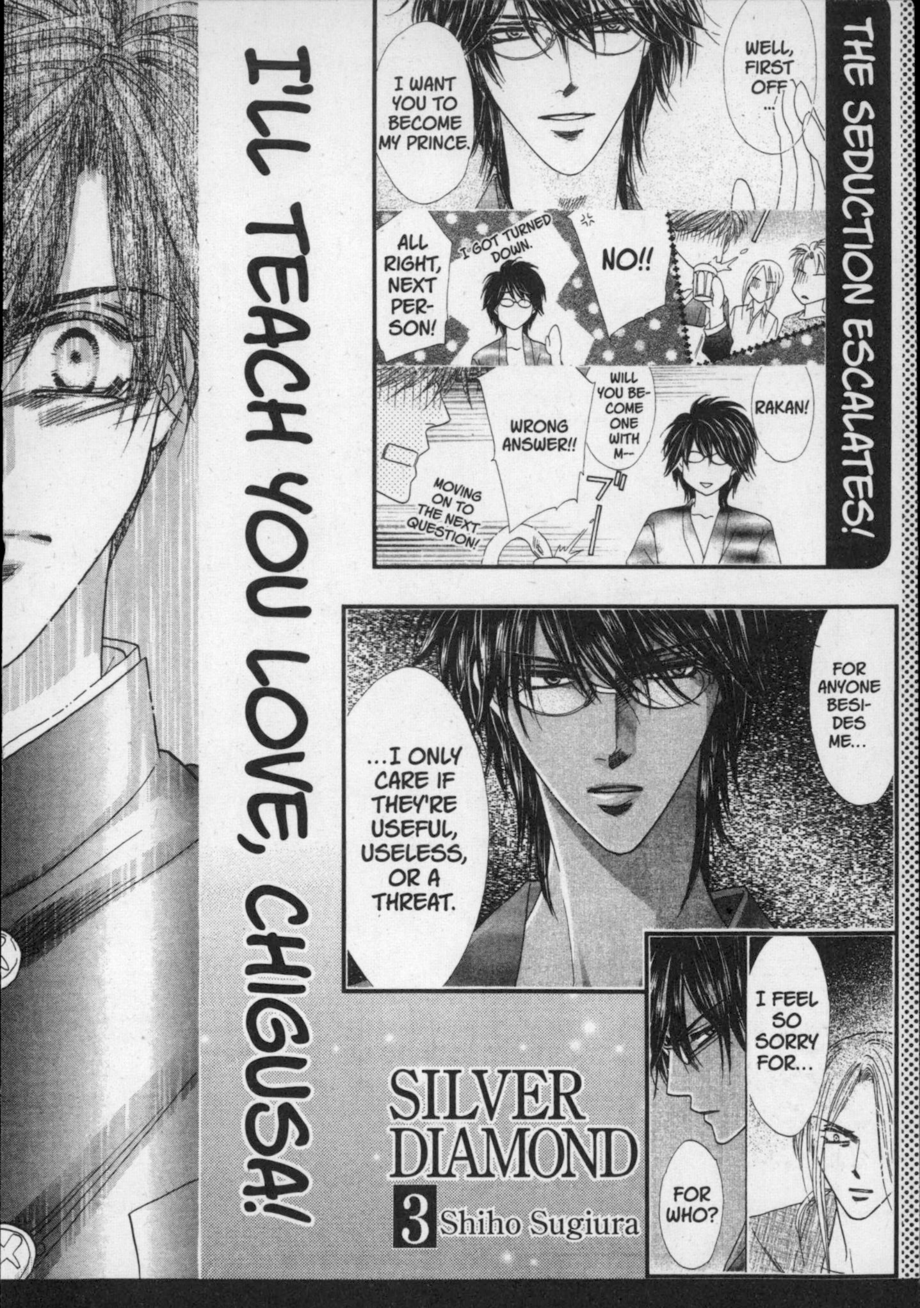

THE SEDUCTION ESCALATES!
WELL, FIRST OFF...
I WANT YOU TO BECOME MY PRINCE.
NO!!
I GOT TURNED DOWN.
ALL RIGHT, NEXT PER-SON!
RAKAN!
WILL YOU BE-COME ONE WITH M--
WRONG ANSWER!!
MOVING ON TO THE NEXT QUESTION!
FOR ANYONE BESI-DES ME...
...I ONLY CARE IF THEY'RE USEFUL, USELESS, OR A THREAT.
I FEEL SO SORRY FOR...
FOR WHO?
SILVER DIAMOND
3 Shiho Sugiura
I'LL TEACH YOU LOVE, CHIGUSA!

VOLUME 3: COMING SOON!!

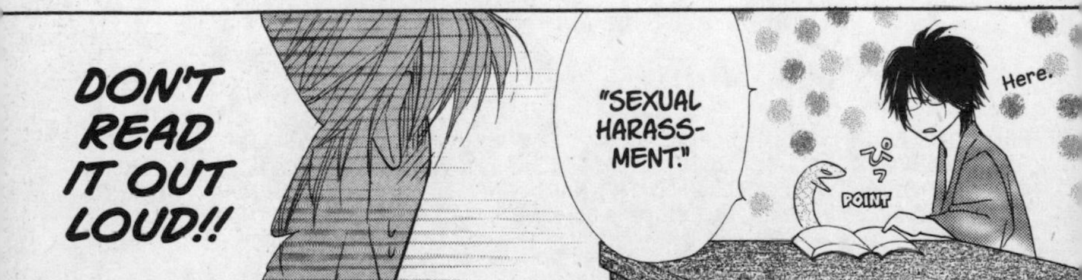
Here.
POINT
"SEXUAL HARASS-MENT."
DON'T READ IT OUT LOUD!!

Inside the World of...

SILVER DIAMOND

THIS SECTION HAS BEEN CREATED TO EXPLAIN AND ANALYZE THE COMPLICATED WORLD THAT IS *SILVER DIAMOND*. HOPEFULLY IT WILL SUCCESSFULLY COVER ALL THE CONFUSING CULTURAL AND LINGUAL ASPECTS OF THE SERIES AND HELP YOU ENJOY *SILVER DIAMOND* EVEN MORE!

honorifics

JAPANESE USES HONORIFICS TO ADDRESS PEOPLE AND REFER TO THEM WITH RESPECT. SIMILAR TO "MR." AND "MRS." IN ENGLISH BUT THERE IS MORE VARIETY IN JAPANESE.

THE MOST COMMON HONORIFICS SEEN IN *SILVER DIAMOND* ARE AS FOLLOWS:
-SAN: VERY COMMON IN JAPANESE AND IS A SIGN OF RESPECT.
-KUN: INFORMAL HONORIFIC USUALLY USED FOR MALES WHEN ADDRESSING SOMEONE YOUNGER THAN YOURSELF.
-CHAN: INFORMAL AND USUALLY USED FOR FEMALES OR CHILDREN.
-SAMA: MORE FORMAL THAN "-SAN." USED FOR PEOPLE HIGHER IN RANK, LIKE THE PRINCE.

p. 22 sekuhara

THIS TERM IN JAPANESE IS DERIVED FROM THE ENGLISH WORDS "SEXUAL HARASSMENT." BECAUSE THE TERM IS PRETTY SELF-DEFINING IN ENGLISH, IT WAS DECIDED TO KEEP THE JAPANESE VERSION FOR THESE PAGES. HOPEFULLY THE JOKE CARRIES OVER IN ENGLISH. CHIGUSA POINTING AT IT IN THE DICTIONARY WHILE KOH SAYS IT OUT LOUD IS PRETTY HILARIOUS!

kinrei/kinre p. 58

YOU MAY HAVE WONDERED WHY KINREI'S NAME WAS CHANGED TO...KINREI. IS IT A MISTAKE? ACTUALLY, WHILE THE NAMES ARE PRONOUNCED THE SAME, THE SPELLING IN JAPANESE IS DIFFERENT. CAN YOU SPOT THE DIFFERENCE BELOW?

金令 -> 金隷

WHILE THE FIRST "REI" SYMBOL MEANS "A COMMAND/ORDER" THE SECOND ONE MEANS "SLAVE/SERVANT." SO AS KINREI IS TOLD ON THIS PAGE, HE HAS NOW BECOME A SERVANT OF GOD. THOUGH, WHILE THE NAME CHANGE MAKES SENSE WHEN ABLE TO SEE THE CHANGE IN KANJI, I WONDER HOW KINREI WAS ABLE TO TELL THE DIFFERENCE WHEN IT WAS SPOKEN TO HIM...?

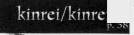

Indoor shoes
p. 102

IN JAPANESE SCHOOLS, STUDENTS TYPICALLY CHANGE SHOES WHEN THEY ENTER AND EXIT THE SCHOOL BUILDING. THIS HELPS TO KEEP THE SCHOOL CLEAN! HERE, RAKAN IS IN SUCH A HURRY THAT HE IS GOING OUTSIDE WITH HIS INDOOR SHOES. HOPEFULLY HE DOESN'T GET DETENTION FOR THAT.

TOHJI'S NAME(WHICH CAN ALSO BE SPELLED AS TOUNO TOUJI) IS WRITTEN LIKE THIS:

Tohno Tohji
p. 125

灯野灯二

AS YOU CAN SEE, HIS NAME FOLLOWS THE TRADITION OF THE OTHER WORLD IN HAVING THE SAME SYMBOL IN BOTH THE FIRST AND LAST NAMES. THE "TOH" PART OF HIS NAME IS THE KANJI FOR "LIGHT." MORE SPECIFICALLY, A LIGHT CREATED BY A FLAME.

THERE IS ALSO DISCUSSION ON THIS PAGE OF A NUMBER IN TOHJI'S NAME. INDEED, THE SECOND PART OF HIS FIRST NAME IS THE NUMBER "TWO." THIS KANJI IS OFTEN PRONOUNCED AS "NI" AND WILL LIKELY SHOW UP LATER IN OTHER CHARACTER NAMES. FURTHER EXPLANATION ON THE NUMBERED CHILDREN CAN BE EXPECTED IN FUTURE VOLUMES.

Join us next time for more revealing tidbits in volume 3!

Silver Diamond
···Fanart···

www.reya.se

Reya···Sweden

An absolutely gorgeous piece of art from Reya.
I love the way she painted the tree. And of
course, Narushige and Tohji look amazing.
Thank you, Reya! Your art is stunning!

Kathy---Los Angeles

What a cute picture! Those Ayame sure have taken a liking to Chigusa! But it looks like they were a little rough on him.

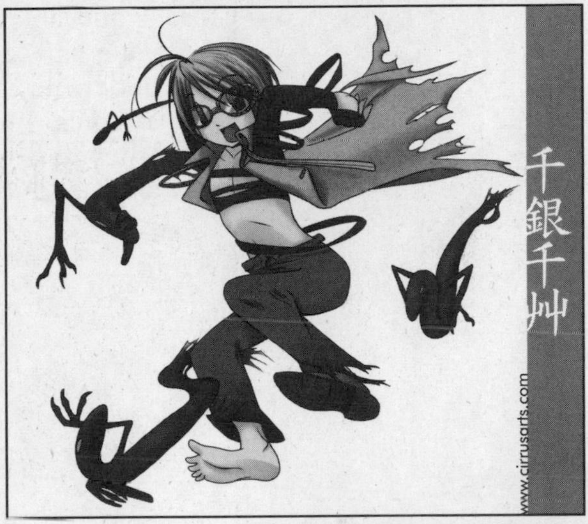
千銀千艸
www.cirrusarts.com

Val---Columbus, Ohio

What great black and white contrast! Rakan and Chigusa are enjoying a relaxing break under a tree.

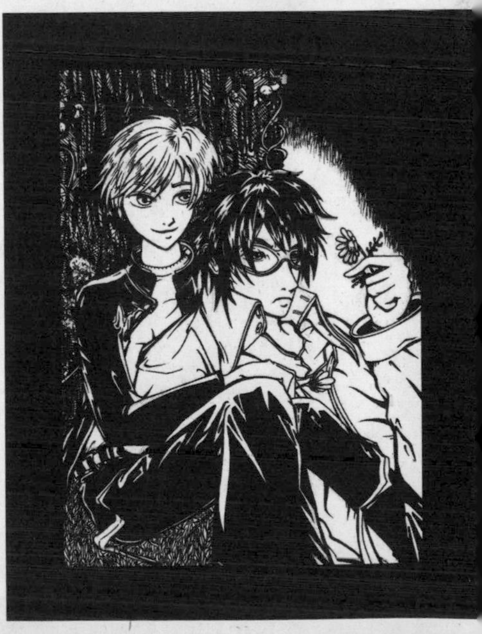

Yen Ting--- Goleta, California

Rakan and Chigusa look adorable as they take a nap together under the cherry blossoms. I wonder if they're dreaming about each other?

Aira---Canada

Rakan is so cute in this chibi version of himself! Perhaps he's waiting for Chigusa to escape the Ayame from Kathy's picture?

Claire---West Sussex, UK

Another picture of Rakan enjoying some time with his plant friends. He's showing off his Sanome powers!

Lechau--- Pickering, Ohio

A beautifully designed piece from Lechau! Chigusa has such a blank stare, what is he thinking? I want this on my wall.

SHOW YOUR LOVE FOR SILVER DIAMOND! NOW ACCEPTING FANART FOR FUTURE VOLUMES!

ADDRESS: *Silver Diamond* Fanart
c/o TOKYOPOP
5900 Wilshire Blvd, #2000
Los Angeles, CA 90036

See http://www.tokyopop.com/legal/fan_art_policy.html
and make sure to follow the proper submission guidelines!

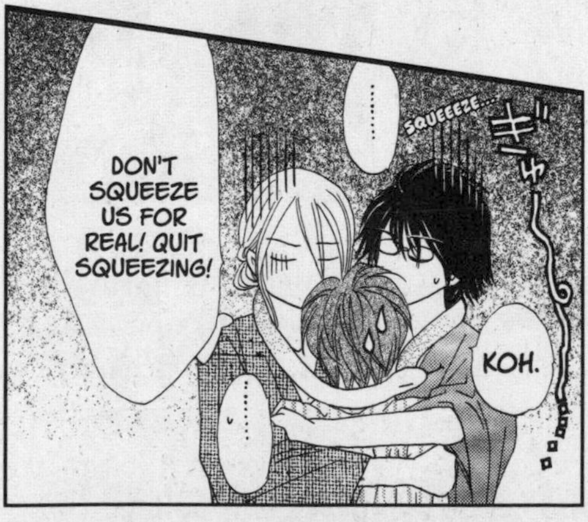
SQUEEEZE...
......
KOH.
DON'T SQUEEZE US FOR REAL! QUIT SQUEEZING!
......

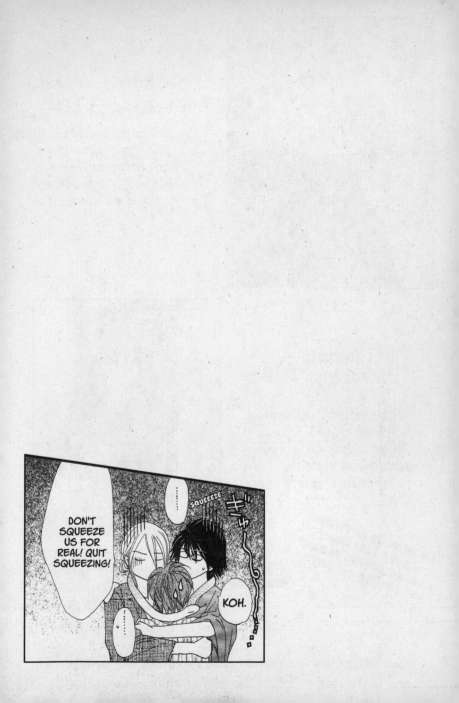

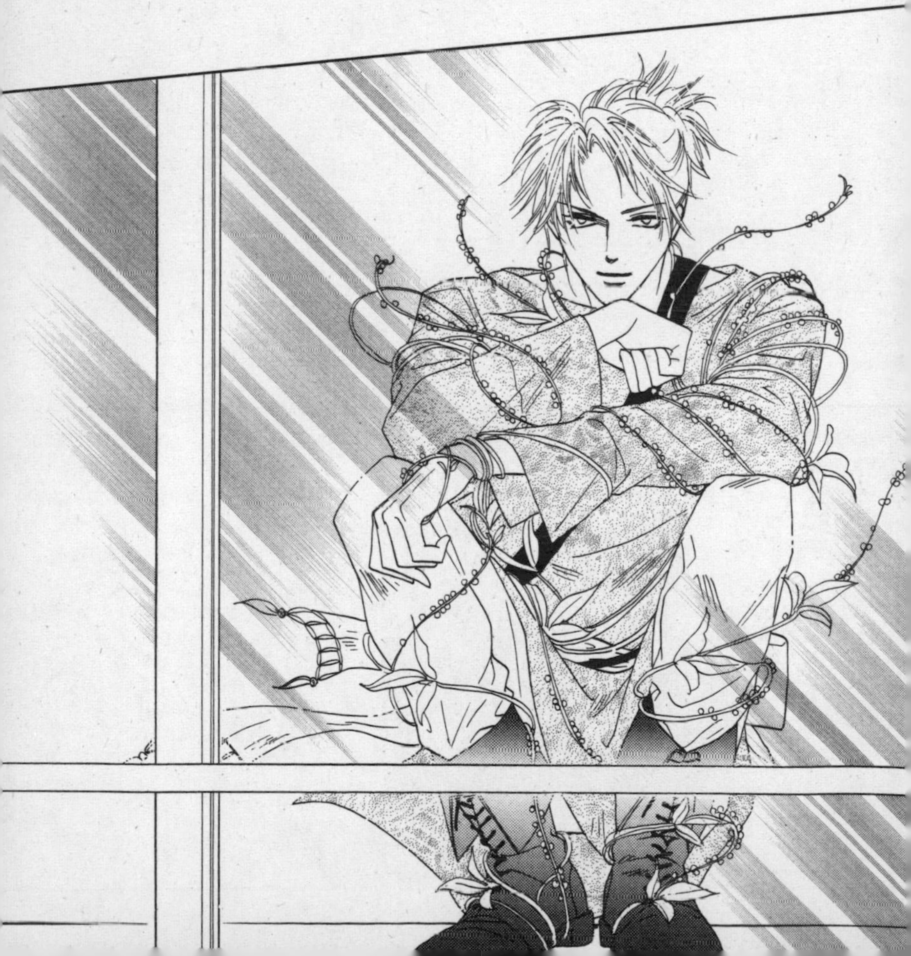

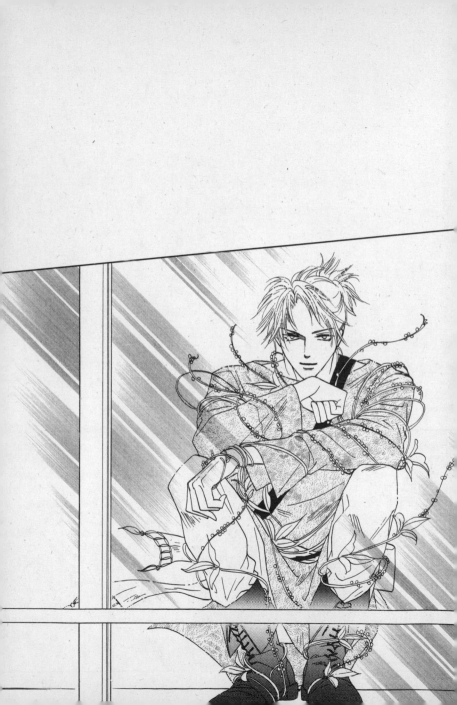

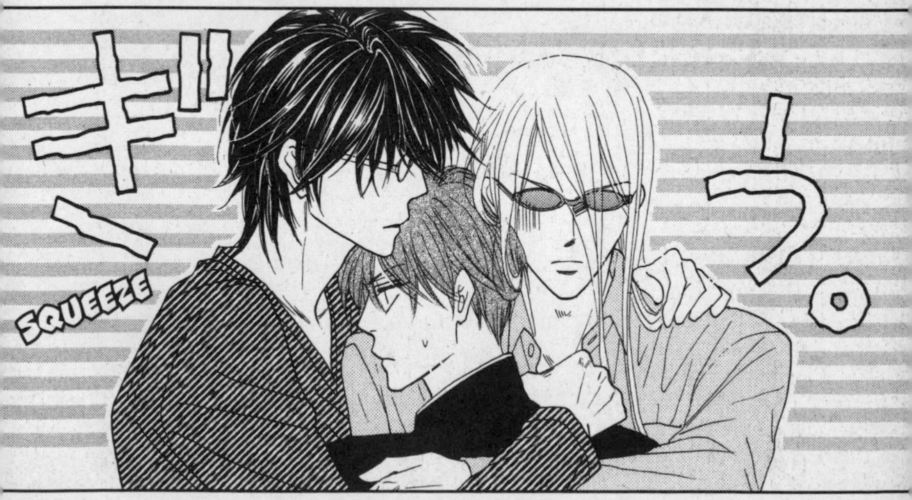
ギュ ーっ。
SQUEEZE

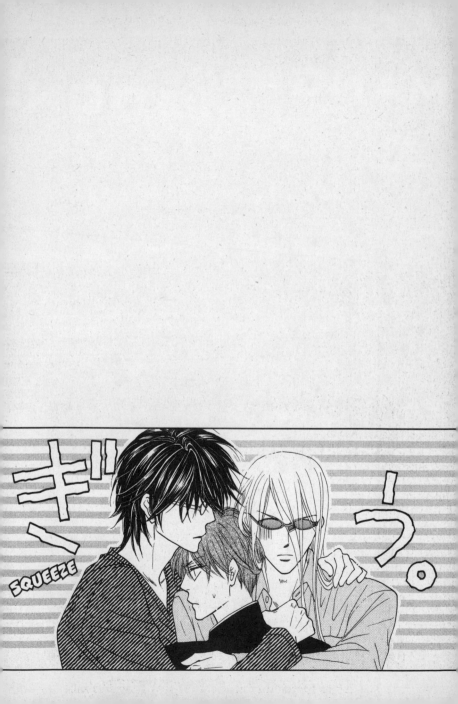

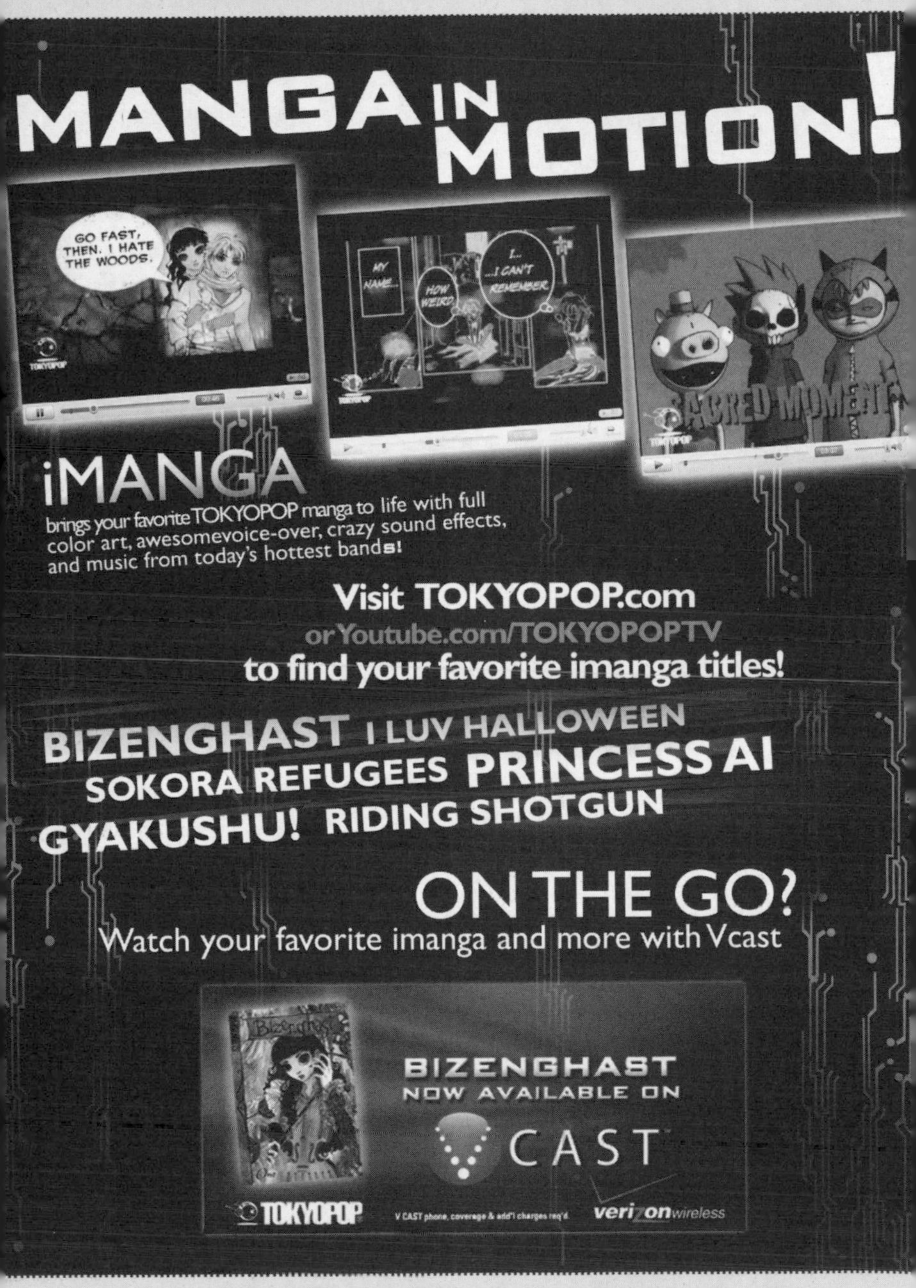
MANGA IN MOTION!
GO FAST, THEN. I HATE THE WOODS.
MY NAME...
HOW WEIRD
I... ...I CAN'T REMEMBER.
iMANGA
brings your favorite TOKYOPOP manga to life with full color art, awesomevoice-over, crazy sound effects, and music from today's hottest bands!
Visit TOKYOPOP.com
or Youtube.com/TOKYOPOPTV
to find your favorite imanga titles!
BIZENGHAST I LUV HALLOWEEN
SOKORA REFUGEES PRINCESS AI
GYAKUSHU! RIDING SHOTGUN
ON THE GO?
Watch your favorite imanga and more with Vcast
BIZENGHAST
NOW AVAILABLE ON
V CAST
TOKYOPOP
V CAST phone, coverage & add'l charges req'd.
verizonwireless

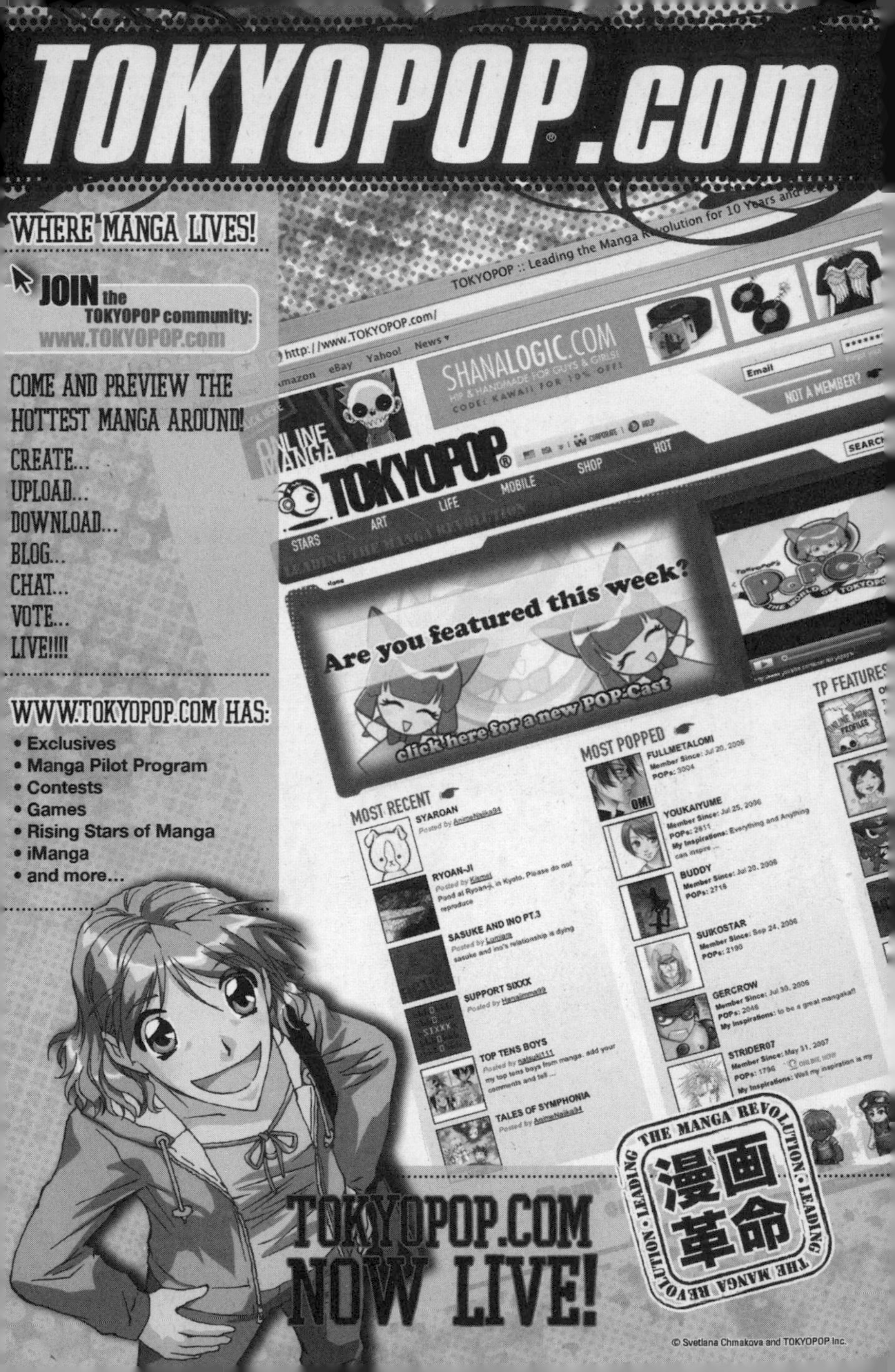
TOKYOPOP®.com
WHERE MANGA LIVES!
JOIN the TOKYOPOP community:
www.TOKYOPOP.com
COME AND PREVIEW THE HOTTEST MANGA AROUND!
CREATE...
UPLOAD...
DOWNLOAD...
BLOG...
CHAT...
VOTE...
LIVE!!!!
WWW.TOKYOPOP.COM HAS:
• Exclusives
• Manga Pilot Program
• Contests
• Games
• Rising Stars of Manga
• iManga
• and more...
TOKYOPOP :: Leading the Manga Revolution for 10 Years and
http://www.TOKYOPOP.com/
SHANALOGIC.COM
TOKYOPOP
STARS
ART
LIFE
MOBILE
SHOP
HOT
Are you featured this week?
click here for a new POP-Cast
MOST RECENT
MOST POPPED
TP FEATURES
TOKYOPOP.COM NOW LIVE!
THE MANGA REVOLUTION · LEADING
漫画革命
© Svetlana Chmakova and TOKYOPOP Inc.

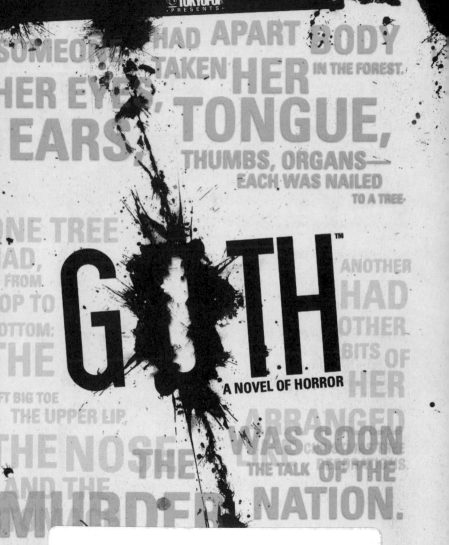

STOP!

This is the back of the book.
You wouldn't want to spoil a great ending!

This book is printed "manga-style," in the authentic Japanese right-to-left format. Since none of the artwork has been flipped or altered, readers get to experience the story just as the creator intended. You've been asking for it, so TOKYOPOP® delivered: authentic, hot-off-the-press, and far more fun!

DIRECTIONS

If this is your first time reading manga-style, here's a quick guide to help you understand how it works.

It's easy... just start in the top right panel and follow the numbers. Have fun, and look for more 100% authentic manga from TOKYOPOP®!